American Capitols

To Peggy

American Capitols

An Encyclopedia of the State, National and Territorial Capital Edifices of the United States

by
Eldon Hauck

McFarland & Company, Inc., Publishers
Jefferson, North Carolina, and London

The present work is a reprint of the library bound edition of American Capitols: An Encyclopedia of the State, National and Territorial Capital Edifices of the United States, *first published in 1991 by McFarland.*

LIBRARY OF CONGRESS CATALOGUING-IN-PUBLICATION DATA

Hauck, Eldon, 1914–
    American capitols : an encyclopedia of the state, national and
territorial capital edifices of the United States / by Eldon Hauck.
        p.   cm.
    Includes bibliographical references and index.

    ISBN 0-7864-1866-4 (softcover : 50# alkaline paper) ∞

    1. United States — Capital and capitol — History.   2. Public
buildings — United States.   I. Title.
NA4411.H38   2004
725'.11'0973 — dc20   90-53609

British Library cataloguing data are available

Cover photograph: Capitol of Texas ©2003 PhotoSpin.

Manufactured in the United States of America

McFarland & Company, Inc., Publishers
  Box 611, Jefferson, North Carolina 28640
  www.mcfarlandpub.com

Preface and Acknowledgments

When the publisher stipulated that my book "must be as exact and factual as possible," my first reaction was, "Where? What source? Who can give me the exact and most factual information concerning the American capitols."

Finally I turned to the chief executives of the states. The governors could certainly give me exact and factual information about their capitols, or if not, they would refer me to someone who could.

I wrote to them. Governors are busy people, but one after another, they responded. Some did not have the information right then, but I received letters to thank me for my inquiry with the assurance, "You will be hearing from us soon." Had it not been for the governors of these United States and Territories, this book could not have been. The Architect of the United States Capitol also responded almost immediately with the latest information.

Like every writer, I am also indebted to those who do historical research and leave their findings recorded for posterity, as well as to bibliographers of original sources: documents, diaries, and books.

My thanks go to the following. **Alabama:** The Hon. Guy Hunt, Governor; The Staff of the Alabama Historical Commission   **Alaska:** The Hon. Steve Cowper, Governor; David Ramseur, Press Secretary to the Governor; Dean Dawson, Reference Assistant, Archives & Records   **American Samoa:** The Hon. Peter Tali Coleman, Governor; John C. Wright, Territorial Archivist   **Arizona:** The Hon. Rose Mofford, Governor; Michael D. Carman, Director, Museum Division, Old Capitol, Department of Library, Archives and Public Records   **Arkansas:** The Hon. Bill Clinton, Governor; W. J. "Bill" McCuen, Secretary of State; Ann Pryor, Information Services   **California:** The Hon. George Deukmejian, Governor; Rodney Palmer, Registrar, California State Capitol Museum   **Colorado:** The Hon. Roy Romer, Governor; Catherine T. Engel, Librarian, Colorado Historical Society   **Connecticut:** The Hon. William A. O'Neill, Governor; Stephen B. Heintz, Commissioner, Department of Economic Development; Jacqueline L. Barron, Administrative Aide, Executive Chambers   **Delaware:** The Hon. Michael N. Castle, Governor; Joan N. Larrivee, Acting Chief, Bureau of Archeology and Historic Preservation   **Florida:** The Hon. Bob Martinez, Governor; Ronald W. Thomas, Executive Director, Department of General Services; Carl L. Morgan, Assistant Director, Division of Facilities Management   **Georgia:** The Hon. Joe Frank Harris,

Governor; Max Cleland, Secretary of State; Dorothy Olson, Director of Capitol Events and Tour Program **Hawaii:** The Hon. John Waihee III, Governor; Russel L. Nagata, Comptroller **Idaho:** The Hon. Cecil D. Andrus, Governor; G. Anne Barker, Administrator, Division of Public Works **Illinois:** The Hon. James R. Thompson, Governor; Drinda L. O'Connor, Director, Governor's Office of Citizens Assistance; Mark W. Sorenson, Assistant Director, Illinois State Archives **Indiana:** The Hon. Evan Bayh, Governor; Terri Roney, Correspondence Manager **Iowa:** The Hon. Terry E. Branstadt, Governor; Richard M. Vohs, Administrative Assistant **Kansas:** The Hon. Mike Hayden, Governor; Larry Jochims, Historic Preservations **Kentucky:** The Hon. Wallace D. Wilkerson, Governor; Jolene Greenwell, Executive Director/State Curator, Office of Historic Properties **Louisiana:** The Hon. Charles "Buddy" Roemer, Governor; Staff, Department of Culture, Recreation and Tourism **Maine:** The Hon. John R. McKernan, Jr., Governor; David S. Silsby, Director, State House and Capitol Park Commission; Dale F. Doughty, Director, Bureau of Public Improvements; Richard Davis, Superintendent of Buildings **Maryland:** The Hon. William Donald Schaeffer, Governor; Ellen Kendall, Manager and Frances Severn, Editor, Office of Tourism Development; Joan Vahlkamp, Senior Guide Supervisor; Chris Allen, Archivist; Toni Dietrich, Secretary; Dr. Henry Miller, Director of Research **Massachusetts:** The Hon. Michael S. Dukakis, Governor; Alice M. Pierce, Director of Correspondence **Michigan:** The Hon. James J. Blanchard, Governor; Richard H. Austin, Secretary of State; Le Roy Barnett, Reference Archivist, Bureau of History; Kathe Rushford Carter, Director, Office of Support Services **Minnesota:** The Hon. Rudy Perpich, Governor; Carolyn Kompolien, Historic Site Manager **Mississippi:** The Hon. Ray Maybus, Governor; Elbert R. Hilliard, Director, Department of Archives and History; Anne Lipscomb, Head Librarian; Michael Beard and Richard C. Cawthon, Assistants, Archives and Library Division; Thomas C. Petrone, Director of Administration **Missouri:** The Hon. John Ashcroft, Governor; Karlene A. Spencer, Director of Constituent Services; Martin E. Shay, Missouri State Museum **Montana:** The Hon. Stan Stephens, Governor; David Walter, Reference Librarian, Montana Historical Society **Nebraska:** The Hon. Kay A. Orr, Governor; Deb Thomas, Director; Ken Fougeron, Administrator, State Building Division **Nevada:** The Hon. Richard H. Bryan, Governor; Acting Governor Bob Miller; Robert A. Nylen, Curator of History, Nevada State Museum; Terry Sullivan, Director, Department of General Services; Daun Bohall, Photographer **New Hampshire:** The Hon. Judd Gregg, Governor; James L. Garvin, Division of Historical Resources **New Jersey:** The Hon. Thomas H. Kean, Governor; Cheryl Halvorson, Reference Librarian, New Jersey State Library **New Mexico:** The Hon. Garrey E. Carruthers, Governor; First Lady Katherine Carruthers, Connie Weston, Executive Secretary to the First Lady; Ms. E. J. Evangelos, Project Administrator, Capitol Renovation Project **New York:** The Hon. Mario M. Cuomo, Governor; Maureen Di Anni, Executive Assistant, State Commission on the Restoration of the Capitol **North Carolina:** The Hon. James G. Martin, Governor;

Raymond L. Beck, Historian, North Carolina State Capitol **North Dakota:** The Hon. George A. Sinner, Governor; Jeffrey Eslinger, Director of Constituent Services; James Sperry, Superintendent, State Historical Society; Roiann Baird, Reference Specialist; Robert Mitchell, Archeology and Historic Preservation **Northern Mariana Islands:** The Hon. Pedro P. Tenorio and The Hon. Lorenzo D. L. Guerrero, Governors; Frank S. Rosario, Public Information and Protocol Officer **Ohio:** The Hon. Richard F. Celeste, Governor; Jettie Hess, Correspondent; Kathleen M. Fox, ASIA, Executive Director, Capitol Square Renovation Foundation **Oklahoma:** The Hon. Henry Bellmon, Governor; Mary Ann Blochowiak, Assistant Editor, Publications and Education, Oklahoma Historical Society **Oregon:** The Hon. Neil Goldschmidt, Governor; Dea Knickerbocker, Supervisor Tour Guides, Visitor Services; Cecil L. Edwards, Legislative Historian, Legislative Administration Committee **Pennsylvania:** The Hon. Robert Casey, Governor; David L. Jannetta, Secretary, Department of General Services; John Cosgrove, Director of Special Events; Jane E. Gazette, Chief Guide, Capitol Tour Guide Service **Puerto Rico:** The Hon. Rafael Hernandez-Colon, Governor; Jaime B. Fuster, Delegate to Congress; Marylin Garcia, Director, District Office, Washington, D.C.; Carmen Lausell, Public Relations, House of Representatives; Luis Ortiz Espinosa, Superintendent of Capitol **Rhode Island:** The Hon. Edward D. DiPrete, Governor; Jennifer M. Soper, Administrative Assistant, Governor's Office **South Carolina:** The Hon. Carroll A. Campbell, Jr., Governor; Paul Begley, Acting Supervisor, and Staff, Reference Services, Department of Archives and History **South Dakota:** The Hon. George S. Mickelson, Governor; Jeff Stroup, Commissioner, Bureau of Administration **Tennessee:** The Hon. Ned Ray McWherter, Governor; James A. Hoobler, Curator of the Capitol; Ann Toplovich, Executive Director, The Tennessee Historical Society **Texas:** The Hon. William P. Clements, Governor; Allan McCree, Architect of the Capitol, State Preservations Board **Capitol of the United States:** President George Walker Bush; George M. White, FAIA, Architect of the Capitol **Utah:** The Hon. Norman H. Bangerter, Governor; Darin G. Bird, Constituent Services, Office of the Governor **Vermont:** The Hon. Madeleine M. Kunin, Governor; David Schutz, Curator of State Buildings **Virgin Islands:** The Hon. Alexander A. Farrelly, Governor; Ron de Lugo, Delegate to Congress **Virginia:** The Hon. Gerald L. Baliles, Governor; Robert B. Jones, Jr., Special Assistant to the Governor; Wendell Seldon, Director, Department of General Services **Washington:** The Hon. Booth Gardner, Governor; K. Wendy Holden, Director, General Administration; Grant Fredricks, Deputy Director, Facilities and Administration; Bob Armdt, Planning Manager, Facilities **West Virginia:** The Hon. Gaston Caperton, Governor; Frederick H. Armstrong, Associate Director, Archives and History **Wisconsin:** The Hon. Tommy G. Thompson, Governor; James Klauser, Secretary of the Department of Administration; Dale W. Dumbleton, Capitol Bureau Director, Neal Steinhoff, Assistant, Division of Building and Grounds **Wyoming:** The Hon. Michael J. Sullivan, Governor; Staff Members, Archives, Museums & Historical Department

Department of Defense: The Hon. Richard B. Cheney, Secretary; Janice Sims, Writer/Editor, Office of Assistant Secretary for Public Affairs **Department of Interior:** The Hon. Stella G. Guerra, Assistant Secretary, Territorial and International Affairs **Libraries:** Central Library of Anaheim, California, for their continuous assistance in unearthing specific facts and finding sources which, without them, would never have been known; Orange County California Public Library System for their special assistance and the punctuality in finding volumes through the nation's inter-library loan system; and Salt Lake City, Utah Public Library for the distinctive help of the reference librarians in finding sources of material.

I am extremely thankful for and indebted to the member libraries in the Inter-Library Loan System that graciously make their books available to researchers throughout that great system.

But I am most grateful to my wife, Peggy, for her understanding and support throughout this project.

Eldon Hauck

Table of Contents

ALABAMA
The Heart of Dixie

HEIGHT: 119'   FACADE: 387' 6"   DEPTH: 218'

For nearly 130 years the Alabama State Capitol has overlooked downtown Montgomery from its majestic hilltop setting. During this time its great neo-classical portico has witnessed stirring historical events.

On December 14, 1819, Alabama became the twenty-second state admitted to the Union. The territorial capital had been at St. Stephens, where government officials met in the local hotel; the newly formed state government moved to Huntsville, where its officials met in a privately owned building for the first two years.

In 1821, because of the influx of thousands of cotton planters to the rich soil in the Black Belt of the south-central section of the state, the legislature permanently relocated in this wealthy, newly populated area and chose the infant town of Cahawba for Alabama's capital city. It was here, near the juncture of the Alabama and Cahawba rivers, that the state's first official capitol was constructed.

Because of Cahawba's location, it was badly flooded by the swollen rivers three times in five years, which made another move necessary. Alabama's first capitol was razed in 1830, and today Cahawba is the center of archeological research.

Seven years after the formation of Alabama as a state, the location of the state's capital became a political struggle between the settlers of the northwest along the Tennessee River and those of the Black Belt's Alabama River. Finally a compromise was reached and Tuscaloosa, located on the Warrior River about midway between the two factions, became the third capital city.

A British-trained architect, William Nichols, designed and built the new capitol. Based upon Roman architecture this classical structure housed the government of Alabama until 1847, when a shift in the state's population demanded it be vacated. The building was put to use as a seminary for women until it was ravaged by fire in 1923.

The shift in population was caused by the opening-up to white settlement

1

of the Indian Territory in eastern Alabama adjacent to the Georgia border. An 1832 treaty forced thousands of Indians off their land and relocated them on federal reservations to the west. This caused the settlers to move eastward to buy and take over the rich farmland. Tuscaloosa was no longer central to the state's populace, and once again political pressure demanded another site.

Located on the Alabama River, Montgomery was a fast-growing center of trade. It was near the center of population and its roads led to and from all areas. These features alone should have made it the proper site, but they weren't enough.

Determined to make Montgomery the seat of state government, one of that city's founding fathers, Andrew Dexter, reserved Goat's Hill, a high slope overlooking the Alabama River, for the location of its state capitol.

To further increase their chances to have the capital city, the citizens of Montgomery raised $70,000 to finance construction of the capitol.

After some heat and much competition the contestant cities were pushed aside and Montgomery was chosen in 1847. Dexter's site for the capitol was confirmed.

Money for its construction having been raised by the people of Montgomery, Stephen D. Button of Philadelphia was retained as architect and the state's capitol became a reality. But on December 14, 1849, almost two years after its completion, the capitol was destroyed by fire.

George Nichols of Philadelphia was chosen to design the central portion of the present capitol, partially built upon the foundation of the destroyed statehouse. Completed in 1851, its construction cost of $64,000 was financed by the state. Fashioned after the United States Capitol, the structure's facade holds six towering Corinthian columns.

The rotunda rises three stories and is crowned by an immense dome soaring 119 feet above the earth. Inside, twin stairways curl upward to reach the third floor. They are entirely supported by the perfect balance of one step upon another. There is no vibration when ascending. This marvelous architectural creation was mastered by the 33-year-old Button. Through such works he achieved national acclaim.

Alabama seceded from the Union on January 11, 1861, and in its capitol on February 4 delegates from throughout the South convened to organize the Confederate States of America. On February 18 Jefferson Davis of Mississippi was inaugurated the president of the Confederacy.

The Alabama State Capitol served as the provision seat of the Confederate States until its government moved to Richmond, Virginia, in May.

The first major renovation of the capitol's interior occurred in 1868–71. It included installation of gas lights, ornamental fresco work and primitive indoor plumbing.

A three-story east wing, designed by W. T. Walker, was built in 1885 to house the Supreme Court's judiciary offices and library, and a landscaping project for the capitol grounds was approved.

In 1889 a nationally eminent landscape architect, Frederick Olmsted, Sr., was commissioned to prepare a complete landscape design for the grounds, but a lack of funds prevented it.

Designed by Montgomery architect Frank Lockwood, in consultation with the Capitol Building Commission and distinguished New York architect Charles Follen McKim, a south wing was added in 1905–1906. Concurrently the rotunda area and corridors were redecorated. The north wing, also designed by Lockwood, was added in 1911–1912.

The completed building's facade had grown to a length of 387 feet, 6 inches. Its exterior depth measures 218 feet. The height of its dome remains 119 feet.

Its principal building material is brick which is covered with stucco and scored to imitate stone.

The three neoclassical additions to the original Greek Revival design have proven highly compatible and, with its location on Goat's Hill overlooking the city, the capitol glistens. With its background a clear blue sky punctuated with brilliant cumulus clouds, when a stiff northerly breeze unfurls and spreads the three flags atop the flagstaff springing out of the dome: Old Glory, Confederate, and Alabama, in that order from the top, the scene of no other capitol is comparable.

The Alabama Capitol is not only alphabetically first in this book, it is, of all our capitols, the only one to claim two historic events. From all over the world, people come to Montgomery to visit the cradle of the two greatest upheavals in American history—the Confederacy, already noted, and the civil rights movement.

One century and 14 years after the completion of the central portion of the capitol, the historic civil rights march, from Selma to Montgomery, ended on the steps of the Alabama Capitol. It was led by Dr. Martin Luther King, Jr., pastor of the Dexter Avenue Baptist Church situated one block below the capitol. His leadership started the movement which began with the Montgomery bus boycott.

The Alabama State Capitol is claimed to be the most historic building in the South. It is the superlative old statehouse, was the Capitol of the Confederacy from February to May, 1861, and on its portico, Jefferson Davis was inaugurated as the first and only president of the Confederacy. A bronze star marks the spot where he stood on that occasion. He returned in 1886 to lay the cornerstone for the Confederate Monument which rises high above the trees on the north lawn of the capitol. Claimed as one of the tallest in Alabama, it was unveiled 12 years later on December 7, 1898, the day following Davis death.

Another tribute to the tumultuous days of the Confederacy, the marble monument contains life-size figures of Confederate soldiers and sailors who are guarding its four corners. At its top, a hero-like woman holds the Confederate flag and a sword, both of which remain as symbols of that period of history.

Inside the capitol, inside the original Supreme Court room, is a plaque marking the spot where the body of Jefferson Davis lay in state.

Immediately behind the capitol, across the street, is the White House of the Confederacy. It is a tranquil, homelike, white frame structure surrounded by old-fashioned gardens. It was the "many memoried," executive mansion of Confederate President Davis and his family.

The Confederate White House contains relics of the Jefferson Davis family and their period of occupancy. It is authentically restored with the original Davis furniture and contains priceless items from the War Between the States.

Teachers bring their classes to the Confederate White House, which provides a colorful excursion into the past with attendant ladies of the South clothed in that era's dresses.

But regardless of its historic realm, a building must be maintained and renovated. During the late 1920s Alabama's capitol rotunda was extensively redecorated and included eight large wall paintings depicting the history of the state. Paintings and the design were the work of artist Roderick MacKenzie of Mobile. The 1940s witnessed an extensive remodeling of the east and south wings and the House and Senate chambers. This included elevators, central air conditioning, and electrical voting boards, as well as the erection of marble front steps to replace the narrow stairs of the 1880s.

In 1981 restoration of the building's exterior was completed, and 1986 prompted the interior's restoration which continues at this writing. It is scheduled for completion in late 1991, at which time it will again be accessible to the public.

ALASKA
Land of the Midnight Sun

HEIGHT: 96' ⅝"   FACADE: 181' 5 ¾"   DEPTH: 118' 3 ¾"+

Many refer to Sitka in the state of Alaska as "the old Capital," but Sitka was never the capital of Alaska. Since there was no legislature in that city, there was no capitol; therefore the designation of capital for that city is a misnomer.

When the United States purchased Alaska from Russia in 1867 for $7.2 million, about $.02 per acre, it was made the Military District of Alaska with headquarters at Sitka. On May 17, 1884, Congress passed an organic act that stated, "Alaska shall constitute a civil and judicial district ... [and] ... the temporary seat of government of said district is hereby established at Sitka."

On June 6, 1900, Congress, in the Carter Act, expanded the court system in Alaska and provided that "the seat of government for the District of Alaska shall be in Juneau as soon as suitable buildings become available there." This change in location came about through action of the greater population in the Juneau area with insufficient opposition from the people of Sitka. Governor John Brady, a Sitka resident, was unable to find suitable buildings in Juneau, so for six years, until he was replaced, Sitka remained the government's seat.

His successor, Governor Wilford Hoggatt of Juneau, requested permission of the Secretary of the Interior to rent suitable buildings in Juneau for living quarters and an office. In July 1906 he opened his office. His staff, with the governmental files, joined him in September.

In 1911 Alaska's delegate to Congress, James Wickersham, procured a $200,000 appropriation for land and a building. Of that amount $20,000 was allocated for the land, which was purchased from the Presbyterian Board of Missions. The governor's office was moved into a building vacated by the mission on the northern half of Block 19. It remained there until 1925 when the building was severely damaged by fire and was then moved to rented quarters in a concrete building.

Congress passed a second organic act for Alaska on August 24, 1912, to create the Territory of Alaska; but this action did not authorize a court system or the creation of counties and their governments as had been allowed in other territories of the western United States. It did provide for a two-house legislature of 24 members, their salaries to be paid by the federal government. They would meet for 60-day sessions in odd-numbered years, all expenses paid. The act also named Juneau "Capital of Alaska." It was the first time any city had been designated a capital by the United States Congress.

The Elks Hall of Juneau became the first territorial capitol of Alaska. Rented by the federal government, the first session of the territorial legislature met there in March of 1914. Built in 1908, the Elks Hall still stands in Juneau. The architect and builder are unknown.

For the next eight sessions, 1915 through 1929, the legislature assembled in rented quarters: another fraternal hall, an office building, a building vacated by a furniture store, and finally—a movie theater.

Through this period of time a hold had been put on building a capitol. The amount appropriated was insufficient. More land was needed. The people of Juneau and members of the legislature agitated for a capitol. As an incentive to expedite and assure its construction, the people of Juneau raised $23,000, purchased the privately owned, southern half of Block 19, and deeded it to the federal government in 1913.

In 1923, with more money appropriated, James A. Wetmore, a supervising architect of the federal government, directed architects of the U.S. Treasury Department in drawing plans and specifications for the Federal and Territorial Building in Alaska.

In April 1929, bids were called for and on August 17, a contract for $712,000 was awarded to N. P. Severin Company of Chicago. With furnishings and extras, it was estimated the total cost would be a million dollars.

The Alaska State Capitol: formerly the territorial capitol of Alaska, but presently serving Alaska's state government. — Department of Archives and Records.

Ground was broken September 18, 1929. The building was completed on February 2, 1931, and formally dedicated on February 14, 1931.

On its completion, federal offices occupied its greater part: Juneau Post Office; U.S. Customs; Army Signal Corps (telegraph service for Alaska); Department of the Interior (the territorial governor and secretary of Alaska); U.S. district court, marshal, attorney, commissioner, and the court's library; the Bureau of Fisheries; Geological Survey; Forest Service; Weather Bureau; and the Bureau of Indian Affairs.

Two rooms were provided for legislative chambers which were used for two months during odd-numbered years. The territorial offices in the building were the library and museum, the attorney general and the treasurer of Alaska.

Alaska's constitution, 12,000 words in length, was ratified on April 24, 1956.

When President Dwight D. Eisenhower signed the Alaska Statehood Bill into law, the Federal and Territorial Building became Alaska's property and, when Alaska became a state on January 3, 1959, it gained possession. But many federal offices, including the post office, did not vacate until 1965 when a new federal building was completed.

The Alaska State Capitol is built of reinforced concrete, faced with a brownish-yellow brick. Indiana limestone was used in the lower floor and trim.

The four great columns at the entrance as well as the interior trim are of light and dark Tokeen marble from the quarries on Marble Island in southeastern Alaska. Some of the marble trim was removed during renovations that started in 1959, when the state took possession. Also, a heavy, decorative cornice of Indiana limestone around the top of the original building was removed. This left the building with a boxlike, unfinished appearance.

Except for interior renovation and remodeling of the entrances, the only additions to the building are two fire escapes at the rear.

Service-minded tour guides are schooled, willing, and available to give visitors a greater perspective on the structure and its contents.

In front of Alaska's capitol is a replica of the Liberty Bell. It was presented to Alaska and dedicated by Secretary of State John W. Snyder in 1950, in the hope that it "will serve forever as a symbol to the people of the United States of the independence which is their priceless heritage."

Through the capitol's front entrance into the lobby, the visitor walks on terrazzo flooring laid throughout the building's corridors by Italian workmen, brought there for that purpose. This is the ground (first) floor of the capitol's six stories. Throughout the building, Alaska's sources of income: oil and gas, fish and its processing, wood products, minerals, tourism, hunting, and trapping are depicted in Indian carvings and paintings. There are also carvings of the numerous animals found in the state.

Inside the lobby are two sculptures of stone-fired clay. "Harvest of the Sea" presents fishermen on Alaskan coastal waters; and "Harvest of the Land" displays Eskimos with Winchester rifles hunting in the interior. Also on this floor are several legislators' offices, the document room, a printing shop, and a legislators' supply room.

The second floor has several committee rooms and offices occupied by some Senators with their staff members. A colorful painting faces the stairway and depicts the formal transfer ceremony of Alaska to the United States by the Russian Imperial Government which took place on Castle Hill at Sitka October 18, 1867. Several photos along the corridor allow a look at members of the first territorial legislature during sessions in the Elks Hall in 1913.

The third floor has a press room; the offices of the speaker of the House, the chief clerk, and the Senate secretary; and the Senate and House chambers. Today's two-house legislature contains 60 members: 20 senators and 40 representatives; and the legislative sessions are held annually, commencing in January. Senators are elected for four-year terms; representatives, two-year. Adorning the walls are photographs dating from 1891 to 1945, taken by Lloyd Winter and Percy Pond of Juneau. The entire floor contains pictures of territorial governors, legislators, Senate presidents, and U.S. senators.

The offices of the governor and lieutenant governor are on the fourth floor and also a most unusual map of Alaska. It was cut out of a piece of pipe, 48 inches in diameter, the same used in the contruction of the trans–Alaskan pipeline. A double-joint weld traces the 800-mile route of the pipeline from Prudhoe Bay to Valdez. The double doors into the governor's office are hand-carved from black birch with carvings representing all of Alaska's major industries. Toward the lieutenant governor's office is the Hall of Governors containing pictures of former governors, both territorial and state.

The attorney general's office and those of several legislators are on the fifth floor.

As one departs the first office elevator in Alaska on the sixth floor, a guide will point out below a white house with a red roof, and explain it was the residence of Judge James Wickersham, "Alaska's outstanding statesman." An historian, pioneer judge, and delegate to Congress, Wickersham came to Alaska to establish the first courts and government in its interior. He presided in the territorial courtroom, now the Senate Finance Committee room.

Entering that room, the visitor's attention will be directed to the before and after picture showing what the room looked like before it was restored to the original. The benches of those early days have been returned. In a showcase is a Russian samovar, a reminder of Russian heritage. Another reminder of early days is a railroad time clock of 1860. The Senate committee's table is of central significance. Constructed in five parts, its center is walnut edged with Honduran mahogany. Ebony and rosewood make up the inlaid detail of its surface.

There is also a House Finance Committee room, also restored to the original with before and after pictures. The wall panelling is of Honduran mahogany and the windows support an excellent view of the State Office Building, the Alaska State Museum, Douglas Island, the Federal Building, and the Public Memorial Library.

As this ends the tour, a guide thanks visitors for coming and asks them to stop in the lobby to sign the guest register and receive a walrus pin, compliments of Alaska.

AMERICAN SAMOA

HEIGHT: 32'   FACADE: 180'   DEPTH: 150'

The Samoan Islands are divided into two parts, eastern and western. The eastern islands are American Samoa; Western Samoa is a self-governed nation. From sherds of decorated pottery found in the Mulifanua Lagoon on Upolo Island, it is believed the islands were settled circa 1,000 B.C. by Polynesians; and certain characteristics in the natives' language indicate they came from Tonga.

Jacob Roggeveen, a Dutch navigator, is credited with having discovered the Samoan Islands in 1722. Some time afterwards (1768), a Frenchman, Louis de Bougainville visited the islands and named them the Navigators Islands.

Apparently the French were occasional visitors, but after 11 members of the La Perouse French expedition were massacred by the natives in 1787, the islands were avoided by Europeans for a 40-year period during which they were a haven for runaway sailors, mutineers, and escaped convicts.

After Otto von Kotzebue's visit in 1824, Germany placed representatives on the islands in 1847, 1853, and 1861 thereby fixing a definite interest.

Christianity entered the islands when two missionaries from the London Missionary Society arrived and established a mission in 1830. Others followed and through the 1830s Christianity became an influence in the lives of the natives.

During 1839 an American expedition led by Charles Wilkes landed and stayed long enough to rename the islands Samoa. Years later (1872) the USS *Narragansett* dropped anchor and Commander Richard Meade made an agreement with Samoan High Chief Mauga for a coaling station for United States ships. Although the agreement was never ratified by Congress, it helped to keep the other nations out.

In January 1878 the United States signed a treaty with the Kingdom of Samoa which gave them a naval station at Pago Pago. By this time Great Britain, Germany, and the United States had established definite interests in the islands.

During 1899 in a tripartite treaty among the United States, Great Britain, and Germany, Great Britain yielded claim to the islands. Germany and the United States divided them, east and west, and the United States acquired commerce and commercial rights in American Samoa. In 1914 during World War I New Zealand claimed Western Samoa from Germany and eventually gave them independence.

On April 17, 1900, the High Chiefs of the islands of Tutuila and Annu'u formally ceded those islands to the United States. On July 16, 1904, the High Chiefs of the Manu's Islands: Ta'u, Ofu, Olosega, and Rose ceded those islands to the United States and Congress, formally and retroactively, ratified both deeds of cession in 1929. Swains Island had become part of the American Samoa group by a joint resolution of Congress during 1925.

Today American Samoa is an unincorporated and unorganized territory administered by the Department of the Interior. It remains unincorporated because not all provisions of the United States Constitution apply to the territory. It remains unorganized because Congress has not provided an organic act with which it could organize its government. However, when Congress gave the Department of the Interior plenary authority over the territory, the Secretary of the Interior allowed the American Samoans to draft a constitution for their own government under which its functions are carried out.

During September 1979 the Government of American Samoa created the Second Temporary Future Political Status Study Commission which recommended "for the present, American Samoa [will] remain an unorganized and unincorporated territory of the United States . . . [and] that this issue be reassessed in 10–15 years."

Their constitution provides for an elected governor and lieutenant governor, elected for four-year terms, and a legislature comprised of a Senate with 18 senators of four-year terms and a House of Representatives (20 members) elected for two-year terms. Swains Island has one non-voting member who is elected in an open meeting of its residents. The legislature meets semiannually in sessions of 45 days.

The judicial branch is independent with the Chief Justice and Associate Justices appointed by the Secretary of the Interior.

American Samoa was given representation in Congress by a 1980 legislation for one non-voting delegate with power to vote in committee.

What should be considered the territorial capitol of American Samoa was built in 1904 by Joseph Jewett, a builder for the United States Navy. It served as the Naval Government Headquarters until 1950. That year the American Samoan Government was established and organized.

The executive branch took over the Navy Headquarters building. The legislative branch, known today as the Fono, had to find another building for its chambers.

American Samoa's first capitol housed only the executive branch. It was constructed in island colonial design of concrete block, painted white. Its two stories were covered with a hip roof. The facade had a balcony of frame construction with balustrades running its full length. Its supporting wood columns likened its appearance to the colonial homes in the antebellum South. A central portico rose through the second floor to a frame pediment.

One of the oldest buildings on the island, it soon became dilapidated to the extent that the executive branch was moved into the original hospital building in 1976. By 1986, with the old hospital's walls crumbling, Governor A. P. Lutali initiated a proposal for a new Executive Office Building.

G. M. Meredith and Associates of a Western Samoa engineering firm was retained for design. Gary Jones of Australia designed the building with critical input from Joseph Weilenman, FAIA, Public Works.

Ground was broken in 1987. The triangular-shaped building was completed in November 1990, at a cost of $14 million.

Its three stories contain 85,000 square feet. To achieve a harmonious hill-valley impression, each floor overhangs the lower floor on the facade of the main entrance. The roof is sloping with wide overhangs to compete with the heavy tropical rainfalls. This feature also eases the visual impact on the building.

A central, skylighted atrium rises through each floor's encircling balcony giving access to stairs and elevators.

Its steel-framed roof and floor structure meet seismic standards and wind velocities up to 130 mph. Its foundation is a shallow concrete grid that "floats" upon low load-bearing soil of pre-historic lagoonal fill. The entire building is of steel and concrete and modern in every respect, but with a standby generator for safety and operation of the computer center.

The new facility will allow greater proficiency in government operations and services and is quite different from the old "leaky, termite and pest infested, dangerous electrical, unhealthy plumbing, and inadequate air conditioning" building previously occupied.

The legislature, the Fono of the American Samoa government, took up quarters in the Old Sailors' Barracks; and from 1950 to 1970 held its sessions, housed its staff, and kept its records in the two-story frame building.

Currently, a new government building is under construction. The American Samoa capitol's executive branch of the government. —John C. Wright, Territorial Archivist.

In late December 1970, a few days before the Fono's regular session was to start, faulty wiring sparked a fire that gutted all of the ground floor and most of the second. New quarters were needed immediately, but nothing could be done until the Fono was organized with new leaders. This was done in the courthouse. With their organization complete and the governor's assistance, the second floor of the Police Headquarters (the old Fitafita Barracks) was quickly renovated.

A sliding curtain separated the two chambers in the large, open room. The Senate President and the House Speaker offices wre at each end in the hall. Staff members found office spaces by partitioning the veranda.

Every member was excited with the knowledge that the fire had created the golden opportunity to build a new Fono building. Of immediate and paramount need during the first sessions, bills were introduced and resolutions made on a site and proposed types of a new building. The two houses formed a joint committee.

The new Fono "compound" was completed and dedicated in October 1973. That event was the Fono's twenty-fifth anniversary and also the meeting of Pacific Conference of Legislatures held in American Samoa.

The new offices and the chambers would give the public greater access to their full-time representatives and the government.

Oval in shape, the building has three parts. The central part of two stories houses the Senate and House chambers. Attached to the central structure by a covered breezeway, one-story wings extend from each side with one holding the Senators' offices and auxiliary services, the other the Representatives' offices and their auxiliary services.

The central structure is 32 feet high, 110 feet wide, and 90 feet deep. Each of the identical wings is 20 feet high, 35 feet wide, and 150 feet deep. This would make the Fono building (excluding the covered breezeways) 32 feet high, 180 feet wide, and 150 feet deep.

The architectural design is the traditional Samoan Fale following the design of the Samoan house with narrowly spaced, slender posts around the perimeter and the main structure's interior. It has a rounded roof and semicircular ends.

Its concrete foundation rests on pilings. The concrete ground floor was poured over earth fill. Concrete columns, fashioned to represent Samoan Fale posts, support heavy laminated wood arches and the superstructure. The roof is cedar shake laid over a heavy tongue and groove decking.

ARIZONA
The Grand Canyon State

HEIGHT: 92'   FACADE: 182' 6"   DEPTH: 80'

In a division of the New Mexico Territory, the United States Congress established the Arizona Territory on February 24, 1863. It didn't come easy. After years of pleading the people of the area, led by the capable Charles D. Poston, the "Father of Arizona Territory," finally persuaded Congress to create another territory and pass the bill which President Abraham Lincoln signed into law.

With John N. Goodwin at its head, an itinerant government, sent out of Washington, D.C., entered the new territory and formally organized the government at Navajo Springs on December 29, 1863.

On January 26, 1864, Territorial Governor Goodwin established a temporary capital at Camp Whipple near Prescott. A small, walled tent served as the territorial capitol. In July the first territorial legislature met in Prescott in the governor's house, a large, two-story log house with a two-window gable centered in the front roof. Officially, on September 26, 1864, the territorial government capital became Prescott; the log building, its capitol.

In 1867 the statehouse was moved to Tucson into a small adobe building on Ochoa Street where it remained for ten years. On March 23, 1877, the government moved back to Prescott to remain there for 12 years. Finally, on February 4, 1889, the government moved to Phoenix to occupy a hurriedly prepared space on the second floor in the Phoenix City Hall.

The move to Phoenix was probably influenced by Marcellus E. Collins, Moses H. Sherman and his wife, Hattie, when they offered the territorial government ten acres, centrally located, for a capitol. Eight years later a deed was signed and the property was transferred to the territory for the sum of $1.00.

Sherman was an educator and banker. Both he and Collins were land developers and invested in street railway systems. They developed the property surrounding their gift as the "Capitol Addition." Collins remained in Phoenix, but Sherman moved to California where he developed the property now known as Hollywood.

Another two years witnessed the territorial assembly's arrangements for bonds and appropriations to finance construction for building a capitol and, finally, work started in 1899. The building was completed August 4, 1900, and dedicated the Arizona Territorial Capitol on August 17. It was designed and constructed for $135,744.29.

James Riley Gordon of San Antonio, active in the design of many public buildings in Texas, designed the classical–Spanish building and Tom Lovell of Denton, Texas, was awarded the construction contract.

Most of the materials used in construction are native to Arizona, especially the exterior stonework: the porous rock, tuff, came from Yavapai County; grey granite from the Salt River Mountains; and malipi from the Camelbacks. The dome, 44 feet in diameter, was coated with copper-colored paint until 1976, when the Arizona Mining Association donated 15 tons of copper and the Anaconda and Cities Services turned it into 2 x 8-foot sheets for sheathing the dome.

If the gaining of territorial status was difficult, statehood was almost impossible. The people of the territory began agitating members of Congress as early as 1872. Congress, with political aptitude, listened with closed ears. A constitution was needed. Arizona wasn't civilized. Indians, gunslingers, cattle rustlers, and bandits dominated the land.

By 1890, with the Indian menace removed, with economic progress showing, and experience in territorial government advanced, things looked better. In 1891 a constitution was submitted to and ratified by the people and sent to Congress.

The United States Senate objected and continued to object until the territory sent a new constitution. It was not until 1910 that Congress, heeding their cry, passed an enabling act prompting a constitutional convention.

Presided over by George W. P. Hunt and dominated by Progressive thinking, the convention produced a model document for Congress and statehood was approved during the summer of 1911.

But their bill was vetoed by President William Howard Taft, who objected to a clause that permitted the people of Arizona to recall presidentially appointed judges. With the removal of that clause, statehood was granted on February 14, 1912, with George W. P. Hunt the governor.

With statehood, the territorial capitol became the Arizona State Capitol

The Arizona State Capitol has been restored and now serves as the "Old Capitol" Museum. — Museum Division, Department of Library, Archives, and Public Records.

and because the state's population had nearly tripled over two decades, 1900–1919, an addition was completed in 1919 to take care of expanding services and staff. Similar circumstances brought about another addition to the original structure in 1938. The added space made room for offices and the Supreme Court. The additions raised the construction cost $813,470.71 for a total of $949,214.

This building is still the legal capitol of the state even though it is surrounded by buildings that house the working machinery of state government. Since 1974, when state officials moved to new adjoining quarters, the Arizona State Capitol has functioned as a museum on the history of Arizona's government; it was listed on the National Register of Historic Places that year.

Known as the Arizona State Capitol Museum, it is a part of the Museum Division of the Arizona Department of Library, Archives, and Public Records.

In order to preserve the structure and effectively present the history of Arizona's government to the people, an ambitious restoration program was started in 1976. It was completed in 1981 at a cost of nearly $4 million.

Today, guided and self-guided tours and various activities are provided visitors of all ages and, when possible, there are opportunities to visit the offices of the governor, secretary of state, and representative or senator from their district.

In the original plan, entrance to the building was on the second floor by way of monumental granite steps, but lack of funds changed it to the ground floor.

Inside the entrance is the rotunda, 22 feet in diameter with a light shaft reaching to the dome. Arizona's state seal of mosaic tile is inlaid in the floor.

Its design includes three of the five C's that created Arizona's economy: copper, climate, and cotton. What happened to cattle and citrus remains a mystery.

The Supreme Court chamber, off the rotunda, is quite small and there is no record of the court having occupied this space. In territorial times the justices and their clerks did occupy the building to have access to the law library.

The 1974 restoration of the capitol returned it to the 1912 era with the offices of the governor and secretary of state, and the library, now used for traveling exhibits, on the second floor.

The third floor houses the legislative and judicial branches with the Senate and House chambers occupying the north and south wings.

The House and Senate galleries, overlooking those chambers, are on the fourth floor. All floors have exhibits; and the furnishings throughout the building are 1912 originals or reproductions.

A 16-feet-high wind vane, in the form of a quarter-ton sculpture of a statue modeled in classic Greek, crowns the gleaming copper dome. Installed in 1899, "Winged Victory" holds a torch in the right hand, a laurel wreath of victory in the left. "A fitting choice for the seat of government, as it turns with desert winds, so Arizona turns with the winds of political change." (Arizona Capital Museum brochure)

In 1988 Arizona spent $4.7 million and employed 165 persons to maintain the building and grounds of the state capitol complex: the Arizona State Capitol Museum and 32 buildings surrounding it.

ARKANSAS
The Land of Opportunity

HEIGHT: 230'   FACADE: 437'   DEPTH: 167'

Approaching today's Arkansas State Capitol, one is amazed at its resemblance to the United States Capitol in Washington, D.C.

When a Congressional enabling act permitted Arkansas territorial power in 1819, Robert Crittenden of Kentucky was appointed acting governor. Arkansas Post became the seat of government and its capitol. The fort, constructed of logs, had a corner blockhouse with a flag rising from its peak.

In 1820 the government moved to Little Rock into a two-story frame building. They remained through 1835, the last year of Arkansas' territorial legislature. On January 4, 1836, Arkansas' First Constitutional Convention met in the Baptist church in Little Rock. Arkansas was admitted to the Union

June 15, 1836. The first state legislature convened on September 12 in a new capitol.

The movement for a new capitol started with the United States Congress in 1831. Legislators set aside ten sections of ground to be sold by the territorial government with the proceeds going toward the building of a capitol. At that time Crittenden, territorial secretary, offered his brick home, suitable for a capitol, in exchange for the grant; and he influenced the territorial legislature to pass a bill to that effect. John Pope, who was appointed territorial governor in preference to Crittenden by President Andrew Jackson, successfully vetoed the bill. Angered, Crittenden claimed that Pope had won over the legislature by offering its members 30 fine hams from his smokehouse. Faced with the governor's stubbornness, Crittenden induced the legislature to petition Congress to remove Pope from office. Jackson refused.

By 1833 enough money was raised from the sale of land to start building. Gideon Shyrock of Kentucky drew the plans. A site was offered and accepted, but Crittenden tried to stop the capitol's placement by deeming it to be an Indian burial ground. He enforced this with the rumor that Jean Lafitte had buried several of his men there in hollow logs. This had little effect on Pope who replied, "We will build, then, a monument to their memory."

Completed, constructed of hand-made brick, covered with mortar, the new Arkansas State Capitol received its government easily, but the square-shaped building, with six columns supporting its centered portico, soon became crowded. By 1842 two wings had to be added. Now it boasted a usable floor space or nearly 35,000 square feet. The building is 57 feet high, 147 feet deep, and its facade is 203 feet in length. With one exception it served as the Arkansas Capitol until 1911, when the government offices moved into a new, unfinished capitol.

With Arkansas' secession from the Union, and the Union troops advancing, legislative action of March 17–22, 1862, authorized moving the capitol from Little Rock. In September 1863 Governor Harris Flanagin ordered the seat of government moved to Washington in Hempstead County where a two-story frame building, with a central, covered portico and a single, front door entrance, became the capitol. Union troops captured Little Rock in 1863.

The Confederate government of Arkansas ended May 26, 1865. From January 7–14, 1868, the Fourth Arkansas Constitutional Convention met at Little Rock and on June 22, 1868, Arkansas was readmitted to the Union.

When the new capitol was occupied in 1911, the old statehouse was designated the War Memorial Building. Today it is the Museum of Arkansas. Standing for more than 150 years it contributes to the antebellum architecture of the South.

Another struggle ensued before a new capitol was guaranteed. In 1897 former Arkansas Attorney General Daniel W. Jones became governor. On April 14, 1898, at Jones' urging, the legislature passed a law providing for the construction of a new capitol. The law set up six commissioners to procure an architect and complete plans and specifications for a building not to exceed

The Arkansas State Capitol is used by many states as an architectural model for their capitols. Most of the exterior stone is Batesville marble; the remainder, Indiana limestone. — Secretary of State.

a cost of $1 million. They appropriated $50,000 to clear the penitentiary off the land and directed the penitentiary commission to find a new location for their building.

The new attorney general, Jefferson Davis (not to be confused with the president of the Confederacy), charged the law to be a "bare-faced fraud." He called his legislative foes "high-collared roosters" and "the silk-stocking gang." When the purchase of a new site for the penitentiary at the price of $5,000 became known, he made known his emphatic opposition: "Five thousand dollars! Fifteen acres of land! That land is so poor that two drunken men couldn't raise a difficulty upon it. It is so poor that you could not raise an umbrella upon it. It is so poor that you have to manure it to make a brick out of it."

Though Davis' exemplary and unusual rhetoric is believed to have taken him into the governor's seat in 1900 (where he would remain for three terms), the new capitol project went forward with additional legislative acts.

Section 7 of the Acts of Arkansas, 1899, providing for construction stated, "the State Penitentiary Board shall turn over to the Board of State Capitol Commissioners, such a number of convicts as can be advantageously worked upon the construction of the Capitol Building and the manufacture of brick and the quarrying and cutting of stone therefore, not exceeding 200 in number."

That year, 1899, planning commenced. On Independence Day, 1899, groundbreaking ceremonies were held. Foundation work with convict labor started in 1901. In 1903 $1 million was appropriated and a contract awarded. By 1908 the money was used up. Construction was halted. Governor George W. Donaghey, elected that year, promised the people it would be finished. His leadership brought additional appropriations. Although the 1911 Arkansas legislature met there, the new Arkansas Capitol was not finished until 1914 at a cost of $2,205,779. It had taken 17 years for the people of Arkansas, through the elected legislature, to obtain their new capitol. The building was dedicated in 1915.

Architect George R. Mann of St. Louis designed the building in the neoclassical style of the United States Capitol in Washington, D.C. Thinking that Mann wasn't using safe-enough construction, in 1909 Governor Donaghey dismissed him and brought in a New York architect, Cass Gilbert, to revise the plans and rebuild the upper part of the building, especially its dome.

Except for two grand staircases at the north and south ends, most of the interior was finished. These were redesigned to a ten-foot width by Gilbert and, with more money appropriated, built with marble. Today, they are two of the most impressive marvels in the capitol.

The dome presented the most ironic change. Governor Donaghey asked Cass Gilbert to copy the dome he believed had been designed by Theodore Link for the new Mississippi Capitol. He didn't know that that dome was the only part of the capitol Link did not design, that it had been designed by Link's friend, the recently fired George R. Mann.

The original contractors were Caldwell and Drake. In 1908 William Miller and Sons was contracted to complete the work.

Of neoclassical design, the Arkansas Capitol is constructed of Arkansas marble from Batesville and Bedford granite from Indiana. With four floors, including the basement, it commands nearly 275,000 square feet of floor space and is recognized as one of the finest capitols in the nation. Many states have used its example for their own capitols.

Mann's work was restricted under the million dollar budget allotted, but it included many impressive details.

With intricate craftsmanship and design by Tiffany's of New York, the six front doors were made of four-inch-thick solid brass. Their price was $10,000. On today's market, if available, they would cost hundreds of thousands of dollars.

Also from Tiffany's came a brass chandelier, 16 feet in diameter, which hangs over the rotunda. To be cleaned, it needs to be lowered 185 feet to the first floor. A smaller replica of bronze hangs over the House chamber and one of copper overhangs the Senate chamber.

Circular, stained glass skylights were built over both chambers on the third floor; and murals were painted around the lunette windows of the fourth floor to depict justice, war, education, and religion.

Located on the first floor, the gift shop offers more than 200 items promoting the historical and cultural heritage of Arkansas. There is an information center. Public tours are conducted daily and the visitor can experience a unique perspective on Arkansas history, government and culture. Geological specimens and historical artifacts, on display throughout the capitol, offer unusual insight into Arkansas' history and people.

Because of constant growth, the Supreme Court needed new quarters and other governmental offices expanded. Today, the capitol complex includes the Justice Building, the Art Ford Education Building, and the Multi-agency Building, all on a beautifully planned and landscaped 40-acre plot.

Of all the rooms in the capitol, the Supreme Court room is the most completely restored with its brass railing around the bench and the mahogany railing bordering the room. Since the court moved in 1958, this room has been used for legislative committee and public meetings.

The governor's office is on the second floor as is his conference room with its walnut conference table that was made from a tree planted by Governor Donaghey's father.

In 1988 maintenance of the buildings and grounds of the capitol complex required 48 employees, including 12 inmates, and cost the people of Arkansas $1,542,978.

CALIFORNIA
The Golden State

HEIGHT: 220'   FACADE: 320'   DEPTH: 164'

A bronze plaque, installed during California's Capitol Restoration Gala in January 1982, commemorates the history of its capitol. It shows the years of the original building's construction period, 1860–1874 and that it was built under the supervision of three different architects.

It is claimed that fires, floods and the Civil War stifled its completion. To those factors should be added that of the human political nature.

The plaque is, in part, in error. Originally, the work on the capitol was started in 1856.

On March 15, 1856, Senator William J. Ferguson introduced a bill to construct a state capitol in Sacramento. Passed by both houses and signed into law by Governor J. Neely Johnson on April 18, 1856, the act provided for a Capitol Commission of three persons including the secretary of state and the state controller; that the cost would not exceed $300,000, and it would be ready for occupancy not later than January 1, 1858.

On August 13, 1856, Reuben Clark's architectural design for the capitol was chosen from among those submitted in California's statehouse competition. As a carpenter from Maine, Clark had worked for contracting builders of capitols in Maine and Alabama during the 1830s, after which he formed his own architectural company in New Orleans. Boarding a ship for the gold fields of California, and finding himself poorer for that effort, he returned to carpentry, then architecture in San Francisco.

Ground was broken December 4, 1856, and work started, but was halted on December 15 by the California Supreme Court, which declared the legislative act had exceeded the limit of state indebtedness and was unconstitutional.

From that $300,000 in 1856, the amount of the appropriation was continuously lowered: $200,000 in 1858, $120,000 in 1859, and $100,000 in 1860; but nothing more was done until 1860, when Governor John Downey urged the legislature to action "for a fine capitol." That year $500,000 was appropriated with a provision for new designs in a second competition.

Returning from San Francisco that spring, Clark paced the corridors of the Sacramento Court House waiting for a decision from the new Capitol Commission, the members of which needed something different from Clark's winning design. Seven architects, including Clark, entered the competition. The judging took place in May 1860, and from all accounts the commission was still not interested in Clark's design. That of Miner F. Butler was chosen, and when five of the architects stormed the commission with angry protests, they were given a two-week extension to revise and improve their plans.

Butler's new plans followed those he believed would be the finished United States Capitol. When he was declared winner, he was accused of copying the facade of another architect. An investigation followed. Only Clark appeared in Butler's behalf and, when it was over, Butler's second design was declared the winner to receive the $1,500 prize. Clark, over others, was appointed superintendent of construction with a salary of $300 per month.

Unable to get building supplies from the East because of the Civil War, Clark sought them from California and the Sandwich Islands. His suppliers charged higher prices, his dealings with the Capitol Commissioners were rockstrewn and almost constantly conservatives in the legislature demanded varied estimates of desired changes and additions to the structure. As a result, Clark was hard on his subcontractors.

In the spring of 1862, the Sacramento River flooded the capitol's foundation, destroying the files and all plans. Clark received $500 from the commission to redesign the plans, and he increased the height of the foundation six feet through the help of the new governor, Leland Stanford.

Stanford's enthusiasm, bolstered by political pressure, caused Clark to speed up the work. If money ran low, the governor forced taxes through the legislature. Clark's revision of the specifications found his numerous changes accepted and approved by Governor Stanford.

Reuben Clark refused to leave the job for a short rest and labored night and day, worrying about delays in the shipment of materials, and poring over the working drawings; and there was always the criticism of certain politicians and political factions.

On September 4, 1865, he was granted a leave of absence until January 1, 1866, "provided he employs G. Parker Cummings to superintend the work during his absence, without expense to the State."

The reason for his leave was not stated, but assumptions have been made: he was subjected to the pressures of increased cost estimates, and do-gooders of Sacramento accused him of disloyalty to the United States because he had been heard to say, "I don't care which side wins. . . ." He was also accused of employing "known secessionists" on construction of the capitol.

Unable to recoup his health during the leave time, Clark was relieved of his duties by a resolution in the minutes of the Capitol Commissioners on January 2, 1866. He was committed to the Stockton Insane Asylum on February 2 and admitted February 6, 1866. He died there on July 4, 1866.

G. Parker Cummings replaced him as architect of the state capitol. Because of financial problems, work was suspended after January 1870. With income from the sale of state bonds forthcoming, it resumed in August. Cummings was not rehired. Instead the Capitol Commissioners appointed a former partner of Clark's, Henry Kenitzer of San Francisco, and A. A. Bennett of San Francisco.

Hampered again by finances, from December 20, 1871, to May 8, 1872, construction proceeded without architectural services, but no major work was undertaken. Then, with assurance of money in hand, the State Board of Examiners unanimously elected George P. Cummings "to take charge of, supervise, and complete the State Capitol." Work resumed on May 15, but before actual construction commenced on June 5, 1872, the Board adopted a hard and fast set of 13 rules and regulations toward greater control of the project and its employees.

Work progressed until stopped, time after time. Cummings was the last supervising architect on the job. There has never been a date established as to the capitol's completion, but since Cummings and others were released on February 4, 1874, that date is used as the completion date. It is finally noted that maintenance work on the capitol commenced before the building was completed.

Constructed of granite from California quarries, it covers an area of 52,480 square feet. Its brick foundation, copied after that of a Spanish fortress in Panama, extends many feet below the basement floor and was, at that time, the strongest foundation construction known.

California has had many capitols. The Monterey Presidio served the Spanish and Mexican governments from 1770 until the Americans took over in 1846. The Presidio was last used as a capitol by California's Constitutional Convention in October 1849. The first California legislature met in San Jose in December 1849, in a two-story adobe, but failed to designate a permanent location.

As a result, several towns vied for the privilege of serving as the state capital. When Mariano J. Vallejo of Sonoma offered to lay out a new city and give adequate land with sufficient funds to the state to build public buildings, the people voted to have the capital in Vallejo. That was in 1850.

Admitted to the Union in 1850, the second legislature met again in San Jose in 1851, but from there, in quick succession, the state's lawmakers moved to Vallejo for a few days, then to the Sacramento County Courthouse, back to Vallejo for a month where Senor Vallejo asked to be released from his pledge. The Benicians offered their city hall, "an imposing structure for such a small town," and offered to introduce the legislators to their "twenty or thirty marriageable young ladies."

On February 4, 1853, Vallejo was freed of his obligations and the legislature resolved to adjourn and reconvene at Benicia on February 11.

The Benicians were delighted and lost no time moving the archives and furniture across the strait. A boardwalk was built from the business section to the new capitol. A grand ball was held in its assembly hall and a military band played far into the night. The remaining time of the fourth legislature was spent there.

Before the fifth could meet January 2, 1854, a drive to move the capitol back to Sacramento was already under way. There, they would have free use of the courthouse, fireproof vaults for state records, and acreage for a capitol was promised.

The Benicians countered with more attractions. They reminded that great body of the vast expense to the state and extended objections as to its legality, but to no avail. A bill was introduced, approved by Governor John Bigler on February 25, and on the same day the legislators adjourned to reconvene in Sacramento the following week. With kit and caboodle they boarded a steamer the next day, were greeted in Sacramento by a burst of artillery and the cheers of thousands and, when festivities ended, went back to work in Sacramento's new courthouse.

A flood forced them to reconvene in San Francisco's Exchange Building until the waters receded, then back they went to Sacramento's courthouse and remained there until 1869 when they moved into the new, unfinished capitol.

Possibly, California's capital city could have been Vallejo had Senor Vallejo's money held out and the electorate's will been complied with. Or Benicia could have been named the capital, had that city had the foresight to build a steel vault for the archives and supply adequate accommodations for the legislators, not to mention "marriageable young ladies."

During the years 1856–1860, while work was stopped, the instability of California's legislature is evident in the bills proposed to move from Sacramento to Oakland! to San Francisco! to San Jose! The corker came during the construction era of the 1860s, when another bill would have left the capitol unfinished and moved the capital to San Jose.

Regardless of its moving history, the construction of California's capitol has maintained a constant, costly, financial record. During construction and

Restored during a six-year period at a cost of $87 million, the California statehouse presents a rich new character to its citizens. – Author's photograph.

before the end of 1863, it became evident the appropriated $500,000 wouldn't be enough to complete the project. The state legislature levied a five-cent property tax at that time and another in 1866. Both were continued until the building and its landscaped grounds were complete. The final cost is given at $2.6 million.

Since that time the original building has had three major remodeling jobs costing over $3 million. In 1954 an east wing was completed for another $7.5 million and then came the major restoration.

In his 1863 annual message, Governor Leland Stanford said, "The State Capitol of California, that is to endure for generations, should be a structure that the future will be proud of, and surrounded with beauty and luxuriousness that no other Capitol in the country could boast."

By 1972, with its continuous remodeling, the building had lost its structural strength. A seismic study declared it unsafe in the event of a major earthquake. In 1975 the legislature elected to restore the doomed building to its 1900 stature rather than build a new capitol.

Bit by bit, brick by brick, at a cost of $87 million, the building was taken apart with each part strengthened, renewed, restored and replaced. Today, California's capitol functions as a strong, modern building and retains its original appearance and beauty.

Returned to Stanford's ideals, the California State Capitol is said to be one of the most beautiful and substantial in the United States. It is, without a doubt; and it *is* regal. It is crowned with a ball of copper, originally plated with gold coins which were removed in the recent restoration and replaced with better, longer-lasting gold plating.

Of Roman-Corinthian design, some say "modified Renaissance," others "Republican," its four stories and great, copper-covered dome and golden crown rise 220 feet into the sky.

No other capitol's landscaping can compare to its surrounding park that contains nearly 50,000 trees, shrubs and flowers. It has been stated that a visitor to the capitol, from any part of the world, can find a plant native to his land.

Inside, in the center of the rotunda is a statue of Columbus kneeling in his last appeal to Queen Isabella of Spain. The surrounding walls carry murals of the state's historic events and include the driving of the golden spike at Promontory Point, Utah, when the ribbons of steel joined the East and West in 1869. That was the year the capitol was first occupied by the governor, state officers and the legislature.

The California State Capitol is an exciting place to visit. Restored to its original condition it continues to serve as the working seat of government. The State Capitol Museum provides an opportunity to tour the entire building, to see how laws are made and to visit historic offices that were once occupied by the governor and other officers of the state.

The museum offers four different tours for groups numbering 10 to 40 as well as self-guided tours. California residents are encouraged to visit the six-story East Annex. Completed in 1952 at a cost of $7.6 million, it houses the offices of the governor and most of the legislators' offices.

In spite of the fact that other cities, from time to time over the years, have sought to become the state capital, Sacramento will remain the legislature's meeting place. The capital city can court lawmakers with exceptional accommodations.

COLORADO
The Centennial State

HEIGHT: 276'   FACADE: 384'   DEPTH: 315'

Within 50 years of Columbus' discovery of America, Spanish explorers, led by Coronado, came out of Mexico into that area which is now Colorado. Seeking gold and fabulous cities but finding none, they went elsewhere.

Captain Zebulon M. Pike was the first official explorer of the Colorado region. In late November 1806, he made an unsuccessful attempt to climb the mountain that bears his name. He was the first of several government explorers that included Fremont and Gunnison.

The first white settlements were in the San Luis Valley. The town of San Luis in Costilla County, founded in 1851, is considered the oldest continually occupied town in Colorado.

Extensive settlement in Colorado started with the discovery of gold on Little Dry Creek near its junction with the South Platte River. That discovery, by members of the Green Russell party from Georgia, caused the "Pikes Peak or Bust" gold rush of 1859, for those hurrying to get their share; and the "Pikes Peak Humbug" for those who gave up and returned home.

Some who stayed and searched further were not disappointed. One of these was John H. Gregory, who discovered gold near what is now Central City. His discovery on May 6, 1859, caused the spread of mining over that area and swelled the population.

At least one town had law and order during the late 1850s. St. Charles, named after Charles III, was progressive and growing. In 1858 officials of the Kansas Territory made General William Larimer a commissioner of the area and gave him authority to change the name of St. Charles to Denver, after the former territorial governor of Kansas, General James W. Denver.

At that time, the land that would become Colorado was within the territories of Kansas, Utah, Nebraska, and New Mexico. Believing they should have a government of their own, Denver residents, often referred to as "The Pikes Peakers," created the Jefferson Territory.

Using the Northwest Ordinance of 1787, which admitted public domain into the Union, their territory took in all of present-day Colorado as well as parts of what are now Utah and Wyoming. With the Jefferson Territory came their government with its laws, but the territorial laws were ignored by the miners who made their own laws and elected officials to enforce them. Jefferson Territory and its government existed less than a year. They were gone before the end of 1860.

With pressure inflicted by their Washington agents, territorial status was created by Congress on February 28, 1861. President Lincoln appointed Colonel William Gilpin governor. Even though Colorado City, now Colorado Springs, was designated the territorial capital, the first territorial government assembly met in Denver on September 9, 1861. From among several names submitted, the territory was named after the river that heads in Colorado and flows through the Grand Canyon into the Gulf of California.

In 1862, the capital was moved to Golden.

Submitting to the pressures of statehood, Congress passed an enabling act for statehood in 1864, but Colorado voters turned it down. When they approved statehood the following year, it was denied them by Congress. In 1866 President Andrew Johnson vetoed Congress' statehood for Colorado. Was it not meant to be?

In 1867, Denver was named the permanent capital of the Colorado Territory.

Finally, in 1875, a Constitutional Convention convened in Denver and the following year, on July 1, 1876, with *men only* voting, Colorado's constitution was ratified by popular vote, four to one. One month later, August 1, 1876, President Ulysses S. Grant declared Colorado to be the thirty-eighth state in the Union with Denver its capital and John L. Routt its governor.

Even after statehood with the capital designated as Denver, there were wishful opposition and hope that a different town would become the state's capital. In 1877 in Galena City, George T. Lee had built a mansion designated to become a future governor's place of residence. He wanted the name changed from Galena to Capitol City; and he firmly believed that its population would swell to a point beyond that of Denver's which would force it into becoming the capital. The population of that mining settlement never exceeded one thousand.

The problem was settled for all time on November 8, 1881. Denver was made the permanent capital by a vote of the people.

In 1874, when a ten-acre site in Denver was offered by Henry C. Brown to the territorial legislature as a site for a capitol, it was eagerly accepted; but the excavation did not begin until July 5, 1886, almost ten years after Colorado was granted statehood.

With money for the capitol's construction appropriated by the legislature, Elija E. Meyers was engaged as architect. Work progressed slowly. A 20-ton cornerstone was set with a Masonic ceremony on July 4, 1890. Within its mass were buried a Bible, an American flag, the United States and Colorado constitutions, countless state records and historical data, a collection of coins and a walking stick made from a piece of the keel from *Old Ironsides*.

Throughout that period, from its statehood until occupation of its capitol, Colorado's legislature met in cramped and uncomfortable rented quarters as necessary and available.

Offices in the building were first occupied in 1894. Apparently, as an architect, Meyers was inadequate. He was discharged and replaced by Frank E. Edbrooke in 1898. The last wing of the capitol was completed in 1907.

Twenty-two years in its building and at a cost of $2.8 million, Colorado's capitol will last for ages. It can be called sturdy for it has long-lasting qualities. Built of Gunnison granite, the outer walls are five feet thick. This granite is of such fine quality, the capitol's builders maintained it would stand for more than a thousand years. Inside those walls, backing the granite, is sandstone from Fort Collins. Sandstone was also used for the foundations.

Inside the capitol, the pillars and wainscoting are a pinkish-brown, rose onyx from Beulah, Colorado. The floors and stairs are laid with Colorado yule marble. To do the required stonework it was necessary to bring more than 200 stonecutters from California, Maine, Texas, and Vermont.

The original dome was copper, but residents began to complain that copper was not native to Colorado, that something native should be on the dome.

Believing it to be a proper native ore, the miners contributed 200 ounces of 28 carat gold amounting to $14,680 to gild the dome in 1908. Its regilding with gold leaf during 1950 became a problem when swarms of gnats flew into the adhesive that covered the dome. This condition sometimes prevented the workers' affixing the thin sheets of shiny metal. But the job was finished at a cost of $22,000.

The dome was last gilded in 1980. It required 45 ounces of gold made into sheets, one-thousandth of an inch thick.

The capitol's floor plan resembles a Greek cross, one formed by two equal, intersecting lines crossing at their midpoints to form right angles. There are four entrances leading to the rotunda and its grand staircase of brass-embellished marble.

Visitors to the capitol's interior remain impressed with its attractions. The governor's suite, paneled in walnut and highlighted with chandeliers, is on the first floor.

There are eight murals on the first floor rotunda walls, and 180 feet above them the interior of the dome covering the rotunda is colored green and gold.

Inside the dome, springing from the rotunda 150 feet below, there is a sunburst; and, surrounding the dome, near the top is Colorado's Hall of Fame: the portraits of 16 Colorado pioneers who helped in the growth and development of the state. Amid much political arguing and dispute, they were placed there in 1900. Only one person in the Colorado Hall of Fame received a unanimous vote. That was the Chief Ouray of the Ute Indians, who had deeded land to the United States. The portraits are in stained glass, intricately pieced together so that they resemble oil paintings.

The Senate and House chambers were refurbished in 1972. Entered on the second floor, both have the green and gold motif, from floors to ceilings from which hang identical great chandeliers each weighing three-quarters of a ton and containing 56 light bulbs.

Two other features of the capitol are pronounced unique. One is the door knobs of intricate brass design on many of the doors. Centered in the knob is the Colorado state seal. The escutcheon displays the state flower, the columbine. The brasswork of the entire building was manufactured in Cincinnati, Ohio. The other feature is the elevator doors. The history of Colorado is portrayed within their eight bronze panels: from the beginning before man, through Indian occupation, the discovery of gold and the settlement of Colorado, and the state's growth into modern times.

The elevators run from the basement to the third floor and are located in the east wing behind the rotunda. There are telephones and water fountains near the elevators.

Visitors are welcome and may climb into the dome from the third floor entry in the north wing Monday through Friday from 9 A.M. to 4 P.M. There is no charge for capitol tours conducted throughout the year for groups; and individuals are welcome to join a group tour. Summer tours are conducted every half hour, 9 A.M. to 4 P.M.

During legislative sessions (approximately January through June) visitors may view the activities of the Senate and House by entering their galleries on the third floor and are also welcome to attend Senate hearings in the third floor meeting rooms. During their sessions legislative printed materials are available and free and may be picked up in the basement.

The basement has restrooms; and exits in the north and south wings of the capitol provide ramps for those who cannot or prefer not to climb stairs.

CONNECTICUT
The Constitution State

HEIGHT: 257′ 2″   FACADE: 295′ 8″   DEPTH: 189′ 4″

The year 1988 marked the 350th anniversary of representative government in Connecticut.

The state of Connecticut was first explored by the Dutch, who founded trading posts; the first permanent settlers there were English: the Puritans coming out of Massachusetts in 1633.

Among them was Reverend Thomas Hooker who, in a sermon delivered on May 31, 1638, suggested to the people that certain principles of government should be executed only through the voice of the people. Out of his examples, the people fashioned and adopted a constitution known as the Fundamental Orders of 1639. Based upon the will of the people, that document is considered the first written constitution of a democratic government.

Although Connecticut is known as "The Constitution State," George Washington named it "The Provision State" because of the supplies contributed to the Continental Army by Governor Jonathon Trumbull who, by the way, was the only colonial governor supporting America's independence.

Connecticut's soldiers fought in battles ranging from the Carolinas into Quebec, Canada. It was here hero General Israel Putnam at Bunker Hill gave the order, "Don't fire until you see the whites of their eyes." It was Connecticut's patriot, Nathan Hale, who uttered, "I regret that I have but one life to lose for my country," before being hanged by the British as a colonial spy.

In 1638 the colonial government met in Hartford in a meeting house. It was a rectangular-shaped, frame building of two stories with a third tucked underneath a gambrel roof holding a cupola. The structure was representative of a modern barn topped by an immense hayloft. Its entrances were without porticos.

The Connecticut capitol is home to the governor, the legislature and secretary of state. It is a treasure house of decorative and architectural accomplishment. — Author's photograph.

From 1701 to 1875 Connecticut had two capitals: New Haven and Hartford with each taking its turn housing the government every other year. As a result, each city had its own capitol. This arrangement for two capitals was further enforced in 1818 when an enactment of the general assembly placed it in the Connecticut constitution.

Hartford's first permanent capitol, designed by Charles Bullfinch, architect for the United States Capitol, was first occupied by the general assembly in 1796. New Haven's first capitol was put into service the same year.

Both of these buildings were replaced with newer ones: Hartford's, completed in 1879, continues to serve the state; New Haven's, completed in 1875, was used until 1879.

For some time during the 1861–70 decade, certain factions of the population posed the question, "Shouldn't Connecticut have but one capital city?" Eventually the subject of the capital's location caused strife among the citizens. Some cried there should be but one and that it should be Hartford because of its central location. Others wanted New Haven because of its greater population and commercial wealth.

In the ensuing debates over the issue two factors were obvious. The use of two cities was inconvenient and onerous; and the buildings currently used as statehouses were in disrepair.

Hartford's offer of $500,000 to the state for the construction of a new capitol forced upon the people, in 1873, a referendum to choose their capital. Hartford was chosen. The people's choice lost in only two counties: New Haven and Fairfield.

After the legislature issued $1 million in bonds to buy land and build, the city of Hartford bought Trinity College and announced its land would be the site for the capitol. A new State House Commission was appointed by Governor Marshall Jewell to organize and manage the project and its building funds. Thirteen architectural firms submitted designs and plans in competition. Those of Richard M. Upjohn of New York were selected and he was appointed capitol architect April 18, 1872.

His design in High Victorian Gothic was built of New England marble and granite by James G. Batterson. Topped with a 12-sided, gold leaf dome, rather than the clock in Upjohn's original design, and completed in 1879 at a cost of $2,532,524.43 (plus furnishings at $100,000), the Connecticut Capitol in Hartford became the seventh building to serve as a meeting place for Connecticut's legislature.

The "Genius of Connecticut," a bronze, female statue, designed and manufactured in Italy by sculptor Randolph Rogers and cast in a German foundry, offered her symbolic wreaths of oak and laurel to Connecticut's citizens from high atop the dome's lantern. Her sister statues, representing agriculture, commerce, force, law, music, and science, ringed the dome at a lower level.

The capitol exterior is faced with white marble from the quarries of East Canaan, Connecticut. Polished granite columns from Westerly, Rhode Island, with white marble capitals, support each of the four entrances. Its interior columns, climbing the stairs, are of pink granite. All the marble and granite of the interior was quarried in Maine, Vermont, Rhode Island and Connecticut. The interior woodwork is comprised of oak, black walnut, and ash.

The building's foundation is brownstone, cement, and brick. Its roof is slate. The facade is ornamented with statuary and historic scenes in bas-relief. One of the subjects is that of the Charter Oak Tree: In 1687, the charter granted Connecticut by Charles II in 1662 was threatened with seizure by forces of King James II. During testy negotiations the candles lighting the room suddenly went out. In the darkness Captain Joseph Wadsworth made off with the document and hid it in a giant oak tree where it was kept until the danger had passed. Years later, when the tree was felled by a storm, part of its wood was used to construct the Charter Oak Chair which occupies the center of three chairs at the rostrum of the Senate chamber.

Off the rotunda, the skylighted, rectangular arcades or atria in the east and west wings are enclosed on each story's level by connecting balconies. Given a courtyard effect, these open areas were filled with hand-painted columns, stenciled beams and stained glass ceiling panels. Italian marble covers the floors. Surrounding the open space on their respective floors are the chambers of the general assembly and the offices of its members.

In its setting, the capitol overlooks Bushnell Park laid out by Dr. Horace

Bushnell, and by Frederick L. Olmsted, designer of Central Park in New York City and acclaimed as first landscape architect in the United States. Both men were residents of Hartford.

Through almost a century of continuous use, the capitol had deteriorated to the point that something had to be done. Would it become Hartford's second "Old State House"? During 1972, the United States Department of the Interior declared the aged capitol a National Historic Landmark. This action started legislative procedures to allocate $38 million for its restoration.

By 1980 workers from the region were giving advice and providing skills to do the work. The accumulated dirtiness from the environment was cleansed from the exterior. The dome, regilded twice, is no longer crowned with the "Genius of Connecticut," but the original plaster model for the bronze statue now stands in the north entrance hall. A new copper roof was installed. Whatever was needed to regain the original structure's beauty and decor was obtained. The entire building, inside and out, was completely restored under the careful supervision of Hartford architect D. C. Cimino.

Because of changes made to the interior without professional advice, as well as the need for additional office space to accommodate the growing government, extensive remodeling and refurbishing were included.

The present Senate chamber was originally the state library. When it was moved into the new Library and Supreme Court Building in 1910, galleries for the public were added to the east and west walls. As the years passed, much of the decoration was destroyed or covered up. Restoration recovered the original elements to blend with the additions.

Modernization of every feature and mechanical system was accomplished and once again Connecticut's Capitol can claim the distinction of being one of the most beautiful architectural treasures in the nation.

The capitol has over 500 windows and 200 doors, many decorated with stained glass and intricately designed hardware. Throughout the building are decorative details at every scale and of every material.

A public information office is found in Room 101 on the main floor, which also features a spectacular view of the rotunda up through the central core of the capitol to the spiraling pattern of the dome's ceiling.

Hartford's Bullfinch-designed "Old State House" served as the seat of Connecticut's government, alternating annually with New Haven during the years 1796 until 1879. When the new capitol was finished, the old one was turned into a museum.

Today, with an annual budget of $500,000, the "Old State House" has been engulfed by Hartford's financial towers that have risen around and above it. Realizing its value as a scenic object for those persons whose tower windows overlook their museum and, according to an article in the *New York Times,* 4,154 windows do overlook the museum, state legislators have set a fee of ten dollars per viewing window, per year.

Because Connecticut's government outgrew its capitol's space, its legislature brought about the construction of a new structure, probably the most modern and electronically designed in existence today. For 20 years legislators had dreamed of an environment that would enhance their work, their commitment to the people, and the legislative process, and make it possible for the citizens of Connecticut to take part in that process.

With the need for specialized committees and task forces to accomplish their work, there came a need for meeting places, places for study and research, places for listening to people with different needs, and problems.

The Legislative Office Building answers those needs. It brings the public into the legislative process and is oriented to the capitol for it is there that ideas, refined in committee in the office building, will be debated, enacted into law, and signed by the governor.

The building is connected to the capitol by a terraced walkway as well as a 500-foot underground concourse containing a moving walkway. A covered passage connects it to the garage.

Its five floors are contained within an irregular-shaped pentagon with an atrium, "the heart of the building," in its center. Night and day, the glistening gold of the capitol's dome shines through the atrium's curved glass wall.

The first floor contains five public hearing rooms; the second, five committee hearing rooms. No two hearing rooms are identical, but are of different size and used as public capacities demand. Besides the hearing rooms, the first floor contains committee offices and maintenance space; the second, committee offices. The remaining floors, with larger space on the third and fifth for committees and state offices, are leaders' and individual House members' offices.

The building is designed to accept technological changes that will occur during its lifetime. There are hearing rooms that have lights that will illuminate an individual speaker, a committee, or the entire audience.

Video screens display the time and place for every event. Visitors to the bill room can pick up bills, journals, calendars, and official documents. No one need miss a hearing. When crowds overflow a hearing room, the proceedings may be watched on video screens in other hearing rooms or the atrium.

DELAWARE
The First State

HEIGHT: 90′   FACADE: 250′   DEPTH: 141′

On October 27, 1682, William Penn landed at New Castle in what is now Delaware. The colonists "subscribed an oath of allegiance to the new proprietor, and the first general assembly was held in the colony."

The following year, Penn ordered the laying out of Dover as the seat of Kent County, a city that would eventually become the capital of Delaware, the first state to ratify the federal Constitution, thereby the "First State" in the United States.

It started in New Castle in the old court house which stands upon the evidence left by its predecessor that was built between the years 1682 and 1689, and destroyed by fire in 1729. In 1731 the central part of the old court house was erected on the site. Small wings were added at the east and west ends in 1765. An addition to the east wing was made in 1802; and, in 1845, the west wing was torn down and replaced with a fireproof wing for the county's records.

Delaware's first capitol was the center of the state's history. It was here, in July of 1776, that the soldiers of Colonel John Hazlet's First Delaware Regiment, the "Blue Hen's Chickens," "took out of the Court House all the insignia of the Monarchy . . . all the baubles of Royalty . . . set fire to them and burnt them to ashes . . . and a merry day we made of it." This act was followed by the framing of the constitution of the "Delaware State" with its antislavery clause, the election of Dr. John McKinley as the state's first president, and the naming of New Castle as the first capital on September 23, 1776.

When the capital was moved to Dover May 12, 1777, the old court house continued to flourish with meetings of the state and federal courts. It was used as a place of assembly for public discussion of the problem of the day; and, for more than a hundred years, the Delaware courts handed down decisions from within its hallowed walls before it languished into disuse and neglect until 1950, when the New Castle Historic Buildings Commission induced its restoration. Today it is one of New Castle's foremost tourist attractions.

During the entire Revolution only one engagement was fought on Delaware soil. This was a skirmish at Cooch's Bridge near Newark on September 3, 1777. The British met no resistance as they occupied Wilmington on September 13, 1777. Even though Delaware's population was small, 4,000 men were raised for the Continental Army, and they fought in most of the important battles from Long Island to Yorktown.

It was from Dover that Caesar Rodney, a Delawarean hero and patriot, was called to sign the Declaration of Independence and assure the state's adoption of the document. A galloping horse brought about his famous ride from Dover to Philadelphia during the night of July 1, 1776, where he cast Delaware's deciding vote in favor of Lee's Resolution for the Declaration.

After the war Delaware's capital thrived. Its population grew to 600 in 1785. It had a lively appearance, about 100 houses, principally of brick, and considerable trade with Philadelphia.

Dover was given new status in 1829 by being incorporated. For 30 years it prospered. The railroad arrived in 1856, and Kent County's crops were shipped to Philadelphia by rail causing a decline in river traffic.

Today, Dover Green remains the heart of that city. Defined by Penn in his 1683 order for Dover and laid out in 1717, it remains confined to the original space that has served as a meeting and market place for the people. The courthouse, built soon afterwards, was ordered, in 1691, "Burnt to get the nails." From about 1722 to 1863 a tavern, with a long series of owners, occupied the site. Today that ground is covered by the Kent County Courthouse that was erected in 1874.

The Kent County Courthouse that was built in 1722, and served as the state government's seat from 1777, was completely rebuilt in 1787–1792. Every salvageable brick and construction material from the old building was used in building the new. During this construction period, with no place to meet, the convention met under the sky near the site to ratify the federal Constitution on December 7, 1787; and this, according to historians, was the most important single event to occur in Dover. Delaware became the first state in the new republic.

A new state constitution was adopted and Delaware's last state president, Joshua Clayton, became her first governor in 1792.

Since its completion in 1792, what was then Delaware's new capitol has become known as "the jewel of the Green." Today it is "the Old Statehouse" and contains many of Delaware's historic treasures. Among these are portraits of former governors and the bell that hung in the Kent County Court House and was rung to assemble "the freeholders of Kent . . . to take into consideration the acts of the British Parliament in shutting up the Port of Boston."

During the Civil War it was used as quarters for troops from Maryland who had been sent to Delaware to disarm suspected Delaware militia companies. Although Delaware was a slave state, it had refused to secede from the Union despite great pro–Southern sympathy. Delaware men fought on both sides and some people were suspect.

Located across the street from the Green, the "Old Statehouse" continues, in part, to function in the government by housing Delaware's Supreme Court.

The Green, laid out in 1717 according to William Penn's orders of 1683, remains as was ordered. It has been the center of life in a county seat and state capital. Formerly the site of fairs and markets, today it is political rallies and public events and, in May each year, it's the central point of the Old Dover Days celebration.

On the Green stood the pillory and the whipping post, used as a means of punishment. The pillory was abolished in 1905, but the whipping post was retained.

It was on the Green that Delaware's Continental Regiment was mustered for the Revolution. The troops marched from the Green to join Washington's Continental Army. It was here that the Declaration of Independence was read to the public, precipitating a celebration that included the burning of George III's portrait. And it was on the Green, January 23, 1800, that John Vining delivered his encomium on the death of George Washington.

Several years before 1933, Capitol Square had been laid out and money for a new capitol appropriated. The creation of the capitol complex was in keeping with Penn's original vision of his seat in Kent County. Today's broad, tree-lined avenues, shady side streets, expansive greens and the parks along the meandering St. Jones River blend into Dover's Georgian architecture and colonial history.

Completed, the new capitol, Legislative Hall, became the home of Delaware's government. Designed by William Martin of Wilmington, the exterior is of handmade red brick following the Georgian architectural pattern of Dover. The exquisite woodwork embellishing the interior, so much detailed in eighteenth century buildings, is of seemingly strict simplicity. The new capitol was opened January 3, 1933. It was enlarged in 1970 to make room for growth in government.

The first floor holds the Senate and House chambers as well as offices for their members. The offices of the governor, the lieutenant governor, the secretary of state, and the governor's reception area are on the second floor.

Throughout its corridors and offices are displayed the heroes and patriots of Delaware's history.

Other buildings on Capitol Square house portions of the government. The Hall of Records, home of the Division of Historical and Cultural Affairs, is the depository of historical documents preserved through the years. One display of 1787 records the action which made Delaware "the state that started a nation" by its unusually fast ratification of the federal Constitution. Another document of 1691 is an order for the new courthouse in Dover.

The departments of Natural Resources, Environmental Control, Health and Social Services, and the Colonel John Haslet Armory occupy other buildings around Capitol Square.

FLORIDA
The Sunshine State

HEIGHT: 322′ ±   FACADE: 371′ 8″   DEPTH: 195′ 8″

The history of Florida's discovery and colonization is most interesting, but too lengthy for a capitols' preview. Yet consideration must be given to that area now comprising Florida's capital city, Tallahassee. Although threatened, it has withstood the pressure of political relocation several times over the years and so must be considered Florida's first and only capital.

Based on conjecture, Ponce de Leon landed in or near the area during

1521, the same year Indians kept him from landing at Charlotte's Harbor. This was a long time after his landing near St. Augustine in 1513, to claim the land for Spain and name it *La Florida*.

It has been established that Panfilo de Narvaez was there in 1528; but historians are absolutely certain that Hernando de Soto spent the winter of 1539 at, or very close to the site of Florida's capital city, Tallahassee.

How and why this place was selected is a good story with a practical and lucid ending. When the Spaniards arrived, the area was inhabited by the now-extinct Apalachee Indians. They were hostile to the Spaniards. It took nearly 100 years for Franciscan friars to get them friendly enough to attempt their Christianization; and in 1675, there were seven Franciscan missions in the area. Some of these were destroyed at the turn of the century by raiding South Carolinians and Creek Indians. The Apalachee villages were destroyed. Their residents scattered before the onslaught.

Eventually the Seminole Indians populated the area, but were considered unfriendly to the United States because, among other things, they harbored runaway slaves. This caused Andrew Jackson and his army to invade Spain's colony to burn Seminole villages. Undaunted, the Seminoles rebuilt as soon as he left and were there when the Tallahassee site was chosen for Florida's capital city in 1823.

Under Spain's rule two provinces, East and West Florida, were governed from St. Augustine and Pensacola, respectively. Spain surrendered Florida to the United States in 1821, and Andrew Jackson took possession as military governor. Jackson resigned shortly afterwards and on March 30, 1822, when the Territory of Florida was established from the two provinces, William Duval was appointed governor. He, along with a legislative council of 13 leaders of the region appointed by President James Monroe, comprised the government of the new territory.

In 1822, the territory's first legislative council met in Pensacola. The following year, 1823, the second met in St. Augustine. Because of the loss of one councilman and the hardships encountered by others who had to travel 400 miles to attend, this legislative council authorized Governor Duval to appoint two commissioners to select a site for a permanent capital that would be centrally located "somewhere between the Suwanee and Ochlockonee Rivers. . . ."

John Lee Williams of Pensacola sailed eastward in a small boat along the coast. Dr. William H. Simmons of St. Augustine traveled westward on horseback. They met at St. Marks, traveled north about 20 miles, looked around and selected an abandoned Indian village that Williams described as "a more beautiful country can scarcely be imagined." The exact site was a group of hills near a stream and waterfall, the place Tallahassee now stands.

Soon afterward, Governor Duval made it known that the next legislative council would meet there; and he ordered that accommodations be built for the government. John McIver of North Carolina arrived at the new capital site with a few settlers on April 9, 1824. Judge Jonathan Robinson and Sherrod

McCall, neighboring planters from what is now Gadsden County, brought slaves and built three log cabins. One of them, accommodating the third legislative council that convened November 8, 1824, became Florida's first capitol.

Congress granted a quarter-section of land to be sold to finance a new capitol for the territory. Within this quarter-section the council directed that a town be laid out and named after the Tallahassee Seminole Indians occupying the area. The southeast corner was designated as that point from which all surveys in Florida were to be made. Within Tallahassee's city limits today, a monument stands at the intersection of the base parallel and meridian lines from which all townships and ranges are numbered: north, south, east, and west. A county was created and named Leon after Ponce de Leon. Tallahassee was named as the county seat.

The town was laid out symmetrically with its center designated as Capitol Square. The first lot was sold in April 1825. By September of that year, within that wilderness area there were more than 50 occupied houses with commercial, social and industrial support, including a church and schoolhouse. The city of Tallahassee was incorporated December 9, 1825, and soon became the trade center of the area with the St. Marks port as its shipping point. The Federal Road: Pensacola to St. Augustine through Tallahassee, was opened that winter and by 1838, for lack of an engine that would work, there was a mule-drawn railroad from the capital to its shipping point, St. Marks, 18 miles away.

Before construction was started on a second capitol at Capitol Square in 1826, the log building was removed and the council met in rented quarters. The new building was designed by Colonel Robert Butler, a former military aide to General Jackson. Work started after the legislative council had specified its construction would be in two parts with the first section completed before the second was started.

The cornerstone for the first section was laid with full Masonic ceremonies on January 7, 1826. When the second section was started, it was discovered that all the money from the sale of land had been spent. The completed section, a 26 × 40 feet, two-story, frame structure had four columns supporting porticos on each story. It served as the capitol for nearly 20 years before Florida's second territorial governor, John H. Eaton, complained his office was "without the comforts which should belong to it."

His complaints and the political pressures in 1838 caused Florida's territorial delegate to Congress, Charles Downing, to contend that the Florida capitol was dilapidated and falling apart, that the people wanted something they could be proud of when Florida took its place with the other states in the Union. His plea, among those of others pressuring for statehood, effected a $20,000 appropriation from Congress, March 3, 1839, and opened the way for territorial officials to sponsor an architectural contest for the third Florida capitol.

The design by Carry Butt of Mobile, Alabama, was chosen. It was for a three-story building of Greek Revival design with six-columned porticos at the east and west entrances. Once more Capitol Square was cleared, but the construction of a new capitol, begun in 1839, was hampered by fiscal, social, and natural disasters. Yellow fever struck Tallahassee in 1841. Hurricanes struck the capital city in 1842 and 1843. In 1843 a fire ravaged the downtown district, destroying many businesses. About this time, the $20,000 congressional appropriation had been used up.

With another $20,000 appropriation from Congress in 1844, work resumed and the building was completed in time for Florida's admission to the Union as the 27th state, March 3, 1845. The inauguration of William D. Moseley as the first elected state governor occurred in June.

Now known as the 1845 capitol, its total cost was $55,000. Its facade measured 151 feet; its depth, 53 feet. The exterior walls were stuccoed and scored to resemble hewn stone. Its ridge roof, covered with slate, had gabled ends. The main entrance had double bronze doors set in classical surrounds.

Because its 23,000 square feet supplied more room than Florida's government needed, basement offices were rented out to professional people, including an artist; but the government's continued growth ended this practice in 1860.

Florida seceded from the Union on January 10, 1861. Its government, under the Confederacy, continued in Tallahassee until July 4, 1868, when it was readmitted with a new constitution. Throughout the Civil War, Tallahassee was the only Confederate capital east of the Mississippi to remain free from invasion and capture by Union troops.

Florida's government grew with its population and by 1900, with the population ten times that of 1845, something had to be done about the capitol. In June a Democratic Convention met in Jacksonville, nominated a governor and with the building of a new capitol in mind, resolved to move the capital to a more central location. Jacksonville, Ocala, and St. Augustine were placed on the ballot with Tallahassee. The people's decision came on November 6, 1900. Their choice, by a wide margin, was Tallahassee.

William S. Jennings was elected the first twentieth century governor and, to start the century properly, Florida's legislature appropriated $75,000 for the renovation and expansion of its capitol.

Frank P. Milburn of Columbia, South Carolina, was chosen as architect. With knowledge of Florida's conservative fiscal policies, his design was plainer than that originally considered. His dome, the most prominent addition, soared 136 feet above the ground and was covered with copperized iron oxidized to a natural green color.

Constructed by the J. E. Parrish Company of Lynchburg, Virginia, the project was completed in late 1902, within the budget of $75,000. Although its floor space was doubled, by the time it was occupied, it was crowded. As a result, separate buildings were authorized and the 1902 capitol was the last to completely house the state government.

With increased government bulging its walls after World War I and crescive desire for an addition to the capitol, the 1921 legislature appropriated $250,000 for another project and Henry J. Klutho of Jacksonville was retained as architect. Substantially enlarged, the building retained Cary Butt's original theme and included Frank Milburn's embellishments. To accomplish this, Klutho added east and west wings and, by moving the porticos, reshaped the capitol into a cross. This practically doubled the floor space again, but in the following decade the walls of the 1921 capitol bulged again.

Under the architectural direction of M. Leo Elliott of Tampa, a north wing was added for the House chamber in 1936. At that time, a similar, south wing was planned to house the Senate, but was delayed by events leading to World War II. It was finished and occupied by the Senate in 1947.

By 1950 the state's government had grown so rapidly that a complex of office buildings surrounded the capitol. Governor and cabinet staffs were so scattered their work and efficiency were threatened. Office space within the capitol had become a desirable commodity. Enlargement was considered, but its age, its several additions, its maintenance, and the changes within its walls brought about by governors and legislators without architectural advice or legislative approval had induced structural failure in many parts. These stoppers prompted consideration of a new capitol.

About 1955, a commission, chaired by Supreme Court Justice Harold Sebring, recommended a new capitol. For nearly 20 years government officials argued and worried before accepting the recommendation.

In 1972 a 22-story, tower capitol was finally approved by the governor, his cabinet, and the legislature. It was designed by Edward Durell Stone of New York in association with the Jacksonville firm of Reynolds, Smith and Hills. Its construction would take four years at a cost of $43 million. Their decision brought about another problem, one which fostered political enemies, enraged the populace, and led to litigation within governmental ranks.

And what about the old capitol? What should be done about the 1845, the 1902, the 1923, the 1936, the 1947 capitols?

So sure were the architects that the existing capitol would be demolished that the new building was constructed within inches of the old. Governor Reubin Askew, the House speaker and many legislators argued that the old building would detract from the new and the cost of its restoration would be more than its worth.

When the 1972 legislature approved the new capitol, it also stipulated that a decision on the old capitol would "be put off until later."

Architect Stone recommended that the old one be torn down and new, full-sized replica of the 1947 capitol be built. The Supreme Court ruled the building could not be destroyed without approval and funding of the legislature.

In a "Save the Old Capitol" crusade, thousands of Floridians signed petitions; service, fraternal, and social clubs vocalized; school children joined the fray. When the newly elected secretary of state, Bruce Smathers, refused to move his office from the old building into the new, the fire marshal intervened

The "old capitol" remains centered before the "new capitol" — the newest in the United
States. — Division of Tourism, Department of Commerce.

to classify the bulding as a fire trap. When a structural engineer attested that
a strong wind would topple the tower, Smathers was evicted. Before leaving
he held a "Save the Capitol" party in the building which was deemed "the most
significant public event to focus on the building's fate."

Overwhelmed by the dissension raised against demolition through the
constant clamor from the people, the opponents about-faced and joined in
ironing out a solution. Out of several proposals, it was decided to demolish all
parts of the building added after 1902 and completely restore Milburn's 1902
capitol.

The Senate approved the restoration in 1977, but the House did not come
to a decision until the final days in May 1978, when an appropriation of $7
million was made to cover all costs including a plaza between the old capitol
and the new.

Research and restoration required four years. Working outside, archeologists discovered numerous features associated with the past. Inside, researchers recorded all the parts of the building that were to be demolished. Demolition for the removal of 80 percent of the structure was started in 1978.

Today a marble tablet on the northeast corner of the 1902 capitol bears, in part, these words: "The Masons of Florida laid cornerstones for additions to the Capitol in the years 1902, 1923, 1936, and 1946 and these stones are now incorporated in the restored Capitol and were reconsecrated this 19th day of July, A.D. 1980, A.L. 5980."

In November 1973 construction of Florida's new capitol was started. It was dedicated in August 1977. It rises 307 feet above the main entrance level to a public observation deck on the twenty-second floor. Within its body are 3,700 tons of structural steel, 2,800 tons of reinforcing steel, and 25,000 cubic yards of concrete, enough to cover 16 football fields, to a depth of one foot. There are three stories below the plaza level. About 3,000 people work there on a normal day, 4,500 during legislative sessions.

The plaza floor contains the Welcome Center, the Religious Heritage Chapel, and the Governor's Reception Room. The House and Senate chambers are on the fourth floor and their public viewing galleries are on the fifth. These floors and the observation deck are public areas. Government offices occupy the remainder of the building.

The public areas have terrazzo floors. The walls of the plaza floor hallways and those surrounding the rotundas are travertine marble from Italy. The foundation of the Great Seal of Florida, centered in the plaza rotunda, is *verde aver* marble from Val d'Aosta, Italy. Bronze medallions around the seal represent the five nations in Florida's history: Spain, France, England, the United States of America, and the Confederacy. Murals, photos, and portraits of people and historic events are displayed throughout the public floors.

Open to everyone, free of charge, the observation deck is probably the most popular attraction to visitors and employees. On a clear day, you can see Georgia to the north and the St. Marks Lighthouse to the southwest, 28 miles away. The view of surrounding Tallahassee is found spectacular by crowds of tour groups as well as brown baggers "lunching it." Absent of the crowd, deserted, it is a place for quiet, meditative review of one's life.

On May 29, 1978, the Florida Senate passed Senate Bill 678. Section 5 of that bill states: A plaque shall be placed in the lobby of the new capitol and shall be inscribed as follows: "This plaque is dedicated to Senator Lee Weissenborn, whose valiant effort to move the Capitol to Orlando was the prime motivation for construction of this building."

In 1988, four people were employed to maintain the building at a cost of $85,000.

GEORGIA
The Empire State of the South

HEIGHT: 272' 4.5"   FACADE: 347' 9"   DEPTH: 272' 4.5"

At the entrance of Georgia's capitol a plaque reads: "This Capitol was Erected Under the Act of the General Assembly, Approved September 8, 1883, Completed in February, 1889."

On July 4, 1989, Georgians celebrated the centennial of their capitol, the last in the rich history of Georgia and its founders.

Named after King George II of England, which was one of the terms of the charter granted to James Edward Oglethorpe and trustees on June 9, 1732, Georgia was the last of the 13 British colonies established along the Atlantic Coast.

Oglethorpe, with 114 settlers landed where Savannah now stands on February 12, 1733. The new colony was to act as a buffer between South Carolina and the Spaniards threatening approach from Florida. That menace was stopped on July 7, 1742, when Oglethorpe, general and commander in chief of the forces of South Carolina and Georgia, defeated the Spanish in the Battle of Bloody Marsh. The following year Oglethorpe returned to England, never to return.

When the trustees gave up their charter in 1752, the king appointed a royal governor, John Reynolds, who arrived in 1754. A legislature of two houses was formed to govern the colony. Its upper house was appointed; the lower house, elected. Savannah became the first governing city of Georgia.

When Georgia declared independence from British rule in 1776, the Revolutionary government caused the election of an executive council with the capital at Savannah.

The capture of Savannah by the British in 1778 drove the government to Augusta. When Augusta fell in 1779 it moved to Heard's Fort until 1782, then returned to Augusta, briefly, before moving back to Savannah, vacated by the British.

But before the legislators could get to Savannah, they had to stop at the German settlement of Ebenezer several days to take care of necessary business.

Georgia's assembly rotated between Augusta and Savannah during the years 1783 to 1785. The two governors elected during those years, Lyman Hall and John Houston, divided their official residences between the two.

This unusual practice was caused by the 1783 legislature passing an act to move the capital to Augusta because it was close to the center of the state. The general assembly's last meeting in Savannah was held on February 2, 1785.

Founded in 1735 by Oglethorpe's men, Augusta was first a fort, then a trading post that grew into a settlement. It was here on January 2, 1788, that a convention called by the legislature unanimously ratified the Constitution of the United States and became the fourth state of the Union.

Still dissatisfied with their location, a legislative commission was appointed to find "a suitable, accessible, and central location for a new capital city." It directed that it be built near Augusta "within proximity of the Indian trading post called 'Galphin's Old Town.'"

The new capital was named Louisville in honor of King Louis XVI of France in appreciation of French aid in the Revolutionary War. It was here that the first permanent capitol was constructed. Completed in 1796, this red-brick, two-story structure of eighteenth century Georgian design witnessed two significant acts of the legislature.

On February 15, 1796, the infamous Yazoo Act was rescinded and a public burning of the act was held on the capitol's grounds. Passed in 1795 in Augusta, the Yazoo Act permitted the sale of Georgia's lands to private individuals and companies. It was here during the session of 1799 that the Great Seal of Georgia was adopted.

A continuing westward expansion of the population caused a third historic act of legislation in 1804. The act provided moving the capital city nearer to the geographic center of the state. When the state government moved, the Augusta capitol became a public arsenal, a county courthouse, then it was destroyed.

The new capital city, located on the Oconee River, was named Milledgeville. A brick, Gothic style building was constructed at a cost of $80,000. The general assembly's first meeting in the new capitol occurred in 1807. For 61 years, the state government occupied this capitol and saw one historic event precipitate another.

America's first gold rush in northern Georgia's mountains near Dahlonega increased the population. The lust for gold farther north caused invasion of Indian land, prompting their removal and ended in the tragic "Trail of Tears" in 1838, which exodus finalized Indian ownership of property in Georgia.

But the most important legislation occurred when Abraham Lincoln was elected president. A special state convention voted to secede from the Union on January 19, 1861. A few months later Georgia joined the Confederate States of America.

In 1864 during Sherman's advance and March to the Sea, a confused legislature adjourned to later reconvene, briefly, in Macon. When the war ended, the legislature was allowed to reconvene at its capitol in Milledgeville.

Through the years, Atlanta, having started as a transportation center, had steadily gained a reputation as a commercial, cultural and financial center for the Southeast; it had been considered as a capital site by the general assembly as early as 1847.

During the Constitutional Convention held in Atlanta in 1867, its city

The cornerstone of the Georgia State Capitol is the only piece of Georgia marble used on the exterior. All the rest is Indiana limestone. — Secretary of State.

council lobbied for the state capitol with the promise to donate suitable lands and buildings for the state government. Their proposal was accepted and ratified along with the fourteenth amendment. Federal troops left the state. Atlanta was named the state capital on March 11, 1868.

On July 4, 1868, the Georgia legislature met in Atlanta and convened in the combined Fulton County Courthouse and Atlanta's City Hall.

Because the courthouse was too crowded a suitable substitute, the Kimball Opera House, was rented and was later purchased for use as the capitol. Because of the electorate's dissatisfaction with the Constitutional Convention's selection of the capital city, a new convention, convening in Atlanta in 1877, agreed to submit to the people the permanent change of the capital in a separate election to be held the same day as the election for the ratification of the new Georgia constitution. Lively competition between proponents of the old and new capitals took place over the following weeks and the problem was finally settled when the electorate chose Atlanta by a two-to-one margin.

The legislature chose the Courthouse/City Hall location for a new capitol in 1879, but because of a shortage of funds, money was not available until 1883. One million dollars was appropriated.

A board of five commissioners, with Governor Henry Dickerson McDaniel as ex-officio chairman, were named to supervise the project. This commission selected the Classic Renaissance design submitted by the architectural firm of Edbrooke and Burnham of Chicago. The firm of Miles and Horne of Toledo, Ohio, contracted for construction.

Five years after construction started in October 1884, a vast throng attended the dedication of the new Georgia Capitol on July 4, 1889. Because of the tremendous expense of quarrying Georgia marble, the outer walls were constructed of Indiana oolitic limestone. Georgia marble was used for the interior walls, floors, steps and the cornerstone.

Due to the economical persistence of the contractors, 450,000 bricks out of the courthouse were used in its building; the cost of the capitol's construction stayed within the million dollar appropriation and left $118.43 in the treasury.

Facing west, the main entrance is a four-story portico with its stone pediment supported by six Corinthian columns set on large stone piers. High above, on the pediment, the Great Seal of Georgia is engraved. The gilded dome rises to a height double that of the four-story portico. Inside, the open rotunda rises to a height of 237.33 feet above the second story's floor.

The cupola above the dome holds a Greek-inspired, female statue, "Freedom." Placed there to commemorate the dead, she holds a downstroked sword in the left hand and a torch in the raised right. Fifteen feet tall, she weighs 2,000 pounds.

During the restoration of the capitol, authorized in 1957, it was necessary to redo the dome's gilt. The citizens of Dahlonega and Lumpkin County donated 43 ounces of native gold to be applied to the dome. The gold arrived in Atlanta by wagon train and was presented to Governor S. Martin Griffin on August 7, 1958.

In 1981 the dome was restored to its original brilliance during the "Make Georgia a Shining Example" campaign. The campaign originated with the Jaycees of Dahlonega and Lumpkin County, then spread throughout Georgia's Jaycees to allow all citizens of Georgia to contribute to the gilding of the dome.

During National Historic Preservation Week in 1977, the capitol was dedicated as a National Historic Landmark and was cited by the National Park Service as an architecturally and historically outstanding structure.

Originally consisting of three main stories with a basement used as a stable, the spread of government converted the stable to office space. The floors were renumbered and the basement became the first floor. This placed the entrance on the second floor with the offices of the governor, lieutenant governor, and secretary of state.

The third floor is gained by grand stairs of Georgia marble leading upward from the north and south wings off the rotunda. It contains the legislative chambers with the House to the west and Senate to the east. Visitors may enter either chamber's gallery from the fourth floor.

Hanging from the fourth floor's railings in the Hall of States in the south wing are the flags of the 50 states of the Union arranged in alphabetical order. The Hall of Flags, to the north of the rotunda, presents the flags that have flown over Georgia.

The museum exhibits are on the first and fourth floors, chiefly; but commemorative plaques of Georgian history and marble busts of the men who made it are placed throughout the capitol on every floor.

The capitol's Guide Service provides tour Monday through Friday from 9 A.M. to 4 P.M. The capitol is open to the public on Saturday (10 A.M. to 2 P.M.) and Sunday (1 to 3 P.M.). The service provides special events to thousands of guests throughout the year. Major emphasis is given to student tour groups who desire knowledge of Georgia's history and government.

Through its tours and special events, the Capitol Guide Service perpetuates the principle that the capitol belongs to the people of Georgia. They welcome all visitors to Georgia to enjoy the great heritage and history of the state.

GUAM

Guam is the largest and southernmost island of the Mariana Archipelago. Thirty miles long, five to eight miles wide, it contains about 210 square miles. It is located about 3,700 miles from Hawaii, 1,500 miles from Manila, and 1,500 miles from Japan. The island was formed by volcanic action. The northern part, a plateau of corraline limestone, rises to 850 feet above sea level. The southern part is mountainous with some elevations 1,300 feet. The average rainfall is 90 inches. Temperatures range between 75 and 86 degrees Fahrenheit with May and June the hottest months.

The first Caucasian of record to set foot on the island of Guam was Ferdinand Magellan, a Portuguese explorer sailing under the flag of Spain.

Guam, like other islands in the Mariana Archipelago, had been settled by Indonesian-Filipino (Chamarros) people who had, by A.D. 800, become a complex society capable of manufacturing various wares and erecting stone pillars to support communal housing. When Magellan arrived in 1521 he found a flourishing community. Spain claimed possession of Guam in 1528.

In 1565, General Miguel Legaspi claimed Guam and the remaining Mariana Islands for Spain. At that time there was a population of 50,000 Chamarros on the islands. Apra Harbor on the west coast of Guam became a main stopover for the Spanish galleons plying between Spanish-America and the Philippines.

Financed by Mariana of Austria, Queen of Spain, missionaries arrived in Guam in 1668. Under strict Spanish rule the Chamarros found reason to rebel and an uprising of the people in 1670 initiated 25 years of warfare with Spanish conquest resulting in severe bloodshed. The continual warfare, smallpox and other diseases brought by the invaders, and the typhoons of 1671 and 1693 reduced the Chamarro population to fewer than 2,000 persons by 1700.

During the Spanish-American War, in June 1898 the *USS Charleston* sailed into Apra Harbor, shelled the fort, and captured the island. On December 10, 1898, Guam was ceded to the United States by Spain who sold the remaining Mariana Islands to Germany in 1899.

With possession Guam became a United States naval station. Governed by the United States Navy, the Guam population was rebuilt with a better health plan. Roads and schools were built. Agriculture and trade flourished.

In the Washington Treaty of 1922, with disarmament of world nations popular, Guam was demilitarized.

Realizing it was the only break in their 3,000 mile island barrier, the Japanese attacked Guam five days after Pearl Harbor, which drew the Americans into World War II. Guam was captured on December 12, 1941, and remained under Japanese control until retaken by the U.S. Marines and Army August 10, 1944.

Made into a major naval and air base facility it was used to carry the assault to Japan and remains one of the strongest military operations in the Pacific. During the 1960s U.S. planes from Anderson Air Force Base flew bombing raids over Indonesia; and in 1975, at the end of the Vietnam War, thousands of refugees were flown to Guam to await transport to the United States.

For more than 200 years Guam was under military rule with all political power vested in military commanders. In 1950 Congress gave Guam local self-government and conferred citizenship, without the right to vote in presidential elections, upon the natives.

When Congress provided an organic act in 1970 it was for a government much like that of the states. Today, Guam elects a governor and lieutenant governor for four-year terms. The legislature is unicameral with 21 members elected for two-year terms. The judiciary includes a territorial court and a U.S. district court. Initially appointed by the governor with legislative consent, the territorial court judges' terms are eight years with subsequent terms elected by the people.

It also has representation in Congress by a delegate elected for a two-year term with the right to vote only in committee, and not on the House floor.

During 1982 Congress presented the Guamanians with six options determining their future. In a referendum the people, by 48 percent of the vote, chose to be a commonwealth. Statehood was second choice. Independence won only 5 percent of the vote. In February 1988 a Guam commission, after it had been approved in two separation plebiscites, submitted to the Congress "for its consideration" a Guam Commonwealth Act. The bill was introduced in March of that year. When or if it is ratified by Congress, another plebiscite will be held before the Act takes effect.

Built in Agana by the U.S. Navy during 1947–1948 the building now serving as the Guam Capitol originally was headquarters for the navy administration. It is one story high of concrete construction in modern design with a low hip roof and contains a large assembly room with associated offices. Turned over to the Guamanians in 1950, it served as the capitol for all government branches.

Another building of concrete in modern design was constructed for the courts and when it was completed the courts moved into their new building. It then became the Legislature Building, one in the group comprising Guam's Capitol Complex.

Another building, between this and the government building, houses the governor, and executive offices. It is two stories in height and of the same design with a low, flat roof.

When presidential-appointed Governor Bill Daniel exerted resistance to the Navy's security clearance for anyone visiting the island, that obsolescent restriction was abolished. Its removal paved the way for increased tourism to the island and the Guamanians welcome visitors to the island and its Capitol Complex.

HAWAII
The Aloha State

HEIGHT: 100'   FACADE: 360'   DEPTH: 270'

Hawaii is unique among all the states in that it has only two levels of government: state, with Honolulu as the capital, and county. There are no separate municipalities, no independent school districts or other small government jurisdictions. Local government is vested in one combined city and county, Honolulu, which consists of the island of Oahu and several outlying islets. There are three nonmetropolitan counties: Hawaii, Kauai, and Maui. One area, legally named Kalawao County, is administered by the State Department of Health.

Shortly after the Christian era began, Polynesians from the islands north of Tahiti set foot on the islands of Hawaii. These were followed by waves of Tahitians whose progeny were that populace found by explorer Captain James Cook when he landed there in 1778. He named them the Sandwich Islands after the English lord.

At that time each island was ruled as an independent kingdom by hereditary chiefs. One of them, Kamehameha, consolidated his power on the island of Hawaii in a series of battles in one of which Cook was killed on February 14, 1779.

After gaining control over Hawaii, King Kamehameha I (the Great) conquered Maui and Oahu and, from 1795 until his death in 1819, united all the islands to establish the Kingdom of Hawaii under his rule.

During this period Occidental fur trade, whaling, and missionaries with their families invaded the islands. These intrusions rapidly depleted Hawaiian culture; and the diseases accompanying them, unknown to the islands, decreased the native population, but not that of the islands. The need for laborers in sugar cane production in 1852 caused the importation of people from China, Japan, Korea, Portugal, Puerto Rico, and the Philippines.

Resulting from a dispute between the two countries, cession of the Kingdom of Hawaii to Great Britain was forced by Lord George Paulet in February 1843, but repudiated in July by Rear Admiral Richard Thomas.

In 1845 King Kamehameha III and the legislature moved to Honolulu from the capital, Lahaina, on Maui. The king declared Honolulu the official capital of Hawaii on August 31, 1850.

With control by European nations threatening, American businessmen sought annexation by the United States. In 1885 a reciprocity treaty with the United States brought prosperity to the islands.

After a century under ruling monarchs, a bloodless revolution in 1893 deposed the eighth, and last, reigning monarch, Queen Liliuokalani. A provisional government, led by Sanford B. Dole, was formed. With its request for annexation to the United States denied by President Grover Cleveland in 1894, Hawaii organized a republic with Dole proclaimed president.

An annexation treaty was negotiated during President William McKinley's administration and, on August 12, 1898, with the promise of eventual statehood, Hawaii was officially annexed with formal transfer of sovereignty. With Dole appointed governor, to take office on June 14, it ws organized as a territory of the United States on April 30, 1900. The first territorial legislature convened on February 20, 1901.

Statehood, proposed during the reign of Kamehameha III, became a goal shortly after World War I when a bill was introduced to Congress by Hawaii's delegate, Prince Jonah Kuhio Kalanianaole. More strenuous efforts were made during the 1930s by delegate Samuel W. King. The attack on Pearl Harbor, World War II, the Korean War, and postwar years found its citizens making vigorous campaigns in Congress for the statehood that was promised in 1898. These nisus were continued by delegate Joseph R. Farrington; and after his death, by delegate Elizabeth Farrington, his widow.

In 1947 and again in 1950 the United States House of Representatives passed bills to make the territory a state, but the bills did not reach a vote in the Senate.

In another move for statehood in 1950, the people adopted a model constitution for their state and the advocates for statehood reminded Congress that Hawaii's population was greater than that of most states when they were admitted, it was larger in land area than three of those states, and it paid more federal taxes than ten of them.

To the argument that Hawaii was too far away from the United States, they replied that travel time was less from Washington, D.C., than what it had been to California when it was admitted. Finally, under the leadership of Hawaii's last territorial delegate to Congress, John A. Burns, the eighty-sixth Congress approved statehood and the bill was signed into law by President Dwight D. Eisenhower on March 18, 1959. Seventy years after the promise of "eventual statehood," Hawaii was admitted as the fiftieth state of the Union on August 21, 1959. Territorial Governor William F. Quinn became the first elected governor of Hawaii.

Ioloni Palace in Honolulu, claimed as the only royal residence in America, served as the legislative building for Hawaii during its monarchical, republican, territorial, and state governments. Occupying the site of a less magnificent monarchical resident, the Ioloni Palace was designed by Thomas J. Baker and built under the supervision of Robert Stirling, superintendent of public works. Its cornerstone was laid on December 31, 1879. It was completed in December 1882, at a cost of $350,000. Later changes in its structure were designed in 1930 by C. J. Wall and Isaac Moore at a cost of $16,000. A more recent restoration to its present status gives it the distinction of being the most historical and interesting building in the area.

Designated a National Historic Landmark in 1962, the palace is constructed of brick, concrete, and concrete block. Its architecture is debatable. Whether it is Austrian, French, American Florentine, Rococo, or others cannot be determined, but all agree its charm captures and portrays the spirit of the Hawaiian monarchy.

During the odd-numbered years of the territorial legislature sessions, the throne room was cleared of its furnishings to make room for the legislators. While it served as the capitol, the monarchial bedroom was made into the governor's office, the state dining room became the Senate chamber, and the throne room, the House chamber.

Today, completely restored, it stands as a museum and a National Historic Monument.

Planning for Hawaii's new capitol started in 1960 with a legislative appropriation and the commissioning of a 14-member committee. Belt, Lemon and Lo of Honolulu and John Carl Warnecke and Associates of San Francisco were retained as architects to design the structure. With plans completed by 1964, Reed and Martin, Inc., of Honolulu were awarded the construction contract.

Ground was broken on November 10, and construction started November 15, 1965. With 49,100 cubic yards of concrete poured to cover 3,500 tons of reinforcing steel; and with equipment, furnishings, and fine arts installed, the completed building was dedicated on March 15, 1969. Total cost of construction was $24,576,900.

The entire structure is set in a reflecting pool to symbolize the creation of

Designed in pure Hawaiian style, the Hawaii State Capitol is modern in capacity, beauty and utility. Its legislative chambers are below ground as are parking spaces for more than 200 automobiles. — Office of the Comptroller.

Hawaii's islands out of the sea; the legislative chambers are shaped to represent the volcanoes that gave birth to the islands; and the capitol's columns are designed in the shape of the islands' native royal palms that have supplied the inhabitants with food and building materials over the centuries.

Bronze replicas of the state seal, 15 feet in diameter, each weighing 7,500 pounds, bedeck and beautify the mauka and makai entrances. The capitol's moods are varied from dusk to dawn by using programmed dimmers on the floodlights that illuminate the exterior.

It contains a floor space of 558,000 square feet and, off the ends of the building, there are 440 underground parking spaces.

The basement, also known as the chamber level, contains the Senate chamber on the Waikiki side and the House chamber on the Ewa side; as well as the offices for the legislative auditor and the Legislative Reference Bureau. Each chamber has a balcony-level spectator's gallery with seating for 180 visitors.

The first floor (entry level) has an open court with public entrances to the spectator's galleries in the chambers. The second floor contains the Senate offices; the third floor, the offices of the members of the House of Representatives. The fourth floor (departmental level) contains the offices of the attorney general, the Department of Budget and Finance, and additional offices for members of the House.

The fifth floor (executive level) accommodates the offices of the governor and lieutenant governor with their staffs.

The legislative chambers and executive offices are paneled in koa: a red, native hardwood. It is lustrous and highly valued in the making of furniture.

During 1988, twenty employees maintained the buildings and grounds at a cost of $252,000.

The capitol's hours of operations are 7:45 A.M. to 4:30 P.M., Monday through Friday. Group tours are available during the legislature's sessions, only, from mid–January through mid–April, annually.

IDAHO
The Gem State

HEIGHT: 208'   FACADE: 398'   DEPTH: 224'

The first non–Indian Americans to enter Idaho were Meriwether Lewis and William Clark on their way to the Pacific Ocean in 1805. Returning in 1806, they struggled through the Lolo Pass on the Indian trail in the central part of the state now occupied by U.S. Highway 12.

With its mountains and streams filled with fur-bearing animals, Idaho country became an attraction to those fanciers who sponsored and financed the fur trappers.

Headed by geographer David Thompson, the Northwest Fur Company established a trading post on Lake Pend Oreille in 1809. The following year the Missouri Fur Company built a post near Yellowstone at what is now St. Anthony in southeastern Idaho. About the same time, Wilson Price Hunt crossed the Grand Teton Pass into Idaho leading a John Jacob Astor expedition to settle on the mouth of the Columbia River.

Two years after Spain surrendered its claim to the area in 1819, the Hudson Bay Company of England took over the Northwest Fur Company and controlled the fur trade in the Northwest for nearly 50 years. Meanwhile, Captain B. L. E. Bonneville explored the region to the south.

The continued travels of those seeking furs eventually led to invasion by religious orders. The first of these, with intent to open a mission in Flathead Indian country, was led by Jason Lee. His group accompanied Nathaniel Wyeth's party along part of what became the Oregon Trail. At the junction of the Snake and Portneuf rivers near what is now Pocatello, Wyeth built Fort Hall and raised the American flag in 1834. That same year the Hudson Bay Company built a fort on the Boise River. Two years later the company moved farther south and bought Fort Hall.

In 1843 John C. Frémont was sent to explore the area along the Oregon Trail and the result was a provisional government for the Oregon country. This brought a land boundary dispute between England and the United States which was finally settled in 1846 when England ceded that territory south of the forty-ninth parallel.

Originally, Idaho was a part of that vast area and became a part of the Oregon Territory when it was established in 1848. During the following 20 years Idaho had five boundary changes.

Gold was discovered near the Grand Ronde River in 1852. The Mormons entered the state and built a mission in the Lemhi Valley to which they brought irrigation. They settled the town of Franklin, a few miles north of the Utah-Idaho border, where they opened the first school for white children. In 1860 more gold was discovered on Orifino Creek. Additional discoveries were made on the Salmon and Boise rivers the following year. Each strike started a mining town, but permanent settlement came with the National Homestead Act of 1862. Within two years Idaho's population ballooned to almost 20,000.

On March 3, 1863, during the Civil War, the Congress created and the next day President Lincoln signed the Idaho Organic Act into law and designated Lewiston as its capital. The following week he appointed a friend, William Wallace, as territorial governor. At that time Idaho's land area was larger than that of Texas. It contained all that was left from the Oregon Territory, after the Oregon and Washington territories were removed, including all of Montana and most of Wyoming.

In Lewiston the first Idaho territorial legislature met in a rented store building. The governor was housed nearby in a smaller building. The second legislature voted to move to Boise and, following adjournment, the records and Idaho territorial seal were moved to Boise under military escort.

In 1864, with the territorial government moved to Boise, Congress took away the Montana Territory; and further reduction in 1868, for the Wyoming Territory, gave Idaho a shape like "a pregnant L." Today, surrounded by six states and Canada, Idaho has a length of 480 miles and a width of 46 to 310 miles. It has been termed "a crazy patchwork of a state . . . and a state that should not have been."

In Boise, facilities were rented for the legislature, governor, and Supreme Court wherever attainable. For nearly 20 years the governor's office was housed in the Stone Jug located near what is now Sixth and Main streets. Throughout this period the court and legislature met in several buildings: Hart's Exchange which became the Central Hotel, Good Templar's Hall, Turnverein Hall (an athletic club), and the May and the Brown buildings.

On February 2, 1885, with $80,000 in bonds issued for its construction, a commission of four persons was appointed to supervise the erection of a building to house Idaho's government. E. E. Myers of Detroit was retained as architect. Work started in 1885 and the building was completed and occupied in 1886.

With its foundation and basement walls constructed of cut stone, the building's red brick exterior had a facade of 123 feet and a depth of 81 feet. It rose four stories above ground. The building was heated by steam, "guaranteed to maintain a temperature of 70 degrees throughout the building, day and night, and burn only a cord of wood, daily." Three entrances, east, west, and the main on the south gave access to the capitol's first floor and the territorial governor's office, the territorial library, and the offices for the territorial secretary and treasurer.

The second floor held the judiciary and legislature; the third floor, galleries and committee rooms. The government's growth to a need to use the fourth floor was restrained for years except to go through it to get to the observatory from which one could view the surrounding country.

This capitol served the people until 1919 when it and the old Central School building were demolished to make room for the east and west wings of the new capitol.

Idaho was admitted to the Union on July 3, 1890, as the forty-third state. Its capital was Boise; its governor, George L. Shoup. The population and government of the state grew to the extent that on February 7, 1905, a bill was introduced in the House for an act to modify, enlarge, and improve "the present capitol building at the city of Boise, state of Idaho, or for procuring a new site at said city of Boise, and erecting thereon a new capitol building and making appropriation therefor."

The bill provided for a commission of the governor, secretaries of state and treasurer, and two appointed citizens with the power and authority to enlarge or improve the old or build a new capitol. If the commission decided on building a new capitol, they could procure the adjoining block containing the Central School; and it with the old capitol would be used for state purposes until the new capitol was completed.

The legislation further provided that the new building was to be absolutely fireproof and burglarproof. Construction was to be financed by proceeds from the sale of 32,000 acres granted to the state for the sole purpose of erecting a capitol.

On February 23, 1905, the Appropriations Committee reported favorably on the bill. Read for the third time in the House, it was passed without opposition on February 27; and, sent to the Senate, it was passed the following afternoon. It was signed into law on March 3, 1905, by the governor.

On March 23 the Capitol Commission called for architectural designs "to be in India ink, rendered with brush or pen . . . one-eighth inch to the foot and sent to the Honorable Will H. Gibson, Secretary of State." Further stipulations outlined the building's size and the materials with which it would be constructed and indicated that $1,000 would be awarded for the best design.

By June 22 eleven designs had been received. Those submitted by John E. Tourtellotte were chosen. Herbert Quigley was employed to oversee construction; and Stewart and Company of Salt Lake City was awarded the contract for the main core of the building.

From that point until its completion, the Capitol Commission supervised, directed, and gave approval before each phase of construction, awarding sub-contracts and determining suppliers of building materials. Convict labor was used to clear the ground, in excavating the basement, and laying the foundations. Inmates were also used in quarrying the sandstone used in the exterior walls from the Table Rock Quarry near Boise, purchased by the state for that purpose.

From the starting point in 1905 to completion of the main core in 1912, problems arose. The granite for the foundation and basement walls, contracted from Montana, was having difficulty in arriving. Bad weather, altitude, and labor disturbances were blamed. In January 1909, because of one senator charging gross extravagances in the use of state funds for the capitol, the Senate ordered an investigation. There followed a proposal for a constitutional amendment to provide bonds to finish the building. The commission was asked to furnish an estimate of cost. A senatorial report was submitted showing extravagances against the commission. A bidder on the project alleged a $5,000 bribe was solicited from him by one of the commissioners. The price was lowered to $3,000 but it remained unpaid. Bribery charges, accidents and talks of impeachment seemed constant through the turn of the decade, but work advanced. The commission proposed to rush the work with little delay. Legislation authorized a bond issue. A consulting architect was hired. An occupancy date for the capitol was set for July 1912.

On October 22, 1912, charges were made against the governor, treasurer, attorney general, capitol architect, and supervising architect that there had been reckless and unwarranted disbursement of funds, conversion of state property to private use, failure to advertise bonds and other irregularities concerning capitol construction. A grand jury was called to probe the matter.

Although two months of finishing touches remained, with the executive, legislative, and judiciary factions and most of the functional offices moved in, on December 20, 1912, Idaho's capitol was formally and officially accepted from the contractors. An inaugural ball was held January 7, 1913. The capitol's central portion was complete.

By February 1919, with more room needed, three committees of the House sponsored a bill recommending the addition of two wings with an appropriation of $900,000.

The House approved, the Senate passed, and the governor signed the bill before the middle of March, and the people of Boise passed the bonds to purchase the land approaching the capitol.

Bids to wreck the Central School and old capitol were called on May 24, 1919, and the demolition was started June 3. The Morrison-Knudsen Company of Boise was awarded the construction contract. After excavations, construction started October 15, 1919, with the pouring of concrete colums in the basement. Except for some finishing details, the wings were completed and ready for occupancy by the last week of September 1920. A ball and reception were held for the people on January 3, 1921.

After nearly 17 years at a cost of $2,290,000, Idaho has a capitol that

The Idaho State Capitol. Started in 1905 and completed in 1920, it cost nearly $2.3 million. The capitol is of the same classical architecture as the United States Capitol. — Department of Commerce and Development.

occupies five acres of land donated to the state by the citizens of Boise. Located in the center of Boise, it has access to water from two artesian wells and is heated by geothermal sources. Modeled after the United States Capitol, its usable space is 190,000 square feet.

A green, swirled marble from Vermont lines its interior walls. The floors and grand staircase bear a gray marble from Alaska. A reddish-pink marble from Georgia and black marble from Italy are used in trim and inlaid patterns.

Making the capitol unique in construction, the double, glassed dome floods the four-story, 80-foot-square rotunda with daylight all the way to the first floor. Its massive glass expanse is supported by eight Corinthian columns, five feet in diameter by 60 feet high. Having the appearance of marble, each column's central core is steel. The remainder is a mixture of gypsum and glue called scagliola which has an outer covering 3/16-inch thick containing coloring to imitate veins of marble.

All the capitol's interior columns are scagliola, which process originated in Italy during the sixteenth century. To accomplish this task, an entire family of artisans was brought from Italy.

From the ground floor to its fourth, the rotunda's circular shape is accomplished with loggias supported by lesser columns. The state treasurer's office is located on the ground floor.

Standing on the ground floor, looking up to the dome, a visitor will see 43 stars symbolizing Idaho as the forty-third state. Among them are 13 larger stars, symbols of the original colonies of the United States.

The main, south entrance admits visitors to the second floor where the governor's and lieutenant governor's offices are found with those of the attorney general and secretary of state. Just inside the governor's office is the state seal, the only one in the United States to have been designed by a woman.

Also on this floor is the most unique equestrian statue of George Washington in the world—unique in that it was carved from a single block of yellow pine by an Austrian immigrant, Charles Ostner, who took four years in the process and used a postage stamp as a model. He presented it to the state in 1869.

On the third floor the room that originally housed the Supreme Court is now being used for hearings in the Finance and Appropriations committees. Both the House and Senate chambers are on this floor. Each has a miniature dome and spectators' galleries reached from the fourth floor. Stairs continue through the fourth floor to the dome to which visitors are admitted on certain occasions.

Within Idaho's capitol are displays of historic and current events. Visitors are welcome during operating hours. Special guided tours of the legislative offices, the governor's office, and the House and Senate chambers are available to the public during hours of operation.

Choir groups are sometimes invited to use the rotunda. Printed materials are free and available to visitors.

During 1988, 20 employees of the Bureau of Building Services maintained the buildings and grounds at a cost of approximately $750,000.

ILLINOIS
The Prairie State

HEIGHT: 405' FACADE: 379' DEPTH: 268'

After nearly 22 years of effort, ten deaths on the construction site, and an expenditure of $4,315,591, the people of Illinois were presented a government building that contained all the constitutional officers, boards, departments, military, elected officials—in effect, all things needed for state government as well as three museums, several libraries, and the state archives. On July 11, 1888, the remainder of the construction budget, $6.35, was returned to the state treasurer.

It was the second capitol built in Springfield, the third state capital. It is the sixth and last capitol of the State of Illinois at this time.

In 1673 those accompanying Father Jacques Marquette and Louis Joliet were the first to see and explore the upper Mississippi since Hernando de Soto's discovery 130 years earlier. Paddling downstream, almost to its junction with the Arkansas River, they turned back, struggled up the Illinois, portaged to the Chicago River and re-entered Lake Michigan.

The following winter, as he had promised them, Marquette visited the Illini Indians after which the area was named, and he established a mission, the first in the Mississippi Valley. On the way back to Canada, he became ill and died en route.

The year 1750 found nearly 2,000 Frenchmen living in small posts around Fort Chartres, Kaskaskia, and Cahokia as fur traders, soldiers, settlers, missionaries, and a few Negro slaves. Following the French and Indian War the "Northwest" region was ceded to Great Britain in 1763.

In 1778, during the American Revolution, George Rogers Clark and his Kentucky frontiersmen captured Kaskaskia and Cahokia and the Northwest became a county in Virginia. Territorial government was established in 1787.

In 1789 St. Clair County was created with Cahokia as its capital. The year 1800 found Illinois part of the Indiana Territory. The Illinois Territory was established by Congress on February 3, 1809, with its capital Kaskaskia and Ninian Edwards its governor.

Two things changed the status of Illinois in 1818. It became a state on December 3 with the capital remaining at Kaskaskia; and its northern boundary was fixed at 42 degrees 30 minutes North taking from Wisconsin a 60-mile strip that would become the Chicago area. The twenty-first state's governor was Shadrack Bond.

The Kaskaskia capitol was a simple, two-story brick structure rented by the state for four dollars a day. It had a porchless entrance, a gabled roof with the peak at one end built to support two chimneys. During sessions its 29 representatives met on the first floor while 14 senators occupied the second floor.

Apparently dissatisfied with the conditions, the assembly moved to Vandalia and occupied the second capitol in 1820. Built with taxpayers' money, it was a plain, two-story frame building. It was destroyed by fire and its loss brought about Illinois' third capitol.

It was completed in 1824 for $15,000 in time for the Illinois citizens' campaign to get their capital city closer to the geographic center of the state. Their clamor brought from the legislature an enabling act for the voters of the state to choose from among the rival cities vying for the capital: Alton, Jacksonville, Peoria, Springfield, and Vandalia.

Fearful they would lose the capital, the Vandalians tore down the state's capitol while the legislature was recessed and replaced it with a brick building costing $16,000. After an intense campaign in which Abraham Lincoln is said to have participated, the relentless voters chose Springfield. According to one source, the voting was so close for Alton, Springfield and Vandalia the results were never announced. That's how the Vandalians' building became the state's fourth capitol.

None of those four exists today. The cornerstone of the fifth capitol was laid on July 4, 1837, in Springfield. Some departments of government moved into the building before it was finished in 1853.

Within two years following the surrender on May 26, 1865, of the remaining Southern troops engaged in the Civil War, the need for a new capitol was evident. The fifth capitol was crowded from the governmental activities within. From the time its cornerstone was set, the state's population had increased 500 percent. With 2.5 million people needing services from the government, the departments' personnel increased proportionately. The need for more space demanded a new capitol, but with it came the cry to change the location of the capital city.

These notions were quelled with the passage of a bill signed into law on February 25, 1867, by Governor Richard Oglesby. Within the year a Capitol Commission of seven men was appointed to facilitate and administer construction of Illinois' sixth capitol. Offering a $3,000 prize, the commission called for a national competition for a design and, selecting that of John C. Cochrane of Chicago, appointed him architect and construction superintendent.

To aid construction, a Toledo, Wabash, and Western Railroad spur was laid down Monroe Street to the site.

The month before ground was broken on March 11, 1868, Cochrane formed a partnership with Alfred H. Piquenard, a French immigrant who moved to Springfield and supervised the construction of the capitol until his death in 1876. Two capitol commissioners broke the ground by plowing a furrow around the foundation line. The foundations were set that summer.

Of particular note is the foundation supporting the central part of the building and its dome. It is 92.5 feet in diameter. Its limestone walls are 17 feet thick and rest upon solid rock 25.5 feet below grade level. The depth of the nine-foot-thick exterior foundation walls varies from 11 to 16 feet.

On October 16, 1868, a celebration accompanied the laying of an engraved cornerstone about which Mark Sorenson, associate director of Illinois State Archives, relates how it was quietly removed and replaced with another because of cracks discovered two years after its setting. It was buried without ceremony and its location forgotten until, 70 years later in 1944, it was discovered and unearthed under the east entrance stairs and relocated to the northeast corner of the east entrance.

With construction came the legislative investigations incited by suspicion, resentment, distrust, and spite. Construction costs had risen. Building methods and materials were inferior to those contracted.

Investigation brought change. Convict labor would be used to cut the limestone for the outer walls. Rather than marble, the interior finish would be of common stone, steel and wood. The Capitol Commission was reduced to three members and, with the adoption of the state's new constitution in 1870, the cost of the building could not exceed $3.5 million. Any amount in excess mandated public approval.

Removal of the capital from Springfield sprang into the picture again. Peoria wined and dined members of the legislature in the spring of 1871. Chicago invited the legislature to hold its November session with free-of-charge offerings which they readily accepted, disregarding the constitutional mandate. Had it not been for the Great Fire that October, Chicago could have been the capital of Illinois today.

Eleven years after breaking ground, the assembly convened its first session in the new capitol on January 3, 1877. The interior of the dome, its rotunda, the walls, and ceilings were not yet finished. The money had been spent. An additional $531,712 would be needed to finish the interior.

A request for that amount, submitted to the voters in November 1877, was refused by the people. It was placed on the ballot again in 1882 and again the people rejected it. A third request in 1884 was successful and, with the enabling act's original signer re-elected, work continued.

Governor Oglesby appointed new commissioners who retained W. W. Boyington to take over the construction project as architect.

While work continued inside, Boyington made a change outside. The 37 steps approaching the main east entrance to the governor's office on the second floor were removed. A new entrance to the ground floor, originally the basement, was installed under a columned portico. A similar entrance was placed on the north side.

Overlooking the former demand for the use of common materials, the interior floors and wall wainscotting were finished with imported marble. The floors contained statuary of outstanding politicians. Portraits and historic murals adorned the walls. The dome contained a stained glass state seal and the rotunda's columns were a highly polished, red Missouri granite with bases and capitals of blue granite and marble.

When opened for the public January 1, 1887, gas jets lighted the interior. Elevators operated in the rotunda. Some offices had typewriters and telephones invented a few years earlier. As times changed, so did the furnishings. Electric lamps replaced gas jets.

In the shape of a Greek cross, the building contains 750,000 cubic feet of cut stone, 20 million bricks, 1.4 million pounds of wrought iron, and 3.4 million pounds of cast iron. The outer walls are domestic limestone from Joliet and Lemont. The north and east porticos' pillars are granite. The grand staircase, the columns and floors of the second floor are domestic and imported multi-color marble.

Inside the east entrance on the first floor in the rotunda a bronze statue welcomes the world with open arms. Used to welcome visitors to the Illinois building in Chicago's Columbian Exposition in 1893, it was afterwards presented to the state. From it, corridors lead to other department and commission offices, a newsstand with souvenirs, and a legislative information bureau.

The offices of the governor, lieutenant governor, state comptroller, and state treasurer are on the second floor with capitol security.

The Senate and House chambers are located on the third floor and their public viewing galleries are reached from the fourth.

Tours of the capitol are given on the hour and half-hours from 8 A.M. to 4:30 P.M. on weekdays and from 9 A.M. to 4 P.M. weekends. The capitol is closed on Easter, Thanksgiving, Christmas, and New Year's.

There are public restrooms on all floors except the fourth; telephones are located on the first and third floors. There is also a nurse at a first aid station on the third floor.

All floors and facilities are available to the handicapped. Elevators have control panels in Braille and ramps are located wherever steps might be difficult.

In 1932 the dome was stripped down to its iron trusses. The rotting wood was replaced with precast concrete. The dome's exterior was sheathed in zinc and painted silver. The actual height to the top of the dome is 361 feet. The cupola and flag pole extend the capitol's height to 405 feet.

The restoration of the dome's interior, believed to be the first since the capitol's completion, came in 1988. All the surfaces and artwork were thoroughly cleaned and repainted. The stained glass in the state seal was removed so that each piece could be cleaned and re-leaded.

Nineteen hundred eighty-eight marked the end of 20 years of total restoration of the capitol. That year, with Governor Jim Edgar its custodian, the centennial of its completion was celebrated and the sixth Capitol of Illinois was designated a National Historic Place.

Throughout the building the state's history has been told with representative murals and statuary. Added to those stories, on September 7, 1989, new works of art highlighting the state's history were unveiled to close recognition of the capitol's centennial.

Four murals were unveiled: "Transforming the Prairie" into farmland, by Ken Holder; "The Key" showing social reform and the progressive movement, by Billy Morrow Jackson; "The Rise of Chicago" from the Great Fire, by Ellen Lanyon; and "The First Controlled Nuclear Chain Reaction," by D. F. Bushman. For two years two separate committees: a historic to determine historic themes and an artistic to identify skilled artists were formed to interpret those themes.

Today the capitol complex in Springfield has several buildings besides the state's sixth capitol: a visitors center, a museum, the State Archives, the Illinois State Library, the Supreme Court, the attorney general, the armory, the State Office Building, and the Centennial Building.

INDIANA
The Hoosier State

HEIGHT: 235'   FACADE: 496'   DEPTH: 283'

When Ohio was set apart from the original Northwest Territory of the United States in 1800, the remainder was called the Indiana (Indian land) Territory and included that land presently comprising the states of Illinois, Wisconsin, part of Michigan, and Indiana. The Michigan Territory was taken from its northern part in 1805, then Illinois, including Wisconsin, in 1809, which left Indiana in its present shape.

Indiana's nickname "Hoosier" is said by some to be derived from Hoozer (hill dweller) because many of its settlers were descendants from England's Cumberland County highlanders.

The French at Sault Sainte Marie and then the English first claimed the area in 1671. Shortly after extensive exploration of the Indiana area, Sieur de la Salle claimed the entire Mississippi Valley for France on April 9, 1682, and named it Louisiana. François de Vincennes built a fort on the Wabash River in 1732. It is acclaimed the first white settlement in Indiana.

Through and following three wars, France ceded that land including Indiana to England and England ceded to the United States in 1783. By 1787 the Northwest Territory was organized and settlement of the Ohio Valley started.

On July 4, 1800, Congress created the Indiana Territory. Vincennes was named the capital with William Henry Harrison appointed governor. Harrison procured Indian land for the Territory through several treaties and battles. The building that served as the territorial capitol at Vincennes is now a State Historic Place.

The territorial capital was moved to Corydon on March 11, 1813. When Indiana was admitted to the Union as the nineteenth state on December 11, 1816, Corydon was named as the capital, but only until such time as a centrally located city could be established as the capital. Jonathan Jennings became the first state governor.

Soon after Corydon became the territorial capital, construction on a suitable building to house the government was started by Dennis Pennington. Finished in 1916, its cost of $3,000 came from the sale of land and the Harrison County treasury.

Constructed of blue limestone, the 40-foot, cube shape of the building rose two stories above ground. When the capitol moved from Corydon it became the county courthouse. It was purchased by the state in 1929 and declared a state historic site.

With Indiana's statehood came a Congressional act donating four square miles of land to build a capital city. The land was to be selected from unsold public lands. On June 20, 1820, a legislative committee submitted a site for the new capital. It was approved by the legislature early the following year, after which a debate ensued regarding a proper name for the new capital. From numerous names submitted, among which were Indiana City and Indiola, Indianapolis was finally chosen by the majority.

Layout of the city was begun in April 1821 by Alexander Ralston, a surveyor who had worked for Pierre L'Enfant laying out Washington, D.C. In 1825 the government moved from Corydon to Indianapolis. For 11 years the legislature's sessions were held in the Marion County Courthouse while Indiana's third capitol was being argued in the legislature and built. During that period the remaining state offices were scattered throughout the capital wherever space could be found.

Finally authorized in 1832, construction got under way with Ithiel Town and Alexander J. Davis of New York retained as architects. The building was completed in 1835 at a cost of $60,000 raised through the sale of land. Its limestone foundation supported exterior walls, two stories in height, of stuccoed brick walls, scored to resemble stone. Its rectangular shape measured 120 by 80 feet.

During the 1860s, because of Indiana's winters of extreme freeze-thaw conditions, there was evidence of deterioration of the exterior stucco. During 1867 the House chamber's ceiling fell in. Its repair and ensuing problems eventually led to the creation of a committee for a new capitol in 1873. In 1877 a Board of State House Commissioners was designated and given the job of completing a new capitol, its cost not to exceed $2 million.

Two dozen designs for the new capitol were submitted in open competition and that of Edwin May of Indianapolis was selected by the Board as being the most feasible and within the budget. When May died in 1880 his draftsman, Adolph Scherrer, succeeded him as supervising architect.

Influenced by the national Capitol, May's Renaissance Revival with Neo-Greco style design was different by his placement of the legislative chambers on either side of the rotunda rather than at the building's opposite ends, which he reserved for the Supreme Court and the state library.

Bids were opened August 15, 1878, and the construction contract was awarded to Kanmacher and Denig of Chicago. Work began that October. On September 28, 1880, the cornerstone was laid. It was a ten-ton block of limestone from Spencer, Indiana, with the inscription "A.D. 1880." A metal box containing historical memorabilia was set at that time.

By 1881 the foundation and walls of the first floor were complete. Another year found the walls completed to the fourth floor window sills. Work progressed, but not without controversy and problems. Architects whose designs had not been chosen claimed that parts of their designs had been incorporated into May's work. Contractors whose bids had not been favored questioned the qualifications of those who had been awarded the contract as well as the quality of the materials they were using. These controversies led to legislative investigation and litigation, both of which were found fallible because of insufficient evidence.

In 1883 the project suffered a definite setback when the contractors lost the support of their financier. The Board of Commissioners abandoned the contract and then selected new contractors, Elias F. Gobel and Columbus Cummings of Chicago. Work resumed that year. The walls were finished, the roof was completed to close the building, and the last stone was set in the dome on July 3, 1886.

Moving into the interior, it was found possible to use more ornate materials than had been originally designed. For example, the columns and pilasters could now be marble shafts with limestone and granite capitals and bases instead of the limestone and cast iron first planned; stair treads were changed from limestone to marble; and paneled oak replaced baseboards.

The upgrading cost $253,958.55, which sum was later matched by an appropriation to furnish the building. The building was opened to the public on January 6, 1887, when the General Assembly convened its first session, but the work didn't stop until September 1888, after the grounds had been landscaped.

On October 2, 1888, the Board of Commissioners issued a summary of their work and closed their accounts without ceremony. Indiana had its new capitol with a gilded lantern atop its dome at a cost of $2,099,794. Up to that time, Indiana's new capitol was the largest, most ambitiously planned statehouse built in America.

In 1904 its first major refurbishing began. Wall paintings were redone in oils to brighten the original watercolors. The woodwork was refinished. The dome's lantern was regilded in 1906. By 1909 state government had outgrown its space and additions for each end of the building were proposed and turned down. Remodeling occurred between 1917 and 1920 when the first story stables were converted into offices. At that time the lighting was upgraded, from gas-electric fixtures to electric chandeliers on the second floor, the governor's office, and the legislature's chambers. New elevators were installed. The interior designs were repainted, but were then painted over during a 1928–1929 renovation.

By 1931 the automobiles' exhaust and soot from coal-burning stacks over the years had accumulated to the extent that the outside of the capitol had to be steam-cleaned.

A second remodeling in 1945–1948 installed channels in the walls for electrical wiring. Aluminum and glass entry doors were installed at all second floor entrances. The original, monumental oak doors were removed from the north and east sides of the building. Cast iron lamp posts were removed from the retaining wall around the capitol; and fluorescent fixtures replaced the 1919 sconces on the east portico. Electric drinking fountains replaced the bottled water coolers.

The House and Senate chambers received their first remodeling to smaller chambers and decorated with paneled wainscoting with murals above. The chambers were ringed by legislative offices within the same space.

The exterior of the building was cleaned again in 1964, by sandblasting; and the dome was painted with a gold epoxy, more costly than gild, but more permanent. The parking lot was enlarged. To illuminate the building at night, spotlights were installed.

In 1966 the light oak wainscoting in the House chamber was replaced with walnut paneling. In 1974 the Senate chamber was remodeled to a colonial style. In 1968, the original corridor chandeliers that had been cleaned and rewired ten years previously were removed from the third floor and replaced with modern fixtures. The same type fixtures replaced the 1917 lighting fixtures on the second floor; and the sconces on the spandrels of the atriums on either side of the rotunda were removed at the same time.

In 1976, during the bicentennial of the American Revolution, whimsies and fancies of taste began to change. There arose in political circles a felt need to renew and restore historic buildings.

This new trend was expressed in the 1975 restoration of the lieutenant governor's office; and in 1978, the capitol dome was given its first new copper cladding, part of the capitol's first major roofing replacement. In 1984 the art glass dome of the rotunda was cleaned and repaired.

First announced by Governor Bob Orr in his 1985 inaugural address, Hoosier Celebration '88 was conceived as a way to focus attention on a proud heritage and, at the same time, encourage long-term planning for economic and community development.

In 1986 planning commenced on a major restoration of the capitol's original appearance, a prelude to the centennial celebration of completion of the State House as the culmination of Hoosier Celebration '88. Some examples of the capitol's restoration included:

1) Four acres of plastered walls and ceilings, the equivalent of 3.6 football fields, were stripped, painted and decorated with the original 1886 designs.

2) Dutch metal gold leaf amounting to 125,000 six by six inch leaves was used for gilding the skylight, balustrades and plaster details.

3) Four sets of original white oak, monumental entrance doors were restored.

4) Four more sets of white oak monumental entrance doors were replicated to match the originals.

In effect, everything was brought back to the capitol's original, completed features. The cost to restore it to its 1866 appearance was $10,937,292.

Today Indiana's capitol is but one of the state's government buildings. Within its grasp is the State Office Building which houses state agencies that occupied 22 different buildings in and around Indianapolis. Thirteen stories high, its exterior of Indiana limestone contains 2,000 windows of heat-resistant glass. From its basement, containing a 900-seat cafeteria, the capitol, the State Library, and the parking lot may be reached through tunnels.

The State Library and Historical Building contains the state archives and houses the Historical Society and the Academy of Science. The Library's stacks and drawers contain publications in the hundreds of thousands and serve every government entity.

The State Museum occupies the former city hall which was completely restored to accept the historic and natural objects connected to Indiana's history.

There are two memorials of note: Indiana's Soldiers and Sailors Monument and the Indiana World War Memorial. The first is dedicated to Indiana's fighting men up to World War I. Constructed over a period of 14 years, and completed in 1901, it rises 284 feet to the top of a magnificent 38-foot victory statue.

Indiana's World War Memorial is a tribute to her fighting men who served in World War I. Its cornerstone was laid July 4, 1927, by General John J. Pershing. From north to south, it stretches over five city blocks and has a 500-seat auditorium, meeting rooms and offices. Its most noted features are the World War Memorial Shrine and the Military Museum. Centered, an altar to the American flag is guarded by four marble eagles and the shrine is surrounded by colossal columns.

The Military Museum contains relics and artifacts of the wars from Tippecanoe to the Korean; and the archives contain more than 25,000 pictures of battle scenes and soldiers in action. More than 6,000 people visit this memorial each month.

Visitors are always welcome in Indiana's capitol and its supporting buildings where they will gain firsthand knowledge of the workings of the state's government and the political and natural history of Indiana.

IOWA

The Hawkeye State

HEIGHT: 275'   FACADE: 363'   DEPTH: 386'

While traveling down the Mississippi River in 1673, Father Jacques Marquette and Louis Joliet stopped near the mouth of the Iowa River to visit an Indian village. They were the first white men of record to set foot in the state of Iowa.

One hundred fifteen years later (1788) the Fox Indians permitted Julien Dubuque, a French trapper, to mine lead on their land. Dubuque set up a trading post in the area bearing his name and is credited with being the first permanent settler in Iowa. He put Indians to work in his mines, died a pauper, but was given an Indian burial with a chieftain's honors.

During the intervening years the Mississippi Valley has been explored and claimed for France by La Salle; and France ceded to Spain that land west of the Mississippi.

After Spain had given grants of the Iowa land to Dubuque in 1796, Louis Tesson in 1799, and Basil Gerard in 1800, she secretly returned the ceded land to France. This completed the parcel making up the Louisiana Purchase bought from France by the United States in 1803.

When the District of Louisiana was organized March 26, 1804, Iowa was included. From that time on the United States, as the new owner, pressed exploration, not only of its newly acquired lands but of all the land between the Mississippi and the Pacific Ocean.

Lewis and Clark started up the Missouri River toward and into the Pacific Northwest in 1804, and in early August of that year made camp and held council with the Omaha, Missouri, and Oto Indian tribes. They named the camp "Councile Bluff." Years later it became Council Bluffs, Iowa.

Before the Lewis and Clark expedition had gone very far, the government sent Zebulon Pike to explore the upper Mississippi. His reports of tall grass and forests of hardwood trees stimulated migration into the Iowa area. He was later sent to the Southwest.

Both expeditions had touched upon Iowan soil. In 1808 Fort Madison was built for protection from the Indians whose lands, by 1812, had become crowded to the extent that Black Hawk attacked the settlers on Credit Island near the site of Davenport and the following year attacked and destroyed Fort Madison.

Disregarding the Indian's desire to retain his lands, settlement continued. Fort Armstrong was built across the river from the future town of Davenport, which became established in 1834 by Colonel George Davenport. While the emigrants' wagons continued across the river, the steamboat *Western Engineer* fought its way up the Missouri to Council Bluffs in 1819. Being first, it started river traffic which brought more settlers.

When Missouri became a state in 1821 Iowa was left without a civil government. It was not until June 17, 1830, that a group of miners assembled in what became Dubuque and drew up a compact of self-government. After Chief Black Hawk was forced to surrender his claims to the eastern Iowa area in 1833 (Black Hawk Purchase), it was opened to settlement.

Whether caused by the increased population or their exercising vigilante laws, civil government returned to Iowa when the area was annexed to the Michigan Territory in which the counties of Dubuque and Des Moines were organized in 1834.

Two years later, on April 20, 1836, Congress created the Wisconsin Territory, and because the population of Iowa continued to burgeon, it was made a part.

Congress finally created the Iowa Territory June 12, 1838, designating its boundaries to include all that land north of Missouri's border between the Missouri and Mississippi rivers. Burlington was named the temporary capital and Robert Lucas the governor.

No sooner had the southern boundary been declared than trouble started with Missouri. In August 1839, when a Missouri sheriff went into an Iowa county to collect taxes, the farmers refused to pay. When the sheriff returned in November with a sizable force, he was met by a larger force of farmers headed by an Iowa county sheriff who immediately arrested the Missouri sheriff for trespassing and took him to Burlington for Governor Lucas to make a decision.

Missouri's Governor Boggs called up his militia of 2,000 men and prepared to move into Iowa. Three Missourians didn't wait for formal military action, but crossed the line and cut down three trees heavily loaded with honey comb. Thus the "Honey War" was started.

Governor Lucas regarded Boggs' call for militia an act of war against the United States and called up three Iowa divisions to support the United States marshal in protecting the rights of United States citizens.

Both armies were disbanded and civil war was stopped while the issue was being decided in the courts. The Missouri sheriff was released and there were no further attempts to collect taxes. The boundary was settled in favor of Iowa by a unanimous Supreme Court in February 1849.

In the meantime (1839) Iowa City had been selected for the capital and the move was made from Burlington. It was in Burlington that Governor Lucas negotiated with the Fox and Sauk Indians to cede their remaining lands to expand Iowa's frontier. He also pushed for the construction of a capitol for the territory. This he accomplished with the help of a commissioner who not only revised and drew up the original architect's plans but pushed and bullied the contractors, suppliers, and workers until the job was finished.

Appointed by President Martin Van Buren, Governor Lucas remained in office only three years. When William Henry Harrison was elected president of the United States, he appointed John Chambers to replace Lucas.

Lucas is credited with having built the territorial capitol and after retiring, he sat on his front porch watching its construction. While governor he attended the laying of the cornerstone July 4, 1840. In 1842 the building was well enough along that the legislature was able to meet there. When the cupola and spiral staircase were finished in 1851 it was deemed complete. It served as the territorial capitol for 15 years and today is the administration building for the University of Iowa.

Two years after territorial status was achieved, the citizens applied for statehood. Because of the boundary problems it was denied. In 1844 a group of citizens called a convention, wrote a new constitution, and submitted it for statehood. They waited another two years before Iowa was admitted to the Union as the twenty-ninth state on December 28, 1846.

When the permanent capital question was raised in the fifth general assembly in 1854, it was decreed that the capitol should occupy a spot near the river. The exact location was determined with a gift to the state of nine and one-half acres of land in Des Moines.

Commensurate to the move to that city in 1857, a group of citizens built a temporary capitol for the state's use while a permanent capitol was being planned and built. This building was eventually bought by the state and was later destroyed by fire.

In 1870 the General Assembly created a Capitol Commission to choose an architect and plan and proceed with the work of building a capitol not to exceed an expense of $1.5 million of available funds. There was to be no tax increase.

Work started and the cornerstone was set with memorabilia in an appropriate ceremony during 1871, but that winter's weather caused unusual crumbling of the native granite placed in the foundation. Feeling their capitol was worthy of more than frugal construction, the assembly had the poor quality granite removed and replaced with a higher grade of stone. Financing was made more adequate, a new commission was appointed and a new cornerstone was placed during 1873.

With the general assembly's occupation of the capitol in January 1884, the building was dedicated, but the executive office was not occupied until 1885. When the Supreme Court chamber was occupied in 1886, it was accepted that the capitol was complete. The cost: $2,873,294.49.

During 1902 a third Capitol Commission was created and appointed to modernize the lighting and heating and accomplish whatever repairs were necessary.

On January 4, 1904, disaster struck the north wing when a fire from an undetermined source gutted the House chamber. As a result the interior was completely redecorated, raising the total cost to $3,296,256.

Glacial stone from the soil of Black Hawk and Buchanan counties formed the foundation of the building. Granite, limestone, and sandstone from Iowa, Missouri, Minnesota, Ohio, and Illinois were used in the superstructure. Over the years the exterior limestone deteriorated to the point that some of it fell from the building. Replacement of the material and maintenance have continued since 1983.

The interior contains 22 kinds of imported marble from Belgium, France, Germany, Ireland, Italy, Mexico, and Spain; as well as seven domestic varieties of marble from Iowa, New York, Tennessee, and Vermont. A distinctive Iowa coral marble, quarried in St. Charles, is in the Senate chamber.

The grand stairway of marble, with ornate carvings of flora and fauna on the newel posts at its base, could be the keystone of attention in the capitol's art.

All of the interior woods are native to Iowa. Appearing throughout the building are carvings of flora, fauna, and grotesque faces carved in ash, butternut, catalpa, cherry, mahogany, oak, pine, and poplar.

Built in modified Romanesque design with Corinthian supplement, the capitol's main entrance portico is supported by stone columns above which, interrupted by the second floor, are segmented columns to support a sculptured pediment. A colonnaded, circular drum rises above the central structure to a gilded steel dome 80 feet in diameter atop which is a lookout lantern, reached by a circular stairway inside the dome. It is 275 feet from ground level to the top of the lantern.

The original cost of gilding the dome was $3,700. Regilding in 1905 cost $8,800; in 1927, $16,500; the dome was last regilded during 1963 with 22-karat gold leaf at a cost of $79,938. The gilded dome remains one of the largest of its kind.

A smaller dome rises above each of the four corners of the capitol.

Inside the entrance, the rotunda is 67 feet in diameter. High above, suspended underneath the dome, is the Grand Army of the Republic emblem. Painted on canvas by Joe Czizek of Des Moines, it was placed there in 1922 during the convention of the Grand Army of the Republic as a reminder of Iowa's sacrifice to preserve the Union during the Civil War. At that time Governor Nate E. Kendall ordered that it be retained as a permanent decoration.

Throughout the building are paintings and statuary of historic moments in the state's history together with those persons contributing to that history.

The capitol's four stories are arranged with a ground floor and three stories rising above. The main entrance steps rise to the portico and doorways into the first floor for the governor's office, the offices of the secretary of state and treasurer, and the Supreme Court chamber.

Side entrances, beneath the portico, give access to the ground floor for public information, dining areas, the post office, and supporting offices for the governor and the Supreme Court.

From the first floor the grand stairway rises to the second floor containing the Senate and House chambers, the lieutenant governor's office, the Law Library, and supporting rooms and offices including conference rooms, the fiscal bureau, the mail room, and the copy center.

Above the grand stairway to the upper floor is Edwin Blashfield's mural, "Westward," depicting the advance of those pioneers who settled the state. Above the mural are mosaics of colored stone. Made in Venice, Italy, they portray charities, defense, education, and the departments of government: executive, judicial, and legislative.

The Senate chamber's columns are scagliola. Four one-ton brass chandeliers hang from ceilings decorated with frescoes, symbols of agriculture, commerce, history, industry, law and peace. The room's marble wainscoting is complemented with mahogany panelling.

The House chamber is panelled in black walnut rising above marble wainscoting. The walls hold portraits of those persons of eminence of Iowa's history. Elmer Garnsey's paintings in the ceiling depict the governmental resonsibilities. The chandeliers were made in Czechoslovakia. Each has 5,600 crystals. They replace the originals destroyed in the fire of 1904 that were identical to those in the Senate chamber.

The Senate and House galleries and the rooms for their caucus staffs on the third floor are reached by stairs or elevators from the second floor.

Across the hall from the governor's reception room on the first floor is one of the world's largest reproduction photographs. Taken on May 15, 1919, at the capitol's west entrance, it is of the famous Rainbow Division, 168th Infantry, returned from France following World War I.

The ideal example of art in wood carving is displayed in the Supreme Court chamber. The work of William Metzger of Chicago, the Supreme Court bench is alive with carvings of cockatoos, cornucopia, eagles, varied fruits, leaves, and vines. Centered in the panelling, beneath the position of the chief justice, Metzger carved an owl to symbolize wisdom.

The justices have immediate access to the Law Library by way of stairs rising from the court's consultation room. In the library a stairway of iron grillwork circles upward through four levels containing more than 150,000 volumes.

Iowa's capitol complex has grown to 165 acres containing 17 buildings, numerous inspirational monuments, and a vast assortment of flowering plants, shrubs and trees.

Presently, a major renovation of the capitol is in progress. With an expected completion set for 1996 in time for Iowa's one hundred fiftieth year of statehood, it will include restoration of the interior and exterior, new meeting rooms, a visitors' center, a new roof, and improvements to the grounds and monuments. It is expected to cost more than $30 million.

The capitol is open from 8:00 A.M. to 4:30 P.M. Monday through Friday; and from 8:00 A.M. to 4:00 P.M. on weekends and holidays. Guided tours are available only on weekdays and visitors are encouraged to participate to enrich their knowledge of the capitol.

Weather permitting, tours to the dome are offered on weekdays, every hour on the hour, from 10:00 A.M. to 3:00 P.M.

KANSAS
The Sunflower State

HEIGHT: 304′ FACADE: 399′ DEPTH: 386′

"The people of the territory of Kansas, by their representatives in convention assembled, at Wyandotte, in said territory, on the twenty-ninth day of July, one thousand eight hundred and fifty-nine, did form for themselves a constitution and state government, republican in form, which was ratified and adopted by the people, at an election held for that purpose on Tuesday, the fourth day of October, one thousand eight hundred and fifty-nine, and the said convention has, in their name and behalf, asked the congress of the United States to admit the said territory into the union as a state, on an equal footing with the other states. . . ."

Sent to Congress, this act permitted statehood for the people of Kansas. They were admitted to the Union as the thirty-fourth state January 29, 1861. The Wyandotte constitution had established Topeka as capital until a permanent capital could be decided by popular vote. Topeka won the distinction the following November; and remains the capital although numerous attempts were made to move it to a more central location.

From the time it became a territory, May 30, 1854, to its admission as a state, Kansas had seven territorial capitals. The first at Fort Leavenworth, headquartered Territorial Governor Andrew Reeder for 50 days. The move to Shawnee Mission lasted only seven months. Governor Reeder then moved to Pawnee to convene the first territorial legislature on July 2, 1855. Dissatisfied, the legislature adjourned, over Reeder's veto, and returned to Shawnee Mission. The governor followed a week later.

On August 18, the second territorial legislature declared Lecompton the territorial capital and met there from January 12 to February 20, 1857, in a two-story, white frame building with a gabled roof, pediment and stone foundation. An uncovered porch, raised on stone piers with straight stone stairs to the left continues to provide entry to the building and its meeting rooms. It is now a National Historic Building.

The third territorial legislature met there December 7, 1857, but adjourned to Lawrence on January 5, 1858, for one month before adjourning. They next passed an act designating Minneola as the territorial capital, and overturned the governor's veto. The U.S. attorney general ruled it a violation of the territory's organic act, but that ruling was disregarded and the third constitutional convention met there March 23, 1858, before adjourning to Leavenworth.

The fourth territorial legislature convened at Lecompton on January 3, 1859, and adjourned to Lawrence to convene January 7, then adjourned February 11.

The following year, the fifth convened at Lecompton on January 2, and after overturning the governor's veto, adjourned to Lawrence for a 12-day session.

The sixth territorial legislature, and the last, met in Lecompton January 7, 1861, and adjourned to Lawrence the following day to convene as a territorial legislature for the last time. Topeka became the permanent capital.

With the country involved in Civil War and Kansas without public buildings, the state's offices occupied rented quarters. The Senate met on the third floor of the Ritchie building in which Governor Charles Robinson had an office. The House met in several places. Others met wherever space could be found.

In 1864 the legislature and state offices moved into a privately owned building, constructed for that purpose, and remained there until the Kansas Capitol received them. It was in that building, today's Old Constitution Hall on Kansas Avenue, that two actions gave Kansas a capitol.

The first was after Topeka became the permanent capital. Twenty centrally located acres, inside four city blocks, were offered as a gift to the state by the Topeka Association, a group formed in 1854 to develop the city. Their gift was accepted February 7, 1862.

The second was the constant constituent pressure which prompted an act by the legislature to provide for the erection of a statehouse. Their act appropriated funds for its construction and created a Board of Commissioners to do the job.

In its first meeting on March 26, 1866, with Governor Samuel J. Crawford presiding, the Board of Commissioners appointed J. G. Haskell of Lawrence as architect and W. W. H. Lawrence as construction superintendent. After examining the site and deciding that the wings of the capitol should extend east and west, they resolved that the east wing should be built first and its construction should begin immediately.

The following day the Board disapproved the architectural designs of E. Townsend Mix because of its "temporary wooden stairs inside a wooden shed"; but approved them later with acceptable changes.

On May 4, 1866, D. J. Silver & Son of Fort Wayne, Indiana, were awarded the construction contract and the work was begun immediately.

After a street parade of leading citizens, led by the town's brass band and state officials, a metal box containing memorabilia was placed and the cornerstone was laid October 17, 1866, with Masonic ceremonies.

Things went well and without mishap that day; this was declared a good omen. Soon after construction started, however, builders discovered the brown sandstone, chosen with geologists' advice, was crumbling in the foundation and walls. The work was redone with limestone brought from Junction City.

Another problem struck in July 1867 when the contractors quit, but was quickly solved when the Board retained Bogart and Babcock of Topeka.

During the latter part of 1869, except for a lack of sanitary facilities which were not included in the east wing plans, the building was ready for occupancy. To remedy this a stairway, walkways, and a privy "fit to occupy" were constructed from hastily drawn, detailed plans and on Christmas Day the east wing of the capitol was declared completed although there was no portico on the east wing until 1873.

The state offices were occupied that December with the legislative chambers in the hallway, separated by a wall.

During this period of growth in Topeka, the citizens clamored for removal of the "unsightly stone fence" built around Capitol Square to keep the cows and horses out. They wanted it replaced with an "up-to-date" fence so a "five-board pig-tight fence" was built.

April 22, 1875, was declared Kansas Arbor Day in Topeka by Mayor

T. J. Anderson. On that day, the people of Topeka planted 800 trees on Capitol Square. Many of them died during the summer months.

In 1879 the legislature provided for a new Board of Commissioners and appropriations to build the west wing. Immediately following his inauguration, Governor John P. St. John appointed the Board of Commissioners which retained E. T. Carr and George Ropes as architects and awarded the construction contract to William Tweeddale and Company of Topeka. By September the west wing building was well under way and continued with certain degrees of controversy and argument through 1880.

The House chamber was completed and occupied by its members on January 17, 1881. The east and west wings were connected by a covered walkway often referred to as the "cave of the winds." To rectify this situation, that session of the legislature enacted laws to construct the central portion of the capitol, and provided financing with a special tax levy.

Built from bedrock to carry the weight of the dome, the foundation was completed in 1884. On May 8, 1885, architect Carr resigned and was appointed to the Board of State House Commissioners. The original architect, John G. Haskell of Lawrence, was retained. While the center was under construction the east wing was remodeled to include the Senate chamber.

Throughout this period, controversy became a partner to construction. Graft, corruption, and excessive spending caused a special investigation which brought in a new Board of Commissioners. The architect, George Ropes, was replaced by Kenneth McDonald of Louisville, Kentucky.

The year 1889 was eventful: Ropes was back on the job, a roofing contract was let for the dome and main building, a cracking was discovered in the main north arch. It was incapable of bearing the excessive weight. Blame was placed with the plans drawn by McDonald that were strictly followed even though the contractors had foretold the result. It was later decided the crack was caused by differences in settling of the foundations. The arch was rebuilt.

In 1891 the Board of State House Commissioners was replaced with a new Board of Public Works that served until 1895, when the Executive Council took over.

On March 24, 1903, the final voucher was paid for the completed capitol even though work went on until 1906, the year the north portico was completed.

As with any building, from its completion to this day, repair and maintenance have been accordant to its lasting charm and dignity.

Throughout its period of furnishing and touch-up, there were disputes, strife, and contention. Marble and porcelain bathrooms with lavish fixtures were placed in the offices of some of the elected officials; a contest for statuary atop the dome, although completed, was never effected; the wall's murals, said to be of "telephone girl nudes," were in 1902 painted over with others thought to better befit the scope and zeal of Kansas: fully clothed women representing knowledge, peace, plenty, and power.

Of the office bathrooms only one marble wash basin remains. Ceres, the winner of the competition to occupy the top of the dome, was exchanged for a light. She is possessed by the Kansas State Historical Society.

Built of limestone in a combination of French Renaissance and Corinthian style architecture, at a total cost of nine lives and $3,200,588.92, over a period of 37 years while under the supervision of eight architects, the Kansas State Capitol is an outstanding achievement in human desire and perseverance.

The main, south entrance is approached by a long series of stone steps. Similar entries are found at each wing. The building's exterior is limestone quarried from Geary and Chase counties in Kansas. The dome of copper, corroded to a robust green, has a diameter of 66.5 feet. The central building has five stories; the east and west wings, four. The entire structure has a basement.

The interior's finish contains numerous types of marble. The building's first floor wainscoting is Georgian marble; that of the west corridor, Tennessee with inserts of Mandual tile, capped with a chair rail of Italian and a base of Belgium black marble. The floor and wainscoting of the central building are of Tennessee marble. The large upper panels on the second floor are Siena and Lambertin from Italy. The mopboard is rouge Royal from France. The columns' bases and capstones are Numidian from Africa. Tennessee marble is used throughout the second floor with Georgian addressing the third floor rotunda.

In the rotunda on the first floor the visitor is surrounded by eight murals commissioned in 1951 to a Topekan native, David H. Overmeyer who completed them over a two-year period. They depict Kansas' historic past from the Spaniards' search for the cities of Cibola to the coming of the railroad.

Looking upward, the blue of the dome captures the blue of the sky framed in a circle of beige on white. The foreground carries eight flags: six of those entities who claimed the soil and two to whom it belongs. Featured are the flags of England, two of France, Mexico, Spain, Texas, the United States flag with 34 stars, and the Kansas flag adopted in 1927. An old fashioned, cage elevator may be taken up to the second floor.

The offices of the governor, lieutenant governor, and secretary of state are on the second floor. The secretary of state's office contains the only white marble wash basin remaining from the lavish porcelain and marble bathrooms of the 1890s. The governor's office is finished in white mahogany from Mexico; the lieutenant governor's in white oak.

Also on the second floor in the central building are 11 fireplaces having hand-carved, white oak mantels, fascia boards, and architraves surrounded by ceramic tile. The murals by John Steuart Curry, including his dramatic "John Brown," have caused many debates and much controversy, but are generally considered to be the true picture of Kansas' history.

In 1976 the legislature acted to have the second floor rotunda decorated with murals to take the place of those Curry had never accomplished. A Capitol Murals Committee selected a native Kansan to do the work. Accomplished by noted sculptor, painter, and muralist Lumen Martin Winter, who referred to Curry's sketches, eight subjects are depicted: "Colonel John C. Frémont" (addressing Indians); "Sacking of Lawrence" (the destruction of that city); "Threshing" (early years of agriculture); "Sowing" (winter wheat); "Commerce" (cattle drives from Texas); "Well Digging" (a necessity on the high plains); "Education" (a teacher leads pupils from one-room school to a storm cellar); and "Governor's Mansion" (travelers in blizzard approach the governor's mansion at Lecompton).

Moving to the third floor, art and adornment continue in the House chamber. It is surrounded by marble columns with bases of Belgium black marble. The wainscoting is imported marble trimmed with Italian Carrara. Panels of Borcelian marble are interrupted with jasper in the east wall. The speaker's dais is walnut above which are hand-carved urns of solid walnut.

The Senate chamber is considered one of the finest in the United States. The $300,000 cost of its furnishings and decorations set off a furor of criticism which cooled rapidly because nothing could be done about it. There are 28 copper columns, hand-hammered with designs of roses and morning glories. Costly marbles from Belgium, Mexico, and Italy reflect the dark oak and Honduras mahogany fixtures.

Since being vacated by its court in 1978, the old Supreme Court chamber has become a "place of unusual historic interest." That year the legislature passed laws to preserve it. It is now used as a legislative hearing room. Every effort has been made to preserve the priceless artistic decor.

Maintenance and upkeep of the Kansas capitol and its grounds in 1988, using 25 full-time and 14 part-time employees, cost the state $1,197,303 which amount includes salaries, supplies, and utilities.

Since completion, the capitol has met the standards of modern efficiency through central heating and air conditioning, lighting, energy efficiency, and renovation.

Hour-long tours are offered to the public on the hour every hour, Monday through Friday from 9 A.M. to 3 P.M., except noon. Saturdays and holidays: 9 and 11 A.M. and 1 and 3 P.M. There are no tours on Sunday, but the building is open to the public. Reservations are requested for groups.

KENTUCKY
The Bluegrass State

HEIGHT: 210′   FACADE: 402′ 10″   DEPTH: 180′

Kentucky was a part of Virginia when Sir Walter Raleigh received its charter in 1584. The British explored the area to the Ohio River Valley in 1671.

France's La Salle laid claim to it in 1682, but with the discovery of the Cumberland Gap by Thomas Walker in 1750 and further exploration by the British, France ceded the area in 1763, the year George III forbade settlement.

After James Harrod, Daniel Boone, and others explored Kentucky and blazed new trails, Fincastle County of the Virginia Colony (Kentucky) was created in 1772 and settlers flooded the area. Towns sprang up, the Louisville site was surveyed. Through a treaty with the Cherokee Indians a group acquired the land between the Cumberland and Ohio rivers west of the Appalachians and called it the Transylvania Land Company which Virginia declared illegal and renamed Kentucky County.

It is believed their action started the desire to split from Virginia, and following the American Revolution, proponents for separation met in Danville December 27, 1784, in the first of ten conventions.

The Constitutional Convention attaining that goal designated Lexington as the site of the first General Assembly and, when Kentucky became the fifteenth state June 1, 1792, the General Assembly convened there on June 4th to inaugurate General Isaac Shelby as Kentucky's first governor and choose a location for the capital.

A five-man commission, delegated to visit several sites under consideration, would select the capital. Among those under consideration were Boonesboro, Frankfort, Lexington, and Louisville. Influenced to some extent by offers of land and building materials each town promised to donate, the Commission recommended Frankfort, which was declared the permanent capital on December 8, 1792.

Kentucky's first capitol was a three-story stone structure which cost the state about $3,500 with all excess expense raised through public subscription. It was built on the public square during 1793–94 and served until it burned in 1813.

The second Kentucky Capitol, a two-story brick building built during 1814–1816, met the same fate in 1824.

On January 12, 1827, a bill was approved for another capitol on the public square. It was completed in 1830 at a cost of $85,000 and remains today, the masterpiece of Kentucky's architect, Gideon Shryock, as the Old State Capitol.

Constructed of limestone quarried near Frankfort, the building is of rectangular shape about 50 fet high, 70 feet wide, and 132 feet deep. It is patterned after an Ionic temple in the Greek Revival style. Its portico's pediment is supported by six massive, fluted columns four feet in diameter by 33 feet long. A prominent cupola is centered in the copper-clad roof.

Most impressive to the visitor entering its portal is the staircase to the twin, self-supporting stairs leading to the legislature's chambers. A solid upper landing serves as the keystone to the stairs, and it is said that its movement of one-tenth of an inch would destroy the entire structure. The staircase is considered Shryock's outstanding achievement.

With government growth and the need of upgraded maintenance and extensive repair foreseen for the building, talk of a new capitol circulated through its corridors, anterooms, and legislative chambers.

For years the subjects of the proper location of Kentucky's capital and the building of a new capitol had been the center of controversy and political indecision. Two others cities, Louisville and Lexington, believed the state's capital should be relocated to their city.

The new capitol is in Frankfort, placed there after a long and bitter quarrel among the citizens and politicians of Louisville, Lexington, and Frankfort.

It emerged into being through acts preceding and following these words, "It is a fact apparent to all, especially to visitors from other states who come to your capital, that in the matter of capitol buildings, Kentucky is far behind the other states, even those of much less wealth and population."

With Governor J. C. W. Beckham's words ringing in their ears, the members of Kentucky's 1902 General Assembly returned to their constituents to convince them of the need for a new capitol.

Prior to his famous utterance, Governor Beckham had sent C. C. Calhoun of Lexington to Washington as the state's special agent and attorney "to look after, investigate, and collect certain state claims against the national government" which had grown out of the Civil and Spanish American wars. This he did and, in time, Kentucky received $1 million.

This money, matched by an appropriation in January 1904 by the legislature, guaranteed a new capitol. Its location was no longer a question when House Bill 69 passed with only one dissenting vote each from the House and Senate. Frankfort won with the provision that the new capitol would be built on the public square, at that time occupied by the third capitol.

A Capitol Commission was appointed. Frank Mills Andrews of Dayton, Ohio, was named architect. The public square was too small for his building. Governor Beckham called a special session in 1905 which appropriated $40,000 to buy 33 acres occupied by homes and vacant parcels in South Frankfort.

Preliminary work, clearing and excavating started May 25, 1905. The construction contract was let August 10; and excavation for the foundation started on the 14th. The cornerstone was laid on June 16. The work progressed with only one power-operated machine, a steam driven concrete mixer. The crane and steel bender were operated by hand.

In December 1909 the first department moved into new quarters. The legislature first convened in January 1910. The new capitol was dedicated June 1.

Designed in the Beaux Arts fashion, built for $1,820,000 including furnishings and landscaping, the Kentucky capitol's three stories and basement rest upon a base of Vermont granite surrounded by terraced walls that extend 30 to 40 feet beyond. The remainder of its exterior stone is oolitic Bedford limestone. The first story is of large, rusticated blocks. Seventy fluted, monolithic columns, their capitals of Ionic decoration, surround the building, identically matching and spaced exactly on its facade, rear and sides.

The dome's 24 columns encircling its base are similar, but sectioned. The

**Seventy Ionic columns surround the Kentucky State Capitol, dedicated in 1910. —
Office of Historic Properties.**

pediment over the front entrance has become distinguished in its statuary, and
its completion required an extra appropriation from the legislature. Designed
by Charles H. Niehaus, and executed by Peter Rossak of Austria, the heroic
lady "Kentucky" was created. She is surrounded by her attendants: art, labor,
law, history, plenty, and progress — all in bold relief.

The interior is displayed through a spacious nave bordered by 36 mono-
lithic, Ionic columns of Vermont granite with marble captains and bases. Running through the second to the third floor, each is 26 feet tall and weighs ten
tons. The walls and stairways are of white Georgian marble. Light Tennessee
and dark Italian marble cover the floor. The stairways, banisters and
balustrades at each end are modeled after those seen in the Paris Opera House.
On the second floor, looking from one end of the nave through the rotunda
to the other end, the visitor is awed by the perfect arches and clean lines on
display.

Reached by dividing marble staircases to the third floor, the legislative
chambers occupy rooms at each end of the nave. Both House and Senate
chambers are adorned with pink scagliola pilasters resembling marble. Named
after its Italian inventor, scagliola consists of a mixture of marble dust, gypsum, and glue. A lunette above each chamber's entrance contains a mural
painted by T. Gilbert White.

The mural in the west lunette pictures the Treaty of Sycamore Shoals in which Colonel Richard Henderson and Daniel Boone negotiated with Chief Oconostoto of the Overhill tribe of the Cherokee Indians for purchase of the land comprising Kentucky. The east lunette's mural portrays Daniel Boone and his party of Long Hunters atop Pilot Knob getting their first look at the Bluegrass region of Kentucky.

Beneath the capitol's dome the central rotunda, 57 feet in diameter, contains the statues of Abraham Lincoln, Jefferson Davis, Dr. Ephraim McDowell, Alben Barkley, and Henry Clay — all distinguished Kentuckians. The dome is patterned after that one at Napoleon's Tomb in the Hotel des Invalides in Paris.

The offices of the governor, lieutenant governor, secretary of state, and attorney general are located on the first floor.

The second floor contains the judicial branch of the government. The Supreme Court Room is resplendent with paneled walls and coffered ceiling of Honduras mahogany.

The Louis XIV designed State Reception Room resembles the Throne Room of the Charlottenberg Palace near Berlin, Germany. Its walls, hand-painted to resemble woven tapestries, are covered with murals depicting classical scenes. The chairs, benches, and sofas of hand-carved Circassian walnut were upholstered in brocade velvet woven at the convent in St. Cloud, France. The room's center table, carved of the same wood, is topped with Breche Violette marble. A 16-foot by 54-foot rug covers the floor. It was specially designed in the Louis XIV period for the room, handwoven in Austria; and, up to that time, it was the largest, specially designed rug ever woven.

On the third and fourth floors, besides the legislative chambers and their galleries, are the offices for the Senate and House leaders and the Legislative Research Commission.

An annex to the rear of the capitol houses the state treasurer, state auditor, Finance and Administrative Cabinet, the Department of Personnel, and the Revenue Cabinet. There are numerous other state office buildings housing other departments of the state government in Frankfort.

Kentucky's new State Capitol is the state's most visited historic site. Free guided tours are available Monday through Friday, from 8 A.M. to 4:30 P.M.; Saturday, from 9 A.M. to 4 P.M.; and Sunday, 1 to 5 P.M.

During sessions, passes may be obtained to visit the House and Senate galleries. The House chamber is used for joint sessions of the legislature.

Numerous printed materials are made available to visitors.

Upon completion of the new capitol, the Old State Capitol was occupied by the State Board of Control, the Frankfort Public Library and, eventually, the United States Quartermaster Department's Shirt Depot. In 1920 the building was assigned to the Kentucky Historical Society.

With an appropriation of $2 million by the legislature in 1972 the Old State Capitol was renovated. A basement area was added. In the Senate chamber the desks and chairs were replicated to the 1830s based on descriptions

The Kentucky State Reception Room. — Office of Historic Properties.

in a contemporary Senate Journal. Except for the original speaker's chair and three desks, the furniture in the House chamber was replicated. Both still have the original 1840 chandeliers. Their natural light is supplied through hand-blown window panes duplicating those in 1865 pictures. Winning a place as a National Historic Monument, the entire structure is a museum maintained by the Kentucky Historical Society headquartered in the Berry Hill Mansion annex to the Old State Capitol.

Free, guided tours feature the circular staircase and the legislative chambers with their galleries with changing exhibits available Monday through Saturday, 9 A.M. to 4 P.M.; Sunday, 1 to 5 P.M.; and holidays, noon to 4 P.M.

LOUISIANA
The Pelican State

HEIGHT: 433'   FACADE: 322'   DEPTH: 120'

While he campaigned for the governership of Louisiana in 1927, one of the declared principles in Huey P. Long's platform was a new state capitol. The existing neo–Gothic capitol in downtown Baton Rouge had served the state for nearly 100 years. On top of the bluff overlooking the Mississippi, it had served well, but age had scored its structure. It bulged with the government growth demanded during its lifetime by Louisiana's swollen population: from 200,000 to more than 2 million.

Elected in 1928 as the state's fortieth governor, Long's inauguration pulled more than 15,000 persons to the old fortress capitol where they swarmed to witness the great event. Among other things, Long gave top priority to a new capitol and spurred legislation to fulfill that goal before his limited term of office expired. A special session of the Louisiana legislature in 1930 produced the means to build.

There is little evidence that a white man came into the Louisiana area before 1541 when Hernando de Soto, searching for gold, explored and gave Spain claim to its northern part. Following de Soto's death Luis de Moscoso led the group down the Mississippi to the gulf.

In 1682 La Salle followed the river to the gulf, claimed the entire drainage system for France, and named it Louisiana. Subsequent explorations and claims in and upon Louisiana were made by both countries. Pierre le Moyne, Sieur d'Iberville visited the site of New Orleans in 1699; and his brother, Jean Baptiste le Moyne, Sieur de Bienville, founded New Orleans and named it after the Duc d'Orleans in 1718. Four years later New Orleans became the capital. The government's business was transacted in the Spanish Government House.

Settlement came when John Law's Company of the Indies was formed. He advertised "riches in the area," but his company collapsed in 1720. More settlement came in 1760 when the British forced the Acadians from Nova Scotia.

In 1762 Louis XV ceded to Spain the French Crown Colony: "Island of New Orleans," and the land west of the Mississippi. The remainder was given to Britain the following year.

The New Orleans Colony is distinguished as the first American colony to revolt against foreign rule, which the people did under the new owners and declared their independence until a large Spanish force entered the picture August 17, 1769. Ten years later Spain and Britain were at war. In the autumn of 1800 Spain retroceded Louisiana to France.

Through the persuasion of Robert Livingston, America's minister to France, and the efforts of James Monroe representing President Thomas Jefferson, a treaty of purchase was signed on April 30, 1803, and the United States bought Louisiana for about $15 per square mile.

Under ownership of the United States, that part of Louisiana south of the thirty-third parallel became the Territory of Louisiana with its capital New Orleans. William Claiborne was appointed territorial governor.

On April 30, 1812, Louisiana became the eighteenth state admitted to the Union. New Orleans remained the capital and Claiborne its governor. With the British defeated by Andrew Jackson in the Battle of New Orleans, 1815, and Spain ceding claim to the land west of the Sabine River, Louisiana's boundaries were finally established in 1819.

Presumably, the original Spanish Government House was the New Orleans capitol. A second presumption: When the capital was moved to Donaldsonville in 1830, government business was conducted in rented quarters, but not for long. It returned to New Orleans the following year and remained until voted upstream to Baton Rouge.

For some time before it became the official government headquarters, plans for a capitol in that city were in process. A Building Commission was created to assume the responsibility for getting it. The Commission advertised for architectural designs on January 21, 1847, and, within five days, having reviewed his plans, they commissioned James Harrison Dakin of New York as architect and hired him to supervise its building.

Unfinished, it was ready to receive the legislature and was dedicated in November 1849 with Governor Isaac Johnson presiding. The building was completed in 1852 at a total cost of $396,000 and, except for the Civil War years, Baton Rouge has remained the capital.

Of Gothic architecture, the capitol was constructed of cast iron, cast by Knap & Totten Foundry of Pittsburgh, with brick and stone walls. A New Orleans brickyard supplied 4,039,786 bricks for the job. All flooring and the doors were of wood.

In the rotunda a massive, balustrade cast iron staircase rises from the floor and curves upward toward the handmade, stained glass dome. The main floor housed the executive branch of the government, whose titles were chiseled in limestone at the entrances to their offices.

At the head of the stairway the rotunda is Medieval Gothic architecture in its purest form. The arches are cast iron. To the east (left) and west large doorways of cypress are entrances to the Senate and House chambers, respectively. Inside the House chamber subdued light pours into the room through hand-drawn, stained glass windows that were made in France. The room's air conditioning unit is a large vent centered in the ceiling. Like a chimney, it creates a draft sucking the hot air up and out of the room and draws fresh, cool air through the open windows. A visitors' gallery is above the entrance. The room was designed for holding joint sessions of the legislature.

On January 26, 1861, in a 113 to 17 vote, the Louisiana legislature repealed the U.S. Constitution and seceded from the Union and was an independent nation with an elected president, vice president and fully constitutional legislature for 23 days. For mutual protection from the Union, it became the sixth state to join the Confederacy March 21, 1861.

During those years of insurgence the capital was moved from Baton Rouge to Opelousas, 1863; to Shreveport, 1864; to New Orleans, 1864–1882.

During Federal occupation of Baton Rouge in 1862 while Union troops were housed in the capitol, a cooking fire spread from the basement of the southeast tower and gutted the interior.

When the government returned to Baton Rouge in 1882, the capitol was rebuilt by William Ferret of New Orleans, following the original plan as closely as possible.

Ordered by and intended for Emperor Maximillian of Mexico, the furnishings being shipped from Europe did not reach New Orleans for transshipment to Mexico until after the ruler's death. They were reconsigned to Baton Rouge to furnish the capitol.

The capitol was restored in 1938 under the administration of Governor Richard W. Leche.

It was rehabilitated and dedicated a memorial to World War II veterans by Governor Jimmie H. Davis on November 11, 1949. While Earl K. Long was governor it was renovated in 1956; and in 1968, it was completely restored with an expenditure of $800,000, and rededicated by Governor John J. McKeithen "to all veterans who died in our Nation's wars."

Louisiana's old capitol continues to serve the people of Louisiana and all who visit its treasures. Turreted, its Moorish, Gothic, and Norman styles of architecture have provided years of human criticism, praise, and conjecture. Built in the 1840s, burned accidentally by federal troops in 1862, rebuilt in 1882, it is found in downtown Baton Rouge with Louisiana's Convention and Visitor's Bureau Tourist Information Center at the foot of the iron staircase.

Although the New Orleans firm of Weiss, Dreyfous and Seiferth was retained to design the new capitol, Governor Huey Long had three distinct recommendations: (1) It should tower above the flat terrain surrounding Baton Rouge so that it could be seen in any direction by all who entered the city; (2) It should stand as a monument to the state and its people; (3) Finally, and the most difficult to attain, it should be finished before his term as governor ended which left little more than a year.

In unmatched effort, the artisans' skills, combined and coordinated, constructed a building that rose from a rectangular base into a structure towering 450 above the earth.

The project was started in December 1930. Building supplies poured into the area and before the capitol was dedicated May 16, 1932, more than 2,500 train carloads of construction and finishing materials arrived including marble from every producing area, Vermont to Mount Vesuvius.

Thirty-four stories tall and, at that time, the South's tallest building, it could be seen from any direction by anyone entering the city. For the first time since the Reconstruction period all facets of government representing Louisiana's people could be together under one roof. Placed within the ceremonies of its dedication was the inauguration of Louisiana's forty-first governor, O. K. Allen. Governor Long's requests had been met.

This example of Art Moderne architecture is not only symbolic of the state's history, but is functional in design and use. Its tower replaced the traditional dome; a spacious public hall, its rotunda. The executive offices and legislative chambers occupy the large, rectangular base upon which the tower is centered. The remaining public offices and agencies with their employees and appointees are housed in the tower above within easy reach.

Carefully researched by the architects, Louisiana's history and resources

Governor Huey Long's dream for the Louisiana State Capitol was realized during his administration. Finished in 1932, its $5 million cost was indicative of Depression prices. — Author's photograph.

make up the capitol's imagery. Cotton, crayfish, eagles, egrets, magnolias, pelicans and sugarcane are a few of the many artistic motifs. The arts, industry, science, and agriculture are depicted in bronze and stone throughout the building; and Louisiana history is pictured on the walls in every room and corridor.

Forty-eight steps lead up to the capitol's main entrance. With one exception, beginning with the original 13, each step bears the name of a state in its order of statehood. Alaska and Hawaii are inscribed on the landing's surface with the United States motto, *E Pluribus Unum*. This feature was intended to greet visitors from other states with "Welcome."

The building is unadorned to its break above the twentieth floor which supports large pelicans. Four-storied figures stand at each corner to represent art, law, philosophy, and science.

Inside, the capitol tells a story of a land and its people and provides corridors and space where history continues.

Framing the entrance, above the brass doors, the portal highlights the state seal. It is flanked by eagles above the state motto, *Union, Justice, Confidence*.

"We have lived long, but this is the noblest work of our whole lives...," the words of Robert Livingston, negotiator of the Louisiana Purchase, are inscribed on either side.

Directly above the portal are figures representing Indians, Spain, France, Britain, the United States, and the Confederacy. Between these are relief panels illustrating industry, justice, learning, liberty, and power.

Memorial Hall is the main room and and the nucleus of the capitol. Two stories in height and over 100 feet in length, it contains the building's greatest diversion of art. The walls are of dark red Italian marble fragmented with white.

The capitol contains more than 30 varieties of stone from every producing state and some foreign countries: violet French marble; grey from Germany; black-veined with white, rose and yellow out of the Pyrenees Mountains are a few examples.

From Memorial Hall, access is gained to the Senate chamber on the west side or the House chamber on the east.

Occupying the center of Memorial Hall is a great bronze relief map of Louisiana displaying her numerous products. Encircling the map are the names of the 64 parishes within her boundaries.

Directly in front of the map are the elevator doors leading to the tower. Made of bronze, they feature the portraits of 37 Louisiana governors including Huey Long. A bronze bust of Long above the doors is accentuated by the striking colors in the ten flags that have flown over Baton Rouge and Louisiana during its 300-year history. Flanking the doors are vases of Sevres porcelain, gifts from France. Freestanding statues of eminent governors are placed at random about the room.

Overhead the chandeliers feature the native subjects of Louisiana, and the ceiling above is an oak leaf pattern in gold leaf.

At each end of Memorial Hall are murals by Guerin. The Goddess of Agriculture is depicted on the Senate wall; the Goddess of Knowledge on the House wall. The bronze doors leading into the anterooms and chambers contain a total of 156 panels, each showing a specific event or place of importance in the state's history. Above each door is a replica of the Louisiana State Seal.

The Memorial Hall motif is found in the legislative chambers in bronze, stone, and wood. Entering either anteroom, visitors may ascend marble stairs gracefully spiraling to a gallery from where the legislative process may be observed.

From Memorial Hall, elevators speed to the observation level on the twenty-seventh floor where one can have a view of everything surrounding the capitol. On a clear day vision ranges more than 20 miles and the Mississippi River traffic can be followed until it disappears "'round the bend."

Overhead, eagle statuary representing the federal government draws attention to the lantern topping the capitol's crown, a beacon to Louisiana's people for more than 60 years.

Below, surrounding the capitol are its grounds and formal gardens. Centered in the formal garden to the south is the grave of Huey P. Long. To the east is the Old Spanish Arsenal, the oldest building on the grounds, dating from its use as a military garrison. Beyond it, across Capitol Lake, is the governor's mansion.

The Pentagon Barracks, to the southwest, are all that remain of an 1822 military post whose buildings later housed Louisiana State University until its campus was relocated to the present locale before the capitol was built.

The capitol stands as an edifice and memorial to Senator Huey P. Long, who was assassinated in its corridors by a young idealist, Dr. Carl Austin Weiss, Jr., on September 8, 1935.

MAINE
The Pine Tree State

HEIGHT: 185′   FACADE: 300′   DEPTH: 150′

Maine was not admitted to the Union as the twenty-third state until 1820, because she was a part of Massachusetts in the original 13 colonies. Her people fought with commitment and her men of the sea compounded grief to the British naval vessels wherever and whenever they could be found.

The history of Maine's exploration is uncertain. It is believed that Leif Ericsson and his crew explored the Maine coast five centuries ahead of Columbus. It is thought that John Cabot may have sailed into her waters about 1504, but evidence of such a visit is for future discovery. For sure, David Ingram's stories about his experiences along the Atlantic Coast in 1569 increased exploration and caused a number of ships to visit the area, some of them "putting ashore for repair and [to] process fish. . . ."

Human history goes back to the Ice Age and the "Red Paint" people who lined their graves with red clay; but Maine's history really started in 1607 when a group from the Plymouth Company settled Popham and, had it not been for the severe cold of the Maine winter, it could have been the first permanent settlement in America instead of Jamestown.

Several English settlements were made along the coast in the 1620s including Monhegan, Saco, and Agamenticos, which town, later named Georgeana then York, was the first chartered city in America. Because of the climate, Indian attacks during King Philip's War, 1675–1678, and ensuing sacking and burning, many were abandoned. With the toll from King William's War, by 1691 only four settlements remained in Maine.

During those years Massachusetts bought up most of the land claims on Maine, formed a provincial government, and drew a new charter giving the people of Maine greater self-government.

The ownership of Maine continued in dispute between England and France until the 1763 Treaty of Paris following the French and Indian War. With this decrease of Indian interference came Massachusetts' offer of 100-acre plots free to anyone settling in the northern province. By 1763 the population had doubled to 24,000. By 1800 it was over 150,000; and almost 300,000 when statehood was gained.

Maine's contributions to the American Revolution were of major proportion. In 1765 a mob seized tax stamps at Falmouth (Portland) and citizens' attacks on customs agents occurred regularly. In 1774 citizens of York duplicated Boston's Tea Party by burning a shipment of tea in a warehouse. Because of these acts English naval forces concentrated on her coastline and, to teach her unruly citizens a lesson, bombarded and burned the city of Falmouth in 1775. That June a group of Maine patriots captured the British cutter *Margaretta* and, later on that year, men from Maine were with Benedict Arnold in his attempt to capture Quebec.

Freed of British rule, the frontier's settlers were anxious to free themselves from Boston's rule. But the coastal merchants, holding majority political power, resisted separation until, during the War of 1812, they realized Massachusetts could not protect their coastline from British raids. They desired separation, and statehood became a desire of the majority.

In October 1819, with Boston's permission, delegates met in Portland to form a constitution. William King, an eminent shipbuilder and merchant from Bath, presided. After three weeks of argument, Maine had a constitution based upon religious freedom, political independence, and popular control of government.

Her separation from Massachusetts to become the twenty-third state to enter the Union was effected by Congress on March 15, 1820, under the Missouri Compromise, an act to retain a balance between free and slave states in the United States Senate. It provided Missouri freedom to form a state constitution without restriction on slavery.

With Portland designated its temporary capital and William King its first governor, Maine's legislature met in two buildings.

The House met in the Cumberland County Courthouse, next door to the Senate's meeting place, a two-story, frame, federal style building erected by the City of Portland for the state in 1820. The two-story pediment of its portico was supported by four columns. It became known as "the State's House" and was located at Congress and Myrtle streets in Portland. Gutted in the Great Fire of 1866, it was torn down and Portland's City Hall occupies that site today.

Location of the capital was in contention from statehood. It began with the understanding among the legislators that the capital would be moved from Portland to a more central location within five to ten years.

Before the year passed, search for a permanent capital began. Augusta, Belfast, Brunswick, Hallowell, Portland, Waterville, and Wiscasset were popular candidates, but eliminated one by one until the legislature chose Augusta. Governor Enoch Lincoln signed the bill on February 24, 1827, making that city the permanent capital of Maine.

But Augusta almost didn't make it.

In 1821 a joint committee was named to designate a town for the next meeting of the legislature. Hallowell was named, but the opposition desired a different place. In 1822 a governor-appointed commission chose Augusta and recommended that Weston's Hill, previously offered as the capitol's site, be accepted, and that the legislture should begin meeting there by the first Wednesday in January 1827, later amended to 1830.

In 1823 the citizens of Augusta purchased the 34-acre conical-shaped hill from Judge Nathan Weston and presented the deed to the state for ten dollars that December. The Senate accepted it, but the House, in a 12-vote majority, wouldn't consider it until 1827. They subsequently changed the year to 1825.

Contradiction raged from that point to a political brawl in 1827 when enough votes on February 24, 1827, forced a bill through the legislature naming Hallowell the site for the next session of the legislature over Portland and Augusta.

On that same day another bill was passed fixing the permanent capital at Augusta "on and after January 1, 1832," and until that time "the Legislature would meet at Portland." A clause was added annulling the Hallowell legislation.

It must be noted that the support of the Portland and southern legislators passed this bill. Through it they would eliminate Hallowell from the competition and during the 1828 session they would gain enough strength to eliminate Augusta.

But it was during that session that a bill was passed to appoint a building commissioner to plan the Augusta capitol and sell public lots, raising the money to build it. The first governor of Maine, William King, was appointed the capitol commissioner and a land sale brought $60,000. Before the year ended King requested a design from Charles Bulfinch, builder of Massachusetts' capitol and architect for the U.S. Capitol.

Bulfinch responded the following year with a complete set of drawings for

The Maine State Capitol, designed by architect Charles Bulfinch. One-tenth of the cost of construction was paid for by the people of Augusta. — State House Commission.

a granite building in Greek Revival design 150 feet by 50 feet with an arcade and colonnade projecting 15 feet in front and 80 feet in length. The estimated cost was $80,000. It was the last major work of his career.

On July 4, 1829, the cornerstone was laid with Masonic ritual. Underneath were placed a copy of the constitution, various publications, American coins, and a commemorative plate. The celebration began at sunrise with ringing bells and a 24-gun salute and continued through the day into dusk with eminent speakers including Governor Enoch Lincoln.

Even though Commissioner King was replaced by a new administration in 1830 by William Clark who was replaced by Reuel Williams, the work progressed uninterrupted until more money was requested to finish the building and grounds. When an appropriation of $30,434 reached the House it was tabled and the issue of a permanent capital was reopened with Portland making new bids for the seat of government, but these were countered by Augusta.

Only $25,000 was appropriated with conditions that Augusta must furnish a $50,000 bond to cover any cost exceeding the appropriation. To complete the capitol an additional $11,466 was spent from the bond. The total cost, including furnishings, landscaping, and interest was $138,991.34.

Completed in January 1832, Maine had a "building of splendid workmanship and excellent materials as any State in the Union. . . ." But Maine also had a political faction dissatisfied with the capital's location. For years the location in Augusta was disputed, threatened, jeopardized, and narrowly escaped relocation.

The first, the building of a Merchant's Exchange that was started by a group in Portland in 1836, was thwarted by a nationwide financial panic in 1837 when supporters, unable to furnish finances, sold it to Portland.

On November 30, 1839, the *Portland Transcript* said, "a serious effort will be made at the approaching session of the Legislature to remove the seat of government again to this place. It has been seen that a great mistake was made when it was transferred to Augusta. . . ."

Each year it was tried, relocation barely escaped reality with hot argument for and against taking place in the legislature; and each of those years was connected in some way to the refurbishing, repair, and updating of, or adding on to, the capitol.

Bulfinch's plan was first modified in 1853 with an appropriation to remove the fireplaces and document rooms from the corners of the House and Senate chambers for more room and replacing candles with gas lighting.

A capital removal measure was introduced in 1860 and suffered a narrow defeat, but with it came another appropriation to increase the space within the capitol.

Occupied with the Civil War, relocation was postponed. On February 26, 1867, approval was given for an extension at the rear to enlarge the capitol. Designs were submitted, but funds were lacking.

In 1884 the governor and council were instructed to investigate enlargement of the capitol. On July 29 a committee of the Executive Council met with Francis H. Fassett, a Portland architect and requested a wing for the rear of the capitol to be 46 feet wide by 85 feet long. Again, funding was not available.

In 1889 a third try was successful and the addition to the capitol, designed by architect John C. Spofford of Boston, was constructed during 1890–1891 at a cost of $150,000. Designed to conform with that of Bulfinch, the three-story wing provided more office space and a place for the library. Confronting this addition was another attempt to relocate the capital and again it was narrowly defeated.

The issue was brought up for the last time in the 1907 session of the

legislature. Inadequate space in the capitol was the vehicle carrying it to a hea
ing held by the Committee on Public Buildings and Grounds on February 1
1907, "to inquire into the expediency of a change in location of the seat
government and erection of a new state house." After hours of debate it w
recommended that the Augusta capitol be enlarged.

In the 1909 session a Commission on the Enlargement of the State Hou
was created. A competition for designs was advertised in every Mai
newspaper and two in Boston. G. Henri Desmond of Boston was the winnii
architect. The George A. Fuller Company of Boston was contracted. Di
mond's design doubled the length by adding wings to either side, raised tne
dome to 185 feet, and increased the capitol's usable floor space to 102,612
square feet. The only Bulfinch features remaining are the portico at the center
of the facade and the wall immediately behind and adjacent to the portico.
The exterior is hammered Maine granite supplied by H. L. Brown Company
of Hallowell.

Finished in 1911 at a cost of $349,929, those changes marked finality to
two of Maine's major historic political problems: relocating the capital and
rebuilding the capitol.

The south wing entrance to the first floor finds space occupied by four
detailed dioramas showing Maine's flora and fauna. Placed in natural surroundings, the display includes beavers, bears, deer, moose, and many other
animals and birds native to Maine.

A display case shows trophy-size fresh water sport fish caught in Maine.
The State Office Building may be reached through a tunnel from the west
wing. Public rest rooms are on this floor. The upper floors are reached by marble stairs or elevators.

The plan for each of the four floors is similar. Beginning with the second
floor, corridors lead into the north and south wings and a broad hallway leads
into the west wing. All the floors are white marble with a colored border.

The second floor contains the Hall of Flags which is divided into three
aisles by two rows of Doric columns. Maine's battle flags are together with portraits of the state's leading politicians. Offices of the governor, attorney
general, and secretary of state; the Law Library and Appropriations Committee
Hearing Room are also on this floor.

The third floor houses the offices of the legislators' leadership, the Senate
president, the speaker of the House, the Senate and House chambers, and the
State Government Committee Hearing Room.

The Senate and House galleries are on the fourth floor. From this floor
the rotunda rises three stories above to culminate in its domed ceiling. Encircled by narrow balconies with delicate iron railings at two levels, it is designed
in simple lines by paired Doric pilasters and denticulated cornices. Atop the
dome is the statue of a draped female figure of *Wisdom* designed by W. Clark
Noble of Gardiner. It is made of copper and plated with gold.

Commemorative plaques and portraits honoring former governors and
outstanding men and women who have served Maine, grace the walls of the

corridors and every significant room, reminders of Maine's illustrious history and promising future.

Another change took place in 1989 when a Media Center took over space formerly occupied by the heating plant.

A free guide service for the capitol is available from the Bureau of Public Improvements at Room 211, State Office Building or by telephone from the red courtesy phones found in the State Office Building or capitol. Brochures and leaflets are available to visitors.

The total cost for operations and maintenance of buildings and grounds for FY 1988 was $5,944,808.62. One hundred eighty persons held authorized positions to care for the state's properties. Fourteen employees maintain the grounds on the 43 acres.

MARYLAND
The Old Line State

HEIGHT: 200′   FACADE: 119′ 5″   DEPTH: 195′

Maryland's government has grown from a single-family dwelling into a capitol complex consisting of 18 buildings. During 1988 Maryland paid $9,444,810 for the maintenance, security, and upkeep of those buildings and grounds by 220 employees.

The Chesapeake Bay was first charted in 1608 by Captain John Smith of the Virginia Colony, who landed at Georgetown.

Within the borders of what would become Maryland, the first permanent settlement was a trading post on Kent Island. It was started in 1631 by a group from the Virginia Colony headed by William Claiborne. All were Protestant in religion and politics. They protested Charles I's granting a charter to Sir George Calvert who wanted to found a colony in that area for a group of Roman Catholic followers. Eventually, their fears were proven unfounded.

The charter was granted but Calvert, the first Lord Baltimore, died in April 1632 before it was effected. On June 20, 1632, it was passed to his son Cecilius who became the second Lord Baltimore and, after enticing rich noblemen to have their sons join the expedition, he arranged for his brother Leonard to head it. Except for that land cultivated, the charter granted all the land between the Potomac and Delaware rivers, north to the fortieth parallel, and west to the Potomac's headwaters. The chartered land was named Maryland by Charles I for his wife, Queen Henrietta Maria.

In November 1633, 17 gentlemen with indentured servants, making a total of 150 colonists, boarded two small ships, the *Ark* and the *Dove,* and sailed from the Isle of Wight. After countless hardships on the sea, they anchored off St. Clements Island on the Potomac River on March 5, 1634.

As governor of the colony, Leonard Calvert took a few men upriver to find a place to settle, encountered friendly Indians, and gained their permission to live on a site they named St. Mary's City where they built a fort. Within eight years, the population of St. Mary's City grew to nearly 400 people. Numerous permanent structures had been built, but growth was slow.

Those who came to Maryland with Leonard Calvert had been enticed with a promise of free land, a rich fur trade with the Indians, and the possibility of finding precious metals. For each settler, there was the gift of 100 acres of land plus 100 for every worker accompanying him. With the fur trade and gold lacking, they turned to agriculture and, with the Indians' knowledge and help, it became their industry. They were successful in growing tobacco, beans, corn, and other staples that staved off periods of starvation that the Virginia colonists were experiencing.

Three men, appointed by Lord Baltimore, acted as a council of advisors to his brother Leonard, the first governor of Maryland. These four and a secretary became the executive branch of government and St. Mary's City became the first capital of the colony in 1634.

Because the Maryland Charter had given Lord Baltimore the power to make laws with the agreement of the freemen, a general assembly was formed to exercise the power of government.

The Maryland General Assembly held its first session in St. Mary's City in 1635, little more than a year after the arrival of the *Ark* and the *Dove.* That session and those which followed were general in assembly in the strictest sense for they were comprised of every freeman of the colony. This first Maryland legislature was a unicameral body comprised of the governor, his advisors and the freemen. By the third session in 1638 the freemen were instructed to meet and choose their representatives. These men, chosen to represent their communities became known as burgesses. Their legislative body, which became the House of Burgesses, was often called the House of Delegates and referred to as the lower house.

Although they sat as one body, a distinction was made between the governor and members of his council and citizens of the colony at large. An effort was made in 1642 to separate the two groups, but Governor Calvert protested. Their division does not appear in the record until the 1646 session when the upper house is mentioned. The governor and his council exercised both executive and legislative powers.

Maryland became known as the "Free State" after 1649 when the general assembly passed "An Act Concerning Religion." The first of such laws to be passed, it followed the wishes of the first Lord Baltimore and allowed religious tolerance among the original settlers of the Catholic, Protestant, and Jewish faiths. Regardless of the law, throughout the colonial period religious

Completed in 1772, the Maryland State Capitol witnessed several significant events in early American history. — Author's photograph.

involvement by the people swayed the administration of the colony back and forth from the crown's domination to Lord Baltimore's governorship.

Reverting to the Crown in 1689, a group of colonists revolted, seized control of the government in St. Mary's City, and asked Queen Mary for a Protestant government. Calling themselves the Protestant Association, they enacted laws until the arrival of the royal governor.

Sir Lionel Copley, a native of England, a soldier, and a person of some note, was appointed governor August 6, 1691. He arrived in 1692 and after receiving the government from the "Committee of Safety," he called and convened the assembly on May 10, 1692.

Copley died in 1693 and was replaced by Francis Nicholson who, by an act in 1694, caused the capital to be moved to Anne Arundel Towne which was laid out by his design. The name was changed to Annapolis in 1695.

Little is known as to where the general assembly's sessions were held in St. Mary's City prior to purchase of the home of Governor Leonard Calvert by the colony. Bought from the Calvert family in 1662, it became the first official statehouse of Maryland.

It was a frame clapboard building of one story with a finished loft. It had a half addition on the rear, was 40 feet wide by 68 feet long. Its construction cost 250,000 pounds of tobacco.

A capitol was built in 1676 and used until the capital was relocated in 1695. Used as a church until 1829, it was a two-story, gabled, cruciform-shaped, brick structure with a pantiled (curved) roof from Holland.

A replica of that building is in St. Mary's City today. Centered, on each side of the main structure, massive chimneys project well above the roof line. The wings contain three arched entrances. One is centered on each side with a third at the front.

With the government of the Province of Maryland in Annapolis, the conflict between the two houses continued. The upper house clung to the power and privilege of the Crown and Proprietor. The lower house asserted its growing strength for liberty. Their struggle to dominate one another continued until independence from England was won, but it did not prevent advancement of the colony.

It was in Annapolis that the first circulating library, the first postal service, and the first free school were established. *The Maryland Gazette,* first published in 1727, remains the oldest circulating newspaper in the nation.

Settled in Annapolis the assembly's first State House was built in 1697 and occupied until 1704 when it was struck by lightning and burned.

Another, built in 1707 was used until 1769 and vacated to be torn down because of its irreparable condition.

Maryland's Assembly appropriated 7,500 pounds sterling to construct a statehouse on the highest point of land in the city, 58 feet above sea level.

Joseph Horatio Anderson was retained as architect and Joseph Clark was the architect for the interior of the building. Contracts were let to an undertaker, Charles Wallace, and to Thomas Wallace, "a clerk of sorts."

Construction was started in 1772 and completed in 1779 giving Maryland a Georgian style capitol. Constructed of brick, manufactured nearby, it contains a basement, a sub-basement and two stories with a usable floor space of 16,422 square feet. The colonial style plastered walls and turned wood columns remain today as excellent examples of architecture of that period.

With a need of increased space, an annex was added to the rear of the original building with construction starting during 1902. It was completed and ready for occupation in 1905. Designed by Baldwin and Pennington in neoclassical style, it is built of Maryland brick matching the original structure. Henry Smith held the construction contract. Costing $600,000, the annex raised the total floor space to 59,939 square feet.

The interior of the annex, unlike the original, uses matching marble in its walls and columns.

Maryland's capitol is a National Historic Monument and the oldest state capitol in continuous legislative use. A museum now occupies the Old Senate Chamber where many historic events took place with many former patriots participating. It is the room in which George Washington resigned his commission December 23, 1783, before he returned to Mount Vernon following the American Revolution.

From November 1783 to June 1784 the building served as the Capitol of the United States while Congress met there. Events occurred in which James Monroe and Thomas Jefferson took part. The Treaty of Peace with England, which ended the American Revolutionary War and created a new nation, was ratified in the Maryland capitol.

The remaining rooms on the first floor display famous paintings by famous artists, the most celebrated of which are the original "Washington at Yorktown" by Charles Wilson Peale; and "Washington Resigning His Commission" by Edwin White.

Flags carried into battle by Maryland's troops, historic banners, and portraits of Maryland's notables are also displayed for posterity.

Guided tours including the legislative chambers are available every day except when the capitol closes for Thanksgiving, Christmas, and New Year's Day. Because of its continuous business traffic, the governor's office is closed to the public.

It is believed the Maryland State House is the only capitol to contain a complete visitor's center with certified travel counselors. Tours, a ten-minute video presentation, and brochures are also available to visitors.

MASSACHUSETTS
The Bay State

HEIGHT: 59'   FACADE: 454' 8"   DEPTH: 462'

In 1628 Charles I of England granted a colonial charter to Massachusetts which precipitated the "great migration" of Puritans from England. Entering Massachusetts Bay in 1630, a group of Puritans led by John Winthrop landed and settled on three hills. The place was named Trimountane, but renamed Boston after a town in Lincolnshire, England. Boston was made the capital of the Massachusetts Bay Colony in 1632.

When Charles Bulfinch returned to Boston from Europe in 1787, with a desire to be an architect, he was assailed with the desire to draw and submit a design for a statehouse for Massachusetts. Probably this insatiable prompting was produced by the people's clamor for a new statehouse. His appointment as architect may have been coupled with the political knowledge he had gained as a selectman for Boston. During his life he designed many of Boston's buildings and assisted in the design of the United States Capitol.

It was not until 1793 that the Town of Boston and the Commonwealth bargained an exchange of properties for services. For the old State and Province houses owned by the Commonwealth, Boston would provide a new statehouse.

In 1795 the Massachusetts General Court appointed a committee of three, including Bulfinch, with authority to "build and finish a new State House." Said building was to accommodate the legislative and executive branches of government. It would be built on a two-acre plot, then known as the governor's pasture because it adjoined the late Governor John Hancock's garden, which was to be purchased by the town and "conveyed in fee simple to the Commonwealth."

The agreement freed the town from constructing the new building and allowed the committee about $27,000 for construction. The town paid about half that much for the property which was conveyed to the Commonwealth on May 2, 1795. Work commenced in that month and on July 4, 1795, the cornerstone was dragged up Beacon Hill by 15 white horses and laid by Governor Samuel Adams in a Masonic ceremony. He was assisted by Paul Revere, Grand Master of the Grand Lodge of Masons.

Steadily the wooden framed, brick and stone building rose. Especially notable in the construction were the great Corinthian columns made from solid logs. Brought from Calais, Maine, these were 25 feet long and about 30 inches in diameter. Holes were drilled from one end to the other, through the center, and the logs were turned down to 23-inch diameters on a massive lathe. Complete with hand-carved capitals and bases, they remained in their original positions for more than 150 years. In 1960 iron pillars with aluminum capitals took over. In all those years only one had been replaced and that one just two years previous.

Completed and ready for occupancy on January 11, 1798, a procession of the General Court, led by Governor Increase Sumner, walked from the old statehouse to the new where, after ceremonies were conducted inside, it became the Massachusetts State Capitol.

The old statehouse, the seat of royal government for Massachusetts from 1713 through the provincial period and into statehood, still stands at the corner of Washington and State streets. Given up, vacated for a larger "more elegant home to better reflect the prosperous new republic, spacious enough to

The cornerstone of the Massachusetts statehouse was laid on July 4, 1795, by Governor Samuel Adams, assisted by Paul Revere. — Office of the Governor.

acccommodate an expanding government," it is now an historical museum. For 85 years the old statehouse performed for the government. Three brick-framed stories rise above the basement to a pitched roof holding five dormers on each side. A tower, rising above the roof's peak on one end, lends an important air to its history. The wall at the other end supports a pediment.

Probably the desire for a new statehouse was brought about by events leading up to the Revolutionary War. The royal charter granted by Charles I was revoked by Charles II in 1684. This abolished the unique advantage of having the government in Massachusetts rather than England. Back under the dominion of England, the colonists were deprived of many advantages. When William and Mary made Massachusetts a royal colony in 1691, with a crown-appointed governor, the crown's laws denied the colonists the manufacture of essential goods. With taxes and commercial controls put upon them, the merchants of Boston boycotted English goods. This forced the repeal of the taxing laws, but others followed and angry colonists provoked clashes with British troops.

The fateful Boston Massacre of March 5, 1770, took place under the balcony of the old statehouse when angry, resentful colonists taunted British soldiers who fired upon them, killing five.

This act, preceded by the Sugar Act, the Stamp Act, and followed by the

Tea Act, aroused anger-built revenge and the Boston Tea Party in which the colonists, under cover of darkness, dumped valuable ship-laden cargoes of tea into the bay. In 1774 the colonists bypassed the statehouse and met in Faneuil Hall where they voted against the taxation measures.

From here in 1775 Paul Revere made his famous ride to warn the colonists of British troops advancing. The battles of Lexington and Concord on April 19, followed by that of Bunker Hill on June 17, led to the American Revolution and the Declaration of Independence on July 4, 1776. Earlier that year General Washington and his army had driven the British troops out of Boston.

The Bulfinch creation is a rectangular building. The facade of the new statehouse measured 173 feet; its depth, 61 feet. Its shingled, whitewashed dome, 50 feet in diameter and 30 feet high, supported a circular lantern topped with a gilded, hand-carved pine cone depicting lumbering as one of the chief products.

Over the years the dome and its top features have seen several changes. Its leaking roof was coppered in 1802 by Paul Revere & Sons, after which for many years it was painted a "stone-color" gray. From 1861 to 1874 it was painted a gold color. The dome was then gilded with 23 carat gold leaf costing $2,862.50. During World War II it was painted a battleship gray. It was re-gilded in 1969 at a cost of $36,000. With the desire to reproduce its lines and proportions to those of Bulfinch's original dome, it was rebuilt in 1859 and again in 1897. Today the golden dome is used by mapmakers as the official location of Boston. A sign indicating the mileage to Boston may just as well say, "50 miles to the golden dome."

Governmental growth required several additions to the capitol. The first, in 1831, was designed by Isaiah Rogers and added four fireproof rooms for records to the rear of the central portion. This addition was 25 feet high, 25 feet deep, and 90 feet long. The second, 1853–1856, was designed by Gridley Bryant. It extended from the rear and surrounded the first addition with almost the same dimensions as the original structure. This addition provided ample library space and offices for other departments.

About 1878, with the government continually outgrowing its capitol, a bill was introduced to relocate the capital in the geographic center of the state and build a new capitol. The legislature defeated the proposal and voted to enlarge the existing capitol.

Eventually Charles Brigham was engaged to design and build, 1889–1895, a large extension to the rear of the Bulfinch building. This was done after the first two additions. Now known as the Brigham addition, its elegant interior was created out of carved wood paneling, wrought iron and marble.

The last additions are the wings of each side of the Bulfinch building. They were designed by architects R. Clipson Sturgis, William Chapman, and Robert Andrew, and were built during the years from 1914 to 1917.

Each architect did his best to design and build to conform with the Bulfinch design which remains the front, central part containing the main entrance and the dome.

Following the Brigham addition, three architects were appointed in 1895 to survey the original Bulfinch part of the capitol to determine its strength and safety features. They found the exterior faultless, but the interior was a shambles created by contractors and workmen who were turned loose in the building to accomplish the changes desired, in any way which might seem most convenient to them.

Their findings and pronouncement brought about a three-year restoration project which probably not only saved the structure, but greatly increased its longevity. Over the years, in spite of the additions and changes, the native son, the original architect, Charles Bulfinch, continues to be credited with the design of the Massachusetts Capitol.

For example, the red brick walls of the Bulfinch contribution were painted white in 1825. Their color was changed to yellow during the 1850s then returned to white in 1918 to match the white marble of the new wings. Ten years later, in 1928, the walls were cleaned of paint and returned to their original and natural red-brick color.

Visitors are encouraged to take the free tours offered by the Tours and Government Education Division of the Office of the Secretary of State. Available from 10 A.M. to 4 P.M. on weekdays, the tours are conducted by the staff and volunteers, all knowledgeable and well-versed in the history and architectural background of the capitol.

Legislative process tours and foreign language tours are made available with prior arrangement.

Large groups of ten or more, including school classes should be scheduled three weeks in advance. For teachers whose curriculum contains state government, educational materials will be sent on request. For those planning to tour the statehouse with their classes, instructional aids are available and will be sent when the tour is booked.

Visitors to the Massachusetts State Capitol will be overwhelmed with its history and contents. It was in the Senate chamber that Angelina Grimke made political history in 1838, speaking on the abolition of slavery. She was the first woman to speak before a legislative body in the United States.

It was from here, at the beginning of the Civil War, that fighting equipment was distributed to companies of volunteers forming the Sixth Massachusetts. These men of the Sixth, who assembled in front of the statehouse to receive their colors from Governor John Andrew, arrived in Washington, D.C., on April 19, 1861, to become the first organized military assistance President Lincoln received in the Civil War.

Today those flags, returned after the Civil War in a ceremony in December 1865, may be seen in the Hall of Flags. Since that war the Massachusetts flags of every war and conflict, including the Berlin emergency, have been returned to repose in the Hall, which now contains more than 300 flags.

Only the president of the United States, with one exception, may enter or leave the statehouse through the middle doors of the front entrance. This tradition was started by former governor Benjamin Butler who, on his last day in office, January 4, 1884, made the journey alone from the front door down the front steps and established the "Long Walk." Since that time, the only other person who may use the middle doors of the front entrance is the departing governor ending his term of office.

MICHIGAN
The Wolverine State

HEIGHT: 267'   FACADE: 420'   DEPTH: 274'

Before white men entered Michigan it was teeming with game and covered with virgin forests. Its lakes and streams were filled with pure water. It was a rich hunting ground for the Chippewa, Ottawa, and Potawatomie Indians who peopled it. When a few of them loaded bundles of rich furs into their birchbark canoes and paddled down the St. Lawrence River to Quebec they found the French fur trappers.

Samuel de Champlain sent Jean Nicolet from Quebec to open trade with the Indians while he searched for a passage to the Orient. In 1634 Nicolet explored the Great Lakes area. Out of Lake Huron through the Straits of Mackinac, he explored the south shore of Michigan's upper peninsula, continued through Wisconsin to the south end of Green Bay and the Fox River. Through Nicolet's reports the French learned about the land and went there with their traps.

Then the missionaries came. In 1641 two Jesuit priests started an Indian mission at Sault Sainte Marie. It failed, but 27 years later (1668), a French Jesuit missionary, Father Jacques Marquette organized the first permanent white settlement at that location and, in 1671 at St. Ignace he established the Mission of Michilimackinac. That year France claimed possession of the Great Lakes region through Simon Daumont, Sieur de St. Lusson.

The soldiers came with René Robert Cavalier, Sieur de La Salle who built Fort Miami at the mouth of the St. Joseph River in 1679.

When La Salle sailed the *Griffon* up the Detroit River that year he was accompanied by Antoine de la Mothe Cadillac, a soldier of fortune, who was so impressed with the area and the possibilities of building a fort there, he returned to France and sold his idea to Louis XIV. Returning with soldiers and colonists in 1701, he built Fort Pontchartrain which became Detroit 50 years later.

The French flag flew over the region until after the French and Indian War. After France surrendered to England in Montreal in 1760, British troops entered Detroit and within the next three years the English occupied Mackinac, Sault Sainte Marie, and Detroit. A good friend of the French, Chief Pontiac of the Ottawa Indians, resented it. Joining forces with the Chippewa (Ojibwa) and Potawatomie tribes, he attacked and destroyed many of the smaller forts. In attacking Fort Mackinac they killed all except one person who escaped. With his forces Pontiac laid siege to Detroit. When he learned of the peace between France and England he lifted the siege and accepted the English.

In 1775 the first civil governor, Henry Hamilton, was sent to Detroit. Thus Detroit became the capital of the region. During the American Revolution the area now known as Michigan remained loyal to the crown regardless of Indian attacks and public unrest. After the war, in the Treaty of Paris (1783), England granted Michigan to the United States and a border was drawn through the middle of the Great Lakes to separate the two countries.

But the British did not leave Michigan. In 1787 it became a part of the Northwest Territory. General Arthur St. Clair was appointed the first governor. He was faced with the problem of putting a stop to the Indian attacks on the settlements. After failing in a campaign against them, Governor St. Clair was replaced by General Anthony Wayne. Defeating the Indians in the Battle of Fallen Timbers in Ohio in 1794, Wayne succeeded in establishing peace with the Indians and a year later they gave up their lands, nearly all of the Northwest Territory, thereby making way for settlement. When the people of the Detroit area organized a county they named it Wayne in the general's honor.

Not long after Congress organized the Northwest Territory, Britain annexed Michigan to upper Canada. Their troops continued to occupy Detroit although the region was ceded to the United States. Finally, on July 11, 1796, the British surrendered Detroit to General Wayne whose forces backed him up.

When Congress organized the Ohio Territory in 1800, eastern Michigan was made a part of it.

In 1805 Congress organized the Michigan Territory naming Detroit the capital. General William Hull of Massachusetts was appointed governor. When Governor Hull arrived in Detroit on July 1 he saw a few wisps of smoke rising from a pile of rubble, all that remained of the fort and small village. With his hands filled with problems and his mind searching for a solution he had only one recourse. Accompanied by Territorial Judge Augustus B. Woodward, he hurried to Washington for aid.

Receiving authorization from Congress to lay out a new town, he was given an appropriation of 10,000 acres of land adjacent to the burned-out fort. Returning, he gave Judge Woodward the honor of plotting a new town.

Detroit was captured by the British August 17, 1812, during the War of 1812, but was retaken by the United States following Britain's defeat in 1813.

In the treaties of 1807, 1819, and 1821 the Indians surrendered their lands to the United States. Opened for settlement, the population grew and by 1834, the people of Michigan, feeling their strength, petitioned Congress for statehood. Congress refused their petition because of boundary problems with Ohio.

In 1835 Congress awarded the Toledo area to Ohio and the following year made Michigan a present of the upper peninsula. With the boundaries settled, Congress admitted Michigan into the Union as the twenty-sixth state January 26, 1837.

When the Michigan Territory was organized in 1805, Detroit had no building in which the governmental bodies could meet; and until Michigan's first capitol was completed in 1828, the legislature met in various places.

The first capitol, constructed as the Territorial Courthouse, was designed by Obed Wait. Constructed of red brick in Greek Revival design, it was 90 feet deep with a 60-foot facade. Two stories in height, it held an Ionic portico beneath a well-defined pediment above which a tower rose to give the building a height of 140 feet. It was completed at a cost of $24,500 and occupied by the territorial government May 5, 1828.

When Michigan was admitted to the Union in 1837 this territorial building housed the state's first elected governor, Stevens T. Mason, and served as the Michigan State Capitol until March 17, 1847, when the capital was moved to the Lansing Township. Vacated, it became Detroit's Union High School and was used as a library. It was destroyed by fire in 1893.

During a constitutional convention in 1835 the delegates included a provision that a permanent capital would be chosen by the legislature in 1847; and as that year approached, Detroit's citizens did everything possible to retain the capital. Heated debates occupied the legislative sessions. Ann Arbor, Detroit, Grand Rapids, Jackson, and Marshall contended. The people of Marshall were so sure of the capital, they built a mansion for the governor.

The debates turned to argument, quarreling, and discord. A deadlock ensued. With several of the towns eliminated for one cause or other, a land speculator, James Seymour, who owned lumber mills in Ingham County, showed a map of his area to the legislators and pointed out that the Lansing Township would be "a fine site for a new state capital." His proposal had little opposition in the House, but met a bitter fight in the Senate where it withstood two months of debate before being passed.

With the location settled it became necessary to name the new capital. Of those submitted, Michigan was chosen; but by 1848 the redundant "Michigan, Michigan," became wearing on the nerves and was changed to Lansing.

When a capital site was finally selected, workmen hurriedly built a temporary capitol and the legislature's first session met there during the winter of 1847–1848.

Michigan's second capitol, designed by Israel Gillett, was a two-story, white frame structure with clean lines. Its gabled roof supported four chimneys and a cupola. By 1853 the need for more room for the expanding government required the building of a two-story brick structure. This was soon crowded and in 1863 an addition was built. Within two years the requirements for more room caused the original temporary capitol to be extended 16 feet. With this addition the total cost of that capitol was $22,952.01.

When no longer needed the temporary capitol was sold and used for offices and the manufacture of wooden handles until fire claimed it in 1882.

It was not until 1871 that Governor Henry P. Baldwin, hoping to overcome the government's congestion, recommended the construction of a new capitol to the legislature. Concurring it acted to provide for one and also a temporary building to house state offices. The act also empowered the governor to appoint a Board of Building Commissioners charged with the responsibility for design and construction of both buildings. A strict maximum expenditure of $1.2 million was included, which sum would be appropriated by taxing Michigan's residents 16.875 cents per year over a six-year period.

With a deadline set for December 1, 1871, the Board of Commissioners advertised a design competition. Because of the Chicago fire the deadline was extended to December 28. From 22 entries submitted, they finally selected the best and least costly design and on January 25, 1872, announced the winner as Philadelphia-born Elijah E. Myers of Springfield, Illinois. With his acceptance to build Michigan's capitol, Myers moved to Detroit.

The construction contract was let to N. Osborne & Co., Contractors, but before work began the temporary, two-story, brick office building had to be removed from the site and another temporary was built "close to the old Capitol to house government offices during the construction of the new statehouse." Preparations got under way in late August and construction began in September.

The ceremony and celebration in the laying of the cornerstone was one long remembered. By September 1873 Lansing had grown from a "hole in the woods" with eight voters to a town of 7,000. Preparations and planning, long in advance of the occasion, were for a crowd of 30,000 to 50,000 visitors.

On October 2, 1873, a cannon was fired and the ceremony began. Thirty-five thousand spectators watched while 5,000 — Masons, Knights Templar, Odd Fellows, and companies of militia, accompanied by brass bands playing their favorite tunes — paraded through the bunting-decorated streets.

Speeches followed the parade. The liquor flowed freely allowing for several unruly episodes. Some tipplers climbed construction derricks and slid down the ropes distracting the speakers. While Governor John J. Bagley addressed the crowd, a somewhat tipsy lawman posted himself before the podium demanding silence from the noise makers. Finally the five-ton cornerstone was set in place with 48 articles representative of that time period. A cannon roared a salute to the flag and the ceremony ended, but the eventful day had just begun.

There were more people than hotel rooms. Residents opened their doors to the visitors. Throughout the celebration there was never a shortage of food for the crowd. If considered comparatively, that event was surely Lansing's greatest.

Construction of the capitol progressed with few interruptions. Through the winter months most of the work had to be suspended. On one occasion the stonecutters struck for a $.50 raise per day to $3.75, but the contractors had enough cut stone and denied the raise.

The completed capitol, handed over to state officials September 23, 1878, cost $1,427,743.78 including all furnishings and landscaping.

Its official dedication was held on January 1, 1879, with the inauguration of the new governor, Charles M. Croswell. Michigan's third capitol and its 139 rooms were overwhelmed with countless visitors from every part of the state.

Based upon the cross-shaped plan of architecture, it illustrates academic-classical composition of Greek and Roman architecture with the addition of the Renaissance style of Italian architect Andrea Palladio (1518–1580).

Great blocks of limestone from Lamont, Illinois, were cut the width of the walls making up the foundation. The stair railings, pedestals and urns are limestone from Joliet, Illinois, and the remainder of the exterior is Ohio sandstone. Massachusetts granite and Vermont marble were used in the interior.

The capitol's main entrance is the east facade where its design receives the greatest emphasis. Tuscan, Ionic, and Corinthian columns, in that order, rise above the ground story. A two-story portico at the head of the outside stairway rises above the main entrance with its three arched doorways.

The pediment, rising high above the portico, is of primary importance to the significance of Michigan's vision. Designed by Louis T. Ives, modeled in plaster by Herman Wehner and carved under the direction of master stone-cutter Richard Glaister, the central figure is a woman in Indian dress. Representing Michigan she offers a volume to her people while her right hand rests upon a globe.

Seated to her left, a woman holds a cornucopia in her right hand, a laurel wreath in her left as her arm rests upon a plow's handles. A third woman, to her right, is seated on bales of goods with her right arm resting upon an anchor to represent commerce.

Above the pediment, constructed of cast iron with sheet metal covering and topped with an octagon cupola, the white dome rises 267 feet into the sky.

In the three doorways of the main entrance, each contains a pair of identical doors reached by way of an impressive granite stairway leading through the portico. Each glass-framed door, designed by Myers, is 14½ feet high by three feet, one inch wide. The exterior is black walnut; the interior, pine. Each door is a work of artistic ingenuity, bearing intricate carvings and moldings. A set of identical paired doors grace each remaining capitol entrance: north, west, and south.

Fifteen million bricks, made in Lansing, were laid in the interior walls. Some may be seen in the unfinished sub-basement.

Entering the ground floor, a visitor is attracted to the one-ton replica of

Designed by architect Elijah Myers in classic Renaissance style, the Michigan State Capitol was completed in 1878 at a cost of $1.5 million. — Author's photograph.

the nation's Liberty Bell. Cast in France it served as a symbol in the United States Bond drive of 1950. It was presented to the people of Michigan by U.S. Treasury Secretary John W. Snyder.

The core of the rotunda houses the Capitol Security Guard staffed by the Michigan State Police. Surrounding the rotunda are glass cases displaying segments of life in Michigan.

Above, in the ceiling (the first level's floor), are 976 glass blocks measuring from five-eights to three-quarters of an inch thick. Designed to create an optical illusion when viewed from high above, the leaded-glass floor is 44½ feet in diameter.

Upstairs on the first floor, surrounding the walls of the rotunda, glass cases display battle flags from the Spanish American and Civil wars. The south wing houses the governor's public offices and the lieutenant governor's office. The corridot holds three murals from the Michigan State Building in Chicago's 1933 World Fair: "Michigan's Natural Resources" by Paul Honore (lumber, agriculture, and minerals); "Old Chicago Road" by Roy C. Gambles (westward expansion scene portraying Father Gabriel Richard, Governor Lewis Cass, and Sauk Indians); and "Cadillac at the Court of Louis XIV" (asking permission to build a fort at Detroit).

Black and white checkerboard floors of Vermont marble and Michigan slate, running throughout the capitol's corridors, are supplemented with walnut doors having brass doorknobs impressed with the state seal, an apple blossom, or a harvest scene. The ceilings are fresco. The chandeliers, a combination of copper, iron, and pewter, weigh 400 pounds apiece and were designed by Tiffany's of New York.

On both sides of the rotunda, grand staircases lead to the upper floors and the second floor's rotunda contains the gallery of governors. The portraits are of the eight most recent governors. Each has chosen his artist and paid for the work and, when he leaves office, his portrait is hung in the gallery. The oldest is removed to be hung in a hallway or in the Historical Museum.

The east wing contains the governor's office; the north wing, the House chamber; and the south wing, the Senate chamber. The galleries to the legislative chambers are reached from the third floor where the Supreme Court chamber is located.

Virtually unchanged from the time of its first session, the Supreme Court chamber is believed to have the best interior design within the building. When the Court moved, the chamber was put into use as a legislative committee hearing room. At the east end is a long, elevated justices' bench with a mahogany-paneled wall behind. It should be noted that most of the interior wood of the capitol is pine hand-painted to resemble walnut.

The fourth floor is divided into meeting and hearing rooms. During dedication time there was "The Pioneers Hall" where the fathers and pioneers of Michigan assembled from time to time to discuss current and future problems and reminisce about the past.

In the rotunda's cone panels above the fourth floor are eight paintings donated by Louis T. Ives who designed the pediment. They represent agriculture, the arts, commerce, communications, education, law and justice, labor and industry, and science.

The remainder of the building is used for legislative offices and the supporting activities of the government.

During fiscal 1988–89, the budget for capitol operations totaled $1,380,200 which included state and contracted personnel salaries, utilities, equipment, and supplies for maintenance and upkeep.

At one time the capitol housed all the departments of Michigan's government. Today it contains only the executive and legislative branches. Currently underway is a restoration program which will renew the building to its original grandeur. Setting aside $45 million for the project in 1988, the program includes the grounds and landscape which are noted for the nation's largest catalpa tree. It was large during the capitol's construction and has had more than 100 years to grow larger. There are two ginkgo trees: one planted in 1880 in memory of Governor Epathrodatus Ransome; the second in 1934 by Mrs. Eleanor Roosevelt.

In October 1988 the Senate and Friends of the Capitol started restoration of the Senate chamber and its adjacent areas. Finished January 10, 1990, it was the first completed project of the restoration. Underway at the same time, the House chamber and its adjacent area were completed April 24, 1990.

The ground floor's east and west corridors, begun in July 1989, were completed during June 1990. Plans for the upper corridors and rotunda were made in December 1989, but the work didn't start until July 1990. Because of scaffolding to reach hard-to-get-at places, it could be finished until 1991.

The Supreme Court chamber's restoration, started during the summer of 1990, was completed in 1991. Planning on the Executive Wing, used by the governor and his staff, was begun in January 1990, but the actual work was not to begin until 1991.

The repair of the dome and replacing the capitol's roof, the repair of the exterior steps, and repair and cleaning of the sandstone exterior, which cannot be done in bad weather, was underway as of 1990.

During the restoration period visitors are welcome, but are asked to observe all signs posted for their safety.

The Capitol Tour Guide and Information Service conducts scheduled tours seven days a week and is a ready reference for questions pertaining to the historical and contemporary information on the capitol and legislative process during hours of operation: Monday through Friday, 8 A.M. to 4 P.M.; Saturday and holidays, 10 A.M. to 4 P.M.; and Sunday, noon to 4 P.M.

Besides the capitol, Michigan's capitol complex includes the new Michigan Library and Historical Center with the State Archives. There is no charge for tours, but advance arrangements must be made for groups of ten or more.

MINNESOTA
The Gopher State — North Star

HEIGHT: 223′ FACADE: 434′ DEPTH: 229′

The Minnesota Capitol overlooks St. Paul's business district. Ranked among the most impressive capitols in the United States, it is the state's third and has been the state's seat of government since 1905.

The first white men to visit the Minnesota area left proof of their visit on a stone found in 1898 near the west central town of Kensington. The stone bore an inscription in runic characters indicating Norse explorers had camped there in 1362. The authenticity of the stone remains uncertain, but it has rested undisturbed with the Smithsonian Institution in Washington, D.C., since 1948.

French fur traders came in 1660 and the French explored and claimed the area for France, settling there until 1762, when France ceded all its lands west of the Mississippi to Spain. The following year, England won the eastern portion from France; then, in the 1783 Treaty of Paris, the British ceded it to the United States.

Spain had secretly returned their gift of land west of the Mississippi to France in 1800. Being part of the Louisiana Purchase, all of Minnesota became United States property, but remained in jeopardy until the Treaty of Ghent closed the War of 1812.

Prosperity in the lumber industry brought more settlers into the area during 1840. One group built a church in 1841, named it St. Paul, and that name was given to their settlement.

A land office opening at St. Croix Falls in 1848 flooded that area with settlers. A convention was called at Stillwater on August 26, 1848, and plans were under way for the Minnesota Territory.

Created by Congress on March 3, 1849, the first session of the Minnesota territorial legislature was headed by Governor Alexander Ramsey. They met in the Central House Hotel in St. Paul from September 3 to November 1, 1849.

The assembly consisted of a nine-member council and 18 representatives. Among its accomplishments was a system of free schools. The Central House Hotel was designed by Robert Kennedy and was listed in the city directories until it burned in 1847.

The second territorial legislature met in a three-story brick building on St. Anthony Street, where a bill was passed February 7, 1851, to make the permanent capital at St. Paul. Several plans for a capitol building were reviewed. The design submitted by N. C. Prentiss was chosen. He was paid $50.

Joseph Daniel's bid of $17,000 was accepted for construction of the exterior, the council chamber, the representatives' hall, the governor's office, and rooms for the secretaries and clerks. The United States Treasurer was to pay $20,000 for the capitol as soon as a permanent capital had been declared and, when the legislature requested an additional amount, the treasurer added $12,500. The actual cost of construction was $31,222.65.

Because the new capitol was not completed, the third territorial legislature met at the Merchant's Hotel on Goodrich Street, convening January 7, 1852.

With the capitol still unfinished, the fourth session met January 5, 1853, in a two-story brick building on the corner of Minnesota and Third Street.

Finally, on January 4, 1854, the fifth session convened in the new capitol. The governor moved into the Executive Office January 21. The completed structure's facade was 139 feet in length. A wing built at its rear, 44½ feet by 52 feet, gave it a depth of 100 feet.

Two changes were made in the building during 1866. Gas lights replaced the candles and steam heat replaced the log-burning iron stoves.

To house the legislature in the growing government, two expansions were built in 1872 at a cost of $15,000. A wing replaced the Greek portico on the facade and the roof and cupola were rebuilt to maintain the building's symmetry.

During the years 1878–1881 a wing was added for the House and space was added to the administrative offices at a cost of $14,000. These additions increased the facade to 204 feet and the depth to 150 feet.

As reported by Alfrieda Gabiou in Minnesota's *Gopher Historian,* fall 1968, on the evening of March 1, 1881, when the twenty-second session of Minnesota's legislature was hard at work, a senator burst into that chamber shouting, "The Capitol is on fire!"

Men jumped from their seats and rushed toward the exit. The stairway leading to safety was afire and filled with smoke. Paralyzed with fear, they stood watching smoke pour into the Senate chamber until one cool head requested that someone should move to adjourn. Others shouted, "Close that door!" Adjourned, with the closed door shutting out the smoke, the Senators busied themselves while determining an action to escape.

Firebrands rained from the ceiling ventilators. The roof of the cupola crashed to the floor blocking the exit. Escape became possible through a small window someone discovered in the chamber cloakroom. The roof of the chamber crashed to its floor just after the last person crawled out the window to the landing and ran down the stairs and outside to safety.

Meanwhile, when a cloud of black smoke swept into the House chamber and the alarm was sounded, "two hundred persons rose as one individual." Terrified, some had to be stopped from jumping out the windows, but one did jump. His fall was broken by a deep snow bank and he suffered no more than a cut on the cheek.

The smoke finally cleared from the hallway and 300 people, including the gallery's spectators, flowed down the stairs and out of the building.

During the three hours the building burned, St. Paul's visitors and citizens were rescuing its contents. Almost everything of value was saved except several thousand law books that did not get thrown out of the library window because the fire and its heat drove a young lawyer and his companion from the library.

A smouldering ruin amid the four walls remained. Some people suspected that someone had deliberately set the fire so that a new capitol could be built in another city.

As the capitol burned, St. Paul's mayor, William Dawson, contacted Governor John S. Pillsbury and offered the city's Market House as a substitute. Within hours it was made ready for them and the twenty-second session of the Minnesota legislature convened there the following day, March 2, 1881, and continued to meet there for the next 22 months.

One of its first acts was an appropriation of $75,000 for a new capitol. Architect Leroy S. Buffington was retained, the rubble and smoke-stained walls of the ruin were removed, construction started, proceeded without interruption, and the second capitol was occupied in January 1883. Immediately it was realized that space was not sufficient. A lack of hearing rooms made it necessary to hold them in nearby buildings. Within eight years of its occupancy offices were crowded, state departments were confined in distant buildings, and the building's ventilation system had brought health problems to its occupants.

In 1891 the Senate president appointed five Senators to a committee to determine the needs for fulfillment of government. The committee favored a new building and all except one recommended it be kept in St. Paul. A cost estimate of $2 million minimum was considered. A bill was introduced and passed in the House and Senate and signed into law April 7, 1893, by Governor Knute Nelson who appointed a Capitol Commission.

The Commission advertised for architectural designs and employed Edmund Wheelwright from Boston to select the best from among the 41 entries submitted. He selected the design of Cass Gilbert of St. Paul. With a legislative appropriation of $4.5 million, a site was selected on a hill a few blocks from the second capitol, ground was broken May 6, 1896, and construction started. The cornerstone was laid in 1898 by Alexander Ramsey who had been Minnesota's first territorial governor in 1849.

Completed, it was dedicated June 14, 1905, in a ceremony of the Grand Army of the Republic conducted by Governor John A. Johnson.

Costing $4,493,000, the capitol's exterior walls and dome are made of Georgia marble. The foundation, terraces, exterior balustrades, and steps are grey granite from St. Cloud, Minnesota. There are six marble statues above the main entrance representing bounty, courage, integrity, prudence, truth, and wisdom.

The dome is topped by a gilded ball. At the base of the dome above the entrance, a gilded, steel and copper sculptured group represents "The Progress of the State." A charioteer holds an upraised banner "Minnesota" in one hand and holds against his body with the other, a cornucopia spilling out the state's products to represent prosperity. His horses symbolize the power of nature. Two women leading them depict civilization.

The interior is filled throughout with the works of nationally renowned artists. More than 20 types of imported marble are used in the corridors, chambers, and on the stairways as well as several types of stone from Minnesota's quarries. Motifs of the state's agriculture, flora and fauna, as well as astronomy are symbolized in grill, plasterwork, and stenciled artworks.

The rotunda and interior of the dome are the most outstanding architectural "marvel" of the capitol. Centered in the first floor is an enormous glass and brass star symbolizing the North Star State. Flags carried by the state's soldiers fighting their country's battles are contained in glass cases around its walls.

To illuminate the rotunda with its 95 bulbs during special occasions like the governor's inauguration, an Austrian crystal chandelier hangs high above the rotunda floor. Weighing a ton, this six-foot wide by seven-foot high creation containing 38,844 glass crystals is suspended from the center of the dome on a 28-foot chain. It can be entered through a door to change a burned out bulb, but must be lowered to the floor for cleaning. Between the column-supported arches above the second floor are four panels containing paintings by Edward Simmons entitled "The Civilization of the Northwest."

The Governor's Reception Room on the first floor is considered the

Designed and built by Cass Gilbert of St. Paul, the Minnesota State Capitol was dedicated June 14, 1905. — Office of Historic Sites.

outstanding room in the capitol. It is resplendent in Minnesota white oak and gilded plaster moldings. Its light comes from two chandeliers made of Austrian crystal and German silver wire. The fireplace is encased in French and Italian marble. Above it is "The Treaty of Traverse des Sioux" by Francis D. Millet; and on the opposite wall is "Father Hennepin Discovering the Falls of St. Anthony" by Douglas Volk. The side walls carry historic scenes of Minnesota regiments in the Civil War by noted artists. The ceiling is covered with gold leaf. An information desk, the attorney general's office, and several hearing rooms are also on the first floor.

The second floor contains the Supreme Court, Senate and House chambers, and the offices of the Clerk of the Court, the Clerk of the House, and the Secretary of the Senate. The Senate chamber and the House chamber, the larger of the two, are ornate in statuary, marble columns, murals, and portraiture.

Visitors to the House and Senate galleries are admitted on the third floor. The Supreme Court Library is also on this floor.

Declared a Historic Site by the Minnesota Historical Society in 1969, the Minnesota capitol was listed on the National Register of Historic Sites in 1972.

During 1988 the Senate chamber was restored at a cost of $1.7 million; and the following year the House chamber received the same treatment costing $2.2 million.

The Minnesota State Capitol continues as a working state government building open to the public seven days a week except New Year's, Easter, Thanksgiving, and Christmas. Free, guided tours are conducted by the Minnesota Historical Society. They start from the Information Center on the first floor every hour, on the hour: Monday through Friday, 9 A.M. to 4 P.M.; Saturday, 10 A.M. to 3 P.M.; and Sunday, 1 to 3 P.M. The tours last about 45 minutes.

Reservations, required for groups of ten or more, may be made by calling ahead. Besides a general tour of the building there are a government tour, a history and government tour, a statehood tour, and a veteran's tour; and activities are offered for pre-school and upper elementary school pupils. On request, an architectural/restoration tour is available.

MISSISSIPPI
The Magnolia State

HEIGHT: 180'   FACADE: 402'   DEPTH: 225'

Acclaimed the discoverer of the Mississippi River in 1541, Hernando De Soto of Spain was first to explore in the state of Mississippi. Filled with dreams of gold since boyhood, his chance came when a friend was appointed to govern Panama. Promoted to captain he led expeditions into Guatemala and Yucatan eventually joining Francisco Pizarro to conquer Peru. With pockets filled, he returned to Spain where the king appointed him governor of Cuba and Florida. He returned to the Americas with 1,000 men and, from Havana, sailed into Tampa Bay, explored north into Georgia, turned west to the Alabama River and followed it back to the gulf. Striking north, still searching for gold, they found the Mississippi River.

Encountering numerous Indian tribes, De Soto's severe demands and brutality toward their chiefs turned into battles decimating his troops. His three-year search for gold a failure, he died in 1542 on the Mississippi's shore near the Red River junction. His men built boats, floated to the gulf, and eventually reached Mexico.

Great Britain claimed the area in 1629 with the Carolina grant of Charles I which was repeated by Charles II in 1663.

The region lay unsettled until 1682 when René Robert Cavelier, Sieur de La Salle claimed it for France to start a trend of French settlements on the river.

With the help of the Biloxi Indians, Frenchmen built Fort Maurepas near the site of Biloxi in 1699. The government of French Louisiana was located there until it was moved to Mobile in 1702.

French commander-general Jean Baptiste le Moyne, Sieur de Bienville established Fort Rosalie on the site of present-day Natchez in 1716. When Bienville was recalled to France his replacement's bad temper and quarrelsome attitude held back the colony's growth. The settlement was eventually destroyed by Indians in 1729.

When the French demanded that the Indians surrender their land that year, the Indians attacked them. A counterattack scattered the Indians and when the Yazoo Indians joined the fray, they were annihilated.

In 1732 George II granted a charter giving England's imprisoned debtors the right to settle in Georgia. The British joined the Chickasaw Indians to drive the French from the northern area. Succeeding, the Treaty of Paris gave them rights in 1763; and the following year the British rebuilt the fort near Natchez and renamed it Fort Panmure. With growing settlements near Natchez and Vicksburg, they established schools.

Spanish troops entered the area and occupied Natchez in 1781. They evacuated part of the area after the American Revolution and ceded it to the United States in 1795, but remained in Natchez until the arrival of American troops in 1798.

On April 7, 1798, the Mississippi Territory was organized with the capital at Natchez. The first governor was Winthrop Sargent. The boundaries were set with the Mississippi River on the west, the Chattahoochee River on the east, the thirty-first parallel on the south, and that parallel running through the mouth of the Yazoo River on the north.

In 1801 a treaty with the Choctaw Indians gave the government the use of the Natchez Trace, a wilderness road connecting Natchez to Nashville, Tennessee, and the Cumberland River. With $6,000 appropriated from Congress it was improved, shortened, and became a post and military road. Used by frontiersmen to and from New Orleans, it was important in Mississippi's population increase.

The state's early settlers came on the Mississippi River. The river was a crucial factor in populating every likely site along its course. Natchez became an important shipping center and more towns were built along the Mississippi's shore from which farm products were loaded to be carried downstream to New Orleans and foreign ports.

The territorial government was moved inland, a few miles from Natchez, to Washington in 1802. While the capital was there, the state's permanent boundaries and federal ownership were settled through land purchase and Indian treaties.

With the eastern part of the Mississippi Territory separated to become Alabama, statehood was granted on December 10, 1817. The first state governor was David Holmes. Washington remained the capital until January 23, 1822, when it was moved to Jackson. When Jackson was captured by Union forces May 13, 1863, the government moved to Enterprise, Meridian, Macon and Columbus in that order; and returned to Macon in 1864, then back to Columbus in 1865. When the legislature refused to ratify the thirteenth Amendment in 1865, Mississippi was placed under military rule and readmitted to the Union February 7, 1870.

The first permanent capitol of record was built in Jackson. Located at Capitol and President streets, it was a two-story, brick structure costing about $3,000. It served as the capitol until the government outgrew it. Within ten years the state's population had tripled. The far-sighted legislators knew a larger capitol would be needed and shortly after the Constitution of 1832 assured them the capital would remain in Jackson, a new capitol was authorized in 1833.

Built on Capitol Green at Capitol and State streets, the Mississippi State Capitol is considered one of America's outstanding examples of Greek Revival architecture. The first architect was John Lawrence who was replaced by William Nichols, an English architect whose reputation had been confirmed through the building of other capitols in the southern states. Construction started in 1836.

During the construction period the entire country was overcome by a depression making it difficult to finance construction, but it was done.

Though unfinished, it was first used for a special session of the legislature in January 1839, and was not completed until the following year. The approximate cost was $400,000 financed by legislative appropriations.

The facade has the classic Greek temple front. Six massive Ionic columns rise from stone archways to support the portico. The first story exterior is constructed of stone. Above that was brick under stucco for the two remaining stories. The interior floors are supported with columns of Ionic, Corinthian, and Doric design. The walls of the corridors and rooms are resplendent with decorations. A spacious rotunda rises 120 feet from the ground floor to the dome. From the foyer on the ground floor, twin stairways spiral upward to the third floor ending at the circular rotunda from where the House and Senate galleries can be entered.

But the Senate and House chambers with their impressive Corinthian columns dominate the interior. In these chambers America's first law was passed giving women property rights. It was there also, in 1861, that the Ordinance of Secession was passed; and in 1865 the first constitutional convention in the South was held after the Confederacy's defeat. Further, it was in the Mississippi capitol that 64 years of state government laws were effected until 1903, when it was abandoned and the government moved into the new capitol.

On February 5, 1903, the State House Commission, as it was designated, unanimously adopted a resolution to invite those persons who attended the laying of the cornerstone on the "Old Capitol" to be present for the same event for the "New Capitol." Eight persons responded and attended.

Erected on the site formerly occupied by the State Penitentiary, the new capitol overlooked its surroundings and could be seen from a considerable distance. Construction began on January 1, 1901, and the new capitol was completed on August 20, 1903.

Hereafter called the capitol, a commission was created by an act of the legislature February 21, 1900. Its duties provided for the building of a statehouse: to secure drawings, plans, and specifications; and to authorize and provide all necessary personnel and supplies for its construction with the cost not to exceed $1 million dollars.

After several commissioners had resigned and new appointments made, the commission advertised for architectural plans and specifications. Fourteen designs were submitted by the deadline, April 9, 1900. Unable to reach a decision after weeks of study and quizzing the competing architects, they selected a competent contractor, the builder of the Congressional Library, and handed him the unnamed designs. He made the selection.

Theodore C. Link of St. Louis was their choice if he would revise the plans to fit the budget. He did and accepted a 5 percent fee, not to exceed $45,000.

Because of the costs of hauling construction materials to the site, without cost to the state the commissioners enticed a spur from the Illinois Central Railroad with the help of Governor A. H. Longino.

Bids for construction were received from 12 contractors before the opening date, December 8, 1900; but none were acceptable as the lowest was higher than the law permitted. With plans changed to lessen material costs, the bidders were invited to resubmit. The lowest bidder, the Wells Brothers Company of Chicago, was retained after investigation of its ability, moral character, and financial worth. With a completion date of May 1, 1903, the construction contract of $833,179 did not include plumbing, heating, and electrical wiring.

Operations began on January 1, 1900, but were halted during foundation excavation when, upon reaching marl, a loose, crumbly clay deposit without resisting power, it became necessary to excavate 20 feet deeper which cost $30,641 extra and, including testing every foot of ground, extended the completion date by three months.

From that point the work went so well that it was believed the original completion date would be met, but during that progress, the commissioners restored several changes made before the designs were resubmitted which increased the contract to $872,131.09.

After high bids on the first, a second competition for the plumbing and piping was contracted for $26,577. The electrical work was contracted for $13,200.

With a need for additional funding because of extra costs, the commission appealed to the legislature for furniture: "[It should] be designed by an artist . . . an expert in such matters . . . and in perfect taste and harmony with the room in which it is to be used and [all] furniture . . . placed therein." The commission estimated the cost to be $75,000 and broached the landscaping with a cost of $60,000 to $70,000.

With their plea they submitted a request from the architect for another

$250,000. He substantiated the need by saying "that the various items ...
marble finish, carving, etc...., [and those] features bearing upon the personal
comfort of the occupants of the building ... be restored, and that the appropriations for color, decorations, furniture and fittings be made more liberal
than shown in the first schedule."

The Mississippi capitol was completed August 20, 1903, at a total cost of
$1,093,641 including furniture, grading of grounds, paving and additional
granite steps.

The new capitol of the Beaux Arts style dominating capitol architecture
from 1890 to 1910 was distinctive with detail and various stone finishes,
highlighted by projecting facades with colossal columns supporting attic stories
and a centered lofty Roman portico of six Corinthian columns that supported
the pediment filled with 14 bas-relief sculpted figures depicting the history of
the state.

Above the portico heavy stone finials decorated with lions' heads weight
the corners of the central block that supports the massive dome with its
peristyle of Corinthian columns topped with a lantern. Its wings spread in
flight, a symbolic eagle crowns the lantern. Built of solid copper gilded with
heavy gold leaf, it stands eight feet high with a wing spread of 15 feet.

Each capitol wing terminates in a semicircle of Corinthian colonnades
topped with saucerlike domes covering the legislative chambers.

There are four stories above ground and a sub-basement. The ground
story is of Georgian granite resting upon 3,500 cubic yards of concrete. The
upper walls are Bedford limestone.

Six massive oak doors enrich the entrance and the interior is rich in detail
and motif. The rotunda floor is grey Italian marble interrupted with jet black
marble. Huge piers at four diagonal points rise from the floor, each carrying
two Pavanazzo art columns of scagliola rushing upward to terminate in capitals
and lead the eye into the dome's interior of pure white plaster. (In 1934, color
and gilt were added.)

A semicircular room at the east end on the first floor is rimmed with Ionic
columns and Tuscan pillars. It was occupied by the Hall of History until 1941.
The west end's small, semicircular room contains Corinthian columns. Rose
Claire marble borders a pink mosaic tile floor. It has always been the United
Daughters of the Confederacy reception room.

Maple, oak, walnut, and mahogany, all hardwoods, are used throughout
the interior. The walls of the second floor corridors are Italian marble accented
with Belgium black marble. At either end, the entrance pediments are supported by marble Tuscan columns. These rooms, formerly occupied by the
Supreme Court and State Library, each have stained glass windows framed in
black walnut and oak.

Reaching the third floor by the grand staircase, the importance of the
legislative and executive functions is reflected in the marble wainscoting,
fluted Ionic pilasters and stained glass forming the ceilings which receive their
light from translucent glass blocks in the fourth floor.

The most expensive marble in the building, Numidian marble, is found in the governor's office. Its reception room has a barrel vaulted ceiling with recessed cove lighting.

In the Senate chamber massive Corinthian columns of Breccia violet art marble support the domed ceiling made of oxidized copper, plaster, and Bohemian stained glass. One such glass contains an inscription reminding the Senators of "The people's government — made for the people — made by the people — and answerable to the people."

The walls of the House lobby are of Tennessee pink marble with base and trim of Tennessee Knoxville marble. The chamber walls are Sienna art marble with Belgian black wainscoting. Large consoles supporting the visitors' galleries are framed with semicircular arches. Overhead arches trace an intricate line beneath the domed, stained glass coffers of the ceiling. Four gilded Mississippi State seals, each centered midpoint in the massive arches, dominate the chamber.

Some renovation occurred during the 1930s and extensive restoration back to the 1903–1930 era was accomplished during 1979–1982 when office mezzanines were built over the second story offices to increase staff space. The total cost was $19 million.

Attempts to demolish the old capitol, deteriorating from neglect, were thwarted by women's preservation groups. With the name "The Old Capitol" affixed, it served as a state office building from 1916 to 1954. Abandoned again when the State Board of Health moved from its crumbling interior, bills for its demolition were introduced. Again the preservationists went into action and survival of "The Old Capitol" was assured in 1959 when Governor Jim Coleman initiated its complete restoration to house the State Historical Museum.

With the stucco removed from the brick, completely restored, it was designated the State Historical Museum in 1961 and is on the National Register of Historic Places.

Today its first floor contains the governor's office, the Hall of Flags, and permanent exhibits with text describing Mississippi's history in chronological order.

The second floor holds the completely restored Senate chamber and the High Court of Errors and Appeals. The House chamber has been furnished as a public auditorium.

The third floor houses exhibits in the Senate Gallery and the State Library. A replica of the Jefferson Davis Library occupies the House Gallery.

The capitol is open Monday through Friday from 8 A.M. to 5 P.M.with tours given at 9 A.M., 10 A.M., 11 A.M., 1:30 P.M., 2:30 P.M., and 3:30 P.M. It is open for self-guided tours on Saturday from 10 A.M. to 4 P.M.; and Sunday from 1 to 4 P.M.

The museum is closed on the four major holidays: New Year's, Easter, Thanksgiving and Christmas.

Visitors are always welcome and may procure a copy of the new, full color booklet *Mississippi,* published in 1990.

MISSOURI
The Show Me State

HEIGHT: 262 + '   FACADE: 437'   DEPTH: 300'

In 1971 the roof of Missouri's capitol sprang a leak and rain spotted the ceilings and walls of the Senate chamber beneath. In April the Senate Accounts Committee recommended and requested an emergency appropriation from the general assembly. Although several appropriations were granted, the executive branch was unable to get the roof repaired. During torrential rains in April and May, 1975, several Senators gave yeomen's service to get and place buckets to prevent damage to the rooms beneath the chamber. The roof was finally repaired in 1976.

Then began the restoration of that chamber not only to repair the leaky roof, but also the damage caused by wear and the variances of temperature and humidity over the years. Opinions differed. Some wanted new fixtures, furnishings, and decorations; others, to restore it to the original chamber of 1924. Compromise cost the project $700,000.

The chamber's original chairs, changed from solid legs to a swivel base, were a part of that cost. Their occupants found them difficult to control, lost their balance, and fell to the floor. Two conditions prevailed in restoring those chairs: they were to be made as solid as possible and the squeaks had to be removed. The chamber was rededicated on April 25, 1977, three centuries after Father Jacques Marquette and Louis Joliet explored the upper Mississippi.

Assisted by their reports, René La Salle descended the Mississippi and claimed the entire valley for France in 1682. From that time French trappers invaded the claim to trap; French soldiers to build protective forts; French priests to establish missions and convert the Indians. Settlements sprang up. The discovery of lead in 1715 brought more people. Ste. Genevieve, the first permanent settlement, was founded by the French in 1735. France ceded its claim on the west side of the Mississippi to Spain in 1762. (It was secretly returned in 1800.)

St. Louis was founded in 1764 and the following year the French moved their headquarters from upper Louisiana to that settlement and remained there until the first Spanish governor, Don Pedro Piernas, arrived in 1770.

In 1803, with the Missouri area included, the United States bought the Louisiana Purchase from France. Because the settlers didn't want Missouri to be made a part of the Indiana territory, it was made a part of the Louisiana Territory in 1805.

On October 1, 1812, Congress effected the Missouri Territory. Benjamin Howard was appointed governor and St. Louis was designated the capital.

After its new standing and organization, the territorial legislature met irregularly in St. Louis. The first session was held that year in the home of Pierre Chouteau, Senior. The second session met in the house of Madame Dubrevill on Second Street.

On October 26, 1818, a special session was held at E. Maury's Hotel on Second Street. Its members planned strategy and formed articles demanding and gaining statehood.

The convention called to draft a constitution for the new state of Missouri met on June 12, 1820, in the Mansion House, a three-story brick building considered the most pretentious in the upper Mississippi country. Built in 1816 by General William Rector, U.S. Surveyor General for Illinois and Missouri, it was intended to serve as his residence and office, but he enlarged it and turned it into a hotel. In its dining room, 41 delegates proposed, considered, weighed, and made decisions for five weeks.

During that time they resolved that the capital would remain in St. Louis until October 1826 and be relocated on the Missouri River within 40 miles of the mouth of the Osage River.

The first Missouri general assembly met on September 20, 1820, in the dining room of the Missouri Hotel, a three-story stone building on the southwest corner of Main and Morgan. Four major actions resulted: they canvassed the votes electing Alexander McNair their first governor, elected their first United States Senators, moved the temporary capital to St. Charles, and named a five-man commission to locate a site for the permanent capital.

On August 10, 1821, Missouri was admitted to the Union. Governor McNair called a special session in St. Charles where they convened in the new capitol, a brick, 20 by 30 feet, two-story building with a saddle roof. (This capitol has been restored.) They chose the second of the two permanent capital sites recommended by their Capital Site Committee and set aside four sections of land on Howard's Bluff on the south bank of the Missouri, 12 miles above the mouth of the Osage River. They authorized its survey to lay out the City of Jefferson and the sale of lots to pay for a capitol building.

In their act the capitol would face the Missouri River, be two stories of brick, and not exceed 40 by 60 feet in size. It would serve as the residence of the governor and contain a large room with a fireplace on each floor, suitable for use by the general assembly. Its cost could not exceed $25,000.

Constructed in two years, the governor's house and state capitol was completed on February 18, 1825, at a cost of $18,573.

During the Ninth General Assembly of 1829 a log stable and a one-story kitchen, partitioned for a smokehouse, were added to the capitol.

With increased size in government, on February 2, 1837, the assembly appropriated $75,000 and created a commission to plan and build a new capitol on the site. But before its construction started, fire consumed the existing capitol and all its contents on November 17. Until the new capitol was finished, the Assembly met in the Cole County Court House.

It was finished in 1840 at a cost of $350,000. Its two stories were capped with a dome. Its height was 130 feet; its facade, 192 feet; its depth, 85 feet. It was enlarged in 1888 with the addition of two wings, each measuring 76 feet by 109 feet. The height of the dome was increased to 185 feet. The additions cost $220,000 and increased the floor space to 50,000 square feet.

The capitol was struck by lightning the evening of February 5, 1911. Within the hour the building was in flames, and all but its walls and most of its contents were destroyed. The general assembly, in session at that time, authorized a bond issue of $3.5 million of which $3 million would be used for a new capitol, $300,000 for its furnishings, and $200,000 for purchase of additional land. Presented to the people in a special election August 1, 1911, it was passed by more than three to one.

A Capitol Commission was appointed, additional land including space for a power house was acquired, and a temporary stucco capitol east of the new capitol and costing $51,000 was built. In 1917 it was demolished along with other undesirable buildings.

Meanwhile, as instructed by law, the Capitol Commission visited the capitols of other states and principal stone quarries. They advertised a competitive architectural competition containing two contests under the rules of the Architects Institute of America. Sixty-eight architects responded to the preliminary contest from which ten finalists were chosen. Assisted by a jury of eminent architects, the commission's final choice, decided unanimously, was Tracy and Swartwout of New York City. This firm was finally paid $200,000.

On April 12 a foundation contract of $100,000 was let to T. H. Johnson & Sons of Sedalia. The highest bid was $170,653. Groundbreaking ceremonies were held on May 6, 1913.

A. Anderson & Company of St. Louis County built the power house for $46,000. That highest bid was $85,382. It was completed during the spring of 1914.

With the foundation completed, a contract for the superstructure was let to John Gill & Sons Company of Cleveland, Ohio. With the extras they received $2,944,409. The highest bid had been over $3 million.

The cornerstone was laid with public documents inside a copper box on June 24, 1915, with appropriate Masonic ceremonies after a parade through the city of several bands, eminent citizens, and state officials.

The completion date was delayed because of contention over the stone to be used; and, except for some money reserved to pay sub-contractors and remove stains from the stone caused by pouring salt into the lewis holes, the contractor was paid in September 1917.

The Capitol Commission Board's final report gives the dates of payments from October 11, 1911, to February 5, 1919. Those payments include the land, the building, its furnishings and decorations inside and out, and grounds improvement. It was the Commission's final action.

About a year before the presentation of that report a surplus was discovered in the Capitol Tax Fund. Because the law stipulated it must be used only on the capitol, a Capitol Decoration Commission was created by the forty-ninth General Assembly.

With over a million dollars to spend, the five-member Commission met and organized June 16, 1917. Although the law specified their terms as four years, their final report, December 1, 1928, is signed by the original members who were re-elected each quadrennium.

For more than ten years, assisted by an advisory committee, the Decoration Commission worked for expenses only which averaged $3,640.76 per person, about $30 a month.

Their responsibility included repainting and repair, reconditioning, and restructuring the building wherever and whenever needed, inside and out.

The decorations included murals, portraits, and photographs; sculptures included friezes, pediment figures, fountains, flag poles and relief figures; furnishings including radiator covers, electric lights, brass frames, rails, announcement holders, seats and flags. All these, with tapestries and stained glass windows added, gave the Missouri state Capitol a lavishly decorated distinction.

The building stands on 285 concrete piers that extend to solid rock in depths of 20 to 50 feet. There are 240,000 cubic feet of stone, nearly five million bricks, and 5,200 tons of steel in its structure. Its four stories and basement occupy three acres of land. It contains nine million cubic feet and there are 500,000 square feet of usable floor space. Its cost: $3,591,671.24; with land and furnishings added, $4,044,153.29. This total cost does not include the expenditure of $1,009,003.10 by the Decoration Commission. But it does include the cost of the power house, 94 × 72 × 32 feet high. Built of limestone and concrete it is connected to the capitol by a tunnel 380 feet long.

On a bluff overlooking the Missouri River, this classical structure, with a white crystalline limestone marble exterior, can be seen from miles around. Built with stone quarried within Missouri, its most prominent feature is the dome. It carries 32 columns around its drum, each three feet in diameter by 24 feet high, and is topped with a bronze statue of Ceres, the goddess of agriculture.

There are 134 columns in the entire building. The 14 largest are five feet in diameter by 48 feet high. They are surmounted with five-foot Corinthian capitals and support the porticos, six on the rear portico, eight on the front.

The bronze front door measures 13 by 18 feet. It is claimed to be the largest cast since the Roman era. From the doorway it is possible to see the interior of the dome. Inside, considered the most monumental feature of the building, is the grand stairway of marble. Thirty feet wide, it occupies a space 65 feet wide and extends from the entrance to the third floor. It is lighted from above with a cathedral skylight. Ionic columns of Napoleon gray marble or Phenix stone are in line on each side.

Each of the first three stories can be entered from the main entrances. The bronze state seal is centered in the rotunda on the first floor. Extending from the rotunda through the Missouri State Museum occupying each wing are corridors 60 feet wide and 112 feet long. Restrooms, the information desk, and elevators occupy the first floor. Administrative and legislative offices and a Senate Hearing Room flank the museum's space.

Responsibility for the museum was assumed by the Department of Natural Resources in 1976 and a major program of renovation was started. Today the museum has two spacious exhibition areas. The History Hall tells and displays Missouri's history from the earliest Indians up through World War II; and the Resources Hall portrays and explains Missouri's natural and human resources and their combined effect upon the state's development.

The Governor's Office and Reception Room, centered on the second floor, overlooks the river and can be reached from either of two semi-circular, marble stairs ascending from the floor of the rotunda. The wings contain the Upper Museums flanked by hallways reaching the state auditor, the secretary of state, state treasurer, legislative and Senate offices, and restrooms. The lunettes in the museums and hallways are filled with murals depicting the history of Missouri.

The lieutenant governor and speaker of the house are with the House and Senate chambers at the top of the grand stairway on the third floor. That floor's area is complete with corridors reaching to elevators and Senate offices and lounge on their side and House offices and lounge on their side. The much disputed Benton murals in the House lounge are the only decorations added to the capitol since the final report of the Decoration Commission.

The walls of both chambers continue upwards to their ceilings in the fourth floor and the galleries. Both chambers have supporting columns; and both have stained glass, painted panels, and murals each portraying some segment of Missouri's history.

Throughout the interior and in exterior prominence are word and phrase inscriptions chiseled in stone to remind those who serve why they are there and give their visiting constituents cause to discontinue the service of any who do not believe and follow these precepts.

An example at the entrance to the Senate chamber is "Not to be served, but to serve"; and inside, "Nothing is politically right that is morally wrong."

At the entrance to the House chamber is the maxim "Progress is the law of Life." Inside and extending full length on each side are such words as integrity, honesty, justice, truth, honor, and charity.

Thirty-minute guided tours are recommended for visits to the chambers and principal areas of the capitol, but all floors are open to the public. The building is open from 8 A.M. to 5 P.M. daily except Easter, Thanksgiving, Christmas, and New Year's. Tours are available from 8 A.M. to 11:30 A.M. and 1 to 4 P.M. every half hour on weekdays and every hour on Saturday, Sunday, and holidays.

MONTANA
The Treasure State

HEIGHT: 165' FACADE: 425' DEPTH: 130'

Montana's settlement started with the discovery of gold and other minerals. Exploration and settlement might have resulted from a fur-trading grant issued to Pierre Gaultier de Varennes, Sieur de La Vérendrye for that region in 1738, but history indicates little interest. La Vérendrye's sons, Louis and Francois, crossed the Dakota plains in 1742, followed the Yellowstone, and saw the Big Horn Mountains in Montana's south-central region.

Montana was part of that area east of the Rocky Mountains that France ceded to Spain in 1762 and Spain secretly returned to France in 1800.

Years before his presidency Thomas Jefferson, upon hearing stories about the unknown land, wanted to know more. After becoming president in 1801 he started plans to explore it with an expedition, persuaded Congress to permit such an expedition, and appointed Captain Meriwether Lewis to lead it.

After Congress in January 1803 appropriated $2,500 to finance it, the president permitted Lewis to choose an assistant. Lewis selected William Clark. Preparations were made that winter and the expedition, assembling near St. Louis, left there Monday, May 14, 1804, in a keelboat and two pirogues. Twenty-nine men plus an auxiliary crew of 16 to assist them as far as the Mandans, and equipage, struggled upstream. Fighting the current and the stream's obstacles they averaged less than ten miles a day. October found them 1,000 miles upstream in the Mandan Indian village. They were not yet inside Montana's boundaries.

They stayed the winter, built canoes, employed guides, and started upstream on Sunday, April 7, 1805. Struggling against the spring runoff, it was another month before they saw the mountains, but they were inside what would become Montana. Getting around the Missouri River's great falls required another month and a 16-mile portage transporting canoes and gear in carts the wheels of which were sawed from cottonwood logs. On July 25, 1805, in eight heavily laden canoes they reached the headwaters of the Missouri: the Gallatine, Madison, and Jefferson rivers, where they were confronted with their greatest problem: getting over the mountains.

Back in St. Louis in September 1806, Captain Lewis notified President Thomas Jefferson of their safe return after traveling more than 7,000 miles. Including everything, even the value of land granted some of its members, the expedition actually cost $38,722.25.

While Lewis and Clark wrestled the Missouri in 1805, Francois Larocoque, a North West Company fur trapper, explored the Yellowstone area. In 1806 a geographer, David Thompson of that company, left British Columbia, crossed the Rockies and, for six years, mapped and explored northwestern Montana.

The first American outpost in Montana, Fort Manuel, was built in 1807 at the mouth of the Big Horn River by Manuel Lisa, a Spanish fur trader. Later, with John Colter, Andrew Henry, and Jean Pierre Chouteau, he founded the Missouri Fur Company. More forts were built along the Missouri River.

There followed a series of fur companies vying with each other until all succumbed to John Jacob Astor's American Fur Company. Astor's men and his influence established posts at the Missouri's junctures with the Yellowstone, Marias, and Big Horn rivers and lured steamboats up the Missouri. By the mid-1930s, with fewer furs available, interest waned and inducements changed; but with the fur trade had come the trappers whose quest for beaver brought knowledge of the land they searched. Those remaining in history's drama turned to scouting and guiding the searchers, the pioneers.

During the 1940s a Jesuit priest, Pierre Jean De Smet, started a mission at St. Mary's and planted crops. The northern boundary dispute with Great Britain was settled and all of western Montana below the forty-ninth parallel was part of the United States.

With the 1950s came Fort Owen at St. Mary's; a beef herd was started in Deer Lodge Valley and a sheep herd in Bitterroot Valley; a wagon road over the mountains, Fort Benton to Walla Walla, was being built by Lt. John Mullan; and the steamboat *Chippewa* made it all the way up the Missouri to Fort Benton bringing more settlers, but the cry of "Gold!" brought the avalanche.

Granville and James Stuart are credited as being the first white men to discover gold in Montana. Coming from California, wintering at the mouth of Gold Creek in Deer Lodge Valley, the brothers found traces and panned "a little" gold. By 1862 word had spread and so had prospecting. A later, richer strike at Last Chance Gulch by four Georgians in July 1864 flooded that area with miners who removed more than $20 million from beneath the ground. One strike found 400 people in a camp named Bannack which became the first capital in Montana Territory.

Partial territorial status and government came March 3, 1863, with the creation of the Idaho Territory out of the Washington, Dakota, and Nebraska territories. Idaho, Montana, and Wyoming were included in the area's 325,373 square miles. Lewiston was designated the capital and the following July 10, President Lincoln appointed William H. Wallace governor of the Idaho Territory and W. B. Daniels its secretary. He also appointed Sidney Edgerton as chief justice and A. C. Smith and Samuel C. Parks associates. A delegate to Congress and members of the legislature were elected in October and the first territorial legislature convened December 10, 1863.

All the appointees were Westerners except Edgerton. Wallace dutifully divided the territory into three judicial districts and appointed a judge to each. Because Edgerton was from Ohio and Wallace didn't believe in importing judges from the East, he placed him in the third district comprising Missoula County and the remainder of unorganized Montana. Bannack, the largest community in the district, welcomed Edgerton and his family in September 1863. Edgerton was soon to become the instrument to secure territorial status for Montana.

With $2,500 in gold quickly collected for the purpose, the people chose Edgerton who started east in January 1864 to present their case to Congress and President Abraham Lincoln. Except for haggling over the name Montana, the bill moved through the legislature. An organic act created the Montana Territory and was signed by President Lincoln May 26, 1864.

Appointed territorial governor June 22, Sidney Edgerton named Bannack the temporary capital. He immediately took a census (20,000), called an election and, using the counties formed during Idaho Territory's term, he apportioned the delegates accordingly. With the Act as its constitution, Montana's first territorial legislature met in a log house in Bannack December 4, 1864.

The legislative power was vested in a Council of seven delegates with two-year terms and a House of 13 delegates with one-year terms. In one action of February 7, 1865, it moved the government to Virginia City and created a Capitol Commission to find land for a capitol, the cost not to exceed $200. No capitol was ever built there.

The governor held the executive power and was commander-in-chief of the militia and superintendent of all Indians in his area. The secretary, also appointed for four years, would become the acting governor on the death, removal, resignation, or absence of the governor.

After the appointment of two secretaries who declined, the office of secretary was vacant until filled with the commissioning of Thomas Francis Meagher by President Andrew Johnson on August 4, 1865.

In October Governor Edgerton went to Washington to take care of personal and territorial matters. Secretary Meagher became acting governor, established his office in Virginia City, and called the legislature to its second session March 5 to April 14, 1866. The territory was redistricted and delegates apportioned. One action among many declared that all non-presidential appointed officers were to be elected.

On March 25 Meagher called for a constitutional convention consisting of 55 delegates. After six days in session, a constitution was adopted to present to Congress. Minutes were not preserved, the original copy was lost, and the constitution was never printed.

Meagher set a third session for November 5, 1866. On the sixth, Governor Green Clay Smith, appointed July 13 to succeed Edgerton, delivered his message to the legislature.

An organic act on March 2, 1867, nullified all actions of the second and third sessions.

The influx of people into the area after discovery of gold at Last Chance soon changed its name to Helena. Surpassing Virginia City in population, pressures came to change the site of the capital. A September 1867 election to determine which of the two would be the capital found Virginia City the victor, but it was "not settled."

On January 2, 1869, the legislature called a plebiscite for August 2 with a canvass of the results by the territorial secretary. The election was held and the returns sent by county clerks to the secretary's office in Virginia City, but before the canvass the office and its contents were destroyed by fire.

Still "not settled," agitation brought an act submitting the question to the people in the annual election held on Monday, August 3, 1874. An abstract of the vote in each county was to be prepared by that county's commissioners and sent by the county clerk to the secretary of the territory who, with the United States marshal in the presence of the governor, would canvass the returns. The governor would then declare the results by proclamation.

The electorate had two choices: "FOR Helena" or "AGAINST Helena."

The return from Gallatin County: FOR 96, AGAINST 551, was rejected because it didn't conform to the law. Tabulations from the remainig counties showed a majority of 152 votes against Helena. Unofficial knowledge held that Meagher County's vote, prepared by the commissioners and sent by the clerk to the secretary, had been 561 FOR and 29 AGAINST Helena; but when canvassed the results had been switched to show 561 AGAINST Helena.

The following year the capital was moved to Helena where it remained despite litigation and appeals to the highest court in the land. It remains there today.

In 1879 the legislature requested an act of Congress enabling the people to draft a constitution and be "admitted to the sisterhood of states." Without a favorable response from Congress, a joint resolution was passed and signed by Governor J. Schuyler Crosby calling for an election to choose 45 members of a convention to draft a constitution.

The delegates met January 14, 1884, deliberated, and signed the constitution February 9. It was presented to the people, ratified, and sent with a memorandum addressed to President Chester A. Arthur and the Speaker of the House of Representatives to try to convince them of the sincerity of their request.

An enabling act of Congress February 22, 1889, authorized a constitutional convention. The elected delegates assembled on July 4, 1889, argued out another constitution, presented it to the people for ratification, and sent it to Congress. Montana was admitted to the Union November 8, 1889, with Helena its capital and Joseph K. Toole the governor.

With legislative acts and appropriations meeting the expense and directing the project, work started on the Montana State Capitol during 1899. Centered on a 14.1-acre site overlooking the valley, ground was broken September 10, 1896. Problems with excavation, finances, and architectural drawing agreements halted the project until 1898, but by November foundation work was progressing normally. The cornerstone-laying was conducted in a Masonic ceremony July 4, 1899. Realizing that the completion date could not be met, builders set a new date of January 1, 1902.

At 9 A.M., January 21, 1902, the capitol was turned over to the State of Montana at a cost of $485,000 including furnishings. It was dedicated July 4, 1902, but the landscaping funds were exhausted. The Eighth Legislative Assembly, made aware of this in the Capitol Commission's final report, appropriated $12,000 for 1903 and $10,000 for 1904 for the care and maintenance of the capitol and grounds.

In Greek neoclassic design by architects Charles Emlen Bell and John Hackett Kent (Bell & Kent) of Council Bluffs, Iowa, the exterior is of Montana sandstone. The central dome is faced with Montana copper and topped with a bronze statue of Lady Liberty with a torch held overhead in the right hand and while the left holds a shield close to her body.

The interior decorations: frescoes, stained glass, and murals, are French Renaissance style and the work of F. Pedretti's Sons of Cincinnati, Ohio.

Within ten years governmental needs outgrew the structure. In 1909 the Eleventh Legislative Assembly authorized bonds in the amount of $500,000 to build east and west wings on the capitol. Frank M. Andrews of New York and Link & Hare of Butte, Montana, were retained as architects for the addition. The latter company held the responsibility of supervising construction. Work started in 1909, but progress was slow. In 1910, with building stone selected, a strike of the stone cutters occurred.

The year 1911 started with a strike of laborers lasting nearly all of January. The first quarter of the year saw modifications of plans and numerous changes in specifications.

On Friday, September 27, 1912, during the week of the Montana State Fair, the capitol was left open after eight o'clock for the people's inspection. Throughout that year a Chicago sculptor, Sigvald Asbjornsen, had been hard at work on a life-size model of Montana pioneer Wilbur Fisk Sanders that was scheduled for a niche in the rotunda. Known as the "Mephistopheles of Montana Politics," Sanders had been instrumental in founding law and order in Montana as prosecuting attorney for the territory's formidable vigilantes.

In October 1912 the completed model was cast in bronze in Mount Vernon, New York. Placed in the capitol rotunda, it was unveiled and accepted by Governor Sam V. Stewart on behalf of the state September 24, 1913. The capitol was complete.

The interior murals for the new wings were commissioned to Montana artists Charles M. Russell, Edgar S. Paxson, and Ralph DeCamp.

During the 1930s the rotunda was repainted and the copper dome refaced under the auspices of the Civil Works Administration.

A renovation for earthquake strengthening and modernization began in 1963 and was pursued in 1965 with bids totaling more than $2 million.

Except for the Supreme Court, which moved into a new building in 1983, the Montana Capitol continues to house its government.

At its entrance there is an equestrian statue of Territorial Secretary (twice the acting governor) Thomas Francis Meagher, the Irish revolutionary whose whirlwind actions and tactics in the early days kept the legislators on their toes.

The rotunda's scagliola columns rise from its terrazzo tile floor in which is centered the Great Seal of Montana. Above the Tennessee marble wainscoting are murals showing the driving of the last spike to complete the Northern Pacific Railroad in 1883; and four murals honoring the frontier's heroes: the Indian, the mountain man and explorer, the miner, and the cowboy.

At the end of the east corridor the Governor's Reception Room (1912 addition) is designed in English Tudor with oak paneled walls and upholstered chairs carved with helmets and shields. The fireplace mantels are Vermont marble. The brass doorknobs hold the imprint of the State Seal.

Back in the rotunda and up the grand stairway to the third floor is the original Senate chamber. Vacated and taken over by the Supreme Court from 1912 until 1983, the room is now used for committee hearings. It is dominated by scagliola columns and murals of prominent episodes in Montana's history: "Indians Attacking Wagon Train," "Signing the Enabling Act," "Lewis' First View of the Rockies," "Approval of Montana's Constitution," "Buffalo Chase," "The Last Buffalo," and "Gates of the Mountains."

Another stairway from the third floor leads to the gallery over the Senate chamber entered from the fourth floor. Except for the original mahogany rostrum and paintings, the room received extensive change during the 1960s. The murals add illustrations of the state's history: "The Louisiana Purchase," "Lewis and Clark at Three Forks," "Old Fort Benton," "Nelson Gulch Prospectors," "Father DeSmet at St. Mary's Mission," and "Custer's Last Stand."

The lobby of the House chamber is entered from the third floor. The west wing addition of 1912 holds the largest meeting room, one that escaped extensive remodeling. Its features are dominated with solid columns of Vermont marble, glass skylights, and oak furniture and detail. Its outstanding possession is the 12 by 25 foot Charles Russell masterpiece, "Lewis and Clark Meeting the Flathead Indians at Ross' Hole."

In 1981 the legislature authorized funding of $6.7 million for the capitol's restoration and remodeling and the firm of Crossman, Whitney and Griffin were appointed architects for the work.

NEBRASKA
The Cornhusker State

HEIGHT: 433' FACADE: 437' DEPTH: 72'

Following René La Salle's claiming the land for France in 1862 and Étienne Venyard Bourgemont's exploration of the Missouri River to the Platte in 1714, it is believed that Pierre and Paul Mallet were the first white men to cross Nebraska in 1739.

France gave La Salle's gift of land to Spain and Spain returned it in time for the United States to make the Louisiana Purchase in 1803, which allowed Lewis and Clark to make their expedition in 1804–1805 without fear of trespassing or stepping on another nation's toes. Traveling up the Missouri, they explored eastern Nebraska.

In 1806 Zebulon Pike is claimed to have visited south-central Nebraska a few years before Robert Stuart. As a partner in John Jacob Astor's American Fur Company, Stuart is purported to have discovered and followed the North Platte and the Platte River across Nebraska from South Pass to mark the route which became a westward trail.

In 1819 the steamboat *Western Engineer* plowed through the current of the Missouri River to reach what is now Omaha and three years later the Missouri Fur Company established a post which became Bellvue, Nebraska's first permanent settlement.

Also in 1819, the "Yellowstone Expedition," headed by Major Stephen H. Long, explored the South Platte River to its source, but it was not until 1832 that Captain B. L. E. Bonneville led the first wagon train along the Platte rivers and over South Pass to the west to establish part of the route for future travelers.

Thousands of pioneers walked or rode on horseback or in long lines of covered wagons, struggling westward to explore, claim, and settle the land. To get there they had to follow the trails through Nebraska.

This happened before Nebraska became a territory of the United States. Bills had been submitted twice and defeated twice because of contention between the Northerners who forbade slavery and the Southerners who wanted it.

On May 30, 1854, the Kansas-Nebraska Act of Congress was approved by President Franklin Pierce and created the Nebraska Territory with its boundaries set between the fortieth to the forty-ninth parallel, the Missouri River and the Continental Divide. The act provided that the slavery question would be settled by popular vote of the people.

The new territory included the present states of Nebraska, the Dakotas, and parts of Colorado, Montana, and Wyoming. With the opening of the land to settlement that year, Bellvue was founded and made the capital.

Francis Burt of Pendleton, South Carolina, was appointed the first territorial governor by President Franklin Pierce. He took the oath of office at Mission House October 16, 1854, and died two days later. The appointed secretary, Thomas B. Cuming, became the acting governor. He organized the government and took a census (1854 population: 2,732). At that time, with some political trickery, Omaha rather than Bellvue became the capital of the Nebraska Territory.

Omaha was named for the Omaha Indians of the Hokan-Siouan linguistic stock who ceded all their lands west of the Missouri River to the United States in 1854.

The First Territorial Legislature met in Omaha January 16, 1855, in a small, two-story brick building where its actions included provisions for free schools and organizing the territory. Throughout Omaha's period as capital, the towns of Bellvue and Florence vied for that distinction.

Appointed governor of the territory, Mark W. Izard of Arkansas arrived in Omaha February 20, 1855. By December he announced progress on the construction of a new territorial capitol with himself being "the author of the original plans." It would cost about $80,000. Before the first floor was completed, Congress' appropriation of $50,000 had been used. With other towns lobbying to become the capital, Omaha issued scrip in the amount of $60,000 which circulated as money.

By 1860 the population had grown to 28,841; and the first Homestead Act of 1862, granting 160 acres of free land in the West to settlers, flooded the territory and brought into pioneer lives "Nebraska marble." This term was given to the sod, dug from the earth in square chunks and piled atop one another in brick fashion to construct a house. The roofs as well were of sod resting atop willow structures. These were called sod houses and were necessary because of the plains' lack of trees or any form of lumber.

The creation of the Dakota and Colorado territories in 1861 and the Idaho Territory in 1863 reduced Nebraska to its present size.

The first convention to form a constitution for statehood met in Omaha July 4, 1864, but when a resolution was introduced to adjourn, it did so by a vote of 37 to 7.

Finally created in convention, a constitution was approved by the people on June 2, 1866. Sent to Congress for approval, it was finally passed by the Senate but President Andrew Johnson gave it a pocket veto. It was passed by the House February 8, vetoed by President Johnson on the same day just before the Senate's override, 30 to 9. The House followed suit the next day, 120 to 40.

On March 1, 1867, President Johnson issued a proclamation to declare Nebraska a state. Admitted to the Union as the thirty-seventh state, the capital was moved to Lancaster, a town of 20 persons which was founded in 1864 and settled because of the huge salt deposits nearby. Briefly called Capital City, renamed Lincoln in honor of President Abraham Lincoln, it was made the county seat of Lancaster County and declared the site for Nebraska's capitol.

The land comprising the plat of the original capital was donated by Jacob Dawson, Joseph Giles, Julian Metcalf, John Young, and the United States government. The site for the capitol, chosen in 1867, was on a knoll within the plat. Construction started in 1868. The building was completed in 1869 at a cost of $75,817.59, which was raised through the sale of lots in the new city.

The architect was John Morris of Chicago. His three-story building was 120 feet high, 120 feet on the facade, and 50 feet deep. Native Nebraska stone was used in its construction with its exterior of magnesium limestone and an interior of brown cretaceous limestone.

The Nebraska State Capitol, built over a ten-year period from 1922 to 1932, cost $10 million. In 1948, in a poll of the nation's architects, it was rated in the top five of the 25 finest buildings in the United States. —State Building Division.

When the walls of the capitol began to crumble, the result of poor workmanship and inferior materials, it was abandoned. During the years 1881–1888, a second capitol was constructed around the existing building with additional wings and walls added. The architect was William H. Wilcox of Lincoln. Its total cost was $759,513. Three stories in height, the second capitol was 191 feet high, 300 feet on the facade, and 150 feet deep. It too was built of native stone and abandoned because of crumbling foundations.

The third try was successful. According to architect Talbot F. Hamlin, "A departure from the typical, as daring as it is logical and beautiful, is to be found in the Nebraska Capitol. Distinguished by a great tower of offices, it is visible for miles across the flat country; it exhibits great classic restraint and simplicity but without historical precedent, and a free and daring use of decorative sculpture—bison at the ends of the walls that flank the entrance steps; Wisdom, Justice, Power, and Mercy on the pylons at the great entrance arch; and the figures of the great lawgivers on the buttresses around the Supreme Court windows, all modeled by Lee Lawrie. The whole forms a remarkable combination of architecture and sculpturing, truly American."

It was started by an act of the Thirty-seventh Nebraska State Legislature February 20, 1919, creating a Capitol Commission of five members with Governor Samuel R. McKelvie as chairman. Their first act, a two-phase competition, supplied three Nebraskan winners to compete in a national competition. The final choice was Bertram Grosvenor Goodhue of New York City.

The Commission next built a railroad. Complete with engines, the main line circled the proposed building site and was connected to a switching spur of the C. B. & Q. Railroad. Its cost and operation were financed by the Commission from the mill levy funds.

During March 1921 test holes drilled for stress and load provided information resulting in the footings being built atop the sandstone stratum.

Construction on the new capitol started April 15, 1922, and consisted of five phases in parts. The first phase dug and laid the foundation around the old structure and built the north and south wings. The American Legion participated in setting the cornerstone November 11, 1922.

The second phase demolished the old capitol, constructed the east wing, and built the tower to the sixth floor. The third phase completed the tower; the fourth completed the west wing; and the fifth, grading and landscaping the grounds.

The first parts of the first and fourth construction phases were contracted to W. J. Assenmacher Company of Lincoln. The J. H. Wiese Company of Omaha contracted for the second part of first and second phases; and Peter Kewitt and Sons of Omaha contracted for the third phase. The fifth was contracted by the Metz Construction Company of Springfield. Ernst Herminghaus was the landscape architect.

On April 24, 1924, capitol architect Goodhue died. In November that year the Commission signed a contract with Bertram Grosvenor Goodhue Associates, Architects, to carry on in his stead.

Finished at a cost of $9.8 million, finances through a tax levy on real property, it was dedicated in January 1932 and the first session of the legislature convened in their new chambers in January 1933. Since 1934 Nebraska has used the unicameral system of government. Only one legislative chamber, formerly that of the House, is used. The Senate chamber is utilized for committee hearings or meetings of other groups.

Bertram Grosvenor Goodhue's design gave Nebraska a 14-story capitol containing 175,000 square feet of usable floor space. The floor plan is a cross within a square. Goodhue is famed for adapting Gothic to modern methods of construction and for using sculpture as integral parts of buildings rather than surface ornaments.

His interiors show the same freedom, richness, logic, and charm as the exterior. Great vaults richly decorated and simple bold mass composition below give a character half Byzantine, half Roman, and yet entirely American and modern.

All the finished wood in the building is select American walnut with doors and frames of solid and the matched paneling of veneer walnut. Much of the wood in the Supreme Courtroom is inlaid. The entrance doors of the Senate chamber are thick hardwood built in heavy brass channel frames.

There are numerous bronze doors in the capitol. Made in New York, they were given a Verde Antique finish. Constant use wore through the finish on the doorknobs and handles. With refinishing costly, some of them were simply painted black. Most of the door and hand railings are of brass.

Marble is used extensively throughout the interior with Vermont green slate bordering the concrete floors and doors. Foreign marble is used in the main entrance, foyer, and rotunda. Hand laid in Portland cement, they were finished and polished with heavy equipment. Marble wainscoting is found in the corridors of the first and second floors with Napoleon gray marble from Missouri in the first and Italian marble wainscoting in the second.

The exterior stone is limestone from Bedford, Indiana. The sculpted figures and panels, designed by Lee Lawrie of New York, were reproduced by stone carvers from plaster cast models. With some of them naturalized citizens from Europe, the stone carvers' skills are displayed in the finished products. According to Charles F. Fowler, an engineer on the capitol's supervising staff, "Coke burners were furnished when the weather became uncomfortable and during the coldest part of the winter the carvers vacationed."

On April 24, 1930, while thousands watched, the tower was topped with an eight-ton, bronze statue, *The Sower,* designed by Lee Lawrie. Modeled in the Egyptian custom of sowing grain, *The Sower* stands on a pedestal representing a sheaf of harvested grain which, added to his height of 19.5 feet, increased the height of the capitol 32 feet.

Free tours are available to the public every day except New Year's Day, Thanksgiving and the Friday after, and Christmas. The main floor's central information desk, manned by volunteer senior citizens, provides visitors with information within the building. This offering is not within the capitol's maintenance budget which for 1989 employed 34 persons at a cost of $1,542,757.39.

A tour office on the second floor, manned by public servants, offers tour guides for visits to the building's attractions. Both have information on local and state attractions with handouts, brochures and maps on the capitol and other features.

All visitors are welcome in the Governor's Reception Room, the legislature's chamber and the Supreme Court when they are in session with each presenting untold treasures of art and antiquity in Nebraska's history. And visitors will find attractions besides these inside the capitol. Paintings and murals depict the history and culture of the pioneers who settled Nebraska.

In the vestibule are *The Homesteader's Campfire*, *The First Furrow*, and *The Houseraising*, three paintings by James Penney reflecting the hard lives of the pioneers.

Inside the Great Hall historic mosaics portray "The United States Survey" by Charles Clement; "The First Railroad" by F. John Miller; "The Blizzard of 1888" and "The Tree Planting" by Jeanne Reynal; and "The Spirit of Nebraska" and "The Building of a Capitol" by Reinhold Marxhausen.

Hildreth Meiere's notable mosaics of Italian white and Belgian black marble, laid in the floor of the Great Hall, are: "Spirit of the Soil," "Spirit of Vegetation," and "Spirit of Animal Life."

Three murals in the rotunda by Kenneth Evett round out the history of modern times: "Labors of the Heart," "Labor of the Hand," and "Labor of the Head."

In 1948, 500 quality architects of the nation were polled to select the 25 finest buildings in the United States. Nebraska's capitol was among the top five architectural structures chosen.

NEVADA
The Silver State

HEIGHT: 120'   FACADE: 148'   DEPTH: 98'

Juan de Onate took possession of New Mexico for Spain in 1598. The nothern portion of this vast land area included present-day Nevada; and, other than a brief visit by Spaniards during 1776, no exploration occurred for more than two centuries.

When Mexico won independence from Spain in 1821 it laid claim to the Southwest area, including Nevada.

In Vancouver, Canada, the Hudson Bay Fur Company, looking for new fields of production, sent Peter Skene Ogden and fur trappers into the area in 1825. Ogden explored, discovered, and named a river Ogden.

The following year, while awaiting the next fur season and rendezvous, Jedediah Smith and a few trappers cached their furs and crossed Nevada on their way to and from California.

An early day Rocky Mountain trapper and explorer, Joseph Walker, was the first white man in Carson Valley. In 1833 he camped there "until he could find a pass over the Sierras."

By 1840 two routes of travel across Nevada had become fixed: the southern Old Spanish Trail and the northern Humboldt Trail which followed Ogden River. John C. Frémont renamed the Humboldt during his 1943–1945 explorations. His written reports aroused interest and increased travel into the region.

When ownership was ceded to the United States by Mexico in the Treaty of Guadalupe-Hidalgo, February 2, 1848, there was no great stir of interest in the desert land; but when gold was discovered in California in 1849, Nevada had to be crossed by those who couldn't afford ship passage. They came on the Oregon/Mormon trails, usually through Salt Lake City, then followed the Humboldt Trail to and across the High Sierras to the gold fields.

Also in 1849 the Mormons organized the State of Deseret, which included Nevada. Mormon Station was built in Carson Valley to outfit and supply "forty-niners" on their way to the gold fields of California.

On September 9, 1850, Congress created the Utah Territory which included most of Nevada. A trading post was built in Carson Valley and a mail service started between Salt Lake City and Sacramento.

When Utah's territorial government created Carson County in 1854, most of Nevada was included. Mormon Station's name was changed to Genoa and it became the county seat of Carson County with Orson Hyde heading the government.

By 1857 Carson Valley's population, mostly Mormon, had built homes and employed irrigation to raise crops to support California-bound travelers. With federal troops approaching and threatening war, Brigham Young recalled all Saints to protect Salt Lake City. Those in Nevada, unable to sell their homes, left them. With the threat of battle stopped before it began, they returned to find their lands occupied.

In 1853 Isaac Roop built a sawmill and established a trading station in Honey Lake Valley (then considered Utah Territory) and a community grew around Roop Station to become Susanville, California. Coming to Genoa in 1857, Roop gathered a few citizens together to draw up a constitution for the Nevada Territory. When Congress ignored their petition for territorial status they organized a provisional government and elected Roop governor.

Abraham Curry, of whom it is said "he has built more, worked harder and done more for Carson than any other man," didn't arrive in Nevada until 1858. Finding prices too high in Genoa, he formed a partnership with B. F. Green, J. J. Musser, and F. M. Proctor, purchased the Eagle Valley Ranch for $500 in coin and a few mustangs, plotted a town in which he set aside ten acres for a capitol, and named it Carson City.

Shortly afterwards the gold and silver of the Comstock Lode were discovered in Washoe Valley. Virginia City sprang into life and prospectors flooded the area bringing new life into Carson City.

Congress passed the bill to create the Nevada Territory March 2, 1861. Two days later Abraham Lincoln became president of the United States and immediately arranged for the organization of the Nevada Territory by appointing James W. Nye of New York its governor. Nye, arriving in July, called for an election of representatives to meet in Carson City on October 1.

According to one source, the First Territorial Legislature was without a meeting facility; and Abe Curry offered Governor Nye the second floor of his Warm Springs Hotel. To get the delegates to their meetings, a distance of two miles from the town's Ormsby House where they stayed, Curry built a two-car, horse-drawn railway. On their return to the city, the cars were loaded with sandstone blocks quarried near the hotel and used in constructing Carson City's buildings.

Although Nye designated Carson City a territorial capital, looking forward to statehood, a permanent capital was a prime consideration of the legislature. With Carson City, Virginia City, Silver City, and Dayton vying for that honor, competition flourished with politics. As the county seat over the western part of the Utah Territory, Carson City had an advantage.

William Stewart, a Carson City lawyer, became the factor making Carson City the permanent capital. He had met Nye in San Francisco and escorted his party to Carson City. On the way he convinced Nye why the capital should be in Carson City and not Virginia City. Having Nye as his house guest until he could get settled was the convincer. Nye declared Carson City the territorial capital.

Toward gaining the legislature's consent in making it permanent, it is implied that Stewart asked each county's delegate where he would like his county's boundaries and the county seat in return for his vote for Carson City as capital. With their responses he framed a bill designating Carson City the permanent capital. The legislature passed the bill November 25, 1861.

According to another source this First Territorial Legislature met in a barn-like structure. There was sawdust on the floor instead of spitoons. It was heated with stoves borrowed from Utah's territorial government and the two bodies were separated with a blanket partition.

In 1863, trying to gain a majority in favor of the Emancipation Proclamation, President Lincoln forced an enabling act through Congress to make Nevada a state. All that was needed was a constitution acceptable to its citizens.

Framed in Nevada's first constitutional convention and presented to the people, the constitution was defeated because of a controversial clause taxing the mining industry.

With delegates for a second convention elected, they framed a constitution without mining taxation. Approved by the people, and so urgent was its need to Lincoln, the entire constitution was telegraphed to Washington, D.C., at a cost of $3,416.77. Under the authority granted by Congress, Lincoln officially proclaimed Nevada the thirty-sixth state in the Union on October 31, 1864.

Time was of the essence. Officials had to be elected and Senators appointed by the legislature. H. G. Blasdel was elected governor; H. G. Worthington, representative; and Jame Nye and William Stewart were selected by the newly elected legislature as the first U.S. Senators.

In session in the Ormsby County Court House, an act to provide for a state capitol was introduced to the Third Nevada State Legislature, meeting biannually, on January 20, 1869. Bitter opposition came from geographically centered Lander County whose Senator termed Carson City a swamp and mud hole.

The act created a Capitol Commission of seven persons and limited the cost of the building to $100,000, which sum would be raised through a special tax levy and the sale of 40 sections of public land. It was signed into law by Governor Blasdel.

The Commission's first act was securing an architect with his maximum fee $250. The design by Joseph Gosling of San Francisco was accepted and contractor's bids were opened April 14, 1870. Peter Cavanaugh and Son of Carson City, who submitted the lowest bid of $84,000, were awarded the contract.

Ground was broken on April 21, 1870. With stone from the Nevada State Prison quarry, furnished free of charge to the contractor "to keep the cost down," the foundation was eight feet thick to a depth of five feet below the surface. Following a parade with brass bands, firemen, fraternal brothers, and statesmen, the cornerstone was set in Masonic rites on June 9, 1870. A velvet lined brass box containing several coins, including a Chinese coin minted in A.D. 704, plus effects of the times, was inserted, all before a crowd of 750 spectators and participants.

The Fourth Nevada State Legislature convened in the new capitol in January 1871. One of its actions was an appropriation to furnish the building. The responsibility for selection, purchase, and the amounts to be spent was delegated to the state's secretary, treasurer, and Supreme Court clerk.

Governor L. R. Bradley moved in during February, and the building was considered completed May 1, 1871. Its cost: $169,830.93.

Its description is best seen as excerpted from *Nevada's State Register*, January 1, 1870:

> In the form of a Grecian cross — 148 feet north and south by 98 feet east and west — and is of modern architecture, compounded of the Corinthian, Ionic and Doric. . . . The basement is seven feet in the clear, cut only by such partition walls as are seen on the first floor, and contains the hot air furnaces, store rooms, etc., and is lighted by forty windows. The walls of the first story are three feet thick, and those of the second story two feet, six inches, exclusive of projections — all of silicious sandstone of a durable nature.
>
> The walls are nearly solid and are 56 feet high to the gables; 72 feet to the top of gables; 120 feet to top of cupola, and 155 feet to top of flag-staff.
>
> The roof is covered with tin, with raised joints, laid in courses, and the whole will have three coats of Princess Red [fire proof] paint. The cupola rises 48 feet above the roof, octagon in form, 83 feet in diameter, and is supported by 16 ornamental pilasters and buttresses; is lighted by eight twin windows with crown

The Nevada State Capitol. In its cornerstone, laid in 1870, are a number of coins, including a Chinese coin minted in A.D. 704. — Daun Bohall.

lights, the windows centering upon the columns with Corinthian caps. The cupola has a curved roof, covered with tin, and is formed in sections to suit the octagon base of the structure.

Above the dome a flag-staff will rise 35 feet, mounted by a large gilded globe, which will have an elevation of 155 feet above the ground.

The first floor held the offices of the governor, treasurer, comptroller, superintendent of schools and attorney general. The Senate and House chambers occupied the second floor together with the Supreme Court, secretary of state, and the Nevada State Library.

In its issue January 5, 1873, the *Carson Appeal* described the Senate and House chambers under illumination:

A gorgeous chandelier is pendant from the center of the ceiling of each and having twelve gas jets artistically arranged and surrounded with glass globe burners ornamentally engraved with wreathes and flowers. The chandelier with the aid of seven single jets disposed around the walls and three over the Clerk's desk fill the apartments with light. The furniture is all made new and bright, and the carpets have been thoroughly cleaned and dusted. One would almost be a legislator if for no other reason than to get a seat in one of these attractive chambers. The experiment of heating the building by steam was tried last night for the first time, and proved a complete success.

For the capitol's protection, the improvement of its grounds, and certain repairs the 1875 legislature provided $25,000. The foremost need came from complaints from Carson City's ladies who claimed that the hems of their dresses were dirtied and damaged from the animal droppings covering the square and that an unpleasant odor prevailed.

The contract for construction of an iron fence with gates was awarded to the lowest bidder, H. Clamp, who, instead of a man, turned out to be Hannah K. Clamp, a local school teacher. Manufactured by Robert Wood & Company of Philadelphia, her fence was assembled by a blacksmith with one helper, set in place, painted, and made ready for use by September 1, 1875.

During its 1879 session the legislature appropriated $1,000 to commission artists for portraits of Governors Blasdel and Bradley for display in the capitol and purchased Frank M. Pebbles' portrait of Senator James W. Nye, the territory's first and only governor. This practice has become tradition and the portraits of all of Nevada's governors adorn the capitol's walls.

By 1899 the State Library had expanded into the office of the Supreme Court clerk. With thousands of volumes added, books were stored on shelves in the dome. By 1904 their weight brought problems to its structure. In 1905 a Building Commission was created and authorized $40,000 to choose a site and build a library annex to the capitol.

During that year the governor's offices were redecorated and, according to the *Carson City News*, it was "the first time in the history of the state that the Governor's office had been properly furnished."

The Commission's site for the annex was behind and 25 feet from the east steps of the capitol. The contract was awarded October 28 to Burke Brothers of Reno for $35,979 for an octagonal building in the capitol design, of steel and granite, 90 feet in diameter, three stories high, fitted with steel cases and furniture. After completion in 1906, 94,000 volumes were shelved and added to until 1936 when, before its walls bulged outward, it moved out.

As the library grew, so did the state's government. In 1913 the legislature appropriated $60,000 to add wings to the capitol for Senate and Assembly chambers and office space. The Commission engaged Frederic J. Delongchamps of Reno as architect and awarded the contractor's low bid of $41,420 to C. G. Sellman of Reno.

The next expenditure for the capitol came in 1915 to commemorate 50 years of statehood. A special committee was authorized to spend $1,300 for a portrait of Lincoln, who was considered most helpful in the territory's attaining statehood. Charles M. Shean's "The Nevada Lincoln" was officially dedicated and hung in the Assembly chamber above the Speaker's rostrum on March 14, 1915, and remained there until 1971. Taken to the new legislative building, it occupies the same place.

In June 1917 contracts were awarded to replace, with marble, the corridors' wood floors, wainscoting and door facings at a cost of $6,755.50. The walls and ceilings were cleaned and repainted. An ornamental frieze, painted on canvas 3 feet wide by 400 feet long, was accepted from A. V. Wiggins of Reno.

During the 1960s when Nevada recorded the second highest population gain in the nation, it became necessary to relieve the crowd in the capitol. With an appropriation of $3,422,000 in 1967, a commission engaged the firm of Ferris & Erskine and Raymond Hellman to design and the Walker Boudwin Construction Company to build Nevada's Legislative Building. Once this building was completed, Nevada was one of three states in the Union having a legislative building separate from its capitol. It was dedicated June 9, 1970.

When the 1971 legislature adjourned, the capitol's restoration continued. During 1969 the dome had been completely restored with insulation, fireproofing, and sheathed with fiberglass. The governor's office had been redecorated in its original motif. Beginning in 1971 the legislative chambers, the former Supreme Court, and the corridors were refurbished at a cost of $96,000.

During 1956 the capitol came close to destruction when an engineer reported "serious consideration should be given to the demolition of the present Nevada State Capitol Building and the construction of a new Capitol Building that can continue to grow with the state." His recommendation was based upon the 80-year age of the capitol and its being subjected to earthquake or fire, the odds of survival from either being "slim."

It was rescued in 1959 with an Assembly's Resolution to the State Planning Board "to discontinue plans for the demolition of the building."

With the capitol's longevity threatened, the 1977 legislature appropriated $6 million to have it completely earthquake- and fireproofed. Those objects marked for return to the building were removed and stored. Everything inside the stone walls was removed and replaced with a reinforced concrete structure. Except for the governor's office all windows were replaced with fiberglass as was the exterior wood. The original dome was replaced with one of fiberglass topped by a silver bell. During 1988, 12 employees maintained the capitol and grounds at a cost of $20,000. Today in its original state, preserved for posterity, the Nevada Capitol is open and free to the public. An exhibit in the Senate chamber tells "The Story of Our Capitol." Open from 8 A.M. to 5 P.M. daily, tours are available through the governor's office or the Nevada State Museum.

NEW HAMPSHIRE
The Granite State

HEIGHT: 149.8′   FACADE: 161′ 10″   DEPTH: 185′ 3″

In 1606 King James I of England organized the Virginia Company of Plymouth to colonize the new land. The following year a group settled a colony on the present coast of Maine at the mouth of the Kennebec River, but misfortune caused its abandonment in 1608.

When Captain John Smith's book, *Description of New England,* was published after his exploration of the Atlantic coastline in 1614, it attracted greater attention to the New England area. Eventually, in 1620 the Virginia Company was reorganized and named the Plymouth Council of New England. There followed a flurry of land grants.

The Plymouth Company received a grant for all the land between the fortieth and forty-eighth parallels from the Atlantic Ocean west to 60 miles inland. This preceded the voyages of the *Mayflower.*

In 1622 Captain John Mason and Sir Ferdinando Gorges were granted all the land between the Merrimack and Kennebeck rivers from the coast to 60 miles inland. It was called the Province of Maine and included much of New Hampshire.

Gorges, an adventurer and soldier of fortune, assisted England in the defeat of the Spanish Armada and eventually won a title. Mason had governed New Foundland from 1615 to 1621, during which time he mapped the island.

The first permanent settlement in New Hampshire was made by David Thompson and a group of colonists who landed at Odiorne's Point (Rye) on the east shore of the Piscataqua River in 1623 where they built a fort, traded with the Indians and stayed for a few years. When Thompson left for Boston it was taken over by Mason and Gorges. Moving to the west bank of the river in 1631, they named the new settlement Strawberry Bank which name was changed to Portsmouth in 1653.

In 1629 the Council for New England had granted Captain Mason the land between the Merrimack and Piscataqua rivers which he named New Hampshire after his county in England. He enlarged this area with additional grants and, with Gorges and others, included Lake Ontario and the St. Lawrence River.

Edward and William Hilton and Thompson received a grant in 1631 for the land they settled on the Cocheko River. There they founded a town which is credited with having been the first to have a government and church, which were established in 1633. After several name changes that town eventually was given the name of Dover in 1651.

Two more reputable towns were founded during the 1630s. The first was Exeter about 15 miles southwest of Dover. It was settled in 1638 by John Wheelwright, a Puritan clergyman banished from the Massachusetts Bay Colony. The second was Hampton settled in 1639 by a group of colonists from the Massachusetts Bay Colony.

For greater protection from the Indians and to encourage more settlers, in 1641 the four towns in Mason's New Hampshire attached themselves to the county of Norfolk within and under the government of Massachusetts. Their action was taken without consent of Mason's heirs in England and resulted in disputed ownership until New Hampshire was chartered a royal province in 1679 with Portsmouth designated the capital. John Cutt of Portsmouth was appointed to head its government.

With jurisdiction over New Hampshire retained by the Massachusetts governor, the crown sent Richard Chamberlain from England to be secretary to the Council. The situation became intolerable, caused friction, and brought the first royal governor, Edward Cranfield, to Portsmouth from England in 1682.

The boundary disputes continued until 1740 when the Massachusetts border was established with New Hampshire declared a separate province by King George II. The crown appointed Portsmouth-born Benning Wentworth the royal governor. Although popular, Wentworth aggravated the boundary disputes by giving his friends, and himself, large land grants west of the Connecticut River; these lands were also claimed by New York. Arguments lasted until 1764 when the English crown declared the Connecticut River the western boundary of New Hampshire.

The northern border remained in dispute with Quebec and Canada until a pact between the United States and Canada was signed in 1842 in the Webster-Ashburton Treaty.

Prior to 1758 the provisional government held its meetings in Portsmouth taverns. That year a building committee comprised of Meshech Weare, Richard Jenness, and Henry Sherburne, Jr., were appointed to design a capitol and get it built. Completed in 1766 the building was two and one-half stories (43 feet) high, 30½ feet wide and 80 feet deep with a usable floor area of 6,200 square feet. It cost 25,731 British pounds sterling paid for with funds raised by mortgaging public lands.

Because of the Indian threat very little settlement occurred inland until after Robert Roger's Rangers defeated the St. Francis Indians in the capture of Quebec in 1759. This victory led to colonial expansion under Governor John Wentworth who succeeded his uncle, Benning Wentworth. Appointed governor in 1766, Wentworth funded interior roads and hired surveyors to map the state.

On December 14, 1774, colonial rebels captured Fort William and Mary in Portsmouth, which engagement has often been cited as the beginning of the American Revolution. Governor Wentworth was declared a Loyalist, forced to resign, and expelled from the colony. A Committee of Safety was organized and the first Provincial Congress met in Exeter in 1775.

On January 5, 1776, the Provincial Congress adopted a temporary state constitution and on June 15, 1776, declared independence from England.

New Hampshire sent three regiments to the Continental Army and while her men fought on the land she sent her seamen in privateers out of Portsmouth Harbor to assail and inflict casualties upon the English ships of war. Despite the state's unity throughout the revolution, internal conflict, domestic in nature, was going on.

With their adoption of the provisional constitution in 1776 the Provincial Congress gave the coastal ports better representation than the inland towns.

Meeting in Concord in 1778 a constitutional convention fashioned a permanent constitution which was rejected by the voters three times.

So incensed were the people about this discrimination in representation that, by 1782, 34 New Hampshire towns on the east side of the Connecticut River had seceded and joined Vermont. Later that year President George Washington persuaded Vermont to release those towns and convinced New Hampshire to revise representation that would be satisfactory to them.

His persuasion caused a permanent constitution to be ratified June 2, 1784, and on June 21, 1788, New Hampshire became the ninth state to ratify the Constitution of the United States. John Langdon, who had served as a New Hampshire delegate to the Continental Congress and a judge in the court of common pleas was elected the first governor and served the state from 1788–1789. He was a United States Senator from 1789–1801 and served twice again as governor, 1805–1809 and 1810–1812.

In fear of bombardment from the British during the American Revolution and afterwards, the capital had been moved to a number of towns. Other than Portsmouth the assembly had met in Exeter, Charlestown, Dover, Amherst, Hanover, and Hopkinton.

Meeting in Concord and Portsmouth in 1805, the legislature voted to meet in Hopkinton the following year. In 1806 the House elected to meet in Salisbury during 1807, but the Senate amended this to Concord to which the House did not agree and substituted Hopkinton to which the Senate agreed.

In Hopkinton in 1807 the House voted to meet in Salisbury in 1808. The Senate disagreed so the House voted for Hopkinton. The following day the Senate amended that resolution to vote for Concord and the House agreed whereby Concord became the permanent capital.

Originally called the Plantation of Penny Cook, the actual settlement of the Concord area did not occur until 1727, at which time it was named Penacook. It was renamed Rumford in 1733, Concord in 1765, and became the capital of New Hampshire June 19, 1808.

As reported by Stephen Winship in his *Concord Monitor* column (July 14, 1983), the Town House, built in 1790 to hold the legislature, was bursting at the seams by 1814. It was mean in appearance and destitute of suitable accommodations. If a granite edifice could be built for the state's criminals, the legislature should have one for itself.

A three-man committee was appointed. They voted for Concord and the Town House was recommended for the capitol's site.

The following year another committee demanded that Concord list its donations for a capitol. With this demand they were promised a site on the main street and the delivery of granite to the site.

Contention prevailed for the siting of the capitol between two factions: the North Enders and the South Enders. Countless political maneuvers were crowned with the northerners saying the South Enders' site was a frog pond and their croaking would interrupt the House debates. The South Enders replied with praises about their site and termed the other a sand heap.

Some South Enders led a money drive and raised $4,000 to purchase the 2.6 acre tract for the capitol. Washing their hands of the matter, the 1816 legislature gave the responsibility to Governor William Plummer and his five-man Executive Council. After inspecting both sites on July 3, with one member missing, the vote was 3 to 2 for the South Enders' site. When the missing member returned he demanded another vote. The result was a tie. The South Enders laid the cornerstone three months before the legislature settled the question. They approved the site in December 1816 and since the cornerstone had been laid September 24, 1816, all that was needed was clearing the ground for construction.

During 1815 Stuart James Park, an architect from Groton, Massachusetts, submitted an estimate and an original plan to build the New Hampshire statehouse. Among a number of outstanding buildings from which Park had gained architectural distinction was the New Hampshire State Prison. His design was chosen. The masonry contract was awarded to Park, the contract for the granite was awarded to John P. Gass of Concord, and the interior woodwork contract to Levi Brigham of Concord.

With its exterior stone of granite from Rattlesnake Hill, supplied by the City of Concord, hammered into ashlar blocks by prisoners from the New Hampshire State Prison, the walls rose without interruption. The building was completed and occupied in 1819 at a cost of $64,643.02.

The finished capitol was two stories high with a basement. Its square-shaped dome, centered atop the ridged roof, turned into a circular body with a convex cover upon which, perched on a ball, a large, gilded eagle, carved from wood, kept watch over the grounds.

Hoisted to its perch atop the capitol July 18, 1818, with appropriate dedicatory exercises followed by oratory and numerous toasts to persons and events, the gilded eagle retained his position until 1865 when he was grounded while the capitol was doubled in size. Regilded, returned to his perch, he stood until 1910 when the capitol was again doubled in size, at which time he was regilded.

Six feet, six inches in height with a wing span of four feet, ten inches, the eagle was carved from butternut wood. His wings and head were hinged with wooden pegs. His origin remains unknown. There is no record of his maker nor his provenance. There is record, however, of his sterling character and longevity. For almost 140 years, before being moved indoors, the wooden eagle withstood the elements of New Hampshire's weather without blinking an eye.

In 1957 a copper replica of the eagle was exchanged for the bullet-ridden, badly deteriorated eagle carved of wood which was placed on display in the lobby of the New Hampshire Historical Society a few yards from the enlarged capitol.

Of modified cruciform shape with a facade of 126 feet and a depth of 57 feet, the original capitol gave the government ample space until 1864 when plans were approved for an addition.

With a gift of $200,000 from the City of Concord, architects Gridley J. F. Bryant and David Bryce of Boston were retained, contracts were awarded to

The New Hampshire statehouse features a golden eagle atop its dome. Of unknown origin, carved of wood, it was raised to its perch in 1818. For 140 years it watched over the capitol until, upon being examined in 1957, its bullet-ridden body brought replacement with a copper replica. – Author's photograph.

Lyman R. Fellows for the masonry, the Granite Railway Company for the stone, and Mead, Mason & Company for the woodwork. All contractors were from Concord.

The work started in 1864. The addition was completed in 1866. Breathing easier in the increased space, the government found the building adequate until 1909 when another addition was approved.

Peabody and Stearns of Concord were retained as architects. The Central Building Company of Worcester, Massachusetts, was engaged as the general contractor and the second remodeling/addition to the capitol was completed in 1910 at a cost of $348,901.

With three stories, a basement, and 62,000 square feet of usable floor space, the government sighed in relief. This would surely do them, always. The height had been increased to 140 feet with a much larger, more symmetrical dome. Its Doric colonnaded facade extends nearly 162 feet; and its front to rear depth is over 185 feet.

By the 1930s more space was needed and appropriations were made for an annex to house the increased number of government departments, all of which were necessary to do the work. The annex was completed in 1939.

Murals by Barry Faulkner depicting New Hampshire's history were added to the Senate chamber when it was refurbished in 1942.

Prior to its sesquicentennial in 1969, the entire building and grounds were totally renewed at a cost of $600,000.

The most recent renovations to the capitol began in 1974 in the Senate chamber with new carpeting, chandeliers, and a fully automatic recording system. The furniture in the Senate chamber is a copy of the 1819 originals made from architectural drawings.

The renewal of the Representatives Hall (House chamber) began in 1976 and included a new rostrum with a movable ramp for the handicapped and an adjustable floor.

The governor's office and the executive council chambers received new furnishings in keeping and preservation of the rich mahogany wainscoting, doors and door frames, and window casings of the 1909 builders.

During 1988 seven employees maintained the capitol and grounds at a cost of $448,371.

The capitol is open and welcomes visitors every day to the governor's office, the legislative chambers, museum and all historic displays. Group tours are given and printed materials are available at the Visitor's Center on the first floor. There on display are dioramas of four decisive events during the American Revolution; and historic documents, one of which is an early copy of the Constitution of the United States.

Claiming to be the oldest capitol in the United States with its legislature still occupying its original chambers, the New Hampshire State Capitol houses the executive branch and all other governmental functions except the judicial.

Besides giving access to the State House Annex and Legislative Office Building by way of its tunnels, the basement houses a cafeteria, senate offices, storage and maintenance departments, and health services.

The Hall of Flags inside the entrance on the first floor displays the numerous flags followed by New Hampshire soldiers through the Civil War to Viet Nam. Besides supportive offices and a press room, the Governor's Business and Citizen Services Offices, Senate Finance Committee, and House Appropriations Committee are housed on the first floor.

The second floor is given over to the Senate chambers, Hall of Representatives, governor's office and reception room, the secretary of state, and supporting offices.

The Senate president and vice president, and the House majority and minority leaders occupy the third floor with their staffs and support services.

New Hampshire's 400 state representatives form the third largest parliamentary body in the English-speaking world. Only the British House of Commons and the U.S. House of Representatives are larger.

More than 200 paintings of historic New Hampshire citizens enhance the capitol's walls. Many of them are the work of local artist Frank French.

NEW JERSEY
The Garden State

HEIGHT: 145' FACADE: 165' DEPTH: 67'

During the spring of 1524 an Italian navigator sailing under the French flag sailed around Sandy Hook and anchored in New York Bay. Credited with being the first European visiting the new land, he was followed by a Portuguese sailor, Estavan Gomez, the following year.

It was not until 1609 that Henry Hudson, an English navigator sailing under the Dutch flag, sailed the *Half Moon* up the river bearing his name. His voyage brought Dutch settlers into Fort Nassau (Gloucester City) and Hoboken on the Hudson River during the early 1600s.

The Dutch were followed by Swedish colonists in 1638. Building forts on the east bank of the Delaware River, they remained until 1655 when they were driven out by the Dutch.

The Lenni-Lenape (Delaware) Indians on whose land these whites were trespassing, used every means to drive them out; but apparently were unsuccessful, for in 1758 they were the first nation to occupy an Indian reservation in the United States (Indian Mills).

The first foreign country to make a definite claim on the New Jersey region did so by force. In a war with the Dutch, England claimed the land surrounding the mouth of the Hudson River in 1664. Charles II granted the area to the Duke of York who gave it to Sir George Cartaret and Lord Berkeley. Cartaret, who had been the governor of Jersey, an island in the English Channel, sent a cousin, Philip Cartaret, to govern the colony.

The first colonial assembly met at Elizabethtown, later to become Elizabeth, the colonial capital from 1665 to 1686. From that time dissension in the proprietary government grew until the colonists refused to pay rents to the proprietors and, meeting in 1672, they removed Philip Cartaret as governor and replaced him with another Cartaret named James.

In 1673 in another war with England, the Dutch recaptured the colony, but it was restored to England in the Treaty of Westminster the following year. When Philip Cartaret returned as governor that year, Lord Berkeley's interest in western New Jersey was purchased by two Quakers, Edward Byllynge and John Fenwick; and Edmond Andros, becoming governor of New York, held jurisdiction over New Jersey which ended that colony's independent rule.

When the colony was divided into East and West Jersey in 1676, West Jersey was entrusted to William Penn and the following year Quaker-settled Burlington became its capital.

When East Jersey was placed on the auction block in 1682, Penn and his associates bought the land and sold it to the colonists. Perth Amboy, off the southern tip of Staten Island, became the capital of East Jersey in 1686.

When the governments of East and West Jersey surrendered to England's crown in 1702, New Jersey became a royal colony and was ruled by the governor of New York until 1738. When the New Jersey colony separated from New York, Lewis Morris became the colony's first governor.

In 1774 the First Provincial Congress met in New Brunswick and chose delegates to attend the Continental Congress.

Meeting in Princeton University's Nassau Hall August 27, 1776, the first New Jersey State Legislature adopted a declaration of independence, a state constitution and elected William Livingston governor.

On September 6 of that year a committee was formed to design a Great Seal and until such was accomplished the Seal of the Arms of Governor Livingston was to be used as the Great Seal of New Jersey. In turn the committee retained Francis Hopkinson with instructions "to employ a qualified person to prepare a Silver Seal, which is to be round, of two and a half inches diameter, and three-eighths of an inch thick, and that the Arms shall be three Ploughs in an Escutcheon; the supporters, Liberty and Ceres, and the Crest, a Horse's Head."

Hopkinson presented the desired design to Pierre Eugene du Simitiere, a Philadelphia artist who was at work on seals for the United States, Georgia, and Virginia. Thus the Great Seal of the State of New Jersey was created and presented to the state in May 1777. (In 1928 the legislature resolved to provide for a new and amended seal "because the original brass seal would no longer make a clear impression.")

In 1776 New Jersey men of Greenwich, dressed like Indians, burned a shipload of tea recently arrived from England.

That year Washington retreated across New Jersey into Pennsylvania only to cross back over the Delaware River and capture Trenton. Two battles, fought in New Jersey and won by Washington against British troops, were decisive in America's claim of independence from England. In a battle January 3, 1777, at Princeton General Howe was driven from New Jersey. The other, June 29, 1778, was the battle at Monmouth.

From June 30, 1783, to November 4, 1783, Princeton served as the new nation's capital. Washington gave his farewell address to his army at Rocky Hill. Trenton served as the nation's capital from November 1 to December 24, 1784.

When the Annapolis Convention convened in 1786, New Jersey was one of the five states in attendance. In 1787 New Jersey was the third state to ratify the Constitution of the United States.

On November 25, 1790, the legislature designated Trenton as the official capital of New Jersey, and the following year passed "an Act to provide suitable buildings for the accommodation of the Legislature and public offices of the State." Land was purchased for the sum of 250 pounds, 5 shillings.

Termed "Trenton's Master Builder," Jonathan Doane was contracted and

The New Jersey State Capitol is presently under a reconstruction program that when first talked about in the 1970s was expected to cost $30 million, but which has escalated to $60 million. — Author's photograph.

produced a rough, stucco-covered building, two stories high. Its gabled roof, projecting immense chimneys, treasured a cupola topped by a weather vane and lightning rod. Arched windows gave natural light to the ground floor with rectangular windows, symmetrically placed, above. The finished capitol was 50 by 150 feet. The Senate and House chambers were located at either end with the executive and judicial offices according to space.

Within months it was realized the building was not large enough, and offices for the secretary of state were added by an act on March 4, 1795. It became the first of many additions and modifications made necessary by the state's continuous changes and needs.

Such growth and a new constitution made it necessary to revise and restructure the capitol in 1845. A Philadelphia architect, John Notman, was retained and under his design and supervision, the building was transformed into one of beauty with the addition of columned porticos, a rotunda over which soared a colonnaded drum beneath a dome topped with a cupola. An increase to three floors and extension of the facade completed the work and would meet the needs for years to come.

Two years later the candle lights were exchanged for gas and a fire hydrant was added "just in case."

On a gray, dismal and extremely cold morning, Saturday, March 21, 1885, fire of an unknown origin broke out in the capitol. The Delaware River was frozen over. The water hydrant was frozen solid. Before firemen were able to obtain water, the fire damaged the capitol's front and rotunda.

Started immediately and finished in 1889, repair of the building was assumed by Lewis H. Broome, an architect from Jersey City. When finished, the front section was of gray limestone with a portico supported by columns of polished granite.

Built in 1891, the House chamber's exterior is stone, brick, and iron. The interior is finished in a combination of Italian marble, Trenton tile, and quartered oak.

The Senate chamber was constructed in 1903. Murals on its walls, painted by William B. Van Ingen, portray scenes from the American Revolution and major industrial activities of New Jersey as well as figures of liberty and prosperity.

The capitol complex, prevailed over by the golden dome, is comprised of the State House Annex, built to the west of the capitol during 1927–1930 to provide office space, hearing rooms, and the Supreme Court chamber.

The Cultural Center, completed during the late 1960s, houses the 65 million-item State Library and the State Museum with its planetarium, auditorium, and galleries. The State Library and the State Museum are a part of the State Department of Education which is in a separate building.

The Old Barracks, built by the British during 1758, is probably the most significantly historical building in the complex. In it Trenton and New Jersey have a unique international tourist attraction.

Built of field stone to house British troops during the French and Indian War (1756–1763), it served the British throughout the American Revolution. Hessian mercenaries were quartered in the barracks when General Washington made his surprise attack in the early morning hours of December 26, 1776. The event proved the turning point of the war.

When the war ended, the barracks property was sold for $3,260 after which the rooms were decreased in size and rented for private apartments.

Its longevity has seen it used also as a hospital, a home for elderly women, and a museum which it now is. Purchased in part by the Daughters of the

American Revolution in 1855, the state bought the remainder and restoration commenced. Owned by the state but managed by the Old Barracks Association since 1917, this museum welcomes more than 50,000 visitors a year. During the spring months it is visited daily by almost 1,000 school children.

New Jersey's capitol sits in the center of a richly endowed historic area of the United States. As such it has seen many distinguished visitors, both foreign and native, over the past 200 years. Today it houses the executive and legislative arms of the government with the secretary of state, state treasurer, governor, and the legislature located on the first floor. The remainder of the capitol's space is used for all supporting activities.

One indication of the growth of a bureaucracy was cited by Harvey Fisher in *New Jersey Buildings* (April 26, 1988). It started with the hiring of three legislative aides in 1970. By 1988 the three had multiplied to nearly 120. In addition, the Office of Legislative Services maintains 300 employees serving the 120 lawmakers and their committees.

At the present time a restoration project of the capitol is underway. Started in 1980 it included restoration of the Senate and House chambers and construction of a new legislative staff building to replace a two-story brownstone building that was added to the capitol previously.

Included in the program, estimated at a cost of $30 million, was refurbishment of the executive wing and new wiring and ventilation in the annex that was built during 1929–1930. The program was put on hold for two years in 1986 by Governor Thomas H. Kean because of increased costs.

After many months of dispute Kean put a ceiling of $60 million on the project and it has moved ahead with a completion date of October 1991 for new new legislative building. The program originally included a Visitor's Center, a separate Press Building, and a parking garage, but when the cost was estimated at $200 million, those plans were excluded.

The capitol is open to visitors during business hours. Group tours must be scheduled in advance except during July and August when they are conducted regularly. Information is available from the Bureau of Education, New Jersey State Museum, 205 West State Street, Trenton, NJ 08625.

NEW MEXICO
The Land of Enchantment

HEIGHT: 52′   FACADE: 240′   DEPTH: 240′

Santa Fe is the second oldest city in the United States. It has existed for 380 years. It has the oldest capitol in the United States.

Originally termed "The Palace of Governors," it served as the seat of government from 1610 to 1886 and from 1892 to 1900. In 1909 it was taken over by the School of American Research and has since served as headquarters for the New Mexico Museum and become an outstanding tourist attraction.

The exploration and settlement of New Mexico parallel that of Texas and much of southwestern United States except that its settlement by whites was earlier and more substantial than that of Texas. Cabeza de Vaca came out of Texas and wandered through New Mexico reaching the Gulf of California in 1536 and is considered the first white man to set foot in the area. Hearing his rumors of gold, he was followed by Marcos de Niza in 1539 and Francisco Vasquez de Coronado in 1540, both of whom searched fruitlessly for the Seven Cities of Cibola.

Although unauthorized, the first attempt to colonize was that of a Spaniard, Gaspar de Sosa in 1590.

A wealthy Mexican, Juan de Onate, claimed the area for Spain in 1589 and founded the first Spanish settlement and church in the state. Apparently his settlement was temporary.

The first permanent Spanish settlement was founded in 1609 in Santa Fe by Pedro de Peralta. As the governor of New Mexico he moved the capital there and built a capitol.

Although Santa Fe remained, the Spaniards were killed or driven from New Mexico when the Pueblo Indians revolted in 1680.

Sixteen years later, after four years of struggle (1692–1696), New Mexico's governor, Diego de Vargas, returned to Santa Fe and reestablished his authority.

During the eighteenth century, trails extended from Santa Fe to the major cities of St. Louis, Los Angeles, and San Antonio. Albuquerque was founded and settled.

In 1800 a rich deposit of copper was found in the southwest corner of the state. The Louisiana Purchase of 1803 extended the United States to eastern New Mexico.

Interested in the area, the United States sent Lieutenant Zebulon Pike to explore its western acquisitions in 1806. While in the area where the Rio Grande exits the state of present-day Colorado he was arrested by Spanish soldiers for trespassing on New Mexico territory and was informed that nothing west of the Rio Grande could be considered a part of the Louisiana Purchase. Partly as a prisoner, partly as a guest, he was escorted through New Mexico, northern Mexico, and Texas. In 1807 he was returned, unharmed, to the American army post in Natchitoches, Louisiana.

When Mexico won its independence in 1821, New Mexico became a province, but it was declared a territory of Mexico July 6, 1824. The border between Mexico and the United States was fixed and ratified by Mexico by treaty in 1828.

After several years of boundary disputes starting with the United States annexing Mexico's former Texas territory, the United States declared war on

Mexico in 1846. The war was short-lived and comparatively easy considering the greater strength and leadership of the Americans. It ended when American forces, after defeating the Mexican army, entered Mexico City September 14, 1847.

In the Treaty of Guadalupe-Hidalgo February 2, 1848, in return for $15 million Mexico gave the United States California and New Mexico which included parts of Nevada, Arizona, Colorado, Utah, and Wyoming. That was above ground. Beneath the surface was the vast mineral wealth of gold, silver, copper, coal, oil and all that is yet to be discovered.

In 1850 the Territory of New Mexico was created by Congress. Santa Fe was named the capital and James C. Calhoun was appointed territorial governor by President Zachary Taylor in 1851. That year the Gadsden Purchase added the Gila River territory to New Mexico. The creation of the Colorado Territory in 1861 and the Arizona Territory in 1863 reduced the New Mexico Territory to its present boundaries.

New Mexico was admitted to the Union as the forty-seventh state January 6, 1912. The capital remained in Santa Fe. On January 15 William C. McDonald, in a ceremony on the steps of the capitol, was inaugurated as the first governor of the new state.

There was a time New Mexico claimed to have the oldest and newest capitols in the United States. The Palace of Governors was built in 1610 and remains there today on the north side of the Plaza in central Santa Fe. It is the oldest. The newest capitol, termed the Executive-Legislative Building, was dedicated in December 1966. It was the newest until Florida dedicated its 22-story capitol in 1977.

The Palace of Governors served the governments of Spain, Mexico, the native Americans, and the United States in that order. Its use by Spain, Mexico, and the United States is easily recognized and confirmed. If the reader questions the Americans' use, remember that after the revolt of the Pueblo Indians in 1680, it served as the seat of government for 12 years.

After New Mexico was acquired by the United States and became a territory, the Palace of Governors served its government until it was occupied by the Confederate army in March 1862. It was taken from them a month later following a battle in Apache Canyon near Santa Fe.

Built by Don Pedro Peralta in 1610, it was the first large structure built in *Villa Real de Santa Fe de San Francisco de Assissi.* Surrounded by an adobe wall it contained a chapel and quartered the soldiers, their horses, the government, and its supporting features.

Not long after the Civil War, the territorial government outgrew the Palace of Governors and a new capitol, built across the Santa Fe River, was dedicated in 1886. Rectangular in shape with round corners, it was four stories high topped with a bronze statue representing justice, liberty, industry, and commerce. Six years after its dedication a "mysterious fire swept through it, burning it to the ground."

Pressed for financing, the territorial government had a difficult time getting a new capitol started. When they did frugality was the theme. The stone from the burned edifice was cleaned and reused with parts of the foundation. Special rates were requested from the railroad. Newspapers were asked to reduce their rates in advertising for bids, laborers, materials and construction. Savings came from convict labor, but prison officials presented problems. In a letter to them, the secretary of the capitol board implied they were not cooperating in getting the capitol built. As examples he informed them that the blacksmith's parole required his payment of wages at $3 per day; and when a convict had been on the job long enough to become useful, he was withdrawn. After becoming a proficient carpenter, convict Number 1074 was put to work in the prison bakery, for instance.

Ready for occupancy June 4, 1900, the capitol's dedication was considered one of the greatest celebrations in the history of the state. Decorated for the occasion with festoons of tri-colored bunting along the parade route, Santa Fe took on the character of revelry. Bands, veterans of the wars, uniformed members of the Elks, the National Guard, the new volunteer fire department, and eminent persons joined in the parade preceding the more serious dedicatory address by Chief Justice W. J. Mills.

The new capitol, built at a cost of $140,000, was three stories high and, topped with a silver dome, rose to a height of 60 feet. With a facade of 172 feet and a depth of 80 feet, its 43,000 square feet were soon crowded and in 1907 the territorial legislature appropriated money to build an annex and a governor's mansion.

A wing was added to the capitol in the 1920s and additional buildings were necessitated for the growing government. In 1949 the older buildings were reconstructed to match the territorial architecture of the newer.

The silver dome on the capitol was removed and rebuilt to a height of 105 feet above which rises a 30-foot flagpole flying the state and national flags. The project included the use on the interior of Westland Green Vein Cream Marble from Vermont and Japanese Rift Oak wood paneling in the offices of the governor and secretary of state.

By the 1960s New Mexico's rapidly expanding government required new quarters. The legislature appropriated money, land was purchased for $1,283,000, and the architectural firm of W. C. Kruger and Associates of Santa Fe and Albuquerque was retained. John Gaw Meem, the famous New Mexico architect of Santa Fe, was contracted as the design consultant. Robert E. McKee, General Contractor, Inc., of Santa Fe was awarded the construction contract.

Ground was broken in a ceremony June 18, 1964, and the new capitol, designated the Executive-Legislative Building, was dedicated December 8, 1966, 356 years after the first was built. Constructed at a cost of $4,676,860 the capitol's four stories (levels), two above, two below ground, contain 232,206 square feet.

Built in the traditional territorial design, the building is circular with a diameter of 240 feet. Built of pumice block with a plastered exterior, its design and character present something new in capitols.

The first level, underground, contains the legislative chambers and their supporting facilities: offices, lounges, restrooms, mail and bill rooms, and 167 parking spaces for their automobiles.

Both legislative chambers are elliptical in shape with curved walls at front and rear. The walls are covered with sound-absorbing panels separated by vertical walnut strips spaced six inches apart. The rear wall in each has floor to ceiling drapery in which is centered the Great Seal of New Mexico in cast aluminum.

The legislators' desks are in continuous curved sections with each desk having file drawers, a microphone, and nameplate.

Also underground, the second level is on the grade entrance to the building and contains the Hall of History, the rotunda, the legislative chambers' galleries, and the offices for the state auditor and Board of Educational Finance. A part of each gallery houses a windowed press room and a separate room is provided for editing and news transmission.

Surrounding the rotunda, the Hall of History contains documents in display cases at each entrance. The rotunda is 24½ feet in diameter and rises 60 feet. Its walls are marble: quarried at the Laguna Indian Reservation in New Mexico, cut and polished in Carthage, Missouri, and returned for installation. The north and south walls contain sandblasted indentations in the shape of New Mexico.

Extending outward in four directions from the terrazzo Great Seal of New Mexico, centered in the rotunda floor, are four points of the historic New Mexico Zia symbol.

The third level (first floor above ground) contains the House and Senate committee rooms.

The fourth level houses the governor's offices and those of the secretary of state, the state planning commission, and the department of finance.

Walnut paneling and draperies cover the walls of the carpeted Governor's Reception Room which contains the Great Seal of New Mexico. Five feet in diameter, it was carved from mahogany by a local craftsman, Volker de la Harpe.

From his automobile parked in the first level, the governor can walk a few steps to his private elevator and be in his office in a few seconds.

New Mexico had 59 governors under Spanish Rule, 1508–1822; 16 under Mexican rule, 1822–1846; 30 under United States rule, 1846–1912; and more than 20 governors under New Mexico's rule since statehood, 1912–1990. Since Indian chiefs are not governors, it may be presumed that research was not conducted for that 12-year rule in the late 17th century of the Pueblo Indians.

During fiscal year 1987-1988, 35 employees maintained New Mexico's government buildings and grounds at a cost of $1,394,600.

The "Old" capitol has been renovated to look more "New Mexican" and is now designated the Bataan Memorial Building.

The new capitol, in process of renovation, was closed to visitors during April 1990. The estimated date of reopening for visitors is April 1992.

NEW YORK
The Empire State

HEIGHT: 108'　FACADE: 400'　DEPTH: 300'

The first westerner to set foot within New York state is believed to have been Samuel de Champlain. Coming out of Quebec in 1609 Champlain discovered the lake that bears his name. In September that year Henry Hudson sailed up the river to which he gave his name. Sent by the Dutch East India Company to find a water route to the Pacific, Hudson failed, but his reports brought Dutch fur traders to build an island fort near present-day Albany. Fort Nassau was destroyed by a flood in 1617.

During the 1620s after the Dutch organized the West India Company, they established a province, New Netherland, and sent 30 families of colonists to occupy it. Some of these refugees from Belgium followed the Hudson river and built Fort Orange on land now occupied by Albany.

Other families built a trading post on the southern tip of Manhattan Island and named it New Amsterdam. Some settled on Long Island.

In 1626 the company named Peter Minuit the governor general over the province. With the Manhattan Indians' permission and trinkets valued at $24, he possessed the land and built a fort that became known as the Battery.

Attention to and settlement along the Hudson River were promoted by the Dutch *patroon* system. Anyone sending 50 colonists over age 15 to New Netherland and paying for their transportation and expenses would become a member of the company. In return he would receive his choice: an eight-mile tract of land on both sides of the Hudson or 16 miles on one side, with a depth as far as he cared to go.

The system brought problems contributing to the end of Dutch rule. The *patroons* lorded it over their charges who were much the same as serfs in the feudal sytem. They had complete powers over the estates their colonists occupied, improved, and maintained.

Becoming director general in 1647, Peter Stuyvesant brought prosperity to the New Netherland province, but he also brought intimidation to the settlers with an hauteur made evident through his response to their persistent clamor for more self-government. "We derive our authority from God and the Company and not from a few ignorant subjects" was his attitude.

Through this period the English occupied the eastern part of Long Island, settling Southold and Southampton. When Charles II granted Connecticut a charter with greater rights to more of Long Island in 1662, boundary friction escalated to war between the two nations. New Netherland was captured by the British in 1664. The king gave it to his brother the Duke of York, and New

Amsterdam and the colony were renamed New York. The name of Beverwyck, to the north on the Hudson, was changed to Albany.

Colonel Richard Nicolls, commander of the fleet that captured the colony, was made governor. The colony was recaptured by the Dutch in 1673, but was returned to the English in the Treaty of Westminster in 1674.

After the Dutch were defeated Sir Edmund Andros became the English governor. Recalled in 1683 because of problems with neighboring New Jersey, he was replaced with Thomas Dongan.

In 1683 New York was divided into 12 counties from which 17 representatives assembled and drew up the Charter of Liberties and Privileges granting freedom of religion to all Christians and giving all landowners the right to vote. This, the first bill of rights in America, was signed by the Duke of York. He renounced it when he became King James II in 1685.

On July 2, 1686, Colonial Governor Dongan granted city charters to Albany and New York City and designated New York City as the capital.

In 1686 Andros returned to become governor of the Dominion of New England of which New York became a part under the jurisdiction of Lieutenant Governor Nicholson.

On November 5, 1688, an expedition of 14,000 men landed on England's shore. Invited there, their purpose was to rescue England from the tyranny and attempted restoration of Catholicism by dethroning James II. With the wholehearted support of the English and the Scotch as well as that of the New York colonists, William III and Mary II became rulers of England in 1689, but it didn't improve politics in the colonies and politics favored the crown up to the American Revolution.

All 13 colonies had grievances against England, but because of jealousy and friction among them, little was accomplished. In 1754 at the start of the French and Indian War, leaders called the Albany Congress. Only seven representatives met to bring a united action toward the war and the colonies' government. Nothing was done with the proposals drawn by Benjamin Franklin.

Meanwhile the population grew and by 1770, there were more than 168,000 people in the province of New York with the great majority opposed to and actively protesting the measures being pressed upon them by the English Parliament.

Petitions sent to the Parliament and the King were ignored. After corresponding with other provinces about the "common cause" of their stress, a congress convened in New York City in October 1765. Known as the Stamp Act Congress, its decisions, at that time and later, gave New York prominence in support of a revolution.

When the Assembly refused to provide supplies to the British troops that were permanently stationed in New York, they caused the Battle of Golden Hill which was fought on January 18, 1770, between British troops and the Sons of Liberty who organized to oppose British domination and taxation.

On July 9, 1776, meeting in a White Plains church, the New York Provincial Congress approved the Declaration of Independence.

Throughout the American Revolution New York City and its environs were British occupied. It is estimated that one-third of the battles were fought on New York soil causing the government to move about—from Harlem to White Plains, Fishkill, Poughkeepsie, and Kingston.

The first state constitution was adopted at Kingston April 20, 1777. George Clinton became the first governor July 30, 1777. The First House of Assembly met in Kingston on September 10, 1777. Soon afterwards Sir Henry Clinton's British troops destroyed Kingston, but retreated after Burgoyne's surrender at Saratoga on October 17, 1777.

The Articles of Confederation were signed in Poughkeepsie February 6, 1778. The defeat of the British in the Battle of Johnstown October 25, 1781, ended the Revolutionary War in the state of New York, but British troops did not evacuate New York City until 1783.

Regardless of opposition from many prominent citizens, New York became the eleventh state to ratify the United States Constitution July 26, 1788.

Although the New York legislature first met in Albany's Town Hall (Stadt Huis) in 1781, the capital was not moved from New York City to Albany until 1797 where construction started on the state's first capitol in 1806.

On land purchased by the Common Council of Albany and donated to the state, the capitol was designed and built by Philip Hooker. It cost $110,000, paid for with a lottery and appropriations. Built of freestone obtained locally, it was completed and occupied in 1809. A column-supported dome topped with a statue rose to a height of 50 feet. Within 50 years its two stories and basement were found too small to hold a government supporting a population of nearly four million people.

In 1865 the legislature passed an act authorizing a Capitol Commission and the construction of a new capitol on the same site. The old capitol continued in use until no longer needed; then it was razed. After two architectural design competitions were held, that of Thomas Fuller was chosen. Fuller had designed and built the Parliament buildings in Ottawa, Canada. He never completed his New York Capitol.

Construction started in 1867. A ceremony placed the cornerstone June 24, 1871, and Governor Theodore Roosevelt declared the capitol finished in 1899. Thirty-two years in construction, it cost $25 million and was built to "last forever."

When finished, the capitol was 400 feet long, 300 feet wide, and five stories high with a full basement and an attic. With approximately 300,000 square feet of floor space, it was built of grey granite from Hallowell, Maine. Some of its walls are more than 16 feet thick at their base. It is one of the last monumental structures built in America in which load-bearing construction techniques were used.

The capitol's construction attracted thousands of laborers which significantly affected the social and political life of Albany.

In 1875 an investigation was conducted regarding certain illegal operations

The New York State Capitol took 32 years to build and cost $25 million. — Author's photograph.

in the construction. It resulted in the replacement of the Capitol Commission. The following year, with the exterior walls of the second story complete, Fuller was dismissed.

The new Capitol Commission chairman, Lieutenant Governor William Dorsheimer, replaced Fuller with an Architectural Advisory Board consisting of Leopold Eidlitz, Frederick Law Olmsted, and Henry Hobson Richardson who transformed the Capitol from a good building into a great one.

Each architect brought years of experience and knowledge into the project and each assumed responsibility for definite parts of the building. Construction continued under their supervision with their combined experience, ideas, inspirations, and daring.

Eidlitz was responsible for the east and north sides of the building while Richardson controlled the west and south. Their responsibilities included the interiors. Together they changed Fuller's design of the remaining stories and the roof and adopted the Romanesque and Gothic styles of architecture on the interior in their use of materials.

The Assembly convened its first session in its chamber on the third floor in 1879. The executive chamber on the second floor and Senate chamber on the third were completed and occupied in 1881.

With much of the capitol incomplete, in 1883 a New York architect, Isaac G. Perry, was appointed to the Capitol Commission as architect of the capitol. He replaced Eidlitz, Olmsted, and Richardson, completed their unfinished work, and made many notable contributions that remain outstanding in the field of architecture.

During 1888 while construction was going on elsewhere, the vaulted stone ceiling in the Assembly chamber collapsed and had to be replaced.

Becoming governor in 1898, Theodore Roosevelt declared the capitol complete the following year. In 1911 a significant part of the capitol's west side was destroyed by fire. It was completely reconstructed.

One of the outstanding features of the capitol is the central courtyard, originally an open space completely surrounding by the building. It follows Fuller's plan and was included to give better natural lighting and air circulation.

There is no dome and although Perry proposed and drew plans for a dome in 1894, it was never included in the finished building.

There are four entrances to the first floor. The ceremonial entrance of the capitol is to the second floor where the executive chamber is located.

There are three major interior staircases. The Assembly staircase was the first to be completed. It has Fuller's dimensions and position, but was designed and built by Eidlitz. Finished in 1879, it was somewhat changed by Perry in 1885. The Senate staircase was built in 1884. It was designed by Eidlitz and constructed with a slightly modified design by Perry.

The great western staircase has become known as the million dollar staircase. Under construction nearly 15 years, it was completed in 1897. Designed by Richardson, it was built by Perry. Constructed of Fox Island granite, Indiana limestone, and Corsehill and Medina freestone, more than 500 stone cutters and carvers were employed over the years to carve portraits in the stone to preserve for posterity the historic personages of the state and nation.

As the population grew so did government. By 1920 the state had over ten million residents with a million or more increase every census. In 1917 the Court of Appeals moved out of the capitol to State Hall in the Court of Appeals Building on Eagle Street, nearby. A 33-story state office building, named for Alfred E. Smith was built for additional space.

As additional space was needed over the years, it was provided. Open space was turned into office space. Great vaulted ceilings, paintings, and decorations disappeared under space-saving construction and modernistic floors and ceilings took their place. Openings were closed, blank walls opened. In some places the embellishments, so cherished in bygone years, were covered up, removed or destroyed. In effect the original interior had been somewhat debilitated, marred, and eroded by time and man.

The Senate chamber and its supporting rooms and offices had fallen into this category. Designed by Richardson, it was his most monumental and decorative work. The need for its restoration was felt so strongly that the Senate commissioned an Historic Structure Report which resulted in its restoration started in 1978 and being continued until completed.

The capitol had leaked for 70 years because of spotty sealing of the joints with temporary materials. In 1979 the legislature caused its restoration by having it completely recaulked. Everything inside had suffered damage. More than 500,000 linear feet of joints were cleaned out with high-pressure waterblasting before being resealed. Inspected periodically since that time, the new caulking material has been found to be holding its own.

After the capitol was declared a National Historic Landmark in 1979, much debate took place about its restoration. On January 19, 1982, the legislature enacted a law to create a temporary state commission "to make a complete study and recommend a master plan for the long term restoration and renovation of the state Capitol in Albany."

A master plan was submitted in December 1982 by Orin Lehman, Chairman of the New York State Temporary Commission on the Restoration of the Capitol. It was "the result of a three-year effort of detailed research," analysis, and documentation by architects, engineers, historians, and representatives from all factors concerned.

Restoration of the capitol has started, and continues as of 1991. When it is finished, future generations may look upon it as something not to be found in today's modern architecture. Its carved faces, its interior decorations and finish with sandstone, marble, encaustic tiling, oak, mahogany, bronze, brass, leather, and stained glass—all will hold the rarities of yesterday, portrayed in coordinated, architectural style.

Guided tours are available every day except New Year's Day, Thanksgiving, and Christmas. Tours begin on the hour from 9 A.M. to 4 P.M. at the Senate staircase on the first floor of the capitol. For further information or to arrange for tours of groups with more than ten people, call the New York Office of General Services Visitors Assistance at (518) 474-2418.

NORTH CAROLINA
The Old North State

HEIGHT: 97' 6"   FACADE: 160'   DEPTH: 140'

In 1524 when Giovanni da Verrazzano sailed past Smith Island and Cape Fear along North Carolina's southern coast, he earned the honor of being the first European explorer.

Then came Lucas Vasquez de Ayllon of Spain, a slave trader, who sailed from Santo Domingo with 500 men and women and attempted a settlement which failed. Its numbers were decreased to 150 from disease and starvation in less than a year.

De Soto looked for gold in its western mountains in 1540; and Hernan Boyano and Juan Pardo explored from the Gulf of Mexico to those mountains in 1566.

With Sir Walter Raleigh's influence, England's Queen Elizabeth authorized colonization of the new land. In 1584 Raleigh sent an expedition which explored the coastline between the Pamlico and Albemarle sounds. Their report was favorable, and a second party of 108 men landed on Roanoke Island August 17, 1585. Headed by Ralph Lane they started construction of Fort Raleigh. Faced with starvation and conflicting Indians, that group returned to England the following spring.

Determined, Raleigh sent 124 men, 17 women and 9 children to carry on. Their governor was John White, one of those returned from Roanoke Island. They sailed the next year and took over Fort Raleigh where the first child of English parents born in America was Virginia Dare, White's granddaughter. Forced to return to England for supplies, White was gone for three years. When he returned, no one was to be found. The lost colony of Roanoke Island remains a mystery.

Settlement of the Carolinas actually started in 1650 with settlers coming from Jamestown to take up land in the region around Albemarle Sound.

In 1663 Charles II granted a charter of land extending from Virginia into Florida to a group of eight Lord Proprietors, but it was not until 1689 that a colony of North Carolina was formed. The colony took root and prospered, but its members were distraught over the laws and neglect of the owners. In 1712 one of the original charter grantees, Edward Hyde, became the first governor.

Edenton became the capital in 1722; but years passed before facilities were provided for the government. When the colony became two provinces in 1730, George Burrington was named governor of North Carolina.

During these years Scotch-Irish and Germans were coming out of Pennsylvania to settle the back country. A colony of Swiss emigrants and German refugees from the Palatinate settled New Bern on the Trent River in 1710. They had been there less than a year when the Tuscarora Indians attacked and killed 130 before moving into the Albemarle Sound area to continue the slaughter. This conflict, the Tuscarora War, lasted two years.

With the coming of Highland Scots in 1746, there were 300,000 residents spread over the land from the seacoast to the Appalachians before the American Revolution.

Unable to continue with the imposed taxes and rules of the government, a group of "Regulators" in the western counties rebelled, but were defeated May 16, 1771, in the Battle of Alamance Creek. Undeterred, the rebellion was continued under various leaders and though faced with opposition the North Carolinians organized a provincial Congress in 1774 and developed plans for a government. When news of the Battle of Lexington reached them May 20,

1775, the people met in Charlotte and drew up the Mecklenburg Declaration of Independence for their county.

On April 12, 1776, the North Carolina Provincial Congress sent delegates to the Continental Congress after directing them to vote for independence. After the adoption of the state constitution December 18, 1776, Richard Caswell was elected governor.

North Carolina's delegates to the Convention refused to ratify the Constitution until after the Bill of Rights was included. The twelfth state to ratify, they did so November 21, 1789, and ceded to the United States that land in the state that had failed to form the State of Franklin (Tennessee).

Up to this time the capital of North Carolina had been many places since its first organization. Efforts failed to establish a permanent seat of government until 1766, when New Bern became the first fixed capital. Construction of a capitol, starting in 1767, was completed in 1770. This elegant Georgian building, to become known as Tryon's Palace, served as that governor's residence, his office, and the meeting place of the Colonial Assembly.

New Bern served as the seat of government until 1777 when it was threatened by enemy attack during the American Revolution. To various degrees over time the honor of being the capital was accepted by Edenton, Hillsborough, Wilmington, Halifax, Smithfield, Salem, Tarboro, and Fayetteville.

Neglected through those years, all but one wing of Tryon's Palace burned to the ground in 1798. It was reconstructed from the original plans, opened to the public in 1959, and has become a point of interest in New Bern.

In 1792 a permanent capital site was surveyed, laid out, given the name of Raleigh, and officially declared North Carolina's capital. A central, six-acre square was designated the site for the capitol and plans were started immediately for construction of a two-story, brick statehouse designed and built by Rhodam Atkins. The General Assembly first met in Raleigh in 1794.

Between the years 1820 to 1824 the capitol was enlarged with the addition of a third floor and short central, pedimental wings with enclosed porticos with Ionic columns. A domed rotunda was added to house the marble statue of Antonio Canova's "Washington" acquired in 1821. The additions were the work of architect-builder William Nichols, trained in England then working in North Carolina. Built with state funds, its total cost was $50,000. Its completed height was between 65 and 75 feet; its facade measured 110 feet and its depth equaled its height.

The structure housed the government's bodies until it accidentally burned on June 21, 1831, during the installation of a zinc sheet, fireproof roof. The fire destroyed the "Washington." With the loss the legislature ordered another capitol built on the same site, and specified a larger building of the same design as that burned. An appointed Capitol Commission sought out Nichols who was at work building Alabama's capitol, but sent his agent and William Nichols, Jr., to work with the Commission on a design finally agreed upon and adopted in 1833 by the Commission.

It was to be a three-story, cruciform building of stone in the neoclassical style with a central domed rotunda. Executive offices were to occupy the first floor with legislative chambers, offices, library, and courtroom on the second and third floors. Construction started in 1833. The cornerstone was laid and work progressed without interruption until that August when Nichols was replaced with architects Ithiel Town and Alexander Jackson Davis of New York.

The new architects added fully developed Doric porticoes on the east and west fronts and placed greater distinction on the north and south fronts by adding bold pilastrades, a trademark of their firm. The capitol had been under construction for less than 18 months when Town and Davis found and employed David Paton to be their resident superintendent of construction.

Born in Edinburgh, Scotland, where he trained as a builder and architect before studying under Sir John Soane in London, Paton came to America in 1833 to practice his profession. After becoming the construction superintendent in 1834, he gained the friendship and earned the complete confidence of the Commission to the extent that they appointed him architect of the capitol replacing Town and Davis. The new architect brought changes.

Paton vaulted the first floor offices in masonry, moved the supreme court and library from the second to the third floor to provide space in the east and west wings for legislative committee rooms, and added public galleries to the legislative chambers at the third floor level. Except for the exterior, he is credited with supervising the capitol's construction.

The North Carolina Capitol was erected entirely with muscle power, human and animal. The stones, some of which weighed several tons, were hauled to the site on mule and horse-drawn railway cars on North Carolina's first railway, the Experimental Rail Road. Cut and dressed by hand, they were hauled into position by men using block and tackle. During the capitol's peak construction period more than 300 employees were at work, forming at that time the largest construction force in the state's history.

The capitol was completed and dedicated in 1840 at a cost of $532,682.34 including furnishings. That amount was more than three times the state's annual income.

The exterior walls are built of gneiss, a form of metamorphic granite from a quarry southeast of Raleigh. The paving stones and stair treads are native. The interior walls are of stone and local brick. The ornamental ironwork, door hardware, lighting equipment and marble mantels came from Philadelphia. All the plasterwork was done by William H. French of Philadelphia. The original massive, wooden truss system continues to carry the roof.

The first floor contains eight offices in the north and south wings and smaller rooms in the east and west wings, all of which originally housed the executive branch of the government, six full-time officials. Today, the rotunda contains a duplicate of Canova's "Washington," acquired in 1970, and in the four niches surrounding the rotunda are the busts of three former governors and a senator.

Begun in 1833, the North Carolina State Capitol was built of granite hauled to the site on horse-drawn cars on strap-iron rails and lifted into place by men using block and tackle. — Division of Archives and History.

Stairways in the east and west wings rise to the second floor to gain the Senate and House chambers, their related offices, and the committee rooms.

Besides the galleries of the Senate and House chambers, the third floor contains the Gothic style State Library and the State Geologist's Office in the east and west wings. Both rooms are domed and have top lighting.

From this point things went well in the North Carolina Capitol until a festering sore in the heart of America was in need of attention and healing. A small island in the Charleston, South Carolina, harbor started the process.

On April 11, 1861, when Major Robert Anderson, United States Army, refused to surrender the fort he commanded, General P. G. T. Beauregard ordered his Confederate batteries to fire upon Fort Sumter the following day, April 12, 1861. That started the war between the North and South, the Civil War.

When South Carolina initiated secession from the Union on December 20, 1860, North Carolina, determined to prevent a war, withheld; but after the Fort Sumter incident she adopted the Order of Secession and joined the South May 20, 1861.

With the war starting in North Carolina, one of its last battles took place at Durham's Station. On April 26, 1865, General Joseph E. Johnston

The original House chamber (c. 1840) of the North Carolina Capitol. This statehouse has probably undergone less changes than any other major civic building of its era in America. – Division of Archives and History.

surrendered to General William T. Sherman. The same year, Andrew Johnson, born in Raleigh, became the seventeenth president of the United States. Three years later, July 2, 1868, North Carolina was readmitted to the Union.

Returned to statehood, North Carolina's capitol housed the entire government until 1888 when the Supreme Court and the State Library moved into a new building. Throughout its existence it has seen constant changes with movement of official occupancy and status, both inside and out.

In 1963 the legislature moved into a new building located one block north of the capitol. It claims to be the first building in the nation to be erected for exclusive use by a legislature. Since their departure their chambers have been used for official state gatherings and ceremonies.

Today's occupants of the capitol are the governor and the lieutenant governor. The southwest suite of rooms on the first floor have served as the governor's office since 1840. At certain times it is open for the public to see the furnishings of the 1840–1850 period. Its massive armchairs were handcrafted in 1850.

Members of the governor's staff occupy the southeast suite, used by the treasurer and comptroller from 1843 to 1865. The room nearest the rotunda was used by the treasurer until 1971. The suite is closed to the public.

The northwest suite also is used by the governor's staff and is closed to the public. Its rooms were used by the auditor and secretary of state from 1840 to 1888, and continued as the auditor's office from 1905 to 1958.

The northeast suite contained the office of the comptroller from 1840 to

1843; the Supreme Court chamber, 1843 to 1888; and the state auditor from 1888 to 1905. The secretary of state occupied the rooms from 1905 to 1989. It is now the office of the lieutenant governor.

The north wing on the second floor contains the Senate chamber, related offices, and committee rooms. Its furniture, 50 desks and chairs and the podium, made by William Thompson of Raleigh in 1840, are arranged in a semicircle. Styled in Ionic architecture rising from a carpet covered with large stars, it was used from 1840 to 1961. It will be refurnished in the 1840 to 1865 period.

Called the House of Commons until 1868, the House chamber and its associated rooms in the north wing's second floor were occupied by the House of Representatives from 1840 until they moved into the Legislative Building. The chamber served 120 seated in a semicircle in desks also made by Thompson. In Corinthian style architecture, the chamber's heat was originally four fireplaces. Its rug, believed to have been laid in 1854, is the 31 star pattern symbolic of the states in the nation at that time. There is a painting of Washington in the chamber, an 1818 copy by Thomas Sully of Gilbert Stuart's "Lansdowne" which hangs in the Pennsylvania Academy of the Fine Arts. Sully's painting and the Speaker's chair were saved from the fire of 1831.

North Carolina's Capitol has probably received fewer changes, inside and out, than any major civic building of its era in America. The stonework, ornamental plaster and ironwork, furniture in the legislative chambers, and most of the marble mantels seen today are the original. Between the years 1971 and 1976 the capitol underwent an extensive and careful rehabilitation to preserve and enhance its architectural splendor and decorative beauty.

They replaced the copper roof, cleaned and resealed the exterior stone, and added an entrance for the handicapped. They repaired the plasterwork damaged by roof leaks and replaced the obsolete wiring and plumbing. The heating and air-conditioning were overhauled. The legislative chambers were given a paint job and new carpeting.

Centered in the six-acre Union Square, the capitol's original fixtures and building materials, except for the candles and oil lights, are exemplary of American-Greek Revival design and exhibit American craftsmanship in that period before machinery and mass production replaced the creative skills of stonecutters, joiners, blacksmiths, and cabinet makers.

The grounds supporting it were landscaped with native trees, shrubs, and flowers by the Olmsted brothers in 1928. Since the beginning of the century numerous statues and monuments were installed, surrounding the capitol, to memorialize North Carolina's eminent persons and historic events. All of them were completely restored during 1982.

At the front (east) entrance is Charles Keck's statue of "Three Presidents" of the United States who were born in North Carolina: Andrew Jackson, seventh president; James Knox Polk, eleventh; and Andrew Johnson, seventeenth. The monument was dedicated in October 1948 with President Harry Truman in attendance.

From the "Three Presidents," visitors may take a walking tour around the capitol to engage the remaining statues and monuments.

The capitol is open to visitors 8 A.M. to 5 P.M., Monday through Friday; 9 A.M. to 5 P.M., Saturday; and 1 to 5 P.M., Sunday. The grounds may be visited at any time. Group tours are offered and may be scheduled in advance by calling (919) 733-3456.

The capitol's usable floor space is 24,836 square feet. Approximately $180,000 was spent in 1988 for supplies and seven employees to maintain the building and grounds.

NORTH DAKOTA
The Flickertail State

HEIGHT: 241' 8"   FACADE: 390' 10"   DEPTH: 173' 8"

Furs brought the first Europeans into North Dakota. Pierre La Vérendrye was a French Canadian explorer and fur trader in search of the western sea. He and his sons, Francois and Louis, were there in 1738. On a second visit in 1742 they established trading posts and others followed.

David Thompson of the North West Company came from Vancouver in 1797 and, from two different stations, mapped the area over a two-year period. He was followed by Alexander Henry, Jr., who built a trading post on the South Fork of the Red River in 1800, then moved it to the Pembina's juncture with the Red River in the northeast corner of present North Dakota. Ten years later a number of Scottish colonists came there from Manitoba, built a fort, and increased the trade to make it a major center of fur trade.

The Lewis and Clark expedition, en route to the Pacific, stopped at a Mandan Indian village in 1804, added Sacajawea to guide their party and visited with the Mandans on their return in 1806.

From 1811 to 1843 scientists entered the area to study the land forms, flora, and fauna. Among them was John James Audubon, one of America's greatest naturalists and artists.

Following the Treaty of 1818 in which the area below the forty-ninth parallel was ceded to the United States, North Dakota was included in the Missouri Territory. In successive years that part of North Dakota east of the Missouri and White Earth rivers was included in the organization of the Michigan (1805), Wisconsin (1836), Iowa (1838), and Minnesota (1849) territories. In 1854 the western portion of North Dakota was included in and governed by the Nebraska Territory. When Minnesota was admitted to the Union in 1858 North Dakota was without formal government for three years.

The Dakota Territory was organized in 1861 to extend from the forty-third to the forty-ninth parallels, south to north; and from the borders of Iowa and Minnesota to the Continental Divide, east to west. Dr. William Jayne, President Lincoln's physician, was appointed governor. Yankton (South Dakota) was declared the capital. The first territorial legislature met in Yankton the following year in a two-story, gabled building with a shed-roofed portico.

That region of the territory forming the present state of Montana became a part of the Idaho Territory when it was organized in 1863.

In the meantime settlers had entered the Dakotas, taken up land, and built homes. Farming and ranching replaced the fur trade. Steamboats plied the Missouri and Red rivers. Railroads entered the territory bringing more settlers. The Northern Pacific crossed the Red River near Fargo in 1872; and the Great Northern steamed into the southeast corner at Wahpeton a few years later. The Homestead Act and the railroad's "cheap" land, advertised and offered to buyers including Europeans, brought settlers from Finland, Norway, Russia, Germany, Sweden, Denmark, Canada, and the eastern United States.

Sod houses rose above the prairie land. The United States built forts and filled them with soldiers to protect the settlers from Sioux Indians struggling to save their hunting lands from the advancing hordes depleting buffalo herds.

On May 17, 1876, General Alfred H. Terry left Fort Abraham Lincoln (Bismarck) with his command, including Colonel George Armstrong Custer, to crush the Indian uprising being led by Crazy Horse and Sitting Bull. Shortly afterwards, June 25, 1876, Custer and his troops were permanently eliminated in the Battle of the Little Bighorn.

Because of population growth some factions proposed removal of the capital to a more central location. In 1883 when a removal bill to relocate to Huron was defeated, the Dakota legislature appointed a nine-man commission to find a central site for the capital. To provide money for a capitol building, the commission demanded $100,000 and 160 acres of land from those towns seeking the capital. The commission's nine men were swamped with bids from towns seeking the site.

Aberdeen, Bismarck, Canton, Frankfort, Huron, Mitchell, Odessa, Ordway, Pierre, and Steele made bids. Steele was figured topmost in the running. That town's founder had erected a $15,000 brick building to house the legislature. When his town wasn't chosen, Steele turned the building into a hotel. Some towns offered more money or land than was requested for siting: Mitchell, $160,000; Odessa, $200,000; Ordway, 320 acres; and Redfield, 240 acres.

Bismarck offered $100,000 cash and 320 acres, a gift to the city by the Northern Pacific Railroad. Considered the best offer, Bismarck was chosen on the thirteenth ballot, the reason being, it was believed, that Alexander

McKenzie, the presiding officer over the commission charged with selecting the town, was a resident of Bismarck.

The territory's capital moved from Yankton to Bismarck in 1883. During its first session in Bismarck, the legislature established a capitol commission on June 2, 1883, to set off an area within the acreage and build a capitol.

After studying the designs of a number of well-known architects, the commission chose that of Leroy S. Buffington of Minneapolis who designed the recently completed Minnesota Capitol that cost $300,000.

A shortage of funds demanded the erection of the central portion only; and the bid of $97,600 for its construction was awarded to Charles W. Thompson of Bismarck August 18, 1883. The lowest bid for the design of a complete capitol, including both wings, was $227,200.

The setting of the cornerstone September 5, 1883, was attended by members of the United States Cabinet and Senators; foreign ministers from Great Britain, Germany, Sweden, and Denmark; former President Ulysses S. Grant; Sitting Bull; and a party of Sioux Indians. Most of these, on their way to the laying of the final rail in the transcontinental Northern Pacific Railroad, stopped off to attend the event.

In January 1884 the brick walls were up and the roof intact. Four million bricks were laid, half of them coming from the contractor's brickyard with the remainder from Eber Bly's brickyard near Bismarck.

The commission officially declared the building complete November 13, 1884, at a cost of $150,000, with the balance made up through the sale of lots from the donated acreage. Formal dedication was made during the first legislative session in January 1885.

During that session a bill was passed to move the capital south to Pierre, but that bill was vetoed by Governor Gilbert Pierce. This unusual movement stirred the residents' anger so as to bring about their vote for a division of the Dakotas into two separate territories, which was followed by their adoption of a constitution.

It was approved by Congress October 1, 1889, and North Dakota was admitted as the thirty-ninth state in the Union November 2, 1889, with Bismarck its capital and John Miller its governor.

In 1893, to add space and remove the eyesores in the north and south walls, construction of the capitol's south wing was authorized by the legislature with an allocation of $50,000. Left unfinished, the Sim's bricks in those walls had deteriorated from rains washing out the lime specks in their clay.

To bring the cost within their allowance, the wing was redesigned. The Hancock Brothers of Fargo were hired as supervising architects. For his bid of $23,330, George H. Sheckler of St. Paul was awarded the construction contract.

The new addition included a formal entrance facing Bismarck, new legislative chambers, and the conversion of the old chambers into office space. More than 1.2 million bricks went into the addition. These were made at the penitentiary brickyard by its inmates at "considerable savings." The addition was completed in December 1894 and occupied by the legislature in January 1895.

The north wing addition was authorized in 1903 with an appropriation of $100,000. At the same time $20,000 was allocated for a power plant and a trolley line connecting the capitol to downtown Bismarck.

The power house was completed late in 1903 under the supervision of Charles Foster, a local electrical engineer. The first to be operated in North Dakota and the first and only system in the nation operated by a state government, a trolley car carried passengers February 20, 1904.

Designed by Milton E. Beebe of Fargo, construction on the north wing began with excavation in 1903. It was completed December 1904 in time for the 1905 legislature to occupy its new chamber.

Finally finished in an abrupt mixture of "Romanesque and Classical styles" at a cost of $273,330, the brick and terra-cotta capitol contained three stories over a basement. If its "formal entrance facing Bismarck" of the south wing was considered its main entrance, its facade of 92 feet is surmounted by its depth of 153 feet.

For several years after its completion, legislative bills for a new capitol were introduced and rejected. With the growth of the state's population, from 38,909 in 1880 to 646,872 in 1920, it became necessary to reorganize the government. Many new departments were formed to provide for government control of and service to the swelling population and more space was needed to house them.

This was provided by the 1919 legislature with a $200,000 appropriation for a Liberty Memorial Building which could serve as a memorial to the veterans of World War I as well as provide office space for the newly created government departments.

The bill included a plan for the landscaping of Capital Park to provide for future growth and the spread of government buildings including a location for a new capitol to replace the irreparable, eyesore capitol. One of the new departments created, the Board of Administration, was given the responsibility of getting the job done.

For the landscaping the Board chose Morell and Nichols of Minneapolis who in January 1920 delivered a landscaping plan guaranteed for years of expansion.

For the Liberty Memorial Building the board retained the services and design of architects Frederick W. Keith and William F. Kurke of Fargo. Construction started with groundbreaking in 1920. Completed in 1924, it was occupied by the state's Supreme Court, Historical Society, Adjutant General, and Library Commission.

Escalated labor and materials costs during its building forced the board to return twice to the legislature for additional funds. The final cost of $350,000 so depleted finances that plans for landscaping had to be ignored and thoughts for a new capitol were placed in cold storage until 1929.

During that session the legislature established a Capitol Building Fund which would slowly but eventually finance the building of a new capitol. Their desire for a new capitol by this plan was thwarted December 28, 1930. A fire that was thought to have started from the spontaneous combustion of oily rags in a closet resulted in the building's being destroyed in a few hours.

Pressed by the loss a desperate 1931 legislature acted to provide a new capitol by creating a three-member Capitol Board of Commissioners to be named by Governor George Shafer. This commission would be responsible to select architects, create a design, and contract for construction of a new capitol within an absolutely firm appropriation of $2 million.

Prior to selecting architects the commission surveyed the spatial needs and requirements of the government bodies and departments of the capitol. From the architects who submitted designs, they requested personal portfolios that contained their history, background, makeup, methods of creating designs, and future plans. In the advertising there was no mention of a desire for a monumental building.

Throughout the selection of design, the commission interviewed prospective architects and visited other states' capitols gathering and cataloguing information.

In August 1931 John A. Holabird and John W. Root of Chicago were chosen to head the design team. Their reputation for skyscrapers and public buildings was nationwide and their portfolio submission was outstanding. To conform to their own responsibilities, the commission selected as associate architects North Dakotans Joseph B. DeRemer of Grand Forks and William F. Kirke of Fargo.

Working with the commissioners' catalogued ideas and survey, the architects took nearly a year to complete the design. Several problems confronted the design planning, the uppermost being finances since the Great Depression had reduced the assessed value of properties by 50 percent. Because brick facing of the capitol would be less expensive than limestone, saving about $150,000, and could be supplied from inside the state, bids were advertised for plans and estimates for each facing.

For 60 days following the bid opening the commissioners were approached by brick manufacturers of the state. When it was found they could not supply the brick at the speed required during construction, the brick facing was eliminated.

The lowest bid of $1,570,000 won the firm of Lundoff and Bicknell of Chicago the construction contract. Ground was broken August 13, 1932, when Governor George F. Shafer plunged a shovel into the earth to start the ceremony.

With their knowledge of steel construction, working from the design and specifications of architects Holabird and Root, supervised by associate architect Kirke, and visited periodically by associate DeRemer, construction proceeded normally with elimination of exterior ornament and statuary to cut expense. One incident worth repeating occurred during construction.

After William Langor became governor in 1933, the cornerstone was

North Dakota's State Capitol features a 20-story tower in Art Deco style. The interior's 210,000 square feet of usable floor space, comprising 80 percent of the whole, is more than any other state capitol's. — State Historical Society.

found to be damaged. It had been set early in construction in a ceremony presided over by United States Vice President Charles Curtis. It was removed and the ceremony for its replacement was officiated by Governor Langor. The cornerstone was cut from a 57-ton granite boulder found east of St. Anthony in North Dakota.

Construction on North Dakota's new capitol was completed during 1934. It was occupied by a relieved legislature in January 1935.

For a little less than the $2 million appropriation North Dakota had a 20-story tower (one story below ground) in a style termed Art Deco in transition toward international. With a base of Wisconsin black granite and a facing of Indiana limestone, the capitol has a three-story wing for the legislative chambers that is connected to its Office and Administration Tower by Memorial Hall. Its usable floor space of 210,000 square feet boasts 80 percent of the whole, more than any other capitol in the United States.

The interior finish is a blend of brass, bronze, marble, travertine, and numerous hardwoods. Yellowstone travertine covers the walls in the lobby on the ground floor and the 40-foot-high walls in Memorial Hall. Those floors and connecting steps are Tennessee marble. The walls of the stairs from the ground floor to Memorial Hall and those of the Legislative Hall are rosewood and curly maple. American chestnut is used in the House chamber's walls. Those of the Senate chamber and the attorney general's office are English quarter-sawed oak.

The capitol's interior is furnished throughout in woods of laurel, Honduras mahogany, teak, Prima Vera mahogany from South America, California walnut, and American oak.

The North Dakota Senate chamber's walls are paneled in English quartersawed oak. The rostrum and furniture are made of American oak. — State Historical Society.

After 40 years of use several attempts were made to gain more office space for government operations and the North Dakota Supreme Court by building separate buildings. Finally in 1977 the legislature authorized the construction of a new wing to the capitol. Symmetrical balance was added to the capitol with the construction of the Judicial Wing which was completed and fully occupied in 1981.

Built to blend with the natural beauty of the capitol grounds, it features an exterior facing of Indiana limestone. Mahogany and cream-colored travertine cover the walls in the Supreme Court's portal hallway and the wall coverings of the Supreme Court chamber are African ribbon mahogany and dark wool fabric.

The Liberty Memorial Building, the oldest one on the capitol grounds was completely remodeled during 1981 and 1982 for occupation by the State Library.

During two fiscal years July 1, 1987, to June 30, 1989, 68 persons were employed in the maintenance of the capitol and its extensive grounds and buildings at an expenditure to the state of $1,744,547.

Visitors are invited and encouraged to take the Arboretum Trail to see the capitol, the capitol grounds, and the buildings, all included along the trail.

Arboretum Trail was especially constructed in 1985 for all visitors to the capitol to see a mixture of nature, history, heritage, and architecture. A paved, curving walkway, interrupted with shaded benches, takes its guests through a broad expanse of trees, shrubs, and colorful flowers (in summer) blended with native fauna.

From the parking lot enter and see the capitol, then take Arboretum Trail to the Heritage Center, the newest building on the grounds and the most modern facility of its kind in the United States. It houses North Dakota's museum, historical society, and archives. The museum contains one of the finest displays of Plains Indian artifacts in the world.

The governor's residence, the Liberty Memorial Building, and the Highway Building are additional forms of architecture.

NORTHERN MARIANA ISLANDS

The first territory acquired by the United States since purchasing the Virgin Islands from Denmark in 1917, the Northern Marianas are among a group of islands in Micronesia, Pacific Ocean.

Lying 1,500 miles east of the Philippines, between the Tropic of Cancer and Guam, the 16 islands are scattered to form an archipelago 300 miles long with a land area of 183.5 square miles. Six of the islands are inhabited with a population of about 20,000, most of which is concentrated on the three largest islands: Saipan, Rota, and Tinian. According to the 1985 census, 45 percent of the population was under 16 years of age.

Occupied for more than 3,000 years by Micronesians, Ferdinand Magellan found them inhabited and named them the Ladrone Islands in 1521. While anchored offshore to take on water and supplies, the natives, like thieves, stole from his ships and their crews.

In 1668 Spain annexed the islands, King Charles II named them after his mother, Mariana of Austria, and Jesuit priests settled there permanently to Christianize the natives. After the native Chamarros had grown tired enough to revolt against their new landlords and failed, they were removed to the island of Guam.

When their descendants returned in 1816 to find Carolinians were settled in, they turned to farming while their neighbors fished.

The largest of the islands, Guam, was ceded to the United States December 10, 1898, by treaty following the Spanish-American War.

Germany purchased the Marianas from Spain in 1899 and changed the people's pattern of life by telling everyone what to do until 1914 when the

Japanese took them from Germany during World War I. In 1921 the islands became the official property of Japan by an act of the League of Nations.

In 1941, while it was being used as a naval base by the United States, Guam was captured and occupied by the Japanese, who remained there until Guam was retaken with all the islands during the Battle of the Philippine Sea in 1944. It then became a trust in care of the United States Navy; and the military built roads, docks, government housing and buildings.

In 1962 the headquarters for the Trust Territory of the Pacific Isles relocated on Saipan, the largest of the islands, and the Marianas began receiving United States aid. Of the towns located along the west shore, Garapan served as the capital for the Japanese, and Suspe, in the center of the island, saw the start of a movement toward true independence.

In 1963 the United States Department of the Interior assumed the administrative responsibilities of the Northern Mariana Islands and the trust territory government's headquarters was in one of the government buildings.

On June 17, 1975, a plebiscite adopted a covenant to establish a commonwealth in union with the United States of America. It was approved by Congress in April 1976 and signed that March by President Gerald Ford. A bicameral parliament was organized with a governor, lieutenant governor, nine senators having four-year terms of office, and 15 representatives serving two years.

In October 1977 President Jimmy Carter approved the Constitution of the Northern Mariana Islands to become effective in November 1986. In 1982 the people of the Northern Mariana Islands voted for commonwealth status.

In 1986 President Ronald Reagan issued a proclamation conferring citizenship on the residents of the Commonwealth of Northern Mariana Islands.

When the trust territory government was phased out in 1987, the government buildings were turned over to the Commonwealth and the executive branch of the government occupied a two-story building constructed of concrete. Another, much larger one-story building, 150 feet away, houses the Senate and House chambers together with offices for its individual members as well as office space for staff members and attorneys.

With regard to the buildings' interior art work and decoration, both have paintings that were donated by private individuals. The governor's office has portraits of President George Bush and Vice President Dan Quayle.

Within close proximity of the capitol, there are one hundred houses, formerly occupied by military personnel, that are now used, free of charge, to house contracted professionals (doctors, lawyers, teachers), hired off-island by the government. The occupants are responsible for the maintenance and utilities of their houses.

There are no conducted tours or handouts for visitors, but they are most welcome to visit the capitol during business hours on weekdays.

OHIO
The Buckeye State

HEIGHT: 158'   FACADE: 304'   DEPTH: 184'

The first Europeans coming into the Ohio area were impressed with the forests of oak, hickory, and walnut. To be sure, there were a few small patches of open prairie, but the forests of hardwood? They were for building! Among those trees was a large tree from the horse chestnut family. It had palmate leaves and erect conical clusters of brightly colored flowers. Its large, glossy, brown seed gave Ohioans a nickname for their state, Buckeye.

But the Europeans were not there to build, but to take the treasures of the land. When nothing better was found they took the fur-bearing animals. While seeking them the trappers found other treasures.

During 1669, using the reports and maps prepared by Marquette and Joliet, René Robert Cavelier, Sieur de La Salle explored the Ohio area between the Ohio River and Lake Erie. Through the years the English from the southeast and the French from the northeast came together. Both claimed the land.

In 1683, feeling a need for greater strength against the French, the British made allies of the Iroquois Indians. Also in need of extra strength, the French allied with the Algonquin nation. From time to time each nation exercised its strength, one against the other, whenever it was deemed necessary.

The French built forts and garrisoned them; the English built forts and garrisoned them. One of them, built in 1745, was Fort Sandoski on Sandusky Bay (Ohio). During 1748 a group of Virginians (English) organized the Ohio Land Company and later (1750) sent Christopher Gist to explore that region. In the meantime a Frenchman named Celeron de Bienville was claiming the same area for France. All this time the French and Indian War was going on between the French and English; but desirous of settling down on some of its fine land, settlers were coming into the area and building.

In 1761 Christian Post chose a site near the present town of Bolivar and built what is claimed the first permanent dwelling in Ohio. The forts could not thus be claimed since they were often burned to the ground by enemy forces.

Following the war, in the Treaty of Paris, France ceded all of Ohio to Great Britain. Except for the Indians the land was open to settlement. Joining forces, some settlers defeated Chief Pontiac and his Ottowan Indians in their attempt to drive the unwanted invaders from the land.

On August 24, 1772, a Moravian community was founded by David Zeisheiger at Schoenbrunn. In 1785 Fort Harmon was set up at the mouth of the Muskingum River.

After the defeat of England in the American Revolution, with England's present of the region to the United States, Congress established the Northwest Territory in the Ordinance of 1787. The first permanent settlement in Ohio was the town of Marietta at the mouth of the Muskingum River. It was founded in 1788 by General Rufus Putnam with a group of New England veterans of the revolution.

In July 1788 Arthur St. Clair, the first governor of the Northwest Territory, entered Marietta and established the territorial government. Two years later he moved his headquarters to Cincinnati.

By 1798, with 5,000 white male residents, Congress allowed an autonomous government to be established in that area of the Northwest Territory, now the state of Ohio. A legislature was elected and in 1799 Governor St. Clair and 22 representatives met in Yeatman's Tavern in Cincinnati. By September, when William Henry Harrison was elected delegate to Congress, a new two-story frame building had been build on Main Street to become the territorial capitol.

Before their next session Congress had divided the territory and designated Chillicothe as the capital. The legislature met there in November 1800. Their four-year-old capital's only meeting place was Abrams' Big House, a two-story log structure. The legislature met on the first floor. A barroom occupied the upper floor.

One of its first actions was a statehouse. Started that year, it was built of freestone from nearby hills. When completed it was a solid structure 45 feet square with two stories. An octagon-shaped cupola was centered in its hip roof.

By 1802, with its population exceeding 45,000, Congress authorized an election of delegates to draft a constitution. Convening November 4, 35 delegates labored over a 25-day period and drew up a constitution for the State of Ohio.

On March 1, 1803, Ohio was taken into the Union as the seventeenth state. The new constitution provided that Chillicothe remain the capital until 1808 when the legislature would determine a permanent site.

Determined to have the capital, the citizens of Zanesville built a two-story brick, stone-trimmed capitol for the government and, as a result, Zanesville became the temporary capital in 1809. Meeting in their new capitol, one of the legislature's first actions was that a new capital should be located within 40 miles of the state's geographical center. A committee was named to select a site for a permanent capital.

They remained in Zanesville until 1812. When an earthquake "nearly shook the building down," they moved back to Chillicothe. The Zanesville capitol became Muskingum County's courthouse until it was replaced in 1874.

The committee named to select a capital site was addressed with problems. When the word got out, its members were constantly harassed, singly and plurally. Every village, hamlet, and locale in central Ohio applied whether established or otherwise.

Their task was lightened when in February 1812 they were approached by a syndicate of Franklin County realtors who offered to lay out a town on the east bank of the Scioto River across from Franklinton for the capital. They would convey to the state two ten-acre plots for a capitol and a penitentiary and, in addition, build the two buildings with value at $50,000 and have them ready for occupation before December 1, 1817.

The offer was accepted on February 14 when the legislature voted that after December 1, 1817, the capital would be permanently sited on the banks of the Scioto River.

The capital site was heavily forested and without a name. Ohio City was favored, but one week after its acceptance of the offer, the Assembly chose the name Columbus.

When the Ohio government moved from Chillicothe to Columbus, that capital vacated became the Ross County Courthouse. Outgrown, it was demolished in 1852.

The new Columbus capitol was built of brick with a stone foundation. Its design was somewhat the same as its predecessor's, but its cupola held a bell, purchased in 1817 by Governor Thomas Worthington for use by the legislature. The cupola's weather vane raised the height to 106 feet.

The entrance door opened into a lobby which gave access to the House chamber and two committee rooms and gallery. From the lobby a stairway led to the Senate chamber and two committee rooms. This room had no gallery.

For nearly 21 years the new Ohio capitol in Columbus was large enough to house the government, but soon after Wilson Shannon was elected governor, on January 26, 1838, the legislature acted to provide a new statehouse. The first action of the appointed Building Commission was determining the stone for construction. They decided to use the native stone from a quarry three miles distant and contracted with its owner, William Sullivant.

Their competition for its design was rewarded with entries from 53 of the nation's leading architects. Overwhelmed, the commission decided upon a composite of the designs submitted following Greek Revival style with Doric columns. Henry Walter of Cincinnati, whose design was second choice, was contracted as the architect. The structure was to be 184 feet by 304 feet with a central dome accented with a surrounding colonnade. By using convict labor at 40 cents per day the cost was not to exceed $400,000.

Construction began during the spring of 1839. Ground was broken, excavations for footings were made to a depth of ten feet, and 15-foot foundation walls were laid. The cornerstone was laid at the northeast corner July 4, 1839, by former governor Jeremiah Morrow. Beneath the stone in hermetically sealed glass jars were articles considered appropriate for that day.

Before the end of the year the foundation walls were complete. Work stopped for the winter with energetic plans made for the following year. In February 1840 the legislature repealed its action to provide for a new statehouse. Work stopped for six years while legislators argued over a different location for the capital city.

With their differences finally settled, construction resumed in 1846 with meager appropriations. That and a scarcity of prison labor made rapid progress impossible. In 1848 a new architect, William R. West, was retained and given an assistant. The legislative appropriations were larger and the work advanced more rapidly with steam-operated machinery installed at the quarry and building site. A railway was built from the quarry to haul the ten- and twelve-ton stones to the site.

Larger appropriations became available when the old capitol burned in 1852 and the legislature was forced into temporary rented quarters. One hundred convicts and 135 stone cutters were employed at the site with another 100 convicts at the quarry. By 1854 all the stonework was complete except for the dome.

When the architect resigned because of personality differences with the superintendent, N. B. Kelly was appointed architect and superintendent.

On January 7, 1857, the legislature held their first sessions in the finished chambers.

Declared officially completed, the new capitol was dedicated and opened to the public November 15, 1861, with a dinner celebration.

The final cost of construction was $1,650,000 including furnishings and landscaping. Twenty-two years in its building, of which 15 were actually construction years, Ohio's capitol was constructed under four different boards of Building Commissioners, five architects, twelve governors, and two state constitutions.

Considered "one of the purest examples of Greek Doric architecture in the United States," this is exemplified in eight great columns at the main entrance, 36 feet in length and 6 feet, 2 inches in diameter. The remaining three entrances each have four columns.

Above the entrance a flat-topped cupola rises 158 feet into the air. The originally planned dome was never completed because of legislative bickering over cost and construction details.

Each of the four entrances has double sets of massive bronze doors with high glass panels leading into foyers rising 12 steps to an elevated rotunda. The rotunda is 65 feet, 5 inches in diameter. Its inlaid floor contains 4,892 blocks of marble. Centered in the floor are 13 varicolored marble blocks representing the 13 original states. These are surrounded by three circles and a sunburst of 32 points symbolizing the number of states in the union at the time the floor was laid.

One hundred twenty feet above the floor is the great dome in which is centered the Great Seal of Ohio. Painted by a team of Cincinnati artists, it is in the center of an 18-foot, 8 inch canvas that is brilliantly lighted and surmounts encircling plaques bearing the names and inaugural dates of Ohio's eight United States presidents.

Between the high arches are murals. Two of them, by William Mark Young, "Freedom of Religion" and "Laws of Equity" symbolize the Ordinance of 1787. The other two, by Arthur Crisp, symbolize "Education" and "Basic Laws of Justice and Authority."

Under each mural, bronze display cases present Ohio's historic data, priceless documents, and traditions. The walls on either side of each entrance contain bronze tablets dedicated to the outstanding units and individuals representing Ohio in war and government. One such is the honor roll of the Ohio women who have played a part in national and state public life.

On the main floor the north and south corridors are 24 feet wide with marble-tiled floors and grained ceilings. The governor's office and that of the secretary of state are off the north foyer; those of the auditor and treasurer, the south foyer. From the rotunda, north and south stairways rise to the second floor and the legislative chambers.

The House chamber has a gallery on three sides. It occupies the southeast quarter of the second floor with the Clerk of the House office, Representatives' offices, and committee rooms in the southwest quarter.

The furnishings in the Senate chamber in the northeast quarter are similar to those of the House except that elevated tiers of seats on two sides serve as the visitors' gallery. The clerk of the Senate is housed adjacent to the Senate chamber.

In the foyer of the Senate chamber is the Lincoln Memorial: a Carrara marble bust of Lincoln, the Vicksburg panel, and a marble panel bearing an excerpt from Lincoln's second inaugural address. The group was designed and executed by Ohio sculptor T. D. Jones of Granville.

The northwest quarter of the second floor originally housed the State Library. It was remodeled in 1934 to house the office of the lieutenant governor, Senate committee rooms, and the Legislative Library. The remaining space on the second and third floors is given over to offices and supporting services.

An auto parking facility, constructed under the capitol grounds, provides tunnels to the basement and elevators to the upper floors. Elevators are also available to the parking garage. The basement is also reached from the north and west pedestrian entrances. The basement has been rehabilitated to contain more offices and a glass-enclosed cafeteria and dining lounge.

On the evening of January 26, 1894, a group gathered in the Senate committee room to determine what to do about the need for more room in the capitol. Ohio's population had nearly doubled since the capitol had been finished and the resultant increase in government needs was now forcing some action.

After debate and consideration of every possibility to increase the capitol's space, all were derailed for a possible annex to the building. Samuel Hannaford of Cincinnati was hired to design the addition and the massive limestone walls of his building came from the same quarry as those of the capitol. The cornerstone was set in February 1899 and the annex was opened to the public in January 1902 and received much praise. Governor George Nash presided over the opening reception attended by crowds.

To accept further increase in Ohio's government, a 14-story, neoclassical building of Georgia marble was erected near the capitol in the early 1930s to house the departments of Agriculture, Development, Education, Natural Resources, Public Works, and the Ohio State Library together with their regulatory commissions.

Two more recent buildings flank the Department of State Building to house the State Highway Department and the Bureau of Unemployment Compensation.

Visitors are welcome during business hours and tours are possible for groups if made in advance. The spiral stone staircase to the top of the dome has been condemned as unsafe and is closed to the public.

In 1988 work began on a $68.7 million renovation of Ohio's capitol. During the renovation period it was to remain open as usual. Among the findings during the period of planning was that, over the years, to gain more space the capitol's original 53 rooms had been reconstructed into 317 rooms.

The master plan's five-phased restoration will restore dignity and pride to the capitol in respect to its historical and architectural significance. Work starting on the first phase (Capitol Grounds) in October 1988 was finished in late spring 1990.

The second phase will renovate the Annex, after which it will be known as the Senate Building, and construct an atrium connector between it and the capitol, for visitors and educational programs. Completion date: fall 1991.

Phase three will renovate the three floors of the eastern parts of the capitol and includes the House and Senate chambers. Completion date: fall 1992.

Phase four will renovate the western half of the capitol, add elevators, and improve the entrance from underground parking. Completion date: fall 1994.

Phase five will take care of a detailed restoration of the rotunda and the primary public halls which will remain open during construction. Completion date: spring 1996.

OKLAHOMA
The Sooner State

HEIGHT: 105'   FACADE: 422'   DEPTH: 340'

The height of the Oklahoma State Capitol in Oklahoma City does not compare to that of other capitols, and no wonder. It has no dome. This fact gives it distinction. It is the only domeless capitol in the United States.

The absence of a dome remains unnoticed by the visitor attracted to the sweeping facade with its wings' pronounced Corinthian columns beautifully balanced in classic Greco-Roman style on either side of its central Corinthian portico. With eyes filled with its magnitude the viewer finally realizes then discovers the absent characteristic, but returns his eyes to marvel at the view with a shrug.

Oklahoma's Capitol and capital can make other claims, too, but the state's history, though brief, is filled with all facets of the struggle of men and women for land and power.

Until 1889 that area currently embracing the state of Oklahoma was occupied by the Apache, Comanche, Kiowa, and Osage Indians, but it had visitors. A runic alphabet carving found in the Ouachita Mountains in eastern Oklahoma is believed to be the work of Vikings who were there around A.D. 1000.

In quest of riches, Coronado is believed to have passed through the state in 1541, but factually its first registered visitor was Juan de Onate, a Spanish explorer of 1601. He was followed by a Frenchman, De la Harpe who camped there in 1719. Stephen H. Long, an army surveyor, led an expedition through there to the Rocky Mountains in 1819. It was there that George Catlin painted Indians; and Washington Irving wrote about it after hunting there in 1832.

All of Oklahoma except the "Strip" was included in the Louisiana Purchase in 1803. The "Strip" was a part of the land claimed by Texas in 1848 and sold to the United States in 1850. It was a "no man's land" until it was included in the Oklahoma Territory in 1890.

After the Cherokee Indians of Georgia, North Carolina and Tennessee were invited to move there in 1819, Oklahoma became a part of the Indian Territory created by Congress in 1830. In 1824, preparatory to moving the Indians from east of the Mississippi into the land, Fort Towson and Fort Gibson were built and the relocation of the Indians commenced in 1828.

Brought about by intensive pressure from white settlers in those states, the Indians were forced out of Georgia, Alabama, Mississippi, and Florida. Known as the Five Civilized Tribes, they were the Cherokees, Choctaws, Chickasaws, Creeks, and Seminoles. President Andrew Jackson approved their removal despite a Supreme Court ruling. To become known as "The Trail of Tears," their relocation requied more than 18 years, 1828 to 1846. Thousands died from hunger, exposure, and disease. Malcontent reigned. After countless clashes with federal troops each tribe was assigned its own space of land.

In its own new land each nation was self-governed. Farms were improved. Schools were built. Prosperity was common. Within a few years the Cherokee nation became literate with its own written language made possible by the Cherokee alphabet devised by Chief Sequoyah in 1821.

The Civil War brought more problems. Some Indians owned slaves and sided with the South. After the war the Five Tribes freed their slaves and ceded their assigned lands in western Oklahoma, reclaimed by the Union to give to the Delaware Indians who had been shuffled successively from that state to Ohio, Indiana, Missouri, Texas, and Kansas. Hemmed in, crowded out, the

Five Tribes were further deprived of land by the railroad's acquisition of land for building.

The drivers of wagons on the trails across the area admired the land, and in 1872 when the railroad was finished it became possible to keep whites out of Indian land.

The opening of the Cherokee Strip in 1889 brought a rush of white settlers into the area. Cities and settlements sprang into being, among them Guthrie and Oklahoma City. On May 2, 1890, western Oklahoma was organized by Congress as Oklahoma Territory with Guthrie the capital and George W. Steele governor.

During 1893 the Dawes Commission, chaired by former U.S. Senator Henry L. Dawes, was appointed to wipe out the tribal lands and allocate them to individuals. The Five Tribes resisted this action and, united, they developed their own constitution. In 1905 they applied for statehood under the name of Sequoyah which was denied. By 1906 their lands had been divided into individual holdings and became available to white possession and settlement.

That same year the Cherokee Outlet was opened up to settlement and here was seen the greatest run of settlers to claim land in that area.

More land was made available to white settlement August 6, 1901. The reservations of the Kiowa, Comanche, and Wichita Indians were dissolved and opened up.

In 1906 delegates from the Indian and Oklahoma territories met in Guthrie and drafted a constitution for statehood.

The two territories occupying eastern and western Oklahoma were united and organized into the forty-sixth state November 16, 1907, with the capital at Guthrie. Charles N. Haskell was the first governor.

One provision of the enabling act to statehood was that Guthrie would serve as the capital until 1913, at least.

As a result, a capitol was never built at Guthrie. The governor's office and those of other territorial and state officials were scattered through several office buildings. At different times the legislature met in the Guthrie City Hall, the Logan County Courthouse, and Convention Hall. Convention Hall was eventually sold to the Masons and is now a part of the Masonic Temple in Guthrie.

An election was called in 1910 and voters were given the opportunity to vote for Guthrie, Oklahoma City, or Shawnee.

En route to Oklahoma City from his home in Muskogee, Governor Haskell received word that Oklahoma City was the unofficial winner of the election. He ordered the press secretary to transport the State Seal to Oklahoma City. The seal and important papers were smuggled out of Guthrie in a laundry basket by the governor's chief clerk.

Upon his return to Oklahoma City, Governor Haskell checked into the Lee-Huckins Hotel and declared it the Oklahoma Capitol. The secret removal of the seal and papers caused severe hostility and the Oklahoma Supreme Court voided the election because the ballot's resolution did not include the words "Shall it be adopted. . . ."

The Oklahoma State Capitol is the only such building in the world with an oil well directly underneath. No longer productive, the well was capped and its pumping structure retained as a monument. — Oklahoma Historical Society.

In response Governor Haskell called a special session of the legislature to provide the necessary legislation to make everything legal. Oklahoma City was named the permanent capital of the state on December 16, 1910.

Fifteen acres of land for the capitol site were donated, half by William F. Harn, half by J. J. Culbertson of Oklahoma City.

With appropriated funds and a design from the architectural firm of Weymuss Smith and Solomon A. Layton, work started on the Oklahoma Capitol July 20, 1914. A cornerstone ceremony helped its laying November 16, 1915. The capitol was completed June 30, 1917.

Facing south with entrances on four sides, the capitol was built at a cost of $1,515,000 with the funds furnished on a pay as you go basis. The work up to the second story was accomplished by Oklahoman day laborers supervised by a Citizens Advisory Committee.

Finished, its foundation of Oklahoma granite encases two stories below ground. Its four stories above ground are of Indiana limestone.

Because of the high price of steel there wasn't enough money in the original appropriation for a dome, but the concrete support columns for a dome were included in the building's structure for the dome addition later. Whenever a dome bill was introduced, it was killed in committee.

A saucer dome was added which, from the inside, gives the appearance of a shallow dome; and in 1934 the Oklahoma State Seal was inlaid in the ceiling to enhance and magnify the saucer dome.

But the idea of a dome has never been abandoned. In 1989 another group became organized in support of a dome. When one is built Oklahomans will lose another distinction, but they have others among which is the claim that they possess the only capitol in the entire world with an oil well beneath its structure.

One of 25 wells pumping at one time on the capitol grounds, it was drilled during 1941–1942. The hole was started 431 feet from the capitol in the middle of a flower bed, thus its nickname "Petunia Number One." With the legal name Capitol Site #1, it was drilled to a depth of 6,618 feet ending up nearly one and one-quarter miles directly under the capitol.

After giving its owners, the state and Phillips Petroleum 1.5 million barrels of oil and 1.6 million cubic feet of natural gas, the well was pluged in 1986 in such a way as to give the impression of a working well. It is owned by the Oklahoma Historical Society and preserved as a monument and tourist attraction.

Above the doors of the south entrance is a bronze cast reproduction of the Oklahoma State Seal. Inside, the grand staircase leads to the fourth floor. Above the grand staircase three murals portray those Oklahomans who gave their lives in World War II.

The fourth floor offers an unobstructed view of the rotunda ceiling's State Seal with its surrounding sunburst of leaded, stained glass artwork. Four "living history" murals, from early exploration through frontier commerce and Indian immigration to settlement and the land rushes, adorn the ceiling. They are the work of Oklahoma artist Charles Banks Wilson. His portraits of Sequoyah, Will Rogers, Jim Thorpe, and Robert S. Kerr adorn the walls.

The second floor's rotunda contains busts of the 21 governors who served the state. The governor's office is in the east wing as is his reception area, the Blue Room, used for civil and state receptions. Adjacent to this room is the Governor's Art Gallery featuring the work of Oklahoma artists.

The governor's mansion in the capitol complex is open to the public from 1 to 3 P.M. every Wednesday.

The capitol is open daily from 8 A.M. to 7:00 P.M. The guided tours are available from 8 A.M. to 3 P.M.

Both the Oklahoma Historical Society and State Museum of History are open Monday through Saturday, 9 A.M. to 5 P.M.

OREGON

The Beaver State

HEIGHT: 176′ FACADE: 633′ DEPTH: 240′

Prior to the first Americans entering Oregon with Captain James Cook of Britain in 1778, it is assumed that two Spanish navigators, Juan Rodriguez

Cabrillo and Bartolomé Ferrelo were the first white men to gaze upon its shores in 1543.

They were followed in 1579 by Sir Francis Drake out of England in the *Golden Hind.* Drake sailed to the forty-fourth parallel which would be as far north as Eugene, currently located 50 miles inland. He named the land New Albion and claimed it for England.

It is probable that in 1741 Vitus Bering sailed into Alaskan waters to lay Russian claim to that land, including the Oregon coast. The word "probable" comes from historians' beliefs that Sebastian Viscaino saw the land.

It is a fact, claims one historian, that Juan de Fuca sailed along the Oregon coast before and after exploring the Puget Sound area of Washington by way of the strait that bears his name.

Several sailed along the coast attempting to gain the river named Oregon and a northwest passage across North America, but they either missed it or were stymied by the great bar at the river's mouth. Captain John Meares of England was one of these. Terrified of the breakers at its mouth, he named the inlet Deception Bay and the headland to its north Cape Disappointment.

It took Captain Robert Gray and his ship *Columbia* to overcome the treacherous bar and sail up the river in 1792. Gray renamed the river after his ship and laid claim to the land for the United States. Additional claim came with the Lewis and Clark expedition during the winter of 1805–1806 when they built and lived in Fort Clatsop near the mouth of the Columbia River.

With America dominating the fur trade, in 1811 John Jacob Astor divided his Pacific Fur Company, sent one party by land and the other by sea, to the mouth of the Columbia where they built a trading post, Fort Astoria. Two years later during the War of 1812 the British North West Company took over Fort Astoria renaming it Fort George.

After that war, in 1818 the two countries agreed to joint occupancy of the area and Fort George was returned.

In 1824 John McLoughlin left Fort George, crossed the Columbia and started building Fort Vancouver opposite the mouth of the Willamette River. He later commanded the fur trade and helped in the settlement of the area along the Columbia River.

In 1824 when Russia gave up claim to that area south of the fifty-four, forty, North Latitude, the way was clear for a boundary settlement between the United States and England. Not until 1848 was the forty-ninth parallel extended west to the Pacific Ocean. This happened only because of national concern and the Americans' insistence on "Fifty-four forty or fight!"

Settlement of the land first came with Jason Lee, an American Methodist missionary, who accompanied Nathaniel Wyeth overland. Wyeth, a fur trader and builder of Fort Hall in Idaho, followed the Columbia and Fort William on Sauvie Island. Lee's group left Fort Vancouver and, with McLoughlin's help, settled in the Willamette Valley where Lee, with his brother Daniel, started a mission school for the Indians in 1835.

The following year Dr. Marcus Whitman and the Reverend Henry

Spaulding, with their wives, crossed the plains on the Oregon Trail and started a mission school on the Walla Walla River.

Both Lee and Whitman returned east to interest people in Oregon and persuade them to move there. Oregon Emigration Societies were organized in Massachusetts, Illinois, and other states. A group from Peoria, Illinois, entered the Willamette Valley in 1839 and settled there. In 1842 more than a thousand emigrants followed the Oregon Trail from Independence, Missouri, with some going all the way to Oregon. By 1845 the number going to Oregon had risen to more than 3,000.

Because of problems, the settlers in the Willamette Valley organized a provisional government in 1841 with the seat at Oregon City.

In 1848, two years after England gave title of the land to the United States, the Oregon Territory was created. It extended south to north from the forty-second to the forty-ninth parallel, and west from the Continental Divide to the Pacific Ocean. It comprised the present states of Oregon, Washington, Idaho, and part of Montana and Wyoming.

Oregon City was designated the capital with General Joseph Lane appointed governor. As its first delegate to Congress, Oregon sent Samuel R. Thurston. In 1851 the territorial legislature named Salem the capital. Congress confirmed that location and President Millard Fillmore signed the measure May 4, 1852, making it official.

With an appropriation from Congress on land donated to the state by pioneer leader and missionary Dr. William Holden Willson, construction on a territorial capitol started in 1854. It was finished in time for the Seventh Territorial Legislature to reconvene on December 17, 1855.

It was a rectangular, frame building, 50 feet by 70 feet, two stories high with a gabled roof. A portico of four columns dominated its front.

It was designed by Captain Charles Bennet, soldier and carpenter who had discovered the gold at Sutter's Fort, California. With construction supervised by William H. Richter, it cost $25,000. When it caught fire and burned to the ground during its first legislative session on December 30, 1855, the government moved to Corvalis, but returned to Salem the following year.

In 1857 a convention was called and presided over by Matthew P. Deady. A state constitution prohibiting slavery was drafted and adopted. On Valentine's Day, February 14, 1859, Oregon was granted statehood, joining the Union as the thirty-third state. Salem remained the capital and John Whitaker became the first state governor.

The government of the new state became quartered in the Holman Building which had been adapted to receive it. It was then located in the Nesmith Building and other rented quarters until funds were appropriated and construction authorized by the legislature in 1872.

A Capitol Commission was appointed, an architect retained, and a contract was let. Construction on the Oregon State Capitol started in 1873 on the spot of the former capitol. Excavation was accomplished with convict labor. The pay was 25 cents a day.

The Oregon State Capitol. Construction on this modern, four-story statehouse began in 1935 and was completed in 1938. Total cost of the project was $2.5 million. — Department of Transportation.

A ceremony on October 8, 1873, witnessed the placement of 83 articles inside the cornerstone among which were a silver half crown, a United States half dollar, and the Oregon Constitution and Laws.

At a cost to the state of $190,927, possession was taken by the government August 26, 1876. It was designed by German-born Justus Krumbien of Krumbien and Gilbert in Portland. Joseph Holman supervised the construction.

Porticos with two-story Corinthian columns were added to the building in 1888 at a cost of $100,000; and in 1893 a huge, copper-clad dome was added raising the total cost of the structure to $500,000.

The building had three stories and a basement. The walls of brick made by convicts were faced with sandstone and limestone. The dome brought its height to 187 feet.

To keep pace with governmental growth the capitol's interior experienced many changes and housed all branches until 1914 when additional buildings were needed.

Except for its walls, a fire consumed the building April 25, 1935.

During the height of the Great Depression, on October 21, 1935, Governor Charles H. Martin called the legislature into a special session to initiate plans for a new capitol. With funding supplied by the United States Public Works Administration in the amount of $2.5 million, a Capitol Commission was appointed. After seriously considering building on one of two other sites, it was finally decided to build on the site of the old capitol.

Their decision brought a lawsuit filed by Roy Hewitt, Dean of Willamette University Law School and others to force construction of the new capitol inside the walls of the burned out capitol.

This proposal enraged the state fire marshal, who warned everyone, "don't dare stand too close to those old walls; if you should breathe heavily upon them they are likely to collapse." Because of this, Hewitt withdrew the suit.

The old brick walls were drilled and packed with dynamite. When all was ready, the charges were exploded at four o'clock one morning. It blew the windows out of neighboring mansions, but the old walls merely shuddered and stubbornly remained standing. The process had to be repeated.

Started in 1935, the building was dedicated October 1, 1938. It was of a modern Greek design and built in cruciform by architect Francis Keally of the Trowbridge and Livingston Firm of New York at a cost of $2.5 million.

It is constructed of steel reinforced concrete faced with Vermont white marble out of the Danby quarry. It is the fourth newest capitol in the United States. With four stories and a basement, it contained the branches of government until 1977 when a "Wings" project was completed at a cost of $12.5 million which added legislative offices, hearing rooms, support services, a first floor galleria and underground parking.

Two massive Vermont marble sculptures flank the main entrance of the capitol. Sculpted by Leo Friedlander, the one on the west is "The Covered Wagon"; on the east, "Lewis and Clark by Sacajawea." On the back sides of these are intaglio maps showing the Oregon Trail and the routes taken by the Lewis and Clark expedition. Above the entrance doors are three cast bronze sculptures by Ulric Ellerhusen and inside above the doors are three more.

The rotunda and lobbies are lined with polished rose travertine from Montana. Centered in the rotunda floor is a large bronze replica of the Oregon State Seal by Ulric Ellerhusen. Its remaining floor and the staircases are large squares of Phoenix Napoleon grey marble from Missouri with borders of radial black marble from Vermont.

Eight medallions painted near the top of the rotunda's walls represent the objects in the state seal. Four large murals surrounding the rotunda depict Oregon's historic events. Painted by Barry Faulkner and Frank H. Schwarz, they show Captain Robert Gray at the mouth of the Columbia River in 1792; Lewis and Clark going to the Pacific in 1805; Dr. John McLoughlin in 1836; and the wagon train migration in 1843.

The exterior windows and doors, and the doorknobs are bronze with the latter featuring the Oregon State Seal.

The capitol's dome, rising 106 feet above the rotunda, has a ceiling painted by Frank A. Schwarz that features 33 stars symbolizing Oregon as the thirty-third state in the Union.

The Oregon Provisional Government Seal is above the grand staircase leading to the Senate chamber. The Oregon Territorial Seal is above the opposite staircase leading to the House chamber.

The paneling and furniture in the House chamber are of golden oak. A specially designed carpet features the Douglas fir, Oregon's state tree. A Faulkner mural behind the Speaker's desk shows the meeting of the Oregon pioneers at Champoeg to form the provisional government in 1843.

Commemorating the pioneers who settled the Oregon Territory, this gilded statue standing atop the capitol is 24 feet tall. — Department of Transportation.

The Senate chamber's furniture and paneling are of black walnut. The carpeting contains alternate designs of wheat and salmon to symbolize Oregon's agricultural and fishing industries. A mural by Schwarz behind the president's desk is a street scene in Salem when news of statehood was received in 1859.

Above the galleries in both chambers are friezes inscribed with the names of 158 people who were prominent in the history and development of Oregon.

Between the two legislative chambers on the second floor is the Governor's Suite with a reception room, a public ceremonial office, and staff offices. The Governor's Ceremonial Office is decorated in gold and blue, Oregon's official colors, and is paneled in matched black walnut.

Made possible by a state law requiring 1 percent of construction funds for public buildings be spent for art, a collection of works by Oregon artists is displayed in the new wing additions. The Governor's Ceremonial Office and the galleria provide space for art exhibits.

The grounds as well feature works of art, ornamental plantings, native trees and shrubs, and landscaping. Recent additions to Capitol Park are fragments of the Corinthian columns salvaged from the fire-destroyed capitol. The Willson Park was a city park until 1965 when it became a part of the capitol grounds. Today it is the setting for the Waite Fountain, the Liberty Bell replica, and a gazebo constructed in 1982. The Sprague Fountain, given to the people of Oregon, was placed in the center of the Capitol Mall in 1980. Fabricated of bronze, it was sculpted by Tom Morandi and William Blix.

Atop the dome, looking over Capitol Park and all of Salem, is the "Oregon Pioneer," another work of Ellerhusen's. Cast in bronze, finished in gold leaf, hollow inside, it weighs 8.5 tons. The base of the 24-foot statue is 140 feet above the ground and is reached by 121 steps spiraling upward into the tower from the fourth floor of the building.

In 1988 the maintenance of Oregon's Capitol and surrounding grounds required 26 employees and cost the state $1,656,468.

The capitol is open during regular business hours, daily, with guided tours and handouts of printed materials describing the capitol and events in Oregon's history.

PENNSYLVANIA
The Keystone State

HEIGHT: 272'   FACADE: 520'   DEPTH: 254'

Several European nations were highly interested in the new land of America, especially that now comprising the state of Pennsylvania.

In 1607 the English, led by Captain John Smith, founded Jamestown for the Virginia Company of London. Two years later, after exploring the lower Delaware River and Bay, Henry Hudson established a Dutch claim to the area surrounding that region. In 1614 a Dutchman, Captain Cornelis Hendricksen, sailed up the Delaware to its union with the Schuylkill, a site where Philadelphia now exists.

The next year a Frenchman out of Canada, Etienne Brule, explored the Susquehanna River Valley for France and followed it to the Chesapeake Bay.

Sweden followed years later, bought land from the Indians, built Fort Christina where Wilmington is today, and named their colony New Sweden. Its first governor, a Dutchman named Peter Minuit, was replaced in 1643 by a Swede, John Printz, who established a government with courts, the first in Pennsylvania, and built forts on Tinicum Island and at the mouth of the Schuylkill.

All was well until Peter Stuyvesant showed up in 1651 and, intending to dispossess the Swedes, built a Dutch fort on the site of present-day New Castle, Delaware. Finally realizing Stuyvesant's intent, the Swedes took over Fort Casimir in 1654 only to have the Dutch take it back the following year and drive them out of New Sweden.

The English established rule over the Dutch by force in 1664 and the region became a part of the Province of New York governed by the Duke of York.

Meanwhile in England, to satisfy a debt owed to William Penn, heir to the estate of his deceased father, Admiral Penn, Charles II granted him 50,000 acres of land which comprises most of today's Pennsylvania. Wanting to name his colony New Wales, Penn was overruled by the king who named it to honor Penn's father.

Penn was rich and a prominent member and leader of the despised and persecuted Quakers. In 1681 he sent his cousin, William Markham, with a group of Quakers to colonize the new land and, after leasing more land from the Duke of York, he left for America with another group of Quakers landing there October 27, 1682.

Soon afterwards he negotiated several treaties of friendliness and land settlement with the Delaware Indians. There followed his "most famous" utterance on June 23, 1683, under a monumental elm tree on the banks of the Delaware which stated the English and Indians would "live in love as long as the sun gave light." While other colonies lived in fear of and were at war with Indian tribes, the Penn colonists were at peace for 70 years.

On December 4, 1682, Penn called a general assembly to meet in Upland (Chester in Delaware County). Forty freeholders from the six counties in his province met and adopted a frame of government the provisions of which included a guarantee of religious freedom. A site for the city of Philadelphia was selected and a general assembly met there March 10, 1683, and passed an Act of Settlement which accepted Penn's Frame of Government with a few changes.

Returning to England on a matter of business in 1684, Penn was detained there for 15 years. Suspected of giving aid and comfort to the dethroned James II during William and Mary's War, he was arrested and deprived of his colony in 1692. Two years later with charges dismissed, he regained his colony and returned in 1699 to find numerous changes had taken place. Twenty thousand people inhabited his province. Many didn't know who he was, except that he owned the province.

He granted their demands for a more democratic form of government by

Ruins of the Pennsylvania State Capitol after a fire destroyed the building's interior in 1897. — Department of General Services.

signing the Charter of Liberties and Privileges October 28, 1701. It gave religious freedom and self-government to all the people of the province. For 75 years it remained in force until the American Revolution.

Later that year business forced Penn to leave his beloved colony and go to England. He never returned.

With no place to meet except private homes, taverns, and Quaker meeting houses, the general assembly finally appropriated 2,000 English pounds in 1729 "for the construction of a State House."

Two men, Andrew Hamilton, the Clerk of the Assembly and Edmund Wooley, Philadelphia's master builder, designed and built what is now known as Independence Hall.

Built in the Georgian colonial architectural style, its construction started in 1732. It was finished in 1741 and provided a statehouse with a ground level basement and two stories rising to a height of 50 feet and a tower with steeple soaring 164 feet into the sky. With a stone foundation, the building holds an area of 11,630 square feet of floor space. Its facade is 107 feet in length, its depth 44½ feet.

(Independence Hall was sold to the city of Philadelphia for $70,000. From that time it served many purposes, one of which was the basement's use as a dog pound. Today it is administered by the National Park Service.)

In 1776 Benjamin Franklin presided over a convention that adopted a constitution making Pennsylvania an independent state; and the First General Assembly convened in Philadelphia November 28, 1776. It was a unicameral body from that time until 1790 when the state adopted the bicameral legislature.

In April 1799 the assembly acted and Governor Thomas Mifflin approved moving the capital to Lancaster before November. They had met there briefly while British troops occupied Philadelphia.

They rented and met in the Lancaster County Courthouse located in Penn Square. Designed in Georgian style by Frederick Mann, built between 1784 and 1787, the building's rock foundation supported its rectangular-shaped two stories with the House meeting in the lower, the Senate in the upper. (The building was demolished in 1853.)

Pressured by their constituents, dissatisfied that the capital wasn't close to the state's center, the assembly passed an act in February 1810 designating Harrisburg the permanent capital. Moving there in October 1812, Pennsylvania's government used the Dauphin County Courthouse for nine years.

Located on Market Street and Raspberry Alley, the courthouse had been known as White Hall. Designed by James Mitchell and built at a cost of $6,000 on property donated by John Harris, Jr., the founder of Harrisburg, the two-story structure of brick had a facade of 90 feet and a depth of 50 feet. While occupied by the legislature, a semi-rotunda of brick was added to the front center. When abandoned by the state, it reverted to Dauphin County as a courthouse until 1860 when it was demolished for a new one.

The State House (Independence Hall) was sold to the city of Philadelphia in March 1816 and the money was used to finance a state capitol.

That year (1816) the General Assembly created a Capitol Commission and advertised a design competition for a capitol to be built at Harrisburg. Of 17 designs submitted, the prize of $400 was awarded to Stephen Hills.

With legislative appropriation, sited on land donated by the town's founder, John Harris, Jr., construction started in 1819 on a capitol for the state of Pennsylvania. The cornerstone ceremony, conducted by Governor William Findlay on May 31, 1819, included the placement inside the stone of copies of the Charter of Pennsylvania, the Declaration of Independence, the Constitution of the United States, and the Constitution of Pennsylvania.

The capitol was completed at a cost of $135,000 in December 1821 and dedicated January 2, 1822, in a ceremony with a prayer offered by Reverend Dr. George Lochman including the words "watch over it and preserve it from fire and lightning."

In Hill's Federal/Greek Revival design, the capitol's facade was 180 feet in length and 80 feet deep. A central dome rose to a height of 100 feet. With a brick exterior and a semicircular portico supported by six brownstone columns, the capitol had two stories and a basement. The interior was plaster.

On February 2, 1897, in a blaze lasting two and one-half hours, flames completely consumed its interior leaving only the walls and the portico's

Main entrance of the Pennsylvania State Capitol. The exterior is faced with Vermont granite. — Department of General Services.

colonnade. Luckily the fire's smoke was noticed during legislative sessions and the building was evacuated without loss of life.

Started by an unattended fireplace warming the lieutenant governor's office, the holocaust destroyed an edifice that for 75 years had presented the architectural symbols of American democracy and received nationwide praise. Its life held momentous events, two of which were the lying in state of President Lincoln's body in 1865 and Pennsylvania's constitutional convention in 1874.

A full view of the Pennsylvania statehouse from the southeast shows the building's extensive wings. Designed and built by Joseph M. Huston in Italian Renaissance style, it was dedicated by President Theodore Roosevelt in 1906. — Department of General Services.

Within six days the legislature leased and met in the Grace Methodist Episcopal Church, a Gothic Revival structure of stone built in 1873. Meeting there for five months, they were allowed the privilege of smoking cigars, chewing tobacco, and spitting on church property.

While there they appropriated $550,000 for a new capitol on the same site and advertised a design contest. The design chosen was that of Henry James Cobb of Chicago, whose plan was much the same as Hill's before him, but to be completed in stages.

In 1894 a structure was designed by John T. Windrim and built to house the executive offices, the state museum, and state library. It was given over to legislative offices during the 1980s and in 1986 was planned for refurbishment for the use by the governor and staff.

With the same trowel used by President George Washington in that ceremony for the nation's capitol, a cornerstone was laid August 10, 1898; and although the building was unfinished the legislature held three consecutive biannual sessions starting January 3, 1899.

The legislative chambers' floors were rough-sawed pine planks. The unfinished walls were covered with burlap. By 1903 it became apparent the funding was insufficient and, with its end in sight, the capitol's roof was pine and hemlock covered with tarred felt, pitch, and sand. The open space where the dome should have been was covered with boards to deter the elements. Only 20 percent of the interior was plastered.

That building was never completed.

In another competition open only to Pennsylvania architects, Philadelphian Joseph M. Huston's design was chosen from among those entered. Incorporating Cobb's walls and parts of the superstructure, with $4 million available, a contract was awarded to the George F. Payne Company. Ground was broken November 7, 1902.

Regarding a cornerstone ceremony, one report states it was laid May 5, 1904, while a second holds "At one point [during construction], architect Huston, his assistant architect and the construction foreman held a brief Masonic ceremony in what is today the capital's sub-basement. They placed a glass jar containing a Greek Testament into the wet cement of the dome's northwest corner pillar."

The capitol was officially dedicated October 4, 1906, by President Theodore Roosevelt who pronounced it "the most beautiful state Capitol in the nation...." It stands and is used today.

In Italian Renaissance style, the capitol's exterior is faced with Vermont granite; its interior walls are Vermont marble; its roof, green glazed tile. There are two levels below ground, five stories above, and a mezzanine running through most of the building. It contains 600 rooms.

Its dome is the dominating architectural feature. Inspired by Rome's St. Peter's Basilica, it weighs 26,000 tons and is supported by four pillars sunk seven feet into slate bedrock. At its base each pillar is 29¼ feet in diameter and tapers to 12½ feet at the top.

Atop the dome, standing on a four-foot golden ball, a gilded bronze female statue, "Commonwealth," holds overhead a garlanded mace representing the standard of statehood with her left hand while her right is extended in benediction. Given the nickname "Miss Penn" years ago, it has been assumed she represents William Penn's daughter, Letitia. Sculpted by Roland Hilton Perry, his original model is displayed in the State Museum.

Historians have disagreed on the cost of the building, reported as $10 million then $13 million with the fraud included. During construction and afterwards, overcharges on materials and furnishings were discovered. The quality paid for had not been used.

Charges were brought against those responsible. Among those found guilty were the architect, Huston, who went to prison, and a decorator from Philadelphia named Sanderson, who died shortly after the trial.

At the main entrance the visitor faces two one-ton doors cast in bronze.

Intricate in design and containing heads of persons eminent in the capitol's construction, they were poured into wax molds prepared by Otto Jahnsen and cast by the Henry Bonnard Bronze Company.

Inside the rotunda on the main floor, six glass cases contain 352 historic flags and banners, 200 of which were Civil War banners presented to the state at Independence Hall after being paraded around Philadelphia on July 4, 1866. Placed in the capitol in Harrisburg, moved to the State Museum in 1895, they escaped the fire. They were transferred to the glass cases in the rotunda in 1914.

High above in the dome four paintings in the pendentives by Edwin Austin Abbey represent religion, law, science, and art. Encircling the dome above the paintings are Penn's famous words.

Dominating the rotunda, a staircase of Italian marble rises to a landing, divides, and curves upward to the first level and a balustrade balcony. The lieutenant governor's office is directly above the main entrance.

To the north, off the balcony on the second floor, the Senate chamber is decorated in rare Irish connamara marble accented with gold velvet draperies and intricately designed golden figurines and chandeliers. In the chamber there are four murals by Pennsylvania's outstanding artist Violet Oakley. Two of them, representing "The Creation of the Union" are in the front panels on either side of the podium; and two "The Preservation of the Union" are in panels to the rear on each side of the entrance.

The stained glass windows beneath the ceiling are by W. B. Van Ingen. They symbolize glass blowing, weaving, temperance, peace, railroads, militia, legislature, history, foundries, and architecture.

The Governor's Suite is located on the second floor in the south wing. The reception room is paneled in English crotched oak enhanced with Oakley murals portraying events in the history of religious liberty in England, the rise of the Society of Friends, and dramatic moments in the life of William Penn culminating with his arrival in America on the vessel *Welcome*. Its twin fireplaces of Sienna marble from Italy are highlighted by two one-ton, ornate, gold plated light fixtures. To provide better light its cut glass globes are a crisscross diamond design. The governor's private office is paneled in English quartered oak with gold leaf cornices. Its fireplace is surrounded with red African marble.

Also to the south, off the balcony, is the House chamber. The French marble surrounding it was taken from quarries owned by monks in the Pyrennees Mountains. It took much persuasion for the monks to open the quarry and donate the marble, which was not for sale.

Its paintings are also the work of Abbey who was paid $25 per square foot. Valued at more than a million dollars today they include "Penn's Treaty with the Indians," "Reading of the Declaration of Independence," "Valley Forge," and "The Passage of the Hours." Another and the largest in the capitol is "The Apotheosis of Pennsylvania" which portrays the famous men in the state's history.

Interior of rotunda ceiling of Pennsylvania State Capitol showing artwork radiating from the core. — Department of General Services.

Fourteen circular stained glass windows by Van Ingen portray the state's outstanding commercial and cultural activities during the time the capitol was being built.

The visitors' galleries to the chambers are reached from the fourth floor.

Located in the east wing of the fourth floor, the Supreme and Superior Court Room is resplendent in the solid mahogany fittings from Belize that are considered the finest in the capitol. Sixteen panels painted by Oakley surround the 72 feet by 42 feet room. Dedicated in 1927 they portray the evolution of law through the ages.

In 1982 a legislative act created a Capitol Preservation Committee and Trust Fund and provided for the restoration of the capitol.

Talk for an expansion of the capitol started in 1916 when architect Arnold W. Brunner and a landscape architect, Warren H. Manning, were commissioned to prepare plans for such. The seven-story South Office Building was completed in 1921.

The North Office Building, completed in 1929, is an exact copy, balancing and following the Brunner design.

By the 1930s, with the North and South Office buildings in place, plans got underway to connect the two buildings with the capitol. They were never carried out and the space reverted to a parking lot.

In 1965 the legislature appropriated $32 million to expand the capitol once more. The plans for a five-story office tower in contemporary design were so opposed by the Historical Commission, that the project was abandoned.

In August 1980 plans for an extension and underground parking area were presented by Celli-Flynn Associates and H. F. Lintz Company of Pittsburgh. The plans were approved September 3, 1981, and construction commenced in November 1982. Costing $147 million, the East Wing of the capitol was dedicated December 2, 1987.

Covering one million square feet, the East Wing has two stories above ground containing 100 legislative offices, conference rooms, a media center, state capitol police headquarters and a cafeteria. There are three levels of underground parking with space for 840 vehicles. The East Wing connects the North and South Office buildings with the main capitol building.

During 1988, 39 people were employed to maintain the buildings and grounds of Pennsylvania's capitol complex at a cost of $3,169,000.

Without charge, visitors are given *The Senate of Pennsylvania* and *Pennsylvania House of Representatives,* booklets in color describing their work, the chambers and affiliated offices; *Landmarks of Pennsylvania's Capitol Complex,* a descriptive folder and map; *Welcome to Pennsylvania's Capitol,* a welcome booklet describing each governmental part of the capitol, with the decorations, art, and furnishings; and *Pennsylvania Symbols,* a folded, color leaflet containing the official state symbols.

The Capitol Tour Guide Service operates during business hours seven days a week with tours every hour. The Pennsylvania Historical Museum, formerly the William Penn Memorial Museum, is across the street from the capitol.

PUERTO RICO

HEIGHT: 143' 8"   FACADE: 305'   DEPTH: 144'

On November 19, 1493, on his second voyage, Christopher Columbus anchored in a bay on the west side of an island, claimed it for Spain, named it San

Juan, and found the friendly Arawak Indians. Sailing on to Guadalupe Island, he possessed it in the names of Ferdinand and Isabella and named it San Juan Bautista before rescuing some Arawak Indians from the cannibalistic and warlike Carib Indians.

After two days there, he pulled anchor and moved on to the island of Hispaniola where the first settlement in the new world was established.

The settlement was neglected for 15 years; then, in 1508 Ponce de Leon anchored in the bay off the island Columbus named San Juan and went ashore where he founded a town (Caparra) and turned to mining gold using the friendly Arawaks to do the labor. He gave the name Puerto Rico to the harbor in which he had anchored. Over the years a switch in names gradually occurred with the island taking the name Puerto Rico and the town, San Juan.

Without much success in mining, de Leon turned his workers to agriculture, but because of the cruelty with which the Spaniards had become known in treatment of their Indian laborers, his helpers revolted. That, together with the frequent attacks and plundering of the English, French, and Dutch pirates, brought about the building of forts for protection.

Eventually and years later during the 1830s, with the introduction of the plantation system and African slaves the economy progressed through the production of coffee, sugarcane, and tobacco. The Puerto Ricans were praised by Spain, especially because of their political independence and the abolition of slavery in the latter part of the century.

In 1897 Spain granted the Puerto Ricans broad powers of self-government, but the Spanish-American War prevented them from putting their new government into effect.

In May 1898 Admiral W. T. Sampson bombarded San Juan with little effect on its fortress. That July, General Nelson A. Miles landed a force of 3,500 men, and after a short campaign including the Battle of San Juan Hill, the fighting ceased.

On October 18, 1898, Puerto Rico was turned over to the armies of the United States and General John R. Burke became the military governor. Puerto Rico was ceded to the United States in the Treaty of Paris December 10, 1898; the treaty was ratified by Congress February 2, 1899.

Under military control schools were built and public education started, sanitation with physical facilities was indoctrinated, and construction of roads and buildings was accomplished. The civil government took over on May 1, 1900.

The Olmstead Act of July 15, 1909, placed the jurisdiction of Puerto Rican affairs under that department designated by the President of the United States.

Puerto Rico became a territory under the Jones Act of March 2, 1917. Its natives were granted citizenship and given limited self-government, but because the key officials were appointed by the President, they were beyond Puerto Rican control.

By the 1930s two political parties had evolved, one seeking independence,

In the oldest capital city in the Americas, Puerto Rico's capitol started from an idea in 1907 and was dedicated February 2, 1929. — Oficina de Relaciones Publicas.

the other, statehood. In 1946 President Harry S Truman appointed the first native Puerto Rican to the governership in 1946, which act led to the governor's being elected by popular vote in 1948.

In 1950 Congress offered changes in the laws governing the relationship between the United States and Puerto Rico. A constitution was drawn up and accepted by the people and on July 25, 1952, Puerto Rico became a commonwealth. Today the Commonwealth of Puerto Rico is a self-governing political unit voluntarily associated with the United States.

San Juan, Puerto Rico, has been the seat of government and the capital since 1508 inasmuch as Ponce de Leon *was* the government at that time. From the time a legislature first assembled, it was known as the Chamber of Delegates and held its meetings in a building at the corner of San Jose and San Francisco streets in what is now designated Old San Juan. Later known as the Assembly House, it was moved from San Francisco Street to Puerta de Tierra, a small precinct at the entrance of Old San Juan City.

Tired of being without a meeting place, a few of the delegates listened when the Honorable Luis Muñoz Rivera on February 7, 1907, presented a bill with the proposal that a Capitol building be constructed with an appropriation of $300,000. The bill passed and during the years 1908, 1916, and 1919 additional monies were appropriated for a capitol.

With the land for a capitol site donated by the Puerto Rico government and a design by a Puerto Rican architect, Rafael Carmoega, a contract was let to Francisco Pons and the work commenced. The cornerstone was set by Governor Horace M. Towner on July 17, 1925, the birthdate of Don Luis Muñoz Rivera.

The marble stairs rising from the rotunda floor in the capitol of Puerto Rico. — Oficina de Relaciones Publicas.

Located on a small hill overlooking the Atlantic Ocean to the north and the Bay of San Juan to the south, the capitol was completed and dedicated February 14, 1929.

Constructed of Georgia and Italian white marble, the Puerto Rican Capitol contains four stories in Italian Renaissance design, covers an area of nearly 52,000 square feet, and offers 170,000 square feet of usable floor space.

The south entrance is off Ponce de Leon Avenue. An extremely broad marble staircase ascends to the ground (first) floor level to a landing and continues upward to a heavy portico supported by eight Corinthian columns rising from the main (second) floor through the third floor to a substantial, rectangular roof.

A low dome topped with a lantern surmounts the central roof and moves upward to a distance of 143 feet, 8 inches from the ground.

This entrance admits to a second (main) floor. The first (ground) floor has entrances on either side of the portico.

Inside, on the second story main floor, centered in the marble floor of the rotunda, displayed among other documents in an octagon-shaped glass case is the Commonwealth's original constitution that was accepted in July 1952. Eighty feet above, in the ceiling, are Venetian mosaics representing agriculture, art, education, freedom, health, industry, justice, and science.

Beneath the mosaics, outside the curves of the heavily decorated arches on each side of the four-sided rotunda, are murals symbolizing Discovery of the Island, Conquest and Colonization, the Autonomist Movement of 1887, and the Abolition of Slavery. They are the work of Jose R. Oliver, Jorge Rechani, Rafael Rios Rey, and Rafael Tufino, all Puerto Rican artists.

Four Ionic columns of Italian rose marble stand on each side of the square rotunda to rise majestically to the fourth floor beneath the arches. Between them at the third floor level, in the white Carrara marble, are friezes portraying the history of Puerto Rico from the Indians to commonwealth status. Designed by Oliver and Rios Rey, they are the work of an Italian sculptor.

The art and furnishings throughout the capitol are of the finest workmanship presenting skill, composure, and a distinct prestige.

Only the legislative and judicial departments of government occupy the capitol. The governor's office is located in another building, Castillo de Santa Catalina (also known as La Fortaleza), which is located in the west corner of Old San Juan.

The exact cost of the capitol's construction has never been available, but it is estimated that the construction expenses were about $3 million.

After the commonwealth government was established in 1952, the increase in legislators demanded more space. Completed in 1955 at a cost of $1 million, annexes were added to accommodate the offices and hearing rooms and supporting services for the legislators.

Visitors are welcome in the Senate and Assembly chambers of the capitol. Guided tours are given Monday through Friday, 8:30 A.M. to 5:00 P.M. Group tours, including school students, are by appointment only. Tourists are accommodated, but reservations are suggested.

RHODE ISLAND
The Little Rhody State

HEIGHT: 235'   FACADE: 333'   DEPTH: 180'

The smallest of the United States, Rhode Island is unique in many ways. Within the state's boundaries two colonies were established. Molded into one by the founder of Rhode Island, the government was eventually rotated among five county seats. Its first settlers were outcasts from the Puritan societies of Massachusetts.

The first white men to enter the area came with an Italian explorer named Giovanni da Verrazzano. Hired by King Louis XII of France to explore the new world, he entered what became Narragansett Bay in 1524.

The next persons of note in Rhode Island history came with Roger Williams from Massachusetts. Banished from the Puritan Massachusetts Bay Colony for heresy, cast out because of religious and political dissension in 1635, Williams' group established themselves on the Moshassuck River in 1636 and named their settlement Providence (God conceived as the power sustaining and guiding human destiny). That action distinguished Williams as the founder of Rhode Island; and further actions accorded him the title of proponent and firm advocate of religious freedom.

Within a year the group had drawn up the "Plantation Covenant," by which the colony was governed, and made good friends of the Indians. In 1838 they formed the Proprietors' Company for Providence Plantations and secured deeds to the land from Chief Canonicus of the Narragansett Indians.

William Coddington and John Clark led an Antinomian group out of Massachusetts that year and settled at Pocasset (Portsmouth) on Aquidneck Island. They were soon joined by Anne Hutchinson, "the American Jezebel" who soon took political control from Coddington.

In 1639 the Williams group formed the first Baptist church in America while Coddington and Clark, unable to cope with Hutchinson, moved their group ten miles farther south on Aquidneck Island and established Newport.

Portsmouth and Newport joined into one government. Aquidneck Island became Rhode Island. Samuel Gorton purchased land from the Indians, established a colony at Shawomet, and renamed it Warwick.

Back in England, Williams was granted a charter by Charles I on March 14, 1644, which tied the four towns together as the Providence Plantations.

In May 1647 representatives of the four towns met in Portsmouth to elect officers, make laws, and form the first General Assembly.

After Coddington procured his own charter for Rhode Island in 1651, Williams went to England. Coddington's charter was annulled the following year and Williams' grant was reaffirmed by the English Commonwealth. In 1654 he returned with a commission to serve as the governor of Rhode Island and Providence Planations and, with his help, the four communities were reunited.

New problems arose from Massachusetts and Connecticut whose religious advocates set covetous eyes upon the beautiful area surrounding Rhode Island, stating it had been transformed into "a moral sewer" by its inhabitants. The threat of Connecticut outsiders taking over was quashed in 1663 when the Colony of Rhode Island was granted a new charter by Charles II. After years of controversy the boundaries between the two, as they are now, were agreed upon in 1703 and approved in 1727.

Five counties were formed during the first half of the eighteenth century, and the functions of Rhode Island's government were rotated among the counties' seats: Newport, Providence, Warwick, Portsmouth, and Kingston.

As each county took a turn it became necessary to have a place other than someone's house to conduct government business. The demand resulted in each county seat building a structure to satisfy the needs of the government which gave Rhode Island another unique quality. These structures were called colony houses. Rhode Island had five capitals in the county seats and a capitol in each at the same time.

Of the colony houses the one at Newport was the oldest, and it was there that the newly elected legislature met each year to organize before moving to that next county seat in turn.

Rhode Island, denied admission to the New England Confederation for years, was no longer an outcast when problems arose leading into the American Revolution.

Citizens of Newport scuttled the British ship *Liberty* in 1769 and when England imposed the sugar tax, the colony's ships smuggled around it. Angered, Britain sent the cutter *Gaspee* into Narragansett Bay where it was burned by the colonists June 9, 1772.

A few days after the battles at Concord and Lexington in 1775, Rhode Island's assembly provided an army of 1,500 men under the command of Nathaniel Greene. These men would play an important role in the war with England.

Rhode Island, the first colony to renounce allegiance to England, declared its independence May 4, 1776, and later joined the other colonies in the Declaration of Independence, signing as the state of Rhode Island and the Providence Plantations. Later that year the general assembly adopted the name Rhode Island.

The first naval action of the Revolution occurred off Jamestown, Rhode Island. The British bombarded Bristol and, because it was a major seaport, seized and occupied Newport December 8, 1776. Constantly harassed by Greene's outnumbered army, the British were prevented from further invasion of the state in the Battle of Quaker Hill August 29, 1778. The British fleet finally evacuated Newport October 25, 1779.

The first in many ways, unique in others, Rhode Island became the thirteenth state to ratify the Constitution of the United States May 29, 1790.

Besides the five capitals named earlier: Newport, Providence, Warwick, Portsmouth, and Kingston, Rhode Island's general assembly also met in Pautuxet, East Greenwich, Bristol, and Narragansett.

In 1854 an amendment to the Rhode Island constitution provided that the general assembly would hold sessions only in Newport and Providence. Rhode Island continued to be unique by having co-capitals for nearly 50 years. In 1900 the eleventh amendment to the state's constitution was adopted establishing that all future legislative sessions would be held in Providence. That was the last session in Newport.

The Newport Colony House, the fourth oldest statehouse standing today, was built during the years 1739–1743 to replace Rhode Island's first government building, a frame structure. Upon its completion the much larger brick structure, 40 feet by 80 feet with two stories, became the center of community life. During the American Revolution when the British occupied Newport, it served as a barracks for Britain's troops. When they evacuated, it became a hospital for the colonial-allied French army.

Badly damaged, it was boarded up after the war and the assembly met in the Touro Synagogue until their building was refurbished in 1845. The Touro Synagogue holds the distinction of being the first synagogue in America.

Designated a National Historic Landmark in 1962, the Newport Colony House has undergone a number of restoration projects which continue. Nearly 250 years old, it stands firmly today exuding the historic moments of its life.

It was in the Newport Colony House that a convention ratified the United States Constitution in 1790 after which President George Washington and Secretary of State Thomas Jefferson were entertained.

It was there that the assembly commissioned Gilbert Stuart, a native of Rhode Island, to paint two portraits of George Washington, one for Providence, one for Newport. They hang today, one in Newport's Colony House, the other in Rhode Island's Capitol in Providence.

Providence's first colony house, erected 1730–1731, was a two-story, frame structure. It was destroyed by fire on Christmas Eve 1758.

In February 1759 the assembly ordered a brick courthouse to replace it. Lotteries, planned to finance its construction, were not too successful so money was printed. Construction started in 1760. Occupied in 1762, it was not completed until 1771. Altered over the years, it eventually assumed an appearance much like that of Newport's Colony House. It had also assumed an important role as the community center. It hosted Washington and Jefferson about the same time they were feted in Newport.

Time after time additions were built to accept the spreading government, but within a few years the government had outgrown the new space. In 1901 after Providence became the permanent capital of Rhode Island and the assembly had provided for a new capitol, the Old State House, as it is called today, was refurbished to contain the Sixth District Court.

During 1975 when the court moved out to occupy the new Garrahy Judicial Complex, Rhode Island's Bicentennial Commission and the Historical Preservation Commission moved in. Restored, rejuvenated, refurbished by 1988, Rhode Island's Old State House stands today more than 225 years after construction. It continues to serve the state as headquarters for Rhode Island's Film Commission, Heritage Commission, and the Historical Preservation Commission. There are three more buildings standing today that served as capitols of Rhode Island.

When King's County was created in 1729 its courthouse was built in

Tower Hill. Twenty-five years later prominent citizens of a rival town, Little Rest, talked the assembly into moving the county seat to their town on the promise they would build three taverns to take care of the needs of the legislators while in session.

The move to Little Rest (Kingston) caused construction of another courthouse in 1752 and brought prosperity to the village. Growth and abundance brought the need of a larger courthouse. In legislative action of 1773 the general assembly provided for plans for a new courthouse. It was completed in 1776 and the old building and its lot were sold. The general assembly first met there in 1777 and four years later changed the name from King's County to Washington County.

It was here that a convention was called in March 1790 to ratify the Constitution of the United States. It was here that Rhode Island refused to join the other 12 states in spite of threatened sanctions. (It was approved in May of that year in a Newport convention.)

The General Assembly last met in Washington County's courthouse in 1851. Occupied by the courts until 1894, it was then leased by the Kingston Free Library and in 1959 the General Assembly transferred its title to the library.

The old King's County Courthouse was listed on the National Register of Historic Places in 1974. It was fully restored during the bicentennial and serves today as the Kingston Library.

In 1750 the General Assembly acted to form Kent County from a part of Providence County with East Greenwich county seat provided the people would build a courthouse. A lot was donated and the people raised the money for Kent County's first courthouse, a two-story, frame structure which was satisfactory for near 50 years.

With the old building removed, a new one, costing more than the $2,000 appropriated, occupied the site by 1805. The General Assembly first met in 1806 and continued through 1854 when use of the building was assumed by the courts.

During 1908–1909 the courthouse was rehabilitated and, in the early 1930s, with more room needed by the courts, a one-story, brick structure with a flat roof was added to the rear. In 1970 it was listed on the National Register of Historic Places.

When the courts moved to a more modern structure in 1974, the East Greenwich Chamber of Commerce made the building its headquarters and it stands today, its aged structure resembling that of its predecessors.

Having served as a county seat since 1685, Bristol continued as county seat after boundary disputes were settled with Massachusetts in 1746 and Bristol County, Rhode Island, was formed.

Only presumptions survive about what is believed to have been Bristol's first courthouse, but records show that in 1766 the General Assembly acted for construction of a new courthouse in the same place. Completed shortly afterwards it was a modest two-and-one-half-story, gambrel-roof wooden structure.

It served through the years until after Bristol became an important seaport. The demands of prosperity and growth and governmental need provided a new courthouse completed in 1817.

Built of rubblework stone covered with stucco, the T-shaped building consists of a central, three-story structure with two-story wings off each side and another at its rear, all with hip roofs. A square-shaped tower, at one time probably meant for a belfry, rises above the roof of the central structure.

It was used by the General Assembly until 1852 then occupied by the county's courts.

With renovations over the years and a refurbishment during the 1930s, the structure has undergone many changes. It was listed on the National Register of Historic Places in 1970 and, since the Bristol County Superior Court moved to Providence in 1980, it has continued in use as a county traffic court and headquarters for the Bristol County Sheriff's Department.

Used occasionally by Bristol's civic and political organizations, the Bristol County Courthouse remains a functional building and an asset to Bristol County as well as to Rhode Island and its newest capitol.

Appointed in 1890, with an appropriation of $200,000, the Rhode Island Board of Capitol Commissioners paid $190,000 for a building site to which was added ten and one-half acres donated by Providence.

The board then advertised for a capitol design in a two-stage competition. The first, for Rhode Island architects only, produced three designs that entered a second competition with Boston and New York architects. This was won by the architectural firm of McKim, Mead, and White of New York.

Awarded the construction contract, the Norcross Brothers Construction Company of Worcester, Massachusetts, broke ground in a ceremony on September 16, 1895. The cornerstone was laid October 15, 1896. Construction progressed rapidly under constant review of the plans by all parties concerned.

First to occupy the statehouse in December 1900 was the secretary of state. The governor occupied his office early in 1901 and other departments of the government and the General Assembly as space was completed.

Declared complete on June 11, 1904, the capitol and its landscaped grounds were accepted by the Board of Capitol Commissioners. The final cost was $3,018,416.33 which included furnishings, decorations, and landscaping. During 1988, 19 employees maintained the capitol building and grounds costing the state $211,832.

Built with 327,000 cubic feet of Georgia white marble, the capitol's body contains 15 million bricks and 1,309 tons of steel floor beams.

Designed in the American Republic and High Renaissance in Italy, the capitol has three above and two stories below ground. Its height was incomplete until December 18, 1899, when "Independent Man" stepped onto his place atop the capitol dome.

With a spear clutched in his right hand, the left resting on an anchor's stock, Rhode Island's symbol looks toward downtown Providence and Narragansett Bay. Eleven feet tall, this 500-pound gilded statue was cast by the

Providence claims one of the most beautiful capitols in America. The original was dedicated in 1904. Bronze statues guard its entrance and a gilded sentinel, "Independent Man," standing atop the dome, guards the city. — Office of the Governor.

Gorham Manufacturing Company of Providence with the bronze discarded from a statue of Simon Bolivar which, declared unsightly, had been removed from New York's Central Park.

"Independent Man" was designed by George T. Brewster of New York. So large he had to be cast in five sections, then riveted together, he was to have been a statue of Roger Williams, founder of Rhode Island, but inasmuch as no one knew what Williams looked like and every loyal citizen did know what he stood for, the statue became "Independent Man."

Struck by lightning in 1927, his repair atop the dome required 42 copper-plated stitches. A physical examination in 1951 revealed damage from the elements, included lightning. It was repaired. When the pilot of WGNG Radio Station's helicopter spotted a hole and further damage August 9, 1975, "Independent Man" was coaxed off the dome. After receiving major repairs and a new coat of gold, he stood in the capitol's rotunda where he observed all visitors until July 20, 1976; then, after a small ceremony a large crowd watched while he was put back onto his rightful position on the capitol's dome.

Below the marble dome inside the capitol, centered in the paving is the bronze cast state seal surrounded by the words, "Seal of the State of Rhode

Island and Providence Plantations—1636–." High above, below the dome's oculus is a 50-foot mural painted in 1945 by James A. King of Scituate depicting the settling of Providence in 1636. Giorgio DeFelice of Providence was commissioned to paint medallions in the spandrels. Finished in 1947, his work features four female figures representing education, justice, literature, and commerce.

The legislative chambers occupy the wings of the second floor. Immediately behind each chamber is a lounge. Each Senator and Representative has an individual desk equipped with a microphone and call buttons with which a vote is registered, a page may be called, or a request to speak may be sent. The visitors' galleries for either chamber are entered from the third floor.

The Senate chamber's furniture is mahogany. An arch high above the visitor's gallery is faced with the seals of the original 13 states with that of Rhode Island in the center. Mirrors mounted on the rear walls are there for the gallery spectators to watch the action on the rostrum beneath them and vice versa for the Senate's president.

The House chamber's desks and furnishings are oak. The walls of its lounge support portraits of its past Speakers of the House. Its main architectural feature is the large Doric columns surrounding it.

Also on the second floor are the State Library and the governor's office of which the State Room is a part. Serving as the formal reception room for official functions, the room has a high, ornately gilded ceiling, gold-topped marble columns, large double fireplaces, and crystal chandeliers. The State Room contains many priceless relics and historic artifacts recalling the state's historic contributions to the nation.

In a massive gilded frame over the mantel of one fireplace is Gilbert Stuart's "Washington." Opposite, above the mantel of another fireplace is another full-length portrait by Gary Melchers of General Nathaniel Greene, Washington's second-in-command.

Two more portraits in the State Room by Willard DeFini are of Oliver Hazard Perry, hero of the Battle of Lake Erie in the War of 1812, and Commodore John Barry who is considered the father of the American Navy. Both men were Rhode Islanders.

Displayed in a glass case are personal items that belonged to General Nathaniel Greene among which are his sword, epaulets, a locket, and a signet.

Another case contained a silver service set that was donated to the battleship U.S.S. *Rhode Island* by the state's citizens in 1907. During its display outside the Senate chamber in 1977 it was stolen.

Fortunately it was recovered at a later date and continues residence in the glass case, electronically wired with an alarm.

The remainder of the capitol contains the offices related to government in which the lieutenant governor and the secretary of state play an important role.

The office of the secretary of state arranges tours of the capitol: the Governor's State Room, the State House Library, and the General Assembly's chambers. Conducted by volunteers, tours are conducted Monday through Friday, 10 A.M. to 3 P.M. The tour includes a handbook, *The Rhode Island State House,* which is given to all visitors participating in a tour.

SOUTH CAROLINA
The Palmetto State

HEIGHT: 164' FACADE: 264' DEPTH: 167'

Within 30 years of Columbus' discovery of America the Spanish were exploring South Carolina's coastline. In 1526 under the leadership of Lucas Vasquez de Ayllon, they established a settlement on Winyah Bay where de Ayllon died of fever. Without leadership the colony collapsed because of a severe winter, Indian attacks, and disease.

Another attempt at settlement almost succeeded when a group of French Huguenots landed on Parris Island in 1562. Led by Jean Ribaut they set up a colony. A few months afterwards Ribaut had to return to France where his return to the colony was delayed. Believing themselves deserted, the colonists built a boat and sailed for home. In danger of starvation, they were rescued by an English ship bound for England.

In 1629 Charles I of England granted "Carolina" to Sir Robert Heath whose title, having seen no action, was transferred to eight noblemen by King Charles II in 1663. Known as the province of Carolina, this tract comprised both Carolinas, Georgia, most of Florida and extended "from ocean to ocean." A second charter granted in 1665 limited the region to an area between the twenty-ninth and the thirty-sixth degree, thirty minutes, parallels.

Under the leadership of Captain Robert Sanford and Dr. Henry Woodward, a group landed in Carolina in 1667 to prepare the way for an English settlement.

In 1669 the Lord Proprietors retained John Locke, an English philosopher and secretary and physician to Sir Anthony Ashley Cooper (Earl of Shaftesbury), to draw up a system of government based on the feudal system. This system, modified through practice, encouraged plantations and a slave-holding aristocracy.

The first permanent settlement and seat of government was established in 1670 when English colonists landed at Albemarle Point on the west bank of the Ashley River and named their settlement Charles Town in honor of their king. In 1680 Charles Town was moved to the east bank of the Ashley River.

Carolina functioned without a government building for more than 80 years during which time its administrators used rented quarters or were invited to use friends' houses.

During this period the colonists' resentment toward the Proprietors' government grew into a revolt in which they made James Moore their governor. By 1729 King George I had been persuaded to make Carolina a royal province and, except for one, the Proprietors sold out to the king. In 1730 a preliminary boundary divided the province into North and South Carolina. (The boundary was not fixed permanently until 1815.) With this separation came a treaty with the Cherokee Indians and heavy settlement of the Piedmont Plateau, the "Up-Country," with new townships established by Germans, Irish, Scotch, French, and Welsh.

Not until 1753 is there evidence of a capitol, but in that year on June 22 a cornerstone of a statehouse was laid by Governor James Glen. After this feat members of the Council and the Assembly and "other Gentlemen who attended the Governor" each laid a brick.

When the building was near completion it was discovered part of it covered an old moat that had been built around Charles Town. Too late to change its location because of the expense, it was completed in 1755 at a cost of 59,127 English pounds sterling.

Of two stories, three-fifths of its facade held a heavy portico with a pediment supported by four columns. There were three entrance doors beneath the portico flanked by another entrance at either side. A domed cupola was centered between heavy chimneys above a hip roof.

Prosperity grew under the crown. The population increased. Plantation owners developed a cultured society and built large estates. Charles Town became the center of fashion and fine arts through schools, libraries, and theaters.

With the influx of population into the Up-Country from other areas came the desire to have representation in the government, the same that was held by the people of Charles Town and the coastal plain.

All the colonies were taxed, but resentment did not catch fire in South Carolina until the Stamp Act of 1765. It smoldered and burst into flame when Charles Town residents, continuing their resentment and protest on the Tea Tax, dumped a cargo of tea into the sea November 1, 1774. That year the Provincial Congress elected delegates to the Continental Congress.

The following year the Provincial Congress voted funds for the colony's defense and established a secret "action committee." On July 12, 1775, American Revolutionary forces seized Ft. Charlotte in McCormick County.

During 1776 the Provincial Congress adopted a temporary constitution for the province and on June 28, a British attack on Charles Town harbor was repulsed.

A second constitution was drafted and adopted by the Provincial Congress in 1778 and, following the war, Charles Town, then renamed Charleston, continued as the capital of South Carolina until Columbia was declared the permanent capital in 1786. In that action the General Assembly ordered and made arrangements for the building of a capitol in Columbia to house the government.

Although records indicated frequent requests for finances to complete it, the Charles Town statehouse served the provincial government for 33 years. It burned February 5, 1788. The fire started in the Senate room, and there was no water to quench it, so within a few hours flames reduced the building to a pile of ruins. The building was reconstructed and put into use in 1789 as Charleston County Courthouse. Extensively remodeled in later years, it continued in use as the courthouse.

In the meantime a new capitol was under construction in South Carolina's new capital, Columbia. With their action of 1786 the General Assembly ordered Columbia's commissioners to reserve eight acres for the building of the capitol and to sell 20 percent of the remaining lots to the highest bidders with bids starting at 20 pounds sterling per lot. When enough funds became available a contract was to be let to the lowest bidder for a statehouse of sufficient size and capacity to hold all the government's officers as well as others appointed in the future.

A "house for the governor" was also specified with both buildings being "on the most frugal plan, which in the opinion of the commissioners, the honor and interest of the state will admit of."

Designed by James Hoban, builder of the White House in Washington, constructed over a three-year period, the capitol was occupied on December 1789. South Carolina's General Assembly first convened in Columbia the following January.

After his visit in May 1791, President George Washington described Columbia as "an uncleared wood, with very few houses on it, and those all wooden ones." Described in his diary, the capitol was "also of wood, a large and commodious building, but unfinished."

According to Archibald Henry, writing of the president's visit, a public dinner was held for Washington on Monday, May 23. He was escorted to the House chamber and introduced to "sixty ladies who upon his entering the room rose and made an elegant appearance. The ladies were then led by the gentlemen to the Senate Room, where they sat down together in a well-conceived arrangement, to a farmer's dinner, where plenty abounded...." Sixteen toasts were drunk with enthusiasm through the course of the dinner. Afterwards, a grand ball in the Assembly Hall honored Washington from eight to eleven o'clock.

In 1802 John Drayton credited Columbia with about 80–100 dwellings and said its exciting months were November and December, during the legislative sessions, while there was calm and quiet during the remainder of the year.

Of two stories constructed of plastered brick, the capitol's first floor housed the offices of the treasurer, secretary, and surveyor general. According to Edward Hooker, a teacher at South Carolina College, writing in 1805, there were several other rooms on the first floor "used for little else than lodging rooms for the goats that run loose about the streets, and which, as the doors are never shut, have at all times, free access."

In 1845 the Assembly appropriated $10,000 for repairs and improvement. Through the years the capitol received many notable visitors, supported ceremonial celebrations, and housed religious services. During the mid-nineteenth century the state drifted from its intensive nationalist position, achieved with statehood, to disagreement, discord, and separation from the United States.

On December 20, 1860, South Carolina became the first state to secede from the Union. Through its historic period South Carolina's second capitol had three notable visitors. The first was President Washington during May 1791; the second, General Marquis de Lafayette in 1824 during his second visit to the United States. The third came in the night. On February 17, 1865, returning north after his march to the sea, General William Tecumseh Sherman and his troops burned Columbia and with it South Carolina's Capitol commonly known as the Hoban State House.

Years before it was burned, the Assembly, feeling a great need for a "Fire Proof Building" had acted to build a new capitol. P. H. Hammerskold was retained as architect and work officially started with a cornerstone setting for the first section December 15, 1851. In 1852 the Assembly appropriated $50,000 to complete it and start a second section of the "New State Capitol."

Hammerskold was dismissed from the project for "concealments and misrepresentations and general dereliction of duty" in May 1854 and on August 3, Major John R. Niernsee was elected architect.

After his survey of the structure and its materials, Niernsee reported both unsuitable and the structure was taken down. The total loss: $72,267.

Working with his design, Niernsee estimated completion of the capitol within five years. The General Assembly ordered a new location for the building with the wings extended east and west and the work was started.

Three years later (1857) the work had progressed to the top of the basement windows. On October 1, 1860, at a total expense of $1,240,063, the structure had risen 66 feet above the foot of the foundation. At the same time work on 64 Corinthian capitals of granite was being completed "in a style and finish heretofore unequalled in that line [with] nothing finer in France or Italy."

Still unfinished in 1865, work on the capitol was suspended when Sherman burned Columbia. Although little damage was done to the structure by the shells from light calibre cannons, the burning of the nearby Hoban capitol caused damage estimated at $700,000 by Niernsee. His library of architectural and scientific books, engravings, and thousands of drawings accumulated during 25 years of practice were burned. The detailed drawings and contracts made over a ten-year period were consumed by the fire. The heat destroyed statuary. It cracked church bells stored nearby and damaged the quoin-stones and the basement cornice that were closest to the fire.

South Carolina was readmitted to the Union June 26, 1868. The first governor to be elected after readmission was General Wade Hampton in 1876.

When he attempted to restore the state government to local control, the Reconstruction governor refused to surrender his authority and did not until President Rutherford B. Hayes ordered federal troops to evacuate the state in 1877.

It was not until 1885 that Niernsee returned to Columbia to resume work on the capitol, but he died June 7, 1885. He was succeeded by a former associate, J. Crawford Neilson, of Baltimore who carried on until October 1, 1888. He was replaced by Frank Niernsee, the son of the original architect, who continued, concentrating on the interior, until the project was again suspended in 1891.

In 1900 Frank P. Milburn was retained as architect. He replaced the roof, built the present dome, and constructed the north and south porticos at a cost of approximately $175,000. Senator J. Q. Marshal of the Capitol Commission, opposed to Milburn's appointment, finally brought about the investigation of the work and charges of Milburn and the contractor, McIlvain & Unkefer Company. Sued by the state, in litigation that was declared a mistrial, the case was not retried.

Milburn's dome brought some criticism, for it was much different from that planned by Niernsee. With all drawings lost except prints of a perspective view of the capitol, it was evident that the Niernsee dome would have been a lofty, finely proportioned tower rising through the center of the building, supported by piers and arches from the ground up. It was topped by a "rectangular lantern" somewhat pyramidal in outline, 30 feet square at the base, 180 feet above the ground. It was to have been built at an estimated cost of $200,000.

As a result a Legislative Joint Committee called upon Captain S. S. Hunt, the superintendent of construction in the Washington Capitol, for his opinion. The committee reported the dome to be "infamous, no uglier creation could be devised, and it is nothing short of a miserable fraud."

On April 4, 1904, Charles Coker Wilson of Columbia was retained as architect. With an expenditure of $100,000, under his direction various improvements and changes in furnishings were made in the interior. The terrace and steps on the north facade were finished and the capitol was considered complete in 1907.

The South Carolina State Capitol was constructed in the Roman Corinthian style, and used granite most of which came from the Granby quarry two miles distant. The appropriations for construction from all available records amounted to $3,540,000.

The Corinthian columns of the capitol are among the largest in the world. Cut from a single piece of stone, each stands 43 feet high and weighs about 37 tons.

Each legislative chamber maintains a symbol of authority. That of the Senate is "The Sword of State" that rests in a rack on the rostrum in front of the president's chair during the daily sessions and is carried by the sergeant at arms on all state occasions. The symbol originated in the Commons House of

Assembly of South Carolina on Friday, May 5, 1704, by virtue of an order that "$129 be paid for a Sword of State for the Rt. Hon. the Governor and all succeeding Governors for the Honr. of this Government."

The Sword of State was used by the Grand Council until the government of the Lord Proprietors was taken over by His Majesty in 1719. It is mentioned in 1722 records that it no longer be used, but be given to the City of Charles Town. On March 6, 1776, it was carried by the sheriff preceding the newly elected president of the state, John Rutledge.

Stolen in 1941, it was replaced on March 5, 1941, with a cavalry sword made in 1800. Used in the War of 1812, the sword was a gift from the Charleston Museum. It was returned to Charleston when another sword was presented to the Senate February 2, 1951. The personal gift of Lord Halifax, former British ambassador to the United States, it was made in England and fashioned by master craftsmen of London.

Twice removed and twice returned, the emblem of authority for the House of Representatives is a mace. Made in London in 1756, purchased at a cost of 90 guineas, it is of solid silver with gold burnishing. During the Revolution it was taken from the Charles Town statehouse and offered for sale to the Assembly of the Bahama Islands by British sympathizers. It was found in a Philadelphia bank vault in 1819 and returned to its owners.

During the night of February 3, 1971, it was taken from the locked glass case behind the speaker's rostrum. It was found in Gainesville, Florida, three weeks later by a chief of police and returned. It is now displayed in a vault. On the opening day of a session it is carried by the sergeant at arms, preceding the speaker, and placed on the rostrum to remain until the House is recessed or adjourned.

Visitors are welcome during business hours and tours may be arranged.

SOUTH DAKOTA
The Sunshine State

HEIGHT: 161'   FACADE: 292'   DEPTH: 190'

Claiming the largest Indian population and lowest literacy rate in the nation, South Dakota rose from a region of severe drought and hailstones.

Indisputably the first Europeans to visit the area were the sons of the French explorer Pierre La Vérendrye, Francois and Louis Joseph, in 1743. Proof is in the inscribed plate they buried that was found near Fort Pierre in 1913.

Pierre Dorion is believed to have been the first European resident of the state. Before acting as a guide for the Lewis and Clark expedition, he had settled on the Jams River. The first house is claimed to have been built by Jean Baptiste Trudeau after he set up a trading post in present-day Charles Mix County in 1794.

On their way to the Pacific coast in 1804, Lewis and Clark explored the Missouri Valley. In 1817 Joseph la Framboise, a French trader, built a trading post at present-day Pierre to become the oldest continuously settled site in the state. It flourished during the fur trade, changed ownerships, was rebuilt with name changes: Fort Tecumseh, Fort Pierre Chouteau, and Fort Pierre; and was bought by the United States in 1855.

When the Nebraska Territory was organized in 1854, South Dakota's southern boundary was fixed. When Minnesota became a state in 1858, the eastern boundary was set and the settlers started clamoring for territorial status.

A land rush resulted a year after the Yankton Sioux ceded their land to the United States in 1858; and a provisional territorial government was organized at Sioux Falls in 1859.

When the Dakota Territory was organized March 2, 1861, it included the two Dakotas and parts of Montana and Wyoming east of the Continental Divide. Dr. William Jayne, President Abraham Lincoln's physician, was named territorial governor, with Yankton the capitol. The First Territorial Legislature, known as the "Pony Congress," met there in 1862. The upper house convened in the William Tripp residence while the lower house met in the Episcopal Chapel. (The Tripp residence was removed from the site in 1893 and forgotten. Used as a granary, it was found in 1935, restored, and put into use as a museum by the Yankton D. A. R. chapter.)

Eighteen sixty-two was also the year of the War of the Outbreak in Minnesota. When Indians killed two men in a hay field near Sioux Falls its settlers were removed to Yankton by troops, after which that settlement was plundered and burned.

When the Montana territory was organized in 1864 the western boundary was formed. The discovery of gold in Montana caused an order for a road to be built up the Powder River to the mines. During the progress of its survey, Chief Red Cloud of the Sioux expressed opposition to the road. The Red Cloud War broke out and continued into 1868. The peace treaty of July 25, 1868, decreed all of the Dakota Territory west of the Missouri River was to be a Sioux reservation. The treaty was short-lived.

Claimed as the most important single event in South Dakota's history was the discovery of gold August 2, 1874, by William McKay and Horatio Ross, two prospectors who were with General George Custer on a military expedition into the Black Hills. News of the discovery spread and caused a rush into the Black Hills. One group of 28, known as the Gordon Party, left Sioux City on October 6. After three months of hardship they arrived at the site of discovery on French Creek near present-day Custer and built a stockade for protection from the Indians. Suffering through the winter, they were rescued by a military unit, put under arrest, and removed to Fort Laramie in Wyoming.

After a futile attempt to lease the land in the area from the Indians so that gold could be prospected, the military ignored the components of the treaty of 1868. Settlers poured into the area illegally and, within the year, several thousand men were in the area. Indian attacks resulted in more white–Indian uprisings. Several battles were fought including Custer's last which took place in Montana.

Starting as early as 1872, by 1877 agitation for statehood gathered force. The land boom spread more settlers over the territory. It was necessary to change the location of the capital to a more central location. Pressured, the 1882 territorial legislature appointed a commission to select a permanent site. Bismarck was chosen. In June 1882 a group of citizens met in Canton and appointed a committee to further the demands for dividing the territory. When the proposal was presented to the legislature, a bill was passed calling for a constitutional convention. It was vetoed by Governor Nehemiah Ordway.

The Executive Committee was then called for a delegate convention to be held the following June in Huron. Every county was represented. An ordinance was passed on September 4, 1883, for a constitutional convention in Sioux Falls. Submitted to the people in a November election, the constitution was unanimously adopted. Presented to Congress, it was ignored.

The next territorial legislature called for a new convention in September 1885. The constitution formed in that convention was ratified by the people and, in the same election that November, a complete slate of state officers together with a legislature and a congressman. Two United States Senators were elected from the legislature. The senators and governor petitioned Congress in person and again they were ignored. The reason: the Democratic administration of the nation was unfavorable toward four new Republican Senators to upset the majority power. They would, however, admit the whole territory as a state. Now they were ignored. Help came in 1888 when the Republican National Convention made the admission of the two states a campaign issue.

In 1889 Congress established the division of the territory in an enabling act on Valentine's Day 1889. It was approved by President Benjamin Harrison on Washington's birthday. With a need to amend and resubmit their state constitution, a convention met on the Fourth of July. In a special election on October 1, it was approved by the people.

South Dakota was admitted to the Union as the fortieth state November 2, 1889. That year marked the last of the Indian problems in the United States. Sitting Bull was killed in the Messiah War which ended December 29, 1890, with the massacre of Indians at Wounded Knee in Shannon County in the southwest corner of South Dakota.

Although the convention of 1885 had voted for Huron as the state capital, the enabling act of Congress required that a popular vote must be held to designate a temporary capital. This caused an awesome contest to be waged

After a long battle to determine what city would serve as the state capital, Pierre won. In 1905 the legislature approved a new capitol. Started in 1907, it was dedicated in 1910 and first used by the government in 1911. — Department of Tourism.

during the summer of 1889. Those towns contending for the capital were Chamberlain, Huron, Mitchell, Pierre, Sioux Falls, and Waterton. Pierre won by a large margin, but the issue was not settled.

The state constitution called for a permanent capital to be selected in the general election of 1890. Pierre and Huron were the only contestants. Pierre won again by a large margin, but the issue remained unsettled and eventually became a contest between two railroads: the Milwaukee running through Mitchell and the Chicago & North Western line which ran through Pierre.

It was agreed in the 1901 legislature that a caucus' decision would be upheld. The result: the town of Mitchell was chosen. A filibuster blocked an attempt to amend the constitution and the decision was left for the 1903 legislature. Again the caucus plan was adopted and again Mitchell was chosen. A two-year campaign between the two cities followed with each railroad giving free passes to influential citizens to visit the city it served.

Eventually both railroads gave free passes to voters to visit either of the rival cities. During the summer of 1904 more than 100,000 people were carried to Pierre and Mitchell by the two lines.

In another election Pierre won the capital by 18,000 votes and a convinced 1905 legislature provided for a permanent capitol. Pierre, as the permanent capital of South Dakota, claims the title not only by plebiscite, but by heritage as well. The same site served as the capital of the Arakara Indian Nation for more than 400 years.

South Dakota's first state capitol was built in 1889 when Pierre became the capital. It was designed by George W. Smith and constructed on land donated by the Chicago & North Western Railroad, at a cost of $20,000 paid for by the people of Pierre. It was a frame structure 50 feet in height containing two stories. It served as the capitol from 1889 to 1910 when the new, permanent capitol was completed on a site to its east.

Action for a new capitol started with the legislature passing Senate Bill 142 in 1905 in which a Capitol Building Commission was established to be responsible for the construction of a capitol. The commission consisted of the governor, secretary of state, state auditor, and the commissioner of school and public lands.

Without a design competition being held, two architects, C. E. Bell and M. S. Detweillier of Minneapolis were retained. O. H. Olsen of Stillwater, Minnesota, was contracted for construction of the capitol which was placed under the supervision of Samuel H. Lea, a state engineer.

During excavation of the basement and footings, several graves were unearthed causing great concern until it was learned that they were the graves of outlaws who had been put to rest by vigilantes during the early days. The bodies were removed, properly encased, and removed to the cemetery where they were interred.

The building's foundation, constructed of South Dakota boulder granite, was laid during 1905, and the construction above the foundation started in May 1907. The cornerstone was laid June 25, 1908, with appropriate ceremonies.

On June 30, 1910, the South Dakota State Capitol was dedicated. Built in a modified Greek-Ionic design reminding one of the nation's Capitol, its lower area is constructed of Marquette (Michigan) raindrop sandstone above which the walls are of Bedford (Indiana) limestone. Ortenville (Minnesota) granite is used in the front steps and door casings. Rising four stories above the basement's granite walls, surmounted with a solid copper dome, it was completed in 1910 and occupied in 1911 at a cost of $944,000 including the artwork and furnishings.

Fronting the main entrance, rising out of a circular walkway, a tall standard presents the flags of the United States and South Dakota. Beyond the flag pole, a broad stairway with heavy balustrades leads into a massive two-story portico. There are three double-entry doors.

From the entrance a broad, marble staircase rises to the main floor rotunda from which a corridor runs east and west to the end of each wing. High above the rotunda floor, rising 96 feet to the dome, Victorian leaded, stained glass panels admit a colorful congestion of sunlight. Sixty-three feet beyond is the weather-blackened outer dome made of 20 tons of copper.

In the pendentives are the paintings of four goddesses with the seal of the sovereignty which ruled the land under each. Ceres depicts agriculture (United

States); Europa and Zeus depict livestock (France); Minerva, wisdom, industry, and mining (Spain); and Venus and Cupid, love of the family and love of the state (South Dakota). They are the work of Edward Simmons.

On the second floor the west wing corridor contains portraits of former governors and is known as the Governor's Gallery. Each new governor has the right to commission an artist to do his portrait and when his term is ended, it is hung in the gallery.

Entered from that corridor, the Governor's Reception Room displays mythology and symbolism on the walls and ceilings. The furniture is mahogany. When the signing of special proclamations is in order, they are signed by the governor at the desk in this room. Decorated in red and green with plaster relief, one walls contains "Spirit of the People," a painting by Edwin Blashfield.

The Supreme Court Room was recently restored to its original gold and brown colors. Its walls are panelled with cherry wood. During restoration eight layers of paint were scraped away to reveal the design on the walls. Its decorations and furniture are of mahogany. Acanthus leaves, the sign of wisdom, decorate the arms of its chairs. Five judges preside over the court, in session September through May. On the wall behind them is a Charles Holloway painting, "Mercy of the Law," which shows Mercy guarding over the law process.

The grand staircase of Tennessee white marble leads to the third floor and the legislative chambers. At the top of the stairs in the lunette above the doorway is Edward Simmons' painting "The Advent of Commerce" showing barter in the fur trade in early history.

The Senate chamber in the west wing, designed in horseshoe shape, contains 35 antique roll-top mahogany desks, one for each senator. Fully restored, all the woodwork and furniture are mahogany. The chamber is surrounded with scagliola pillars. The dominating color is a pastel green with elaborate stenciling all of which is highlighted with brass fixtures throughout. Over the Senate chamber Charles Holloway's mural "The Louisiana Purchase" is symbolic of President Thomas Jefferson's transaction with France.

Also created by Holloway is the largest mural in the capitol, "The Peace That Passes Understanding," symbolizing the first prayer given in the state.

The House chamber occupies the east wing. Its 70 members sit at antique roll-top desks in an earth tones environment decorated with stenciling, oak wood, and gold-colored chandeliers bearing white globed lights. At their head is the Speaker of the House. On the wall behind his chair is a painting of a proud eagle. It was uncovered during the restoration by a worker from Pierre.

The visitors' gallery in the Senate and House chambers are reached from the fourth floor.

Like all state governments, that of South Dakota increased to the extent that an annex was added to the north-facing side of the capitol during the 1930s.

Today the main capitol complex consists of 16 buildings, 115 acres of property including a five-acre lake, 48 acres of cultured grass, 3,000 trees, and more than 8,000 flowers. During 1988, 60 people were employed to care for and maintain the buildings and grounds at a cost to the state of $3.2 million.

The replacement cost of the capitol is $53 million. It was listed as a National Historical Place September 1, 1976.

The historically accurate restoration of the capitol, started during 1975, was completed in 1989 to commemorate South Dakota's Centennial Statehood Celebration. The design and color schemes were recreated. The woodwork was refinished. The solid brass chandeliers in the original were duplicated. Exact copies were made of missing items. All paintings were cleaned and preserved. Repairs were made to the terrazzo tile and marble. The mortar joints of the exterior stones were filled with a narrow ridge of fine lime mortar, and the exterior was sandblasted.

On Wednesday, June 14, 1989, in the capitol rotunda where they may be seen today, four prodigious works were dedicated. These statues, created by sculptor Dale Claude Lamphere, represent wisdom, vision, integrity, and courage. In the same order, the first, a mother/teacher extends her hand to little ones offering them the world beyond. The second: The pursuit of vision is a constant process, sometimes fearful which requires courage. The third represents the careful, constant and visible declaration of our intent to honor our ideal; and the fourth is the wonderful gift of moral strength to venture, preserve, and withstand difficulty.

The capitol is open from 7 A.M. to 11 P.M. daily. The visitor information center and security station are located on the first floor at the north entrance. Tours are given at 9 A.M. and 10 A.M. and 1 P.M. and 3 P.M. Monday through Friday. Large groups should make appointments in advance. During the legislative sessions group tours must be scheduled in advance.

The Robinson State Museum, across the street from the capitol, is open to visitors from 8 A.M. to 5 P.M., Monday through Friday; Saturday from 10 A.M. to 5 P.M.; and Sunday, 1 to 5 P.M.

TENNESSEE
The Volunteer State

HEIGHT: 198'   FACADE: 239' 3"   DEPTH: 112'

When the first Europeans explored what is now Tennessee they found the Chickasaw Indians in the west, the Cherokee in the east and the Creek and

Chickamauga Indians in the south. Tennessee was a part of Louisiana, the territory La Salle named for his king and claimed for France.

The Tennessee area was included in that land granted to Sir Walter Raleigh in 1584 by Elizabeth I, the charters to the Virginia Company by King James I in 1606, and to the Carolina Company by Charles II in 1665.

In 1763 James Needham and Gabriel Arthur explored the eastern part of Tennessee for the Virginia Company. That same year Louis Joliet and Father Jacques Marquette came from Quebec and, by the way of Lake Michigan, ascended the Fox River, portaged to the Wisconsin River, followed it to the Mississippi, which they entered June 17, 1673, and followed it as far as the Arkansas River. They were the first white men to see and be on the Mississippi since its discovery by DeSoto in 1541 near the present site of Memphis. They visited with Indians near the same site.

In 1682 René-Robert Cavelier, Sieur de La Salle followed the Illinois and Mississippi rivers to the Gulf of Mexico exploring the land. He built Fort Prud'homme at the mouth of the Hatchie River about thirty miles above Memphis.

In the years following, a French trading post was established near present-day Nashville (1714), a group of Virginians explored eastern Tennessee to the Cumberland River and Mountains (1750), and South Carolinians built Fort Loudon on the Little Tennessee River, 30 miles north of present-day Knoxville (1757). Three years later Cherokee Indians captured Fort Loudon, killing its occupants and the settlers nearby.

In 1763 France surrendered to England all claims to the land east of the Mississippi; and the Iroquois Indians ceded all their claims in Tennessee to the English in 1768. The first permanent white settler, William Bean, built a cabin near the Watauga River in 1769. The first permanent settlement was started in the northeastern corner of Tennessee on the Watauga River. Settlers from Virginia and the Carolinas poured into the Holston Valley and a second settlement formed in 1771 on the Holston River near present-day Rogersville.

Led by John Sevier and James Robertson, residents of the two settlements met in a general convention in 1772, created by the Watauga Association, and adopted a plan of self-government. A third settlement, started on the Nolichucky River, joined the Watauga Association.

In 1775 the Transylvania Company was formed by a few North Carolinians. They bought the Cherokee land and resold it to the occupants, and the Watauga Association became the Washington District.

When the American Revolution started, they requested and received annexation to North Carolina and became Washington County in 1777, with its boundaries those of present-day Tennessee. The first town chartered was Jonesboro. It was named the seat of Washington County in 1779. That year the Transylvania Company founded Nashville.

During the war the troops of Washington County, led by Sevier and Isaac Shelby, were instrumental in the crushing defeat of the Loyalists at Kings Mountain.

With the menace of Indians and Spanish at hand after the war, when North Carolina ceded Washington County to the federal government in 1784, the settlers were so angered they met at Jonesboro and organized the State of Franklin with John Sevier as its governor. The new state was ignored by both Congress and North Carolina and, in 1788 when North Carolina revoked its act to cede the land, Franklin went out of business.

In 1790, when North Carolina again ceded the land to the United States, Congress organized the "Territory South of the River Ohio." Rogersville was named the capital and William Blount, governor. In 1792 Knoxville was named the capital. In 1796 Tennessee was admitted to the Union as the sixteenth state with its capital at Knoxville. Its first governor was John Sevier.

Knoxville remained the capital city until 1812 when an act of the legislature moved it to Nashville. There it remained until 1817 when lawmakers decided to move back to Knoxville. With two cities determined to gain the pleasures of the capital, another town entered the contest and the government moved to Murfreesboro in 1819. Much argument and arm-twisting ensued and finally the capital was returned to Nashville in 1825.

Through all its years of statehood Tennessee's government had functioned in various quarters including school buildings, log cabins, and frame-constructed homes. While in Murfreesboro they were allowed the comforts of a church building. Back in Nashville they eventually had the use of the Davidson County Courthouse.

Incorporated since 1806, Nashville had a mayor who, with his aldermen, bought a piece of land with the idea of giving it to the state for a capitol site. Their gift and the decree made in the constitutional convention of 1834 that a permanent seat of government be fixed in 1843 did the trick. The city of Nashville, awakened to the battle, gave the state a hilltop on which they could build a capitol. In a plebiscite October 1943 Nashville won the distinction of becoming the permanent capital of Tennessee.

On January 30, 1844, the Tennessee legislature acted to create a board of commissioners to start and oversee the construction of a capitol and authorized an appropriation of $10,000, stipulating that convict labor was to be used in the construction.

A six-member board was appointed with former governor William Carroll as chairman. Their first meetings were to decide which quarry would supply the building stone and Samuel Watkin's was leased in January 1845 for three years at $500 per year.

As the quarries were being investigated, a search for an architect was underway. Without money to finance a design contest, the commissioners made inquiries through which they came across an offer from a Phildelphia architect, William Strickland, who was "willing to furnish a plan and superintend the erection of the State House at a salary of $2,500 per annum."

Several other architects had been recommended and advanced offers, but on April 2, 1845, Strickland was asked to come to Nashville, survey the site, and submit a design. The architect was there before the end of the month working on a per diem basis. He was given the job May 20 and contracted to be the architect of the capitol June 18, 1845.

Because Nashville's donated lot was too small, additional land was purchased for $42,150, but before excavation could begin, buildings had to be sold and removed from the site.

A. G. Payne was contracted for the excavation and ground was broken in June 1845. The cornerstone ceremony of July 4, 1845, attended by thousands, was unequalled in the history of that city.

Throughout the entire period of construction numerous problems interrupted the work, the chief being lack of finances. Another appropriation of $32,000 in January 1846 was to be divided equally for that year and 1847. In January 1848 another act appropriated $50,000 for that year and a like sum for 1849. The capitol was being built on a "pay as you go" basis without any rise in taxes. At times the commissioners had to rely upon the next appropriation to pay the bills.

Labor was another deterrent. A public meeting was held to protest the use of convict labor as unfair to the local laborers who "wished to work on the Capitol." Despite their protest both the commissioners and the legislature remained unmoved, knowing that convict labor was imperative to the economy of construction. Within a few days an act was passed allowing for the use of 120 convicts.

During 1846 the commissioners contracted with Payne to furnish 15 able-bodied Negro men at $18 per month, and their overseer at $30 per month. The commissioners would supply housing. Payne would furnish board for them at that price. If others were hired he would board them for a dollar per week.

Skilled stonecutters and setters were also needed and when they complained they didn't have enough work to keep them busy, 30 Negroes were added to the quarry's work force. By October 1849 there were 233 men working on the capitol. During the summers of 1849 and 1850 cholera struck Nashville and almost stopped the work.

Work was interrupted momentarily with a threatened strike by the Stonecutters Association when a group asked that they be given a written guarantee of employment through March 1, 1855. It was rejected without a strike. Two months later they returned with a request for a twenty-five cents per day raise, which was granted.

Nature as well supplied problems with construction when on March 12, 1855, a tornado struck Nashville and tore a sizable quantity of copper sheeting from the roof. Disaster struck again March 29 in a fire that destroyed the stonecutters' shops with all their tools. Had it not been for the fire, all the stonework would have been completed that year.

Disenchanted with the progress of construction one year, the legislature created a committee to investigate the use of funds. Following the investigation it was reported the funds were being spent wisely, honestly, and without waste. On February 28, 1853, the legislature passed a resolution requiring the commissioners "to fit up and furnish in a suitable manner the legislative halls and other rooms" needed for the next meeting of the General Assembly and on October 3, 1853, the legislature convened in the Tennessee capitol.

William Strickland died on April 7, 1854. Only a few weeks prior to his death the legislature set aside a vault in the basement for the architect of the capitol "in honor of his genius in erecting so grand a work." The vault was a space hewn out of solid stone on the east facade on the first floor. The day following his death a large group escorted his body from his home to the capitol. His funeral was held in the Hall of Representatives with more than 2,000 people in attendance. The commissioners paid his funeral expenses and his widow was paid his salary withheld due to absence from his office.

Strickland was replaced by his eldest son, Francis. The previous January the elder Strickland had petitioned the legislature for a salary of $80 a month for his son who had been working unpaid as a draftsman and general assistant to his father since 1849. His request was refused. It is believed this issue started strained relations between the commissioners and the architect. Pressed for time, the commissioners appointed Francis as architect on June 3, 1854, realizing his knowledge of the building would allow him to carry on the work of his father. He was paid $100 a month.

Work continued as before with each specific area of construction — the plastering of walls, the frescoed work, the construction of stairs, selection of interior marble — all components of what would become their desired creation — being contracted out by the commissioners.

To save the salary he was being paid, believing they could get along without an architect, the commissioners informed Francis Strickland during March 1857 that he would no longer be needed after May 1.

They got along without an architect until a design for the library was needed. H. M. Akeroyd, an English architect practicing in Nashville for 15 years, submitted a plan on December 4, 1858. It was adopted. A Library Board was appointed. The board appointed Akeroyd who was to design and do whatever the board requested in finishing up the library in one contract at $500; and design and finish the interior work of the entire capitol in a second contract at $500.

The capitol was completed in December 1859 with the total cost of construction $879,981.48, but the work was not finished. After a year of rest the commissioners met on May 1, 1860, to discuss the exterior landscaping inasmuch as the grounds "are in a most chaotic state, a mere mass of huge broken rocks, together with various dilapidated out houses, altogether a disgrace to the State and city." Prompted by R. J. Meigs' description in the city directory, the legislature acted to provide $100,000 for "improvement of the site."

A civil engineer was hired to make a topographical survey, provide a contour map, and estimate the grading and fill required. A countrywide search for a landscape architect was finally rewarded with William Pritchard of Nashville selected to submit a plan which was adopted after several dissenting votes amended parts of the plan.

All work was ordered stopped by the legislature during the spring of 1861.

The stone for the walls had been delivered. Piled in the streets awaiting the masons, it would remain there for years because of the start of the Civil War.

"The Great Panic" came on Sunday, February 16, 1861. On that day most of Nashville's population fled the city in fear of the approaching Union Army. The governor and the government moved to Memphis. The Confederate Army left also. Two weeks after "The Great Panic" 10,000 Union soldiers entered the city and took the capitol without opposition.

From that day until July 1, 1865, the capitol was in the hands of the Union Army, serving in many ways. During the Battle of Nashville, December 15 and 16, 1864, it was an observation point.

Regained, little repair was necessary other than what might have been required over a five-year maintenance period. A repair survey in April 1866 revealed that the most costly item was $350 for the varnishing and repair of all window frames.

During the 1870s the grounds were landscaped and from that period until 1902, various repairs were made by way of pure maintenance. During the 1901–1902 period the exterior was cleaned and a preservative applied. Paving work was redone on the terraces and porticos. The esplanade walls were refaced with new stonework. New floors of marble and mosaic were laid in the vestibules. Tin replaced the copper roof.

During the 1920s space was so crowded that several buildings had to be rented in the downtown area. Plans were advanced for annexes to the capitol, but dropped.

Completed as it now stands the capitol contains four stories: ground, first, second, and third floors. Doric, Ionic, and Corinthian values are meshed into a Greek Revival design.

Its exterior of Tennessee limestone from the Nashville quarry was laid up in blocks weighing as much as ten tons. The facade measures 239 feet; the depth of the building is 112 feet. It contains 39,909 square feet of usable floor space.

Its cupola, "a slightly modified replica of the Choragic Monument of Lysicrates in Athens," rises above the facade's central portico. Its rectangular base is surmounted by a circular drum or lantern with a colonnade of Corinthian pillars supporting a crown above which rises another structure to give the capitol a height of 198 feet.

The building's exterior, especially the heavy porticos and pediments at either end, resemble Jefferson's Virginia Capitol. It has four Ionic porticos, one on each side.

Inside the building, marble stairways rise from the main (first) floor to the Senate and House chambers on the second floor. The smaller Senate chamber has 12-foot galleries on three sides. These are supported by 12 columns of Tennessee marble.

Surrounding the House chamber, which measures 70 by 100 feet, 16 columns support the ceiling. The State Library and Transverse Hall are also on the second floor.

Because of population growth and crowding, a complex of government buildings gradually rose above the grounds surrounding the capitol to the point that during 1988 the cost of maintaining the buildings and grounds with ten employees was $503,327.65.

Almost 100 years after completion in 1956, extensive repairs of the exterior were needed. Indiana limestone was used to replace columns, pediments, and cornices; and the terrace and steps were rebuilt. New windows were installed. The leaking tin roof was replaced with a new copper roof.

Later in that decade the interior received a going over. The ground floor was enlarged by excavation to supply additional office space and committee rooms. Elevators were added, floors were strengthened and replaced, and ceilings restored.

When James A. Hoobler, executive director of the Tennessee Historical Society, brought the disrepair of the capitol to the attention of the secretary of state, a work project was started during 1984 to repair a leaky roof and some of the stonework on the exterior.

The following year Governor Lamar Alexander ordered a Capitol Restoration Commission which was established in 1986 by the legislature and empowered to "oversee the study of the needs of the building, and to recommend ways of addressing those needs."

In 1986 the former State Library and Archives Chamber was restored and first viewed January 1987. All the work had to be accomplished between sessions of the legislature. The ground floor or basement (now known as the first floor) has been completely refurbished and or restored. The former Supreme Court Chamber was rebuilt. Much of the art work was cleaned, especially in the governor's reception room. This work was completed during 1988. The House and Senate chambers will have been restored; and the goal of complete restoration will have been accomplished before Tennessee's Statehood Bicentennial in 1996.

On July 8, 1970, the Tennessee Capitol was accepted and listed as a National Historic Place to which visitors are always welcome. The capitol is open daily from 9 A.M. to 4 P.M. Tours are scheduled in advance.

The Tennessee State Museum has collected and preserved countless artifacts of historical and material culture of the state and presents these in continuously changing displays for the enrichment of those who visit.

There is assistance for the handicapped and group tours can be arranged in advance.

The museum's exhibits are displayed on three levels in six distinct sections: First Tennesseans, the Frontier, the Age of Jackson, the Antebellum, Civil War and Reconstruction, and the New South. A seventh, the Twentieth Century, opened during the 1990s. A museum store on the upper level has a variety of unique gifts and handmade Tennessee crafts.

The Museum's Military Branch (across the street in the War Memorial Building) contains exhibits of Tennessee's involvement in America's foreign wars.

Admission to the museum and capitol is free, but donations toward its maintenance are appreciated. Hours are 10 A.M. to 5 P.M., Monday through Saturday; 1 to 5 P.M. on Sunday.

TEXAS
The Lone Star State

HEIGHT: 310'   FACADE: 566' 6"   DEPTH: 228' 10"

In the year 1520 an expedition formed by Francisco Garay left Mexico and headed toward what is now Texas. It reached the Rio Grande River in 1523. Because of their treatment by those who explored their lands, the Indians along the Rio Grande prevented further exploration.

One of the earliest Europeans to set foot in that area was Álvar Núñez Cabeza de Vaca who was shipwrecked on an island outside Matagorda Bay in 1528. The 80 survivors, reduced to 15 by disease and starvation, became prisoners of the Indians. Cabeza de Vaca eventually escaped in 1530, but remained in the vicinity to persuade others to leave the Indians and join him to find a Spanish settlement.

Finally, in 1534, joined by two Spaniards and a black slave, he started west and, with support from Indian villages along the way, crossed the Rio Grande above the Pecos River and at last arrived in Mexico City where he met Cortez July 23, 1536.

Except for Coronado's wanderings across the panhandle after the Seven Cities of Cibola and a few trivial expeditions during more than a century, the area was without name and boundaries for more than 200 years after discovery.

After Franciscan fathers founded Guadalupe Mission near present-day El Paso in 1659, settlement came to the area when settlers fled from New Mexico during the Indian revolt in 1680. Thus the area became part of Mexico.

In 1685, after he was unable to find the mouth of the Mississippi where he intended to establish a French colony, La Salle entered Matagorda Bay and built Fort St. Louis which was destroyed by Indians in 1687. His encroachment brought the building of more missions in the eastern part of the region among the Tejas Indians after whom it was named.

More than 25 missions and presidios were established by the Spanish during the nineteenth century, but they had little effect upon the Indians. Under 150 years of Spanish rule, the population was centered in Goliad, San Antonio, and Nacogdoches.

In 1718 Mission San Antonio de Valero (the Alamo) and the presidio San Antonio de Bexar were founded on the site presently occupied by San Antonio. Within four years the presidio Los Adaes was established by Marquis de Aguayo at what is now Robeline, Louisiana. The presidio served as the capital of Spanish Texas until 1772 when it was moved to San Antonio. A province of New Spain since 1723, San Antonio remained the capital during the latter years of Spanish rule and throughout Mexico's rule.

The United States considered east Texas a part of its Louisiana Purchase of 1803, but Spain refused its claim. When an expedition of Americans led by Bernardo Gutierrez and Augustus Magee entered and took over San Antonio in 1812, they were driven out by the Spaniards the following year. With its claim finally recognized, Spain was awarded undisputed control of Texas in the Adams-Onus Treaty of 1819–1821. The American immigration continued.

In 1821 Moses Austin received Spain's permission to settle 300 families in Texas. Upon his death that year, his son Stephen Fuller Austin brought the first families into the lower Brazos country, then under Mexico's rule, in December. By 1823, under the flag of Mexico, San Felipe de Austin had become the capital and, with friendly Mexico granting land to the American settlers, the population expanded.

As immigration increased, Mexico became unhappy and showed resentment in 1826 when a group of Americans formed the Republic of Fredonia in Nacogdoches. By 1830, with the population having grown to 25,000, further immigration was forbidden. Disputes increased between Mexican authorities and the Americans and when Santa Anna established a dictatorship in Mexico the Americans in Texas revolted.

After Mexican troops under Santa Anna stormed the rebuilt mission, the Alamo in San Antonio, February 23, 1836, killing its defenders, a group met in Washington on the Brazos on March 2 and declared independence from Mexico. Using the Constitution of the United States as a model, they framed one for the Republic of Texas. Later that month more than 300 Texans, held prisoners by the Mexicans, were massacred at Goliad.

Still later that same month, when General Sam Houston defeated Santa Anna in the Battle of San Jacinto near the city now bearing his name, Texas won independence. For ten years Texas was recognized as a republic by the United States and foreign nations.

During those troublesome years Columbia was the capital of the republic in 1836; Houston from 1837 to 1839; Austin from 1839 to 1842; and Washington on the Brazos, 1842–1845. Finally, after a bitter struggle over slavery, Congress admitted Texas to the Union as the 28th state December 29, 1845. Austin was named the permanent capital and J. P. Henderson the governor.

The first Texas state legislature met in Austin February 16, 1846, and declared the Republic of Texas abolished.

In the Treaty of Guadalupe-Hidalgo (1848) when Mexico ceded to the United States the territory east of the Rio Grande River, Texas claimed the land which they held in dispute until 1850 when, deeply in debt, they accepted the

$10 million Congress paid for the 100,000 square miles included in the states of New Mexico, Oklahoma, Colorado, Kansas, and Wyoming.

Despite Sam Houston's struggle to keep it in the Union, when the Civil War came Texas seceded to join the Confederacy. After Lee had surrendered at Appomattox, the final battle of the Civil War was fought at Palmito Hill near Brownsville, Texas, May 12 and 13, 1865.

While a republic, Texas didn't need nor could it afford a capitol of magnificence built on a grand scale. Three years after declaring itself a republic, a special commission was appointed to locate a site for the capital. They chose a site on the Colorado River, platted the City of Austin and reserved in its center and on the highest ground a "Capitol Square" upon which the first Texas State Capitol was built.

Built in 1839, the capitol, according to an 1846 newswriter, "is a one story wooden building, made somewhat roughly inside and out, over 100 feet long, and 50 wide. . . . So far as comfort is concerned, no one suffers; and the Texians had no idea of *lavishing* money upon things to look at, just yet."

After paying their debts with the money received in the land payoff, which amount was raised to $12,750,000 with interest, the legislature set aside $125,000 for a new capitol and furnishings and created a Capitol Commission to take charge of its building. A design competition was held and its entries rejected by the Commission after "borrowing" from each for their own plans. The final design is attributed to a local builder, John Brandon.

The Commission contracted with O. J. Nichols for the stone work and Abner H. Cook for the woodwork. Begun in 1852 and completed in 1853, it was constructed in the Greek Revival style. It was an impressive structure with exterior walls of a soft yellow limestone. Three stories in height, the rusticated stones of the lower story stood out in appearance while the walls of the upper stories were smooth. Texans took pride in their new building and were supported by news articles and comments from various dignitaries traveling through the state.

With a facade of 145 feet and a depth of 90 feet, the capitol was entered through a monumental portico from a wide flight of steps. The first floor was occupied by the state's officers, the second by the legislative chambers, and the third by the library and museum.

But by 1870, with the lack of money and maintenance through the Civil War, the building had fallen into a state of disrepair. The legislature hesitated to make appropriations because the 1869 Constitution of Texas required another election for a permanent seat for the state government. An election in 1872 determined that the people of Texas wished to keep their capital at Austin.

Strengthened and composed, in 1875 the legislature set aside 3 million acres of land in the panhandle to pay for a new capitol and, in 1879 enacted legislation setting aside another 50,000 acres to pay for surveying that land. In addition, to administer its construction, a five-man Capitol Board was created, consisting of the governor, treasurer, comptroller, attorney general, and commissioner of the Land Office. This board appointed a building superintendent and two commissioners to select an architect for its design.

By this time the capitol's crowded condition had brought about the appropriations and construction of buildings for the Supreme Court, the General Land Office, and the Treasury Department.

When the outgrown, unwanted capitol was destroyed by fire on November 19, 1881, caused by a faulty stovepipe installation, a number of news articles declared it was a good thing, that the building had become obsolete and was no longer needed. Demands for a new capitol swept through the Senate which met in the Armory and in the House that met in Millett's Opera House.

Soon after its loss an Austin architect, Frederick E. Ruffini, was commissioned to design a temporary capitol to be built at the foot of Capitol Hill. Dedicated January 1, 1883, it was designed in Italianate style with a cut stone facade and had three stories, with the first floor being occupied by the executive, the second by the legislative, and the third by the judiciary departments of government while the new capitol was under construction. When the state government vacated this building the Austin public schools used it until it burned in 1899.

After they appointed the design committee, the Capitol Board retained an Austin architect, Jasper N. Preston, to superintend its construction. Preston was instrumental in writing the notice for the design competition advertised nationwide offering a $1,700 prize to the winner. Eleven anonymous designs and sets of plans by eight architects were entered and, unable to determine the best, the Board brought architect Napoleon Le Brun from New York to make the decision and offer suggestions at a cost of $3,000 plus expenses.

Le Brun chose the design of Elijah E. Myers of Detroit, the builder of the Michigan State Capitol. His plans were made available to bidders on July 1, 1881, with the understanding that payment for construction would be made in land. Two contractors offered bids and the one bidding the smaller acreage, Mattheas Schnell of Rock Island, Illinois, was awarded the contract January 1, 1882.

Afterwards, Schnell assigned his interest to Taylor, Babcock & Co. who assigned their interest to Abner Taylor. Ground was broken and the work started in 1882. The "in the rough" eight-ton cornerstone was set March 2, 1885.

Countless problems, great and small, surfaced throughout construction with the greatest dispute being over the selection of stone for the exterior. When the use of Bedford limestone from Indiana was recommended, the Texans were outraged. Domestic materials must be used. The owners of Granite Mountain at Marble Falls in Burnet County solved the problem by offering the state its Texas pink granite free of charge.

Of course, the press was consistent in enlarging, promoting, and helping to solve problems. Despite difficulties the capitol was completed, but not until after the architect, argumentative Elijah Myers, was dismissed.

On May 16, 1888, the people of Texas received from the contractor their magnificent capitol. Decked in bunting, Austin came alive with civic and military demonstrations. Parades, fireworks, marching bands, pomp and pageantry were the theme and order of the day before and after the capitol was dedicated by the Masonic Grand Lodge.

Occupied in September at a cost of 3 million acres, the Texas State Capitol covers three acres of ground and contains eight and one-half acres of floor space. Its exterior walls contain 15,000 carloads of Texas pink granite, hauled by ox teams and on a specially built railroad from Marble Falls 50 miles away. Its interior and dome walls are of Texas limestone highlighted with seven miles of wainscoting in oak, pine, cherry, cedar, ash, mahogany, and walnut.

The 85,000 square feet in the roof are clad with copper. The remaining original floors are hand-blocked clay tile, glass, and wood. During the 1930s terrazzo was laid in the halls and rotunda with all colors of domestic material except the blue in the United States Seal which was imported from Italy.

With the exception of cherry used in the governor's office, the wood in the doors and window frames is oak and pine.

Classic in design, in the shape of a Grecian cross, the capitol's facade, including the steps, measures 585 feet, 10 inches. The front to rear depth at center, including steps is 299 feet, 10 inches. The height from the basement floor to the top of the 16-foot Goddess of Liberty statue atop the dome is 309 feet, 8 inches.

The first floor is reached through the south (main) entrance foyer. Its terrazzo floor depicts the 12 significant battles fought on Texas soil. Paintings on the walls by Austin artist W. H. Huddle portray the surrender of Santa Anna after the Battle of San Jacinto (left wall) and Davy Crockett (right wall). On each side, entering the rotunda, are marble statues of Stephen F. Austin, Father of Texas, and Sam Houston, the army's commander-in-chief during the Texas Revolution. Both are the work of Texas sculptress Elisabet Ney. A copy of the Texas Declaration of Independence of March 2, 1836, is on the right and opposite is a copy of the Ordinance of Secession of February 1, 1861.

The circular rotunda occupies the center of the capitol. It rises four stories from the floor to the dome. Its walls, on each floor surrounding it, carry the portraits of the five presidents of the republic and the governors that served Texas. Occupying a pedestal on the first floor is a bust of Miriam A. Ferguson, the only woman governor of Texas.

Centered in the rotunda floor is a composite terrazzo design, Seals of the Nations. The Seal of the Republic of Texas forms the center and spaced around it are the Great Seal of the United States, Seal of the Confederacy, and the Seals of Mexico, France, and Spain; the five nations of which Texas is and was a part.

In the governor's reception room in the south wing on the second floor, displayed in a glass case, are the "Six Flags of Texas" that have flown over the state. The governor's office and those of his staff are also on this floor with the legislative chambers.

The Senate chamber in the east wing, known as the Hall of Deliberation,

seats 31 Senators over which the lieutenant governor presides. Two giant scenes
are portrayed to the right and left of the entrance. The work of H. A. McArdle,
his research and work required 40 years of his life and portray "The Battle of
San Jacinto" and "Dawn at the Alamo."

The House chamber in the west wing contains 150 Representatives when
in session. The bills under consideration are read from a podium in front of
the Speaker's desk. Behind the rostrum the original battle flag of the Battle
of San Jacinto is enshrined. A press box is to the left of the rostrum.

The Legislative Reference Library occupies the north wing of the second
floor. It contains all the House and Senate journals from 1900 to date,
newspaper clippings from 1920, and microfilm of the major Texas newspapers
one of which dates back to 1880. It is open to the public as are the chambers'
balconies.

On the third floor, the respective balconies are reached from the rotunda.
The walls surrounding each balcony are adorned with pictures of past members
of that chamber. The north wing contains a display of photos of the capitol's
construction; antique tools; samples of stone, masonry, plaster molds, and
details of the elaborate hand-carved woodwork.

The executive and legislative branches of state government as well as their
support services are housed in the capitol which is surrounded by 16 other
buildings in a Capitol Complex containing government departments.

The landscaped grounds contain 13 statues and memorials portraying and
depicting heroic mementos in Texas history.

Every day during legislative sessions the Texas State Capitol is open 24
hours. A tourist information center in the south foyer is open daily from 8 A.M.
to 5 P.M. The governor's reception room is open Monday through Friday, 8
A.M. to noon and 1 to 5 P.M. Free guided tours are offered from 8:30 A.M. to
4:30 P.M.

Other buildings in the Capitol Complex are open at various times through
the week: the Governor's Mansion, the Texas Archives and Library, and the
Old Land Office Museum.

Public parking in the complex is limited, but there is a two-hour, free
parking lot for visitors in the 1500 block on Congress Avenue, north of the
capitol.

In 1983 a fire destroyed furnishings and damaged rooms behind the
Senate chamber. Following the fire, the legislature created a State Preservation
Board to "preserve, maintain, and restore the State Capitol." To assist, a seven-
member advisory committee was created. The Board was authorized to retain
a capitol architect and devise a 20-year master plan for the maintenance,
preservation, restoration, and modification of the capitol.

In 1986 it was designated a National Historic Landmark.

UNITED STATES

HEIGHT: 287' 5.5"   FACADE: 751' 4"   DEPTH: 350"

Two factors contributed to the founding and creation of the nation that has become known as the United States of America. The first is the rich natural resources of the land. The second and most important is the people who came mostly from Europe to populate the land and put to use its natural resources. It started with discovery, continued with exploration, led to exploitation, and stabilized with settlement.

Leaving Europe because of conditions there, or to fulfill their royalty's desire to increase fortunes or claim holdings by settling far-off lands, the people came from England, Scotland, Ireland, Holland, Sweden, and Germany and grouped in settlements along the Atlantic seaboard.

Within 125 years after the colony of Virginia was founded in 1607, England had 13 colonies. Those settled under her control were Connecticut, Georgia, Maryland, Massachusetts, New Hampshire, North Carolina, Pennsylvania, Rhode Island, South Carolina, and Virginia. Those acquired by England from other nations were Delaware, New Jersey, and New York.

The migration to the new land, originally forced by freedom to worship, became a desire to escape restraints imposed by their homelands. With no relief after colonization, that desire turned into bitterness because of restriction in commerce and boundary expansion. Usurped and restricted by English rule, the colonies united, declared independence, turned against their landlord, and fought the American Revolution.

One major act of resistance came with the Boston Tea Party when colonists, disguised as Indians, dumped a valuable cargo of British East India Company tea into Boston's harbor.

This action was countered by Parliament's five "intolerable acts" of 1774. The first closed the Boston harbor until the tea was paid for; the second took from Massachusetts certain rights of self-government that had been enjoyed since 1691; the third: when accused of crimes, British officials could be returned to England for trial; the fourth allowed Britain's soldiers to be quartered in Boston taverns and unoccupied buildings; and the fifth extended boundaries of the province to give Roman Catholics freedom of religion with protection under French and English laws.

Those acts, together with Parliament's tax laws, were denounced by the First Continental Congress meeting in Carpenter's Hall in Philadelphia September 7, 1774. It was there that Patrick Henry of Virginia claimed to be "not a Virginian, but an *American!*"

The delegates signed a Continental Association agreement intended to stop all trade with England if they didn't accept the denunciation; but England enforced the acts with a military governor and troops. Their rebuttal aroused anger and set rebellion in motion.

In a revolutionary convention called in Virgina the following year, Patrick Henry strengthened the cause for revolution on March 23, 1775, when he proclaimed:

> Gentlemen may cry peace! peace! But there is no peace! The war is actually begun! The next gale that sweeps from the North will bring to our ears the clash of resounding arms! Our brethren are already in the field. Is life so dear, or peace so sweet as to be purchased at the price of chains and slavery? Forbid it, Almighty God! I know not what course others may take; but as for me, give me liberty, or give me death.

On the night of April 18 Paul Revere and William Dawes rode through the country alerting patriots that the "British are coming!" Eight hundred British troops were on their way to Lexington, Massachusetts, to arrest insurgents John Hancock and Samuel Adams, accused of stirring the colonists to rebellion. From Lexington they were to go to Concord and destroy the colonists' store of arms and military supplies.

Reaching Lexington's common, they found minutemen facing them with rifles. When they refused to disperse, the British fired upon them, killing eight, wounding ten. This resulted in confusion and scattered the Americans.

Arriving at Concord at 7 A.M. on Sunday, April 19, 1775, about 200 British troops were met by 400 minutemen at the North Bridge over the Concord River. The British fired upon the Americans and they fired back. The American Revolution had begun. The red-clad British retreated and, during their withdrawal, were fired upon by the minutemen and farmers from behind trees, rocks, fences, and buildings. Returning to Boston, they counted their losses: 285 dead and wounded. The Americans killed and wounded totalled 88.

The Second Continental Congress met in Pennsylvania's State House (Independence Hall) in Philadelphia. On June 17, 1775, they named George Washington commander-in-chief of the Continental Army.

On June 7, 1776, in the Continental Congress, Richard Henry Lee made the motion "that these united colonies are and of right ought to be free and independent states." The resolution was adopted July 2, 1776; and the Declaration of Independence was approved on July 4, 1776.

The Articles of Confederation and Perpetual Union were adopted by the Continental Congress on November 15, 1777.

The war ended October 19, 1781, with General Charles Marquis Cornwallis' surrender at Yorktown, Virginia. Britain recognized the United States' independence during March 1782 and signed a preliminary agreement in Paris on November 30, 1782.

England and the United States signed a peace treaty September 3, 1783, and Washington disbanded the army November 3, 1783. On January 14, 1784, the United States Congress ratified the treaty with England.

Meeting in Annapolis, Maryland, September 11–14, 1786, delegates from five states requested that Congress call a convention in Philadelphia to write a constitution for the 13 states.

The Constitutional Convention convened in Philadelphia May 25, 1787, with George Washington presiding. A constitution was accepted and adopted by the delegates on September 17, 1787, with ratification required by nine of the 13 states.

The ninth state, New Hampshire, ratified the constitution June 21, 1788. It was then adopted and, after ratification by all 13 states, the Constitution of the United States of America was declared in effect March 4, 1789.

After the election of George Washington as president of the United States with John Adams as vice president, on February 4, 1789, the First Congress met in Federal Hall in New York City with its regular session beginning April 6, 1789. Washington's inaugural occurred April 30, 1789. With the government organized, the Supreme Court was created by the Federal Judiciary Act of September 24, 1789, and Philadelphia was designated as the temporary capital. Congress met there December 6, 1790.

If the capital is to be considered that place where a nation's government is located, which it is, the capital of these United States, including direction of the Continental Congress, was moved 11 times and occupied nine cities. Some of the moves occurred during the Revolutionary War when British troops threatened.

Movements of the United States Continental Congress

Philadelphia: September 5, 1774, to December 12, 1776
Baltimore: December 20, 1776, to March 4, 1777
Philadelphia: March 5, 1777, to September 18, 1777
Lancaster, Pennsylvania: September 27, 1777
York, Pennsylvania: September 30, 1777, to June 6, 1778
Philadelphia: July 2, 1778, to June 21, 1783
Princeton, New Jersey: June 30, 1783, to June 3, 1784
Annapolis, Maryland: November 26, 1783, to June 3, 1784
Trenton, New Jersey: November 1, 1784, to December 24, 1784
New York City: January 11, 1785, to August 12, 1790
Philadelphia: December 6, 1790, to May 14, 1800
Washington, D.C.: June 10, 1800, permanently

Four years prior to the adoption of the Constitution and the government's organization, a proposal for a "federal town" was made in the Continental Congress April 30, 1783, in Philadelphia. During the First Session of Congress in 1789 the selection of a site for the capital generated rivalry between North and South factions. The Senate's tied vote, broken by John Adams, decided in favor of Germantown, Pennsylvania. The following year a compromise named Philadelphia the capital for a period of ten years with a permanent site to be named during that time.

During that time, looking to the future and believing their state an appropriate site for the nation's capital, Maryland's Assembly on December 23, 1788, ceded to the United States Congress "any district in this state not exceeding ten miles square."

A year later, December 3, 1789, Virginia also ceded ten miles square. Both were accepted by Congress July 16, 1790. That land ceded by Virginia was returned by an act of Congress July 9, 1846, "as not being required or necessary."

Experimental boundaries of the District were proclaimed by President Washington January 24, 1791. He appointed commissioners and ordered a survey. The boundaries were approved by Congress March 3, 1791, with an amendment indicating public buildings could be built only on the Maryland side of the Potomac.

After an agreement with the land owners on a $66 per acre price for their land, Washington proclaimed the boundaries March 30, 1791, and the cornerstone of the lines of the federal territory was laid "with great solemnity" at Jones' Point April 15, 1791, with the commissioners and a large crowd attending. The new federal city was named Washington.

The commissioners employed Major Pierre Charles L'Enfant to draw the plans for the city. Also, L'Enfant, a French soldier and engineer who had accompanied Lafayette to America, was to design, locate, and supervise the construction of its federal buildings.

For the Capitol's site L'Enfant selected Jenkins' Hill, "a pedestal awaiting a monument" and, to give it unrivaled prominence and visibility, his plan carried major avenues to converge on it. Washington approved L'Enfant's plan for the city although many were opposed to the streets, most of which were 110 feet wide, and especially to one that was 400 feet wide and a mile long.

Expected to design and build the Capitol, L'Enfant refused to produce a plan, claiming he carried it "in his head." When he aroused the wrath of a wealthy landowner by tearing down his new manor because it blocked a view, he was dismissed; his work in designing the city was completed by Benjamin Banneker, an eminent black architect.

Seeking a design for a Capitol, the commissioners were advised by the secretary of state, Thomas Jefferson, to hold a competition. The offer of a $500 prize and a city lot brought designs from 16 architects, none of which were suitable.

During October 1792, long after the competition's deadline, a letter arrived from the British West Indies. It requested permission to submit a design. With permission given, the seventeenth design was submitted by Dr. William Thornton. It was accepted as the winning entry by the commissioners April 5, 1793, approved by Washington July 25, 1793, and ground was broken August 1, 1793.

The cornerstone was set in the southeast corner by George Washington assisted by the Masons from Georgetown and Alexandria in a Masonic ceremony on September 18, 1793. Proceeding doggedly, the foundation work was completed during the winter of 1796.

To implement Thornton's design, three architects were engaged to supervise construction that started on the north wing selection which contained the Senate Chamber. Both Stephen Hallet and George Hadfield were dismissed for attempted changes in the design. The third, James Hogan, became the architect of the White House and was also engaged for its reconstruction after it was burned by the British in 1814.

Finished in 1800, the north wing of the Capitol was occupied by Congress in November. The Supreme Court held its first session in the new Capitol in February 1801.

The year following incorporation of the city of Washington in 1802, Congress appropriated $50,000 to continue construction of the Capitol. The three-man commission was replaced by the superintendent of the city of Washington, Benjamin H. Latrobe, who was appointed architect of the Capitol and the work continued under his supervision.

Modifying Thornton's design of the south wing, Latrobe moved the House Chamber to the second floor, filled the first floor with offices, and replaced wood construction with masonry vaults. With the south wing under way, he completely rebuilt the interior of the north wing when it was found in a state of decay.

The new House Chamber was occupied in 1807 although it was not completed until 1811. The two wings were connected by a frame corridor still in use when the British set the Capitol afire on August 24, 1814, during the War of 1812. Luckily, a rainstorm saved it from complete destruction.

After the fire Congress met for one session in the Blodget Hotel (Seventh and E streets, N.W.), and from 1815 to 1819 in what became known as the Old Brick Capitol, built to house Congress during reconstruction of the Capitol and later razed for the Supreme Court Building.

During this reconstruction disapproving Congressmen attempted to achieve an abandonment of the structure and went so far as to push for relocating the capital to a safer, centrally located area. Their efforts failed and President James Madison was authorized to borrow $500,000 to rebuild. Latrobe ignored a clamor from the Congress for speed and greater economy because delays were beyond his control and costs were above his estimates. When his proposal to vault the ceilings in the House and Senate chambers was not approved, he resigned in November 1817 and left Washington, never to return.

Wondering if two architects would be needed to fill the vacancy, President James Monroe appointed Charles Bulfinch of Boston, third architect of the Capitol, to finish the work. Starting in 1818, Bulfinch continued repair of the existing wings and started work on the central section.

The Supreme Court occupied its chamber in March 1819, and the House and Senate chambers were ready in December. After 37 years under construction, the United States Capitol was finally completed under the supervision of Charles Bulfinch who left Washington under friendly terms in 1830.

The original Capitol, built of Aquia Creek sandstone from Virginia, was 351 feet, 7 ½ inches on the facade, 282 feet, 10 ½ inches in depth, and 140 feet,

7 ¼ inches (approximately) in height. Its total cost, up to the year 1827, was $2,432,851.34 including all repairs, grading of the grounds, and the like.

Except for repainting the exterior to keep the stone from weathering, the routine maintenance of the building and grounds, the addition of running water in 1832, and changing to gas lights in 1840, there was a 20-year lull in construction; but responding to a dire need for expansion due to additional territories' gaining statehood, the Senate Committee on Public Hearings advertised for an architectural design competition in 1850. With a prize of $500 offered, the committee reserved the right to split the prize and use the designs as they saw fit.

None of the entries were outstanding and the money was split five ways. Congress appropriated $100,000 September 30, 1850, and authorized President Millard Fillmore to appoint an architect of the Capitol. Fillmore chose Thomas U. Walter, an eminent Philadelphia architect who had been a contestant in the competition.

Construction on the Capitol extension was started in June 1851. The cornerstone was set in the northeast corner of the House wing on July 4, 1851, by President Fillmore in a ceremony that included an oration by Secretary of State Daniel Webster.

With the extensions under construction it became necessary to increase the height of the dome to preserve architectural proportions. Bulfinch's low wooden dome was replaced with today's cast iron structure designed by the fourth capitol architect, Thomas U. Walter.

Construction on the dome started in 1856 with new masonry, reinforced with iron bands, added to the top of the rotunda. Arriving by rail, cast iron from foundries in Maryland, New Jersey, New York, and Virginia was lifted into place by steam-powered derricks and installed. With more than 7,000 tons of masonry and iron added to its structure, the Capitol awaited its crown.

The additions to the House and Senate wings proceeded without interruption. Finished first, the House chamber was occupied December 16, 1857. The Senate held its first meeting in its new quarters on January 4, 1859.

The Capitol's crown came in the form of a bronze statue, 19 ½ feet tall and weighing 14,985 pounds. Arriving from Clark Mill's foundry nearby, it had been cast in five sections. The first four sections were hoisted to the top of the dome and secured. The finishing section, the woman's head and shoulders, generated a special ceremony.

At noon, December 2, 1863, the operator of the steam hoist threw a lever and the fifth section started toward its final resting place. To reach the top, 300 feet away, required 20 minutes. When the section was in place and secured, Old Glory was unfurled over her head and a 35-gun salute fired from the battery on Capitol Hill.

As the last gun sounded, an answering salute was given by the guns of each of the 12 forts surrounding and fortifying the city. The dome was complete.

With her official name being *Statue of Freedom*, clothed in flowing robes, her right hand rests upon a sheathed sword while the left holds a wreath and a protecting shield. Stars encircle her helmet which is crested with the head and feathers of an eagle.

The empty Senate chamber, hurriedly occupied by the Supreme Court who transferred their Law Library to their vacated quarters, was no problem, but the House chamber became something else. After years of deliberation and discussion with some wanting it changed to two floors for offices, the solution came from a Vermont Congressman, Justin Morrill.

Morrill proposed that the vacated House chamber, which had become "home to a motley assortment of peddlers and hawkers," be transformed into a National Statuary Hall thereby saving Latrobe's creative genius for posterity.

His suggestion became law July 2, 1864, and Congress invited each state to contribute to Statuary Hall two statues of its outstanding citizens who were "worthy of national commemoration." The first statue was placed in 1870. In 1933 when the architect of the Capitol determined Statuary Hall was bearing its maximum weight, Congress authorized the display of the statues throughout the Capitol. Statuary Hall was limited to 33 statues. By 1971 all 50 states had placed at least one statue and by 1980 all but seven states had placed two. Statuary Hall, now used for ceremonial events, was partially restored for the United States Bicentennial Celebration.

From 1865 to 1902 the Capitol kept abreast of times with modernization introduced by Edward Clark, the fifth Capitol architect.

With its walls continuing to bulge with crowded space during the following 50 years, seven major buildings were constructed with additions added. The grounds were enlarged and underground parking provided. As new space was provided, the Capitol received proper maintenance and repair. This work was supervised by Elliott Woods and David Lynn, the sixth and seventh architects of the Capitol.

It was under Lynn's direction, with appropriations of $5,102,000 from July 1949 to January 1951, that major repair and change were brought to the Senate and House chambers. Their roofs and skylights and those of the connecting corridors were replaced with concrete and steel and covered with copper.

During the renovation the Senate met in its original chamber that was vacated by the Supreme Court; and the House met in a committee room in the Longworth House Office Building.

With an appropriation in 1956 of $24 million, under the direction of George Stewart, architect of the Capitol, an extension was made to the east front beginning in 1958; it was completed in 1962. At the same time, repair was made to the dome.

When George M. White was appointed architect of the Capitol by President Richard Nixon in 1971, he emphasized a higher standard of maintenance and technology as well as renewed appreciation of the Capitol's architectural history.

Anticipating the Bicentennial, the Capitol's interior was restored to its

The United States Capitol, located in Washington, D.C. It is estimated that there are more visitors to the U.S. Capitol each year than to all the states' and territories' capitols combined. — Author's photograph.

1850s appearance; but the most ambitious restoration in its history occurred between 1983 and 1987. It involved the restoration of the west-central front from which 40 percent of the original Aquia Creek sandstone was removed and replaced with Indiana limestone. Over 1,000 two and one-half inch holes up to 37 feet in length were drilled through the walls; and stainless steel rods, set in concrete, were installed to reinforce the vaulted structure and foundation.

To conserve energy, all the windows were replaced. A stone strengthening consolidant was applied before the west front was repainted.

Over the years, while additions to the Capitol were being made, land has been added and the Capitol grounds now include 273.7 acres of lawn, sidewalks, streets, and roadways.

Visitors are always welcomed, especially by their senators and representatives.

UTAH
The Beehive State

HEIGHT: 285′   FACADE: 404′   DEPTH: 240′

Unlike most of the regions in the United States, the Utah-Nevada area, because of its desolation, was never considered worthy of exploration; and until 1847 was traversed by Europeans only to get to the Pacific coast.

True, the southeast corner was investigated by Garcia Lopez de Cardenas, sent there by Coronado in 1540 to see what was there. His report of desert and useless land was taken for granted, but because Juan de Onate claimed the New Mexico region for Spain in 1598, that nation held a vague claim to it.

During 1776 two Franciscan priests from Santa Fe, looking for a way to California, found themselves in the Utah area. Traveling to Utah Lake in north-central Utah, their reports started trade between Santa Fe and the Indians.

When Mexico won its independence in 1821, the Utah region was in the land they claimed; and it was not until the 1820s that the Americans showed an interest in the area during the fur trading era of the mountain men. The fur companies sent trappers into the area: Jim Bridger, supposedly the discoverer of the Great Salt Lake, and Jedediah Smith, who led a group of trappers from that lake to California, the first Americans to travel overland to the Pacific.

The 1830s found more trappers and when the fur was trapped out, exploration came under the leadership of Captain Benjamin L. Bonneville, who wrote a description of the Great Salt Lake and gave it his name. Later his name was transferred to prehistoric Lake Bonneville.

By the 1840s enough knowledge had come from the trappers and those traveling across the area that Captain John Bartleson took a wagon train across to California. With Kit Carson as his guide, John C. Frémont explored the Salt Lake area and his reports attracted Miles Goodyear to settle on a site (now Ogden) and build Fort Buenaventura.

Then the Mormons came. Known as members of the Church of Jesus Christ of Latter-day Saints and led by President Brigham Young who replaced Joseph Smith, founder of the restored Church of Jesus Christ, they entered the Salt Lake Valley on July 21, 1847. The next day they cleared and plowed land, diverted irrigation water from the creek, and planted crops. Brigham Young arrived on July 24. The same year the High Council of the Church bought Goodyear's interests in Fort Buenaventura.

During 1848 late frosts and a cricket invasion threatened the crops, but they were saved when large flocks of gulls came off the lake and ate the crickets.

As a result the Mormons built a monument of sea gulls commemorating the event. That year Utah was included in the area ceded to the United States in the Treaty of Guadalupe-Hidalgo, which placed the Mormons under federal control.

Two years after their arrival, with a continuous stream of members of the faith pouring into the valley to strengthen the population, the State of Deseret was organized to include nearly all of Utah and Nevada, a good part of Arizona, and parts of neighboring states Idaho, Colorado, and Wyoming. With Brigham Young as their governor, Congress was petitioned for admission to the Union as a state. Congress rejected the petition.

The discovery of gold in California that year brought the "forty-niners" through the area bound for the gold fields. Sizing up the land and commercial possibilities, many stayed.

In 1850, to supersede the State of Deseret, Congress created the Territory of Utah with the capital at Salt Lake City. Brigham Young was appointed governor. When federal officials arrived in 1851, friction started between them and the Mormons; and when the Mormons avowed "plural marriage" as a rule of the Church, it incited criticism and controversy reaching Washington.

Since their exodus from Nauvoo, Illinois, the converts to Mormonism — from New England, the South, from Europe: hundreds pushing handcarts over the Mormon Trail — continued to flow into Salt Lake Valley until 1860. Arriving, many were sent to pioneer the land surrounding the Salt Lake Valley. They settled in Idaho, Wyoming, Colorado, Arizona, and Nevada to cultivate the land and start settlements that grew into cities.

With the coming of Congress' laws enforcing opposition to polygamy, many Mormons relocated in Mexico. By 1857 the friction between Mormons and non–Mormons in the territorial government increased to the point that President James Buchanan removed Brigham Young from the governorship and sent troops toward Utah to bring about peace. The United States troops were detained through the winter by Mormon forces 300 miles from their objective. When they finally reached Utah, the peace had already been negotiated.

Young's replacement as governor, Alfred Cumming, took office in 1860. After the territories of Nevada and Colorado (1861) and Wyoming (1868) were created, and Congress had ceded more of Utah's land to Nevada (1862 and 1866), Utah's borders were decreased to their present limits.

When a new constitution was drawn for the State of Deseret in 1862, Congress rejected it again. Eventually laws were passed to fine and imprison the polygamists. With the continued pressure hurting members and the Church, plural marriage among its members was forbidden by President Wilfred Woodruff in 1890.

In 1895 a constitution for proposed statehood was framed and submitted to Congress and on January 4, 1896, Utah was admitted to the Union as the forty-fifth state. The capital was placed at Salt Lake City and the first governor of Utah was Heber M. Wells.

Soon after the region received territorial distinction the people insisted upon a capitol. The first assembly of the legislature meeting October 4, 1850, designated the Pauvan Valley in central Utah as the logical place for the capital. The same session created Millard County, designated Fillmore City its seat, and appointed a committee to travel to that city to locate a suitable site for a capitol.

With the site selected, Truman O. Angel was retained to design the capitol. With an appropriation of $20,000 from Congress construction started on what would become the east wing of the capitol. Work progressed slowly. All stone and timbers were hand-fashioned. Because of the excess building going on in the territory, there was a shortage of skilled workers. Three years after starting, the sandstone walls of the two-story building were not yet finished. It was finally roofed during 1855. Finished, the capitol's wing rises 43 feet to the top of its hip roof. Rectangular in form, its facade is 41⅓ feet, its depth 61⅔ feet.

The Fifth Legislative Assembly held its first meeting December 10, 1855. It was dedicated by Brigham Young the following day. That session, with two others of brief duration, was the only complete session Fillmore City saw. Convening briefly in their one-winged capitol, the legislators adjourned to reconvene in Salt Lake City. Fillmore remained the capital of the territory until December 15, 1856, when Salt Lake City was designated the capital.

After abandonment the building was neglected. Turned over to Fillmore City, it was used as an office building, a school, a church, and a jail. In 1927, with its value as an historic building realized, it was turned back to the state and is now maintained by the state as a museum in the town of Fillmore.

During the years prior to and after statehood that they were without a capitol, the territorial legislature met in several rented buildings, some of which remain in Salt Lake City.

They used the Council House, the original Salt Lake County Courthouse, the Salt Lake City Hall, the Social Hall, and the Salt Lake City/County Building which recently underwent restoration. The territorial officers were sometimes housed in other buildings, one of which was the Women's Industrial Christian Home.

Although 20 acres of land had been donated for the capitol site by eminent men of the community in 1888, no action was taken by the legislature until 1909 when they limited its cost to $2.5 million and created a seven-man Capitol Commission to select and retain an architect. The action stopped short when their one-mill tax levy was defeated by the voters.

It started again March 1, 1911, when the state treasury received an inheritance tax of $798,546 paid by the widow of Edward H. Harriman, former president of the Union Pacific Railroad.

The legislature matched it with a $1 million bond and Governor William Spry selected six men besides himself for the Capitol Commission. Immediately, the commission toured several eastern capitols for ideas and studied their plans. Setting a deadline for submissions, they received a number of designs from local and out-of-state firms from which they selected those of Richard K. A. Kletting of Salt Lake City.

P. J. Moran of Salt Lake City was contracted for site preparation and a ceremonial groundbreaking was held December 26, 1912. James Stewart & Company of New York City, with a branch in Salt Lake, was contracted for the building. After purchasing more land, the architectural landscaping of which would conform to the capitol's size and position, construction was started.

On April 4, 1914, a cornerstone was set with an "elaborate" ceremony including a metal box containing photos, newspapers, coins, and church books. At that time the third floor for the convening of the Eleventh Utah Legislature; and on February 11, 1915, one month after it had convened elsewhere, the legislature held the remainder of that session in the capitol.

At two o'clock on the afternoon of October 9, 1916, the executive and judicial officers of the state having moved into their new quarters, the Utah State Capitol was formally presented to its citizens in a dedication ceremony followed by a public reception attended by an estimated 30,000 people.

The building's exterior stone is granite from the Consolidated Stone Company quarry in Little Cottonwood Canyon near the city. The interior contains gray Georgia marble, Utah marble, and Utah onyx in the different rooms' walls, floors, and colonnades. Utah's Sanpete oolite (white sandstone) is used in the walls of the ground floor.

Finished at a cost of $2,739,528, in a classical Corinthian design, rising 285 feet to the tip of a copper-clad dome, its facade and sides contain 52 sectioned granite columns. Reached over a massive stone stairway through the portico, and supported by eight of those columns, the front entrance admits the visitors to the second floor which is designated Main Hall.

A lack of finances during the finishing work of the interior curtailed the furnishings and artwork, much of which was included afterwards. Governmental growth was overcome in the early 1960s with constuction of an office building annex immediately to the north.

The rotunda rises 160 feet to the dome ceiling upon which are painted circling sea gulls with six-feet wingspreads. In the spandrels under the dome, four murals depict great events in the state's history: Father Escalante entering Utah Valley in 1776, Peter Skene Ogden near Ogden River in 1828, John C. Frémont's visit to the Great Salt Lake in 1843, and Brigham Young entering Salt Lake Valley in 1847. Designed by Lee Greene Richards, they were painted by Utah artists working under the federal Works Progress Administration in the 1930s.

A three-ton chandelier hangs from the dome on a 95-foot chain weighing more than the chandelier.

The Main Hall houses the executive branch of government, which includes the offices of the governor, lieutenant governor, secretary of state, and the attorney general. The Gold Room (State Reception Room) is considered the most attractive and elaborate room in the capitol. It was refurbished during 1955– 1956.

Although the land was granted to the Utah Territory in 1888, construction on Utah's capitol did not start until 1913. It was completed in 1915 at a cost of $2.7 million. — Office of Administrative Services.

With its furnishings created by European artisans, the room's golden motif is upheld by 23-karat Utah gold leaf trim throughout. From Birdseye, Utah, Golden Traverse marble of 16 colors, including gold, trims the fireplace and walkway. The floor is covered with a half-ton, single-piece, hand-woven chenille carpet made in Scotland. It is adorned with Utah symbols.

A massive table made of Circassian walnut from the southeastern hills of Russia occupies the center of the room. Purple chairs and love seats from England are upholstered in the queen's coronation velvet. Green brocaded chairs and Italian tapestries are entwined with 14-karat gold thread. Brilliant French mirrors reflect the lights from a thousand-piece French chandelier.

Overlooking the room is the ceiling's painting, "Children at Play." It was painted over a three-month period in 1913 by Lewis Schettle for $3,000.

Matching marble stairs rise to the third floor for the Supreme Court chamber, Senate chamber, and the House of Representatives chamber. Each matches the capitol's ornate decorations and art spread throughout the building. The galleries to the legislative chambers are reached from the fourth floor and visitors are welcome and encouraged to attend their sessions which start in January.

The ground floor (Exhibition Hall) is given over to representative displays of Utah's scenic and recreational attractions with exhibits of education, agriculture, commerce, and special occurrences in the state's history.

Statuary and paintings are spread through the building, and monuments and statues are contained in the landscaped grounds including Memory Grove in a small canyon east of and a short distance from the capitol. Easily accessible, a stairway descends to the park and its monuments, reminders of the nation's fights for freedom.

The capitol and grounds are maintained by ten full-time employees to which are added temporary workers during the summer months. For the maintenance of buildings and grounds during 1988, the state paid $2,436,893.

Visitors are welcome to the capitol during its hours of operation as well as to the many other historic buildings in the immediate area.

The governor's mansion, located at 603 East South Temple, is considered one of Utah's most significant landmarks. The 36-room mansion was built in 1902 by Thomas F. Kearns, a mining magnate and U.S. Senator. It was deeded to the state in 1937 by his widow to become the official residence of Utah's governor. Completely restored in 1977, it is open to visitors a few days each week.

VERMONT
The Green Mountain State

HEIGHT: 136'   FACADE: 176' 8"   DEPTH: 112' 6"

The declaration of independence by people of Vermont in 1774 indirectly started what became known as the Westminster Massacre occuring March 13, 1775, when a group of armed men of Westminster took the courthouse from New York's representatives. During its retaking by New Yorkers, shots fired into the courthouse killed two men. The tombstone of one bears the epitaph "[killed] by the hands of cruel ministerial tools of George ye 3rd."

Vermont's greatest problem in becoming a part of the United States was gaining a definition of its boundaries, of its physical existence.

The problem started with the granting of lands in 1741 by King George II of England. The king's proclamation gave New Hampshire all the land extending westward to the other governments' land. Likewise he gave New York similar grants. As a result Governor Benning Wentworth of New Hampshire assumed his western boundary would be the same as those of Massachusetts and Connecticut while New York's governor, George Clinton, claimed the same land: from the west side of the Connecticut River which included Vermont.

Agreeing to let the king settle the question, both governors gave numerous grants in the disputed area. In 1764 King George III proclaimed the Connecticut River to be New Hampshire's western boundary and the land from there to the west (Vermont) that of New York. The people living in that area held grants from New Hampshire. Now grants for the same lands were being given to New Yorkers.

Some residents recognized New York's title to their lands and offered to buy the properties from New York but were refused. During a long, bitter struggle between the two factions, the Green Mountain Boys led by Ethan Allen were organized. Their actions terrorized the New Yorkers' attempts to claim their lands and eventually brought Vermont on its course to statehood.

In 1776 a group, including some Green Mountain Boys, met in Dorset and declared their area to be independent. The following January a meeting in Westminster established the state of New Connecticut and declared it a free state.

Seventy-two delegates from the New Hampshire grants met in Windsor June 4, 1777, to frame a constitution for a new and independent state.

They named the new state Vermont and signed their constitution July 8, 1777. The Vermont constitution was the first in the nation to give the voting right to all adult males and prohibit slavery. The following year on March 3, Thomas Chittendon was elected governor. The first session of its unicameral legislature met on March 12, 1778. From that day until March 4, 1791, Vermont was a completely independent republic.

The new government was never recognized by the other colonies, the Continental Congress, or even some of its residents. Through the process of ironing out problems, making amends, and paying New York for lands they had possessed, Vermont adopted the Constitution of the United States. Vermont ceased to be a republic on March 4, 1791, and was admitted to the Union as the fourteenth state.

From the day it was founded as a republic, Vermont had no permanent capital or capitol. Over those years the legislature met 46 times in whatever tavern or church was available in 14 different towns.

Montpelier was named the permanent capital in 1805 with the stipulation that all legislative sessions were to be held there. With this action were two conditions: the town must donate land for a capitol and the capitol must be ready for occupancy by September 1808.

Construction on Vermont's first capitol started in 1805 on a site donated by Thomas Davis, the son of Colonel Jacob Davis, founder of Montpelier. Finished in 1808 before the deadline, the three-story, frame building with clapboard siding was claimed to have been "whittled out of use" by legislators' jackknives. Built at a cost of $10,000, of which $2,000 in materials were donated by Montpelier citizens, the capitol was used for 30 years. Steep, circular staircases rose to upper floors. A belfry was centered in its hip roof. Warmed by a two-story stove, the legislators with their jackknives sat on straight-backed, plank seats of pine at pine desks.

Recognizing its gradual deterioration and the need for more space, legislative action started construction of a new capitol of stone during 1834. When it was occupied by Vermont's bicameral (adopted in 1836) government in 1838 the wooden structure was demolished.

Built on higher ground for protection from floods, the second capitol was constructed of Barre granite hauled from the Cobble Hill quarry on drays powered by four horses and a yoke of oxen. The loading, ten-mile delivery, and return required 18 hours. The new capitol was designed in Greek Revival by Ammi Burnham Young using the Greek Temple of Theseus as a model.

Topped by a large dome, it had a six-column-supported portico. It was 100 feet high with a facade of 150 feet and a depth of 100 feet. It contained two full stories above ground. The capitol was built for $132,000 with half of that paid by the people of Montpelier.

On a cold night in January 1857, a stove in the House chamber exploded setting a fire that left nothing but granite walls and the portico.

The walls were knocked down and construction on a new capitol, united with the portico of the second, started about mid-year. With its basic design similar to that of its predecessor, but on a grander scale with Renaissance Revival decoration and ornamentation style, two Boston architects were retained. The first was Thomas W. Silloway, who was followed by Joseph R. Richards. Two and one-half years to completion, the capitol was dedicated in 1859. Its construction cost was $132,000. With furnishings, most of which exist today, the total cost was $150,000.

In 1888 an annex was built to house the Supreme Court and the State Library at a cost of $36,000.

In 1900 a Speaker of the House office was added at a cost of $10,000.

In 1987 an addition was built to house legislative staffs and a cafeteria at a cost of $1,300,000.

Two opposing wings extend from the central structure to form a Greek cross. The pediment of its Greek Revival portico is supported by six Doric columns having six-foot diameters. Above the pediment, centered in the cross, a gilded dome rises above its pedestal to support Ceres, the Roman goddess of agriculture.

In 1938 workmen found the original statue, carved by Larkin G. Meade of Brattleboro, so badly deteriorated that it was in danger of falling from the dome. Ceres was removed and replaced with a duplicate statue carved from pine by 86-year-old Sergeant-at-Arms Dwight G. Dwinell. This 14-foot Ceres had to be cut into pieces, raised to the top of the dome, reassembled, and placed atop her six-foot pedestal. Coated with weatherpoof white paint and topped with a lightning rod, she looks far beyond the capitol's approach.

The capitol dome is made of wood, sheathed with copper and covered with 40 ounces of 23.75 karat gold leaf. It was regilded in 1976 for $20,000.

The third Vermont State Capitol built in Montpelier was completed and occupied in 1859. The governor's chair was carved from the oak timbers of the U.S. frigate *Old Ironsides*, otherwise known as the U.S.S. *Constitution*. — Author's photograph.

On each side of the approach to the capitol's main entrance is a Spanish naval gun. Both were captured from a Spanish cruiser in the Battle of Manila Bay in 1898 by the American fleet commanded by Admiral George Dewey of Montpelier.

Standing on a pedestal of Barre granite at the top of the steps, to greet every visitor to the capitol, is a statue of Ethan Allen. Weighing four tons, sculpted from Danby marble in 1941 by Aristide J. Piccini, it replaced the original which was carved from Italian marble by Larkin Goldsmith Mead in 1861 at a cost of $3,000.

Inside the lobby, to support the dome, four Ionic columns rise from a black and white, checkerboard marble floor. The black, fossilized marble comes from the Isle La Motte quarries near Lake Champlain in the Grand Isle County. The white is from Danby. From the lobby a bust of Abraham Lincoln is found in the Hall of Inscription so named because its walls contain statements of Vermont greats that epitomize the state's character. The Lincoln bust is identical to the one in Lincoln's tomb in Springfield, Illinois. It was sculpted by Larkin Goldsmith Mead.

The capitol's corridors are abundant with portraits of former Vermont notables. Politicians, statesmen, senators, governors, and presidents are framed in dark wood and hung amid the contrast of gleaming white walls. The major rooms are lighted by large bronze chandeliers hanging from sculptured ceilings.

The first or main floor contains the lieutenant governor's office, the sergeant-at-arms, Senate committee rooms, and those of the Legislative Council. At the top of the left-hand stairway on the second floor is H. B. Hall's carving of Governor Thomas Chittendon. Because a likeness of Governor Chittendon was never made, Hall used portraits of the governor's grandsons to make a composite.

The second floor contains the governor's office, the Senate and House chambers and the House committee rooms. The governor's reception room contains George Gassner's copy of Gilbert Stuart's portrait of Washington from where it hung behind the desk of the speaker of the House. It was one of very few items rescued from the fire of 1857.

The governor's reception room is known as the Cedar Creek Room because of the dominating 10 by 20-foot painting of the Civil War's Battle of Cedar Creek. Its artist, Julian Scott, a Civil War veteran cited for saving several officers, was awarded the first Congressional Medal of Honor. Commissioned by the legislature for the sum of $9,000, Scott worked from 1871 to 1875 to produce the painting. With its oak frame it is considered outstanding among paintings of the Civil War.

Room by room a program of restoration has been planned over several years toward completion of the public areas of the capitol before Vermont's Statehood Bicentennial in 1991. The Cedar Creek Room, originally the State Library, serves as the official entertainment room for state officials.

An oak desk chair in the governor's office was carved from timbers removed from the U.S.S. *Constitution* when it was restored during the late 1850s. "Constitution chairs" were made from the timbers and presented at that time to each of the United States. This chair has been the governor's official chair since 1858.

Glass doors admit you to Representatives Hall (House chamber) where Vermont's 150 representatives meet annually from January to May. The House had 246 members, one from each town, almost, until 1965 when its numbers were reduced. All joint meetings are held in this chamber. The light fixtures, once gas lit, are bronze and intricately carved with statuettes of historic personages. The main, central fixture hangs from the center of a lotus ceiling ornament 18 feet in diameter centered in a molded plaster ceiling with double sunk panels.

The Senate chamber has an elliptical, domed ceiling with 20 lobes joined at the center. Like those in the House chamber, the columns are Corinthian. Except for the carpeting and draperies, its furnishings are those of 1859 when the Senators' tub chairs and black walnut desks cost $20 apiece.

The Senate president's desk is elaborately carved with Vermont's coat of arms as is that of the speaker of the House. The bronze lamps on the president's desk were made in France and symbolize the muses of Inspiration and Meditation. The chandelier, restored in 1981, features a maritime theme with sea horses, water lilies, and figures of Neptune.

Spectators' galleries may be reached by stairs from the lobby on the second floor.

Visitors are encouraged to visit the Vermont Historical Society's museum in the Pavilion Office Building near the capitol.

From the first week in July to the third week in October, tours of the capitol are conducted by volunteer guides of the Friends of the Vermont State House, Monday through Friday from 10 A.M. to 4 P.M.; Saturday, 11 A.M. to 3 P.M. In July 1990 Friends of the Vermont State House opened a small gift shop which is open to visitors during those hours.

THE VIRGIN ISLANDS

The Virgin Islands are divided into two groups. One-half mile of water separates the western group (United States) from the eastern (Great Britain). They are located in the Caribbean Sea about 1,000 miles southeast of Miami, Florida.

When on his second voyage to the new world (1493), Columbus landed on St. Croix Island, one of the three largest in the United States Virgin Islands. The other two are St. Thomas and St. John. The group consists of more than 50 smaller islands, islets, and cays some of which are not inhabited.

When Columbus was there, he found St. Croix inhabited by the Carib Indians, a warlike, cannibalistic people who were instrumental in discouraging foreign exploitation. In all probability, the islands were first settled by the Arawak Indians as other islands in that area had been.

During 1555 a Spanish expedition landed, defeated the Carib Indians, and claimed the land for Spain thus paving the way for exploitation and settlement. By 1625 the English and French had settled on St. Croix and were farming. During this time the island had supplied a harbor and become a protective retreat for the pirates of that period.

The Spaniards came again during 1650 and drove out all the English settlers, but the French took the land from the Spaniards the same year, kept it until 1653, then gave it to the Knights of Malta who eventually sold it to the French West India Company.

Denmark entered the islands during 1666 and, claiming the island of St. Thomas, they founded a colony, divided the island into plantations, imported their convicted criminals, and grew sugarcane. By 1671 they were supplying Denmark with sugar, cotton, and indigo.

In 1673 African slaves were imported to work the cane fields and the traffic was started. The first regular consignment of Africans were brought to St. Thomas during 1681. Three years later (1684) Denmark claimed St. John and by 1717 had colonized it with planters who brought slaves to do the work. Things went well until the slaves rebelled (1733), chased the Danes off the island, and held it for six months. That same year Denmark bought St. Croix from the French.

Within 70 years from the time the first African slave set foot upon St. Thomas, there were more than 1,900 slaves on St. Croix alone. Sugar production grew and the plantations prospered. Commerce developed. Slaves were imported from Africa. Rum, indigo, sugar, and molasses were exported to Europe. European goods were exported to the islands. St. Thomas became the major slave market in the Caribbean and Charlotte Amalie was made a free port. By the beginning of the nineteenth century the sugar industry had declined, and that combined with slave revolts and the abolition of slavery in 1848 affected the plantations' industry.

Although the Denmark Crown claimed ownership of the islands, the British occupied them during 1801 and 1802; and again from 1807 to 1815 when they reverted to Danish rule.

The United States' interest in the islands came during the Civil War. The opportunity to buy St. Thomas and St. John from Denmark for $7.5 million came during 1870, but the U.S. Senate refused to approve the purchase.

During World War I when crises threatened the security and shipping lanes of the United States, President Woodrow Wilson effected the purchase of the Virgin Islands from Denmark "with force, if necessary." Wishing to avoid seizure of the islands by the Allied Forces; or worse, their conquest by Germany, the owner of docks, warehouses, steamships (Hamburg American Line), and property on St. Thomas Island, Denmark was willing and the sale was finalized in 1917 for $25 million.

Immediately after purchase, under the U.S. Navy's administration, all military, civil, and judicial power in the newly acquired territory was vested in the appointed governor. The Virgin Islanders were made citizens of the United States in 1927, but cannot vote in presidential elections because they are not a state and are not represented in the electoral college. On February 27, 1931, the control of the Virgin Islands government was transferred to the U.S. Department of the Interior.

The Organic Act of 1936 provided for two municipal councils, one for St. Thomas and St. John and one for St. Croix plus a council for the entire territory.

In 1954 the Organic Act of the Virgin Islands revised the former act to create a central government with executive, legislative, and judicial bodies; and provided for substantial self-government in an elected unicameral legislature with two-year terms. The judiciary is comprised of the territorial court with six judges appointed by the governor and the U.S. district court whose judges are appointed by the President.

In 1968 another act, to take effect in 1970, provided that the governor and lieutenant governor would be elected by the people for four-year terms. In 1970 the last appointed governor, Herbert Evans, an islander of African descent, was inaugurated as the first elected governor.

In 1973 the people had representation in the House of Representatives with a non-voting delegate who can vote in committee.

In 1976 the U.S. Virgin Islands were given the right to draft a constitution subject to approval by Congress and the President. It was completed in 1978, but rejected in 1979 in referendum. Revised and amended, it was brought before the people in 1981 and rejected.

The original and permanent capital of the territory is Charlotte Amalie on St. Thomas Island. The capitol is also the residence of the governor. Constructed at a cost of $33,605, it has three floors. It was completed in 1867 during Denmark's regime and since the United States' acquisition has housed the governor's office on the first floor. The second floor holds a formal reception room, dining room, and kitchen. The governor's residence is on the third floor. The legislature (15 senators) meets in a separate, two-story building.

None of the islands are self-supporting. Tourism is the main industry and visitors are welcome.

VIRGINIA
The Old Dominion State

HEIGHT: 53' FACADE: 146' DEPTH: 84' 6"

Sir Walter Raleigh is credited with being the original force in England's colonization of America which created the United States and Canada. After several of his expeditions a settlement was made on Roanoke Island off the Carolinas. Although it didn't survive, the seed of colonization had been planted.

Naming Virginia after herself, Elizabeth I, England's "virgin queen" set aside this vast territory in America with colonization in mind.

Following her, James I granted a charter to the London Company which sent the *Goodspeed, Discovery,* and *Sarah Constant* filled with people to mine the gold they would find in the new land. Sailing 30 miles up the James River, they landed and founded Jamestown in 1607 as America's first permanent settlement. With Captain John Smith as leader the colony survived. When Smith was wounded he returned to England. Not long afterwards the discouraged colonists sailed for home. En route they met English ships bringing food and supplies, and so they returned to Jamestown.

In 1611 Thomas Dale took charge and ruled with an iron hand. He gave each settler a piece of land for raising food. Discovering that England would pay a good price for tobacco, it became their chief crop.

Sir Edward Sandy became treasurer of the newly formed Virginia Company in 1618. The following year he sent liberal George Yeardley and a new charter to govern the colony. The new charter gave each of the free colonists 50 acres of land and allowed them a House of Burgesses representation; thus the first legislature assembled in America in Jamestown, the first capital.

That same year young women arrived from England to become the brides of the colonists, each of whom paid 120 pounds of tobacco for his wife's passage. During that year the first Negro slaves arrived in the new land.

By 1622 tobacco plantations had spread up the James River, but of the 4,000 settlers who had come into the area only 1,200 remained and that year an Indian massacre killed 350. After the king revoked the Virginia Company's charter in 1624 he sent his own governors.

Sir William Berkeley came in 1642 and ruled until 1652, after England became a commonwealth, and again from 1660 to 1676 keeping the colonists loyal to the Stuart kings. To one, Charles II, the colonists offered refuge in America during his struggle for power. After he gained the throne he always referred to Virginia as his "Old Dominion," which remains Virginia's nickname to this day.

Governor Berkeley kept the House of Burgesses by setting up a ruling aristocracy with predominating power. In 1675 the Indians rampaged again. When Berkeley failed to give adequate protection to the settlers scattered in the Piedmont area, they organized under Nathaniel Bacon, put down the Indians and, turning against the governor, burned Jamestown and drove Governor Berkeley to refuge on an English ship. With Bacon's sudden death the rebellion collapsed. Returning to power, the revengeful Berkeley hanged 20 of the insurgents. With extreme disapproval of his actions toward the colonists, Charles II removed him.

Between 1673 and 1684 Charles II organized the proprietor system for the colony. The capital was moved to Williamsburg in 1699.

For years the English kings had profited from Virginia's commerce and her governors had collected more than substantial taxes. In 1764 when the crown's parliamentary policy of taxation was forced upon them, the Virginians were so angered their opposition produced revolutionary leaders. When each new tax law received protest from the House of Burgesses, the governor dissolved the Assembly.

The Virginians held five successive conventions forming committees and appointing members to the Continental Congress. In May 1776 they passed a resolution requesting a declaration of independence from the Congress and the

Given credit for the design of Virginia's capitol, Thomas Jefferson while in France on government business actually requested the design from French architect, Charles-Louis Clerisseau. His design was sent to Jefferson after he returned to America. — Author's photograph.

following month declared independence from Great Britain, adopted George Mason's Declaration of Rights as their state constitution, and passed Thomas Jefferson's Acts for Religious Freedom and Abolition of the Law of Entail.

The capital was moved to Richmond in 1779 during the American Revolution. Up the James River, 90 miles from the Atlantic Ocean, Richmond was founded by Colonel William Byrd in 1737. Laid out by Major William Mayo, it was granted a city charter in 1782.

The Revolution ended with Britain's surrender at Yorktown in 1781. When the new Constitution of the United States was drafted in 1787, the convention adopted the Virginia constitution as a model. Seven men of that convention were Virginians. On June 26, 1788, Virginia was the tenth state to ratify the United States Constitution.

On April 17, 1861, Virginia seceded from the United States and joined the Confederacy a week later. After a few months in Montgomery, Alabama, the Confederate capital was moved to Richmond. Having ceded its northwestern lands to the federal government in 1784, when West Virginia was admitted to the Union during 1863, Virginia's present boundaries were formed.

Because of pending invasion of Union forces April 2, 1865, Richmond was abandoned. A week later, on April 9, General Robert E. Lee surrendered to General Ulysses S. Grant at the Appomattox Court House and the Civil War ended. Virginia was readmitted to the Union January 20, 1870.

Virginia's First General Assembly met in a Jamestown church during the summer of 1619, 12 years after the founding of the Virginia Colony and more than a year before the Pilgrims landed at Plymouth.

Because of Jamestown's unhealthy climate, the capital was moved in 1699 to Middle Plantation, later named Williamsburg for William III. A capitol, started in 1701, was completed in 1705. Burned in 1747, it was rebuilt in 1751. It was there that Patrick Henry and his fellow patriots sowed the seeds of revolution. The capitol burned again in 1832 and after the capital moved to Richmond, the city of Williamsburg deteriorated. Over the years many of the buildings were vacated and burned or fell into ruin.

After years of disrepair Williamsburg was partially restored and among its buildings is the reconstructed capitol of 1705. Today Williamsburg is joined to Jamestown and Yorktown in the Colonial National Historical Park.

In 1780 the capital was moved to Richmond for greater protection from British troops as well as to provide a healthier climate. Until a Capitol could be built the Virginia General Assembly met in the Cunningham Warehouse.

The site for Virginia's capitol was chosen at that time for its view overlooking the James River. Part of its building site was donated. The remainder was purchased by the state.

In March 1785 the Directors of Public Buildings in Richmond asked Thomas Jefferson, the United States Minister to France, to consult an architect on a plan for a capitol that would "unite economy with elegance and utility."

Jefferson conferred with a well-known French architect, Charles-Louis Clerisseau, and chose as a model for the Virginia Capitol the Maison Carree, a Roman temple built in Nimes, France, during the first century of the Christian Era. It was not long after work had started in 1785 that Clerisseau's plans for the capitol arrived and a year later, they received Bloquet's plaster model of the design Jefferson had chosen. The French artisan's model of the capitol is displayed today in the capitol's entrance hall.

The capitol's cornerstone was laid August 18, 1785, and construction continued under the supervision of Samuel Dobie. The Assembly held its first meeting in the capitol, which was still incomplete, in October 1788.

Completed in 1789 at a cost of 5,000 British pounds sterling, it was a rectangular structure with two stories above a high basement. Built of handmade brick, its walls graduated from five feet to three feet in thickness. Its massive portico was completed in 1790. Its walls were not stuccoed until 1800. At first the House of Delegates and the General Court were housed on the first floor with the Executive and Senate chambers on the second, but during the mid-1880s the Senate chamber switched places with the General Court.

At the south end of the capitol, opening onto the portico, the Senate chamber was described by one writer as a "neat, small apartment — like a drawing room."

During the Civil War, 1861 to 1865, the capitol served as headquarters for the Confederacy but luckily was not damaged when Richmond fell to Union troops February 2, 1865.

On April 27, 1870, disaster befell occupants of the capitol when the weight from an overabundance of spectators attending a Supreme Court case on the third floor caused the floor to collapse sending 62 people to their death while injuring 251.

Between 1904 and 1906 the structure was enlarged with flanking wings for the legislature: an east wing for the House of Delegates and the west for the Senate chamber. Since then the exterior has seen only minor changes.

During 1962 the interior was renovated and remodeled. The corridors into the wings were widened. Stairways, elevators, and offices were added. The attic was partitioned for offices and committee hearing rooms.

The capitol rotunda contains Virginia's most treasured art work: a life-size statue of George Washington, the only one executed from the living model. In 1784 the General Assembly, as a tribute to the great commander, commissioned the statue to be made "of the finest marble and best work-manship."

Governor Benjamin Harrison wrote to the American Minister to France, Thomas Jefferson, requesting that he find an artist for the work; Jefferson suggested French artist Jean Antoine Houdon who visited Mount Vernon, made a plaster bust of Washington's head, took detailed measurements of his body, returned to France, and carved the statue from Carrara marble.

The statue was placed on display in the Louvre in Paris before being shipped to America in May 1796, and it has been on continuous display in the capitol rotunda for nearly 200 years.

Upon viewing the statue, Lafayette, the French general said, "That is the man, himself. I can almost realize he is going to move."

The statue presents Washington erect, bare-headed, a cane in his right hand pressed into the pedestal on which he stands. At his left are a sheathed sword and fasces. Resting his left forearm on the fasces, his spurred right heel presses against a plowshare, with the former representing authority, power, and honor; the latter, the peaceful arts most congenial to his taste and feelings.

Another Houdon bust of Carrara marble in the rotunda is that of General Marquis de Lafayette. Placed there by funds voted by the Assembly in 1784, it is "a lasting monument of his merit and their gratitude." Its duplicate, presented to the people of Paris, was destroyed during the French Revolution.

In the rotunda's wall niches are busts of other Virginians who have served as United States presidents: Jefferson, Madison, Monroe, Harrison, Tyler, Taylor, and Wilson.

In the black limestone of the checkerboard flooring of the rotunda may be seen fossils of snails, shells, sea lilies, algae, and nautiloids. Ornamented in Renaissance style, located 20 feet below the A-line roof, an unusual interior dome with skylights crowns the capitol rotunda. At the base of the dome, pictured in triangles, are the Roman fasces, the symbol of government authority, and the Great Seal of Virginia. Both are encircled with the golden leaves of tobacco rather than the traditional laurel leaf.

Opposite the entrance, off the rotunda, the largest room in the capitol is the Old House of the Delegates. Now a museum, during the delegates' use it witnessed many historic activities. In 1807 Aaron Burr was acquitted of treason; the convention drafting the 1830 constitution held meetings there; the 1861 secession convention met in the room. It was used regularly for church services with Episcopal and Presbyterian members alternating Sundays.

Statuary adorns niches and pedestals around the room and a life-size, bronze statue of Robert E. Lee by Rudolph Evans stands, back to door, in the center of the room, where Lee stood April 23, 1861, when he accepted command of the Confederate forces.

The former Senate Chamber, now used for committee meetings, contains historic paintings rather than statuary. A painting by Griffith Bailey Coale represents the establishment of the first permanent settlement in America by portraying the three British ships that landed the colonizers at Jamestown.

Another, by Louis Eugene Lami, is of the final battle of the American Revolution when the British Redoubt Number 10 at Yorktown is stormed by American troops.

The capitol grounds contain the governor's mansion. Designed by Alexander Parris of Boston, it has been the official residence of Virginia's governors since 1813. Two-storied, hip-roofed with a rectangular widow's walk cornered with chimneys, the building's shuttered windows lend striking contrast to white walls balanced by a harmonious portico supported by four columns.

The Old Bell Tower, built in 1824 for the Virginia Public Guard, is located west of the capitol. With the equestrian statue of Washington atop the monument featuring the seven Virginians with allegorical figures depicting their individual contributions; with the statuary and two spring-fed fountains and rich green, shaded lawn, picnickers find it irresistible in spring and summer when lunch hour entertainment is often provided.

It is said that the Virginia State Capitol is a magnificent monument to Virginia's past and serves well the present needs of the Commonwealth.

Visitors are welcome during hours of operation.

WASHINGTON
The Evergreen State

HEIGHT: 287′ FACADE: 340′ DEPTH: 240′

The history of the finding, exploration, exploitation, and settling of Washington is much the same as that of Oregon for they at one time were a part of the same territory.

Spain laid claim to the Washington part of the Pacific Coast in 1543 through Bartolome Ferrelo who sailed along the coast. A few years later (1579), Sir Francis Drake sailed along the northwest coast of North America and claimed it for England. Leaving the California coast with a few men in a caravel, Juan de Fuca sailed north, entered the strait bearing his name, and described his exploration of the Puget Sound area in 1592.

The fur trade entered the scene in 1670 when England's Charles II granted trading privileges in the Northwest to the Hudson's Bay Company.

One hundred four years later Spaniard Juan Perez visited the coast, saw a high mountain from the strait now bearing Juan de Fuca's name, and named it Monte Santa Rosalia.

When Captain John Meares of England saw the mountain in 1788 he renamed it Mt. Olympus. Sailing farther north, he built a trading post at Nootka on the west-central coast of Vancouver Island. He was visited by Americans Robert Gray and John Kendrick the same year. The following year (1789) Estavan Jose Martinez sailed into Nootka Sound, seized British ships, destroyed Meares' trading post, and built a Spanish fort.

During the last quarter of the eighteenth century, much interest and penetration were indicated. Russia laid claim to the area through Alaska; and Spain reclaimed it. In 1792 George Vancouver surveyed the northwest coast for England and Robert Gray rediscovered and renamed the Columbia River. Before the end of the century Spain signed an agreement with England and relinquished claim to the area.

Prior to the nineteenth century, with one exception, the Pacific Northwest had been reached by sea. In 1789 Alexander Mackenzie, a partner in the North West Company of Canada followed the Mackenzie River from its source to the Arctic Ocean. Again, in 1792, with Alexander Mackay, six French Canadians, and two Indians, he set out from the Peace River to the Bella Coola River and followed it to the Pacific and gained the distinction of being the first white man to reach the Pacific Ocean across the continent.

Helped by the Louisiana Purchase of 1803, President Thomas Jefferson started Meriwether Lewis and William Clark on their way across the continent in 1804. Reaching the mouth of the Columbia River in 1805, they built a fort and established a claim for the United States.

With four nations converging on the area, there was no need to be greedy. In 1819 Spain surrendered all claims to the Pacific Coast north of the forty-second parallel. Russia followed suit in 1824, giving up all claims south of parallel 54 degrees, 40 minutes north. This left England (Canada) and the United States as the only contenders with private companies vying for the fur-trapping territory until settlement started and projected each nation's citizens into land arguments.

In 1811 the Americans built a trading post at Fort Okanogan in north-central Washington. In 1818 the two nations agreed to joint occupancy of the area. The North West Company built Fort Walla Walla in south-central Washington. Free of Russia's claim, Dr. John McLoughlin started building Fort

Vancouver on the north shore of the Columbia, across from the juncture of the Willamette River.

Jason Lee was the first missionary to reach the Northwest. Accompanying Nathaniel Wyeth's expedition in 1834 to open a mission among the Flathead Indians, he arrived at Fort Vancouver and, aided by Dr. McLoughlin, settled in the Willamette Valley in what would become Oregon. He was followed by Dr. Marcus Whitman who founded a mission at Fort Walla Walla.

By 1843 a trail across the continent encouraged settlement and a provisional government, organized in Champoeg (Marion County, Oregon), became the first government established by United States citizens west of the Rocky Mountains. Its first governor, elected in 1845, was John Abernathy.

There ensued a boundary dispute between the two nations during 1844 from which erupted the "Fifty-four forty or fight" slogan. President James K. Polk compromised by accepting the forty-ninth parallel and giving Vancouver to the British, which left the matter of the San Juan Islands in jeopardy.

The climax of disputed ownership of the land came with the "Pig War" of 1859 involving the San Juan Islands located in the Puget Sound between Washington State and Vancouver Island, British Columbia. The dispute kindled when an Englishman's pig escaped its pen to root in a neighbor American's potato patch. The American shot the pig and threatened to shoot anyone opposed to his shooting it. The problem increased when a court of settlement, British or American, could not be determined.

Meanwhile an eager American tax collector forcibly collected a few British sheep for payment of taxes. With the increased heat, both nations landed troops who, through leadership, became friendly to the extent that both British and American garrisons organized and gave parties and banquets for each other. This didn't resolve the issue.

The two nations finally chose Emperor Wilhelm I of Germany to settle the issue. He awarded the islands to the United States in 1872, and they became part of Washington when that state was admitted to the Union.

In 1848 the Oregon Territory was created with Oregon City designated the capital. General Joseph Lane was appointed governor by President Polk. With the Donation Land Act of 1850 providing free land, more settlers came. That year the population of the territory was 13,294 of which 1,200 were counted in Washington. In 1860 nearly 65,000 persons lived in the same are. Nearly one-fourth resided in Washington while the major portion settled around and in the Puget Sound area.

In 1851 the Washingtonians petitioned Congress for separate territorial status, which was granted in 1853 when Congress created the Washington Territory and designated Olympia the capital. The territory included northern Idaho and western Montana. Isaac Ingalls Stevens, a West Point graduate, was appointed governor by President Franklin Pierce. Governor Stevens' party left Washington, D.C., May 9, and on November 25, arrived in Olympia, a "rain-drenched mud hole" as described by a contemporary.

Five years earlier Edmund Sylvester and Levi Lathrop Smith had staked claims along Budd Inlet and named it Smithfield. Preceding them, in 1845 Michael Simmons of Kentucky hacked a trail from Washougal on the Columbia River to the southern tip of Puget Sound and settled at the falls on the Deschutes River (Tum Water) where, for more than 500 years, the Nisquallys had harvested shellfish and salmon. In 1848 Father Pascal Ricard with missionaries built a church and school south of Smithfield near a Nisqually Indian burial ground.

Others came. A sawmill was established at Tumwater by Edmund Sylvester and others who formed the Puget Sound Milling Company, and the settlers built houses rather than log cabins. When Smithfield was dedicated as a town in 1850, its name was changed to Olympia. A public school was built in 1852. When Sylvester platted the town in 1850 his drawings included a park used as a pasture or otherwise until its development and landscaping in 1893.

After Governor Stevens arrived his selection of Olympia as the territorial seat of government was ratified in the first session of the legislature meeting in the Gold Bar Building in 1854. Congress appropriated $5,000 for a capitol and Sylvester donated the land on which to build it.

The second and third sessions of the legislature were held in the Masonic Building, the first session of legislature in the Washington Territory.

Construction on the first capitol of the territory, started in 1855, was interrupted by an Indian uprising. Completed in 1856, it was wood frame covered with rough, whitewashed lumber. Probably designed from a book of architectural plans by the local carpenters who built it at a cost of $5,000, the two-story, rectangular building's facade measured 40 feet; depth, 68 feet; and height, 57½ feet. Its facade carried a portico reaching to the second floor and its gabled roof carried a square cupola rising into a dome. It served as the capitol into statehood.

Washington Territory started a movement to become a state in 1861 which Congress ignored. Repeated in 1867 and again in 1878, both attempts were refused by Congress. Finally, on February 22, 1889, Congress passed an enabling act to draw up a constitution and Washington was admitted to the Union as the forty-second state November 11, 1889.

With statehood and still pleasant in architectural style, the capitol's depth had been extended 22 feet to increase its floor space from 5,116 to 6,876 square feet. It was used until 1901. After it was found to be infested with termites and considered too old to correct, it was demolished in 1911.

Washington's second capitol originated as Thurston County's Courthouse. Costing $125,000, it was completed and occupied by the county in October 1892. Purchasing it from the county in 1901, Washington State used it for a capitol until a new statehouse could be occupied. It has been continuously occupied by Washington State's superintendent of public instruction since state ownership and, with nature's help, made its own history containing incidents both peculiar and extraordinary.

Just short of a century in age, still standing despite nature's attempts at

Known as the Legislative Building, the Washington State Capitol and its surrounding buildings are known as the Capitol Campus. — Department of General Administration.

destruction, it was designed in the Richardson Romanesque style of that day by Willis Ritchie and built of Chuckanut stone from Whatcom County.

Purchased with only one wing, the capitol's original architect, Willis Ritchie, was retained to design another wing for the east side for the Senate and House. This was completed and dedicated January 11, 1905, during the inauguration of Governor Albert E. Mead before a joint session of the legislature.

The addition raised the state's total cost of the building to $350,000 and gave them a four-story building containing 71,000 square feet. Its central octagonal tower, with each side featuring a clock, rose to a height of 150 feet to dominate the 12 conical-shaped towers spaced above the eaves around the structure. Windowed gables punctuate the roof and its 20-foot skylight. Its interior boasted an elaborate grilled elevator which not only carried its passengers to their desired floors but satisfied their appetites from a snack bar.

Ornate in design, the building is listed on both the state and national register of Historic Places and is most deserving. In 1910 the state purchased the entire block surrounding the capitol which housed most of the state agencies until 1919. The legislature moved out in 1928 to occupy new space in the present capitol.

That was the year fire gutted the tower and the fourth floor of the west wing and connecting wings. In 1939 the Works Progress Administration installed new concrete floors in the east wing area previously occupied by the Senate chamber and Gallery. A new steam heating system was installed throughout the building. The elevator was exchanged for one more modern, the restrooms were updated with marble, bronze exterior doors replaced wood, and the electrical system was modernized.

An earthquake in 1949 shook down 10 of the 12 towers and eliminated the House chamber and galleries of the east wing as well as the rotunda in its center.

Even though its life experienced countless changes in the relocation of partition walls, a second earthquake in 1965 caused little damage. During the 1970s after several studies determined the expense involved to keep the building in service, the legislature approved its renovation. The state's employees were moved to the Thurston Airdustrial Park in Tumwater and the work started in March 1981.

Completely cleaned inside and out, with its entire structure seismologically reinforced, the building received new heating and cooling systems installed in two new towers above the front entrance. With new elevators, a new skylight, a new copper roof, doors of oak and oak trim, a lunchroom, and safe conference rooms, the work was finished in February 1983 at a cost of $9 million; it was rededicated on Washington's birthday.

With statehood Washington had received from Congress 132,000 acres of forest land for building a capitol. Some was sold. The remaining 107,860 acres are held in reserve in the Capital Forest west of Olympia.

In 1893 New York architect Ernest Flagg was retained and the foundation for a new capitol was laid, but lack of funds stopped the work in 1894.

Occupying the "Old State Capitol," the 1909 legislature authorized completion of the Flagg capitol but appropriated no funds. In 1911 Flagg proposed the "group concept" for a Capitol Campus. New York City architects Walter R. Wilder and Harry K. White won a nationwide competition. The first building for the Capitol Campus, the Temple of Justice, was authorized and funds were appropriated.

In 1919 work resumed on the 1893 foundations of the Legislative Building. At the same time the outer facing on the Temple of Justice building was being completed. In 1922 the above ground construction was started and the Legislative Building was completed in 1928.

More than 500 builders, including marble setters and stone carvers from all over the world, worked during the five-year period. John Bruce, the chief carver, had 30 assistants using hand tools and sandblasting equipment.

Contracted by Pratt and Watson of Tacoma and the Sound Construction and Engineering Company of Seattle, it was finished at a cost of $7,385,768. The capitol dome rises to a height of 287 feet including the 47-foot "Lantern of Liberty." The exterior of the capitol is Wilkinson sandstone from the Wilkinson quarry in Pierce County. The foundation, steps, platforms, and sills are granite from Index, Snohomish County. All the sculptures, inside and out, were designed by Maxfield H. Keck of New York in a Corinthian-Gothic-Doric style, including a touch of Rococo.

The ground floor with its cafeteria is given over to public use, the Washington State Patrol, and services and support for the House and Senate.

Forty-two steps leading to the main entrance and the second floor are the designees of the 42 states in the Union with Washington the forty-second. Six solid, five-ton, bronze doors at the entrance carry designs submitted by state residents that were interpreted by Keck. They were cast in Pennsylvania and the bas-relief added by the Jackson Brothers in New Jersey. The offices of the governor, secretary of state, state treasurer, and state auditor are on the main floor as is the rotunda.

Centered in the rotunda floor is a four-foot bronze replica of the Washington State Seal that was designed by Charles Talcott who drew a circle around an ink well, a smaller circle around a silver dollar inside it. He then pasted a two-cent postage stamp inside the smaller circle and lettered: *The Seal of the State of Washington, 1889* between the two circles. It was produced by Talcott Brothers of Olympia, the oldest jewelry store in the state. The design is carried on doorknobs and railings throughout the capitol.

The capitol dome above the rotunda floor contains 1,400 cut stones and weighs 15,400 tons. The "Angels of Mercy" chandelier, cast in bronze, contains 202 bulbs. Weighing five tons, it is suspended from the dome on a 101-foot chain weighing one and one-half tons. Two hundred sixty-two steps reach to the top of the dome.

All the furnishings in the capitol were custom designed for the original decor and are made of oak, walnut, and or mahogany. Tokeen and Gravina marble from southeast Alaska are used in the north main entrance, the vestibule, the south main stairs hall, the rotunda, and public corridors.

The third floor is distinctive in its offering of "Ulcer Gulch," a room in which more than 700 registered lobbyists can congregate during legislative sessions to use its message center and meet with legislators.

Visiting dignitaries and heads of state are received in the State Reception Room, the most distinguished room in the capitol. President Harry Truman was the last United States president received here. The room is lined with Italian bresche violetta marble. The entrance floor is Belgian marble. The floor's perimeter is Italian violetta reflection marble.

Made by Mohawk in 1930, the single loom rug measures 25½ by 55½ feet. When completed, the original design was destroyed to prevent copying. Of wool velvet velour, it is one of eight made for the capitol. It lies over a parquet floor of teakwood.

Many of the room's furnishings were donated. Especially noted is a bust of George Washington after whom the state was named. The chandeliers of Czechoslovakian crystal weigh a ton. A Russian Circassion and walnut center table has a base carved in the shape of eagles' legs. The decorative inlay of the table features 52 pieces of native Northwest wood.

The legislative chambers occupy the east and west wings: the House with bronze doors features French escalette marble with garlands of laurel leaves and walnut furniture. Both ceilings are decorated with eagles and the Far Eastern Indian rosette.

The Senate chamber is furnished with German foremoso marble and mahogany. To its ceiling are added Grecian rosettes and Bosh lighting. Visitors may reach the galleries of each from the fourth floor.

Executives and legislative offices and their support offices, hearing and conference rooms occupy the remaining space of the Legislative Building.

The maintenance and upkeep of the capitol campus, its grounds, and all the government buildings required 204 employees during 1988 at a cost of $16 million.

Visitors are welcome every day of the week. The state buildings are open from 8 A.M. to 5 P.M., Monday through Friday; and the legislative buildings are open on weekends from 10 A.M. to 4 P.M.

WEST VIRGINIA
The Mountain State

HEIGHT: 292'   FACADE: 558'   DEPTH: 515'

Unlike most states, West Virginia was at first a part of a state. When James I of England granted a charter to the Virginia Colony, West Virginia was a part of that grant and colony. Then Virginia became a state until 1861 when, in a convention at Wheeling, the people of the West Virginia region refused to secede from the Union. This quashed Virginia's Ordinance of Secession, and a "restored" government was formed for West Virginia.

Because of the mountains little exploration toward inland settlement was ordered, but increased after the New River in southeast West Virginia was discovered in 1641. Thirty years later the New River Valley was explored to the site of present-day Kanawha Falls. In 1770 after the Cherokee Indians ceded all the lands comprising present-day West Virginia to Britain, the area was opened for settlement.

At this time Benjamin Franklin and Thomas Walpole were talking to King George III about creating a separate colony of the West Virginia area to be named Vandalia, but their project was stopped by war. Not until after Dunmore's War was followed by a peace treaty with seven Indian tribes in 1774, did peace come between the settlers and the Indians and then, but briefly. During that year Fort Fincastle was built. Renamed Fort Henry in 1776, it eventually became Wheeling.

During the American Revolution the British incited Indian attacks on the settlers in the West Virginia frontier. These continued into 1782; and the Indians continued sporadic attacks on the West Virginia settlers until 1794 when "Mad Anthony" Wayne defeated them at Fallen Timbers, Ohio. During 1794 Charleston was established as a town.

Tempers flared between the east and west Virginians during a constitutional convention in 1829, but it was not until 1850 that some concessions were granted the western settlers in a new constitution and, in 1861 when the Wheeling Convention was asked to secede from the Union, they balked and in a popular election voted to create a new state.

Washington Hall, "The Birthplace of West Virginia," was the site of numerous assemblies toward statehood. When West Virginia became the thirty-fifth state on June 20, 1863, Wheeling was declared its capital with Arthur I. Boreman the first governor. The Linsley Institute building in Wheeling, built in 1858, became the first capitol of the new state and served for seven years.

West Virginia's first capitol in Wheeling was built in 1858 as a private academy. It was designed by Henry Coen. Rented by the state, its three stories were occupied by the government until the capital was relocated to Charleston. It was used again during 1875–1876 while the government awaited completion of a new capitol. In private ownership, it is currently an office building.

In 1868 the legislature acted to move the capital to Charleston and on March 28, 1870, they boarded *The Mountain Boy*, sailed down the Ohio and up the Kanawha to the new capital to enter and occupy a new capitol building.

West Virginia's second capitol was built in Charleston during 1869–1870. It was designed by a member of a group of "competent architects from Cincinnati" named Garcelon and built by the State House Company at a cost of $79,000. With three floors and a basement, this brick and stone structure was 140 feet high with a facade of 138 feet and a depth of 56 feet. It was there, in its state constitution of 1872, that Negroes were given the right to vote and hold office. Vacated upon the capital's return to Wheeling, it was torn down.

During May 1875 the legislators decided they liked Wheeling best and the capital returned to Wheeling in the same mode of transportation except that two barges and a steamer were required to haul the state's records.

When the citizens of Charleston learned of the move to Wheeling, they tried to stop the removal of the state records with a court injunction, but failed. With their grievance uppermost in mind they started action for a plebiscite.

Returned to Wheeling in 1875, the government rented quarters in the Linsly Institute until the new capitol was ready. Wheeling's second and West Virginia's third, this capitol was designed by architect J. S. Fairfax. Completed and occupied in 1876 its $120,000 cost was paid for with a bond issue by the people of Wheeling. Built of brick and stone, it had three stories and a

The cities of Charleston and Wheeling fought for years to become West Virginia's capital. When Charleston finally was declared the victor, renowned architect Cass Gilbert was retained to design the capitol. The statehouse remains today as it was when dedicated in 1932. — Department of Archives and History.

basement. It was rectangular in shape. Each corner supported a domed cupola. A central, recessed portico of interrupted brick columns was surmounted by a pediment. When the government returned to Charleston it reverted to the Wheeling City/Ohio County Building until it was razed in 1956.

In the meantime an election by the people to determine a permanent site for their capital was held and during the fall of 1877 a proclamation was issued that Charleston, having received the majority of votes, would become the permanent capital of West Virginia.

For the third and last time, the government, with bags, baggage, and state documents, boarded river steamers. Back in Charleston a contract was awarded for West Virginia's fourth capitol in 1880. Three architects had to do with its design and construction: C. C. Kemple, A. Peoples, and S. W. Howard. Its cost of $389,923.58 was financed with the sale of the former Charleston capitol and a legislative appropriation. With four stories and a basement, this brick and stone building's clock tower rose to a height of 194.03 feet. Its facade was 230 feet and its depth was 180 feet. While thousands watched, it burned on January 3, 1921, with excellent, intermittent displays of fireworks caused by the explosion of thousands of rounds of ammunition stored in the building.

Luckily an annex had previously been built to house the Historical Library, Archives, and Museum where many important records and artifacts had been stored.

A fifth, temporary capitol was hurriedly constructed during 42 working days of that year. Contracted by David Dick with a $225,000 appropriation, it was a frame structure of clapboard siding and interior wallboard construction. It was two stories in height containing 166 rooms. Dubbed the "Pasteboard Capitol," its rooms and those rented about the city would serve for several years while a "permanent and enduring monument to West Virginia's statehood" was being built.

The responsibility of building today's capitol, West Virginia's sixth, was vested in an appointed Board of Capitol Commissioners. Seven in number, the board retained architect Cass Gilbert to design the capitol. It was financed by an appropriation of $6,412,373.60 together with the sale and insurance from the old capitol of $3,078,806.63. With the city of Charleston's donation of $1 million toward the land, a new site was selected and prepared at a cost of $2,111,825.43.

As a complex, the capitol was to be constructed in three phases, each with a separate contract. The general construction contract for the first phase, the west wing, was awarded to the George A. Fuller Company. Ground was broken January 7, 1924.

A railroad spur from the New York Central curved to the building site. Over it were hauled the cranes used in construction, the steel, and the great stone blocks. Steel workers assembled the superstructure and on May 1, 1924, the cornerstone was laid in the west wing. Built during 1924–1925, its finished cost was $1,218,171.32. Its 84,000-foot floor space created permanent quarters to be occupied by many departments moving from their rented quarters.

The east wing was built during 1926–1927 by the James Baird Company starting work in July 1926. The cornerstone was set November 30, 1926. Its design was exactly the same as that of the west wing, but within the plans were the Supreme Court chamber and the treasurer's office which were planned for the west wing, but the state treasurer would not accept the plan, as it was not safe enough for the treasury of the state.

He wanted and got an impregnable office. The floors, walls, and ceilings of the room containing the vault were lined with three layers of half-inch steel. The vault was completely surrounded with 18-inch walls reinforced with Wheeling crete steel. The vault contained 40 safes, each with a double combination lock. The door to the vault was solid forged steel 15 inches thick and weighing 15 tons.

During March 1927 the Pasteboard Capitol burned down, necessitating a speedup of work on the east wing which was finished and occupied in January 1928 at an increased cost of $1,361,425.

Some effort was required before the central section, tying the two wings together, could be built. During a two-year period the legislature acted to appropriate the money by a special levy taxing all the property in the state, not to exceed during any year more than five cents per $100 of assessed value. The cost was not to exceed $5 million. (The finished cost was $4,482,623.21.)

With the architect's plans approved by the commission, the George A. Fuller Company broke ground March 6, 1930, a few months after the nation's most smashing economic depression was started across the country by the collapse of the New York Stock Exchange.

But on November 5, 1930, in a short ceremony, the commission secretary placed in the cornerstone a small copper box holding memorabilia of the state and the cornerstone was set in place and sealed by masons.

During construction every tree on the site, every flowering shrub, every bush that was in the way was boxed, carefully saved, and its location marked on the contractor's maps, to be replaced when the work was finished.

Completed, dedicated by Governor William G. Conley June 20, 1932, West Virginia's capitol is built of Indiana buff limestone in classical design, more correctly termed Renaissance. The main unit contains three floors and a basement. Each wing contains four stories and a basement. The main building's facade and depth are 558 feet and 120 feet, respectively. Each wing's facade is 300 feet, its depth 60 feet.

Each wing is connected to the main unit by basemented, one-story sections measuring 95 feet in length by 56 feet in depth, to form a U-shaped capitol containing 535,000 square feet of usable floor space. The building remains as it was dedicated in 1932. Its dimensions: height, 292 feet; facade, 558 feet; depth, 515 feet.

The total cost for the completed capitol, including the land, construction, furnishings and decorations, and landscaping: $9,491,180.03.

During 1988 the buildings and grounds were maintained by 31 employees for $112,000 (estimated). A part of the work was contracted to private firms.

The main entrance to the capitol is on the south side facing the Kanawha River. A similar entrance is on the north side. Each is approached by a broad flight of steps up to and through a Corinthian portico with massive, 86-ton, limestone columns rising two stories to a pediment above which towers a gilded dome.

Originally gilded in 1931 at a cost of $23,700, the dome has since been regilded with paint. The dome is crowned by a lantern topped with a bronze staff upon which stands a golden eagle with raised wings.

At each north and south entrance are sliding entry doors weighing 2,800 pounds apiece and made of bronze and copper. They open to a circular, arched rotunda on the second or main floor. On this floor, centered in the rotunda, is a well surrounded by a balustrade of white marble.

Through the west and east arches of the main (second) floor, corridors lead to the foyers of the Senate and House chambers, respectively. Entered through massive marble columns, each foyer's ceiling is embellished with square-coffered panels containing bronze-colored, plaster leaves to resemble West Virginia's hardwoods. The walls are Vermont white marble above which are carved symbols of West Virginians' heritage.

Offices and committee rooms to support the legislators surround the corridor and respective chambers. Stairs rise to the left and right of each chamber to the spectators' galleries framed by massive arches on three sides with a fourth above the dais.

Except for the dome-shaped skylight in the Senate chamber and the rectangular-shaped skylight in the House chamber and the arrangement of furnishings, the two are almost identical. Rock crystal chandeliers hang from the center of their skylights. The furniture is made of the famous West Virginia black walnut.

The Supreme Court chamber occupies the entire third floor of the east wing. The planning and design of its decorations and furnishings were given the utmost attention by architect Gilbert. The ceiling above the chamber is a rectangular opening of stained glass and bronze carvings depicting the "Scales of Justice" and the "Book of Law." Columns of white Vermont marble with bases of Belgian black marble surround the room. The steps leading to the dais are made of Vermont verd antique marble.

The general plan of the wings provides for practical business offices. Inside the east or west entrance, a corridor extends the full length of the building. Offices are located on both sides. Each of the four floors, except for the Supreme Court chamber in the east wing, is treated likewise. Given over to the court, the two top floors of the east wing contain a suite of rooms for each justice, a consultation room, library, clerks' offices, lawyer's consulting room, clerk of the court office, and other minor offices.

The first or ground floor is reached from the east and west entrances or from those allowing access from the north and south main entrances.

The executive departments of the state occupy the first or ground floor of the Main Building. Circling the rotunda, columns of solid marble weighing 34 tons apiece form a colonnade rising from the floor to support the main floor above. From the rotunda floor it is 180 feet to the top of the dome. High above from its center hangs a two-ton chandelier of beveled Czechoslovakian crystal. Powered by 800 light bulbs, this eight-foot creation is lowered every four years to clean each piece of crystal in time for the governor's inaugural ball.

The governor's suite is found on the ground floor. The governor's office is finished with American walnut panelled walls and furniture with harmonizing carpet and draperies. His reception room is Georgian in architecture furnished appropriately. The ceilings of both rooms are of ornamental plaster. The natural lighting of each is supplemented with crystal chandeliers, similar in design.

Architect Cass Gilbert drew master plans for a complete capitol complex including drawings of sculpture, specific furnishings, landscaping, and recommendations for acquiring additional land to prevent encroachment of unattractive structures.

Today the capitol complex with its parklike landscape is a source of beauty and inspiration for all who visit. Most of Gilbert's recommendations have been carried out. Additional ground surrounding the complex was purchased thereby preventing intrusion on the decor. A boat landing on the river and steps were included. Streets were widened and improved. Across the Kanawha River the University of Charleston is insurance against objectionable land-use intrusions.

The capitol is open to the public during regular office hours, evenings until 7 P.M., and on weekends. A visitor's center has printed materials with information on the capitol, governor's mansion, and the capitol complex besides literature on state government and culture, recreation, and travel in West Virginia. Guided group tours to the capitol and governor's mansion may be arranged.

The newest addition to the capitol complex is the Cultural Center adjacent to the capitol. Simpler in design so as not to detract from the capitol, it holds varied exhibits and festivals, both historical and artistic and contains the state's museum, archives, and library. It is open seven days a week: Monday through Friday, 9 A.M. to 8 P.M.; Saturday and Sunday, 1 to 5 P.M.

WISCONSIN
The Badger State

HEIGHT: 285.9' FACADE: 438.8' DEPTH: 438.8'

Looking for a route to China during 1634, a French explorer guided his canoe into a Lake Michigan bay, landed near the site of present-day Green Bay and asked his way of the Winnebago Indians. Jean Nicolet did not find China, but he was shown a trail that, with a short portage, would lead him to great waters. It became an historic passageway from the Great Lakes to the Mississippi River by going up the Fox River into and through Lake Winnebago, portaging a mile and a half to the Wisconsin River and following it into the Mississippi.

Twenty-five years later French fur traders Pierre Esprit Radisson and his brother-in-law, Medard Sieur de Groseilliers explored the southern shore of Lake Superior while spending three winters around Chequamegon Bay in northern Wisconsin. Rene Menard established a Jesuit mission there in 1661.

After the region was claimed for France by Simon Daumont, Sieur de St. Lusson in 1671, another Jesuit mission was established at De Pere.

The first Europeans to cross what is now the state of Wisconsin were a Jesuit priest, Jacques Marquette, and Louis Jolliet, a Jesuit priest turned fur trader who had been directed by the government of New France to find the

Mississippi and take Marquette with him. Using the route Nicolet learned from the Winnebagos, the party of seven men in two canoes reached the Mississippi June 17, 1673, with written descriptions of the land and accurate maps.

One hundred years later following the French and Indian War between the two nations, the region was ceded to Great Britain in the Treaty of Paris (1763). Prior to the war the French had built forts at Green Bay, Prairie du Chien, and La Pointe, and French Canadians settled around them.

In September of 1766 a surveyor, Jonathon Carver of Massachusetts, set out with a small group to explore the area. Like those before them they followed the portage route, but went up the Mississippi. Much was learned from Carver's reports and writings.

When the United States won independence and the lands that came with it through the 1783 Treaty of Paris, there was little change even though Congress established the Northwest Territory to include Wisconsin in 1787. The French Canadians continued to take their fur and the English continued their trade. In 1800 Wisconsin was included when Congress created the Indiana Territory; and it stayed a part of the Illinois Territory when it was created in 1809.

During the War of 1812 the British captured Fort Shelby at Prairie du Chien in 1814 and didn't leave until the following year. But the war completed the land transaction and American forts were built at Prairie du Chien and Green Bay, encouraging more settlement.

When the Michigan Territory was created in 1818, Wisconsin was attached and the territory was divided into four counties with Brown County surrounding Green Bay and Crawford County surrounding Prairie du Chien.

Lead was discovered in the Fever River area. It was followed by heavy mining, prospecting and settlements. A misunderstanding brought about the Winnebago War in 1827, which opened lands for mining and settlement in southwestern Wisconsin. When the Sauk Indians were defeated in the Black Hawk War (1832), that and the Removal Act of 1930, which moved the Indians to the west of the Mississippi, opened more Wisconsin lands to settlement.

Congress created the Wisconsin Territory in 1836. Henry Dodge was appointed governor by President Andrew Jackson. Governor Dodge organized the territory at Mineral Point July 4, 1836. On October 25, 1836, the legislature convened at Old Belmont (now Leslie in Lafayette County). After a long, heated struggle Madison was chosen as the site for the capital even though it was only a town on paper.

The territorial capitol, rented for the occasion from John Atchinson, was a framed, two-story, false-fronted, white-painted building measuring 25 feet by 42 feet.

In June 1837 work was begun on a capitol in Madison. The cornerstone was laid with ceremony on July 4. While their capitol was under construction the legislature met in a Burlington (now Iowa) building until a fire forced them back to Madison.

When completed at a cost of $60,000 the capitol's outer structure was stone from the Maple Bluff quarry, ferried across Lake Mendota. Its oak interior came from trees on the site planned for the governor's mansion. The facade was 104 feet in length, 54 feet in depth, and 30 feet high.

When Congress passed an enabling act for statehood in 1846, a constitution was framed in convention, but when voted on the following year the people turned it down because it contained radical provisions relating to the rights of married women. The following year a more conservative constitution won their approval and Wisconsin was admitted to the Union as the thirtieth state May 29, 1848, with Madison the capital and Nelson Dewey the first governor.

With statehood the government grew and by 1857 the capitol proved so inadequate the legislature appropriated funds to increase its size. Work beginning that fall finally led to the dome's completion in 1869, but as new departments were organized, the government outgrew its space again and in 1882 the legislature provided $200,000 to make room for the State Historical Society, Supreme Court, State Library and more staff offices.

Finally completed with wings added to the north and south sides, the capitol's facade measured 396 feet, its depth, 226 feet, and height, 225 feet to the eagle atop the dome's flagstaff. The final cost for its construction, enlargements, and park landscaping by 1904 was $900,000.

Having realized the capitol no longer served their purpose, the 1903 legislature provided for a Building Commission to determine needs and implement consideration of a new, larger capitol. Before the commission started its chore, a fire beginning February 27, 1904, destroyed most of the capitol's interior.

The 1906 legislature, with limits on its size and cost, directed the commission to find an architect for a new capitol. The commission presented a program to five leading architectural firms inviting them to submit designs and plans. The firm of George B. Post & Sons of New York was chosen to do the job.

Implications in government finances and work space made it necessary to carry construction over a number of years with only one wing built at a time. Work on the most damaged west wing started in late 1906. It was completed in time for the 1909 legislature. The east wing was built during 1908–1910; the south, 1910–1913; the north, 1914–1917; the rotunda and dome, 1911–1915.

Occupying the original site in the center of Capitol Park on an elevation, Wisconsin's capitol holds a commanding position between Lake Mendota and Lake Monona.

The exterior is White Bethel Vermont granite, the hardest stone used, and the most durable. It is surrounded by a balustrade of white granite from which lighting is conveyed to grouped statuary surrounding the building. Extending from the central rotunda and dome, each of the four identical wings faces a street pointing to a cardinal point of the compass; while four avenues, each intersecting the central core between two wings, leads to the entrances.

Each wing is 125 feet wide, 85 feet high, and 187 feet long; and each terminates in a portico of six Corinthian columns supporting pediments. Within each tympanum of the pediments is a granite statuary harmonious to Beaux Arts architecture. The work of German-born sculptor Adolph Weinman, the statuary in the north pediment depicts "Learning of the World"; the south pediment, "The Virtues and Traits of Character"; the east, "Liberty Supported by the Law"; and west, "The Unveiling of the Resources of the State."

Surrounding the dome, high above each entrance overlooking the avenues, are additional groups of statuary. Designed and created by Karl Bitter, born and trained in Vienna, they represent "Faith," "Prosperity and Abundance," "Strength," and "Knowledge."

The dome is considered the wonder of the capitol and as far as anyone knows it is the only granite dome in the United States supported by 2,500 tons of structural steel.

Standing atop the colonnaded lantern above the granite dome is "Wisconsin," a 15⅓-foot, three-ton statue symbolizing "Forward," the state motto. A badger crests the helmet of her slightly bowed head. The open right hand of her outstretched arm reaches forward and slightly upward. Her left hand holds a globe upon which stands an eagle with spread wings. "Wisconsin" is the work of the renowned French sculptor Daniel Chester French.

Another "Forward," a bronze statue on a granite base at the north wing entrance to the capitol, was cast from a plaster model by Jean P. Miner of Madison for the Chicago Fair of 1893. When the fair closed, Wisconsin's women collected funds for casting the model in bronze and presented it to the state.

A second statue, of Hans Christian Heg, a Civil War hero killed in the Battle of Chickamauga, stands at the east wing entrance. It was modeled by Norway's Paul Fjelde, cast in Norway, and presented to the state in 1925 by the Norwegian Society of America.

The approaches to the capitol are completed with granite copings and steps. Semicircular, granite seats, bronze flower vases and drinking fountains complement the landscaping.

The pavilions, reached through the main entrances, offer an immediate and impressive view of the rotunda. Two hundred feet above, in the crown of the coffer dome, is a painting by Edwin Howland Blashfield of New York. Trained in Paris, Blashfield used a seven-foot bowl to get the perspective, made a model inside the bowl, and enlarged it to 34 feet in diameter.

Beneath and between the four great arches are four pendentives each decorated with a panel of mosaic glass. The work of Ohio-born Kenyon Cox, each panel measures 12 feet high by 24 feet long. Comprising 400,000 pieces of glass furnished by the Decorative Stained Glass Company of New York, they were placed under the supervision of the artist. It is believed to be the first attempt of mosaic in such monumental proportions. In the center of each mosaic is a seated, dominating figure with the four symbolizing the three divisions of the Wisconsin's powers: executive, legislative, and judicial; and liberty, the foundation of all powers in a free country.

From the rotunda, grand stairways lead to the upper floors and the executive chamber on the first floor of the east wing. Designed in the Venetian Renaissance style following the council chamber in the Doge's Palace in Venice, the art work and decoration in the governor's conference room is that of Hugo Ballin who studied in New York, Florence, and Rome. A nine-foot circular painting centered in the ceiling is especially noteworthy in its representation of "Wisconsin" surrounded by her attributes: beauty, strength, patriotism, labor, commerce, agriculture, and horticulture. His murals depict historic scenes in Wisconsin's history.

The Supreme Court chamber on the second floor, east wing, is 43 feet square. Daylight filters through a large, central skylight of low-toned, leaded glass in its 30-foot ceiling. The walls are finished with Italian Botticino marble punctuated with panels of gold-veined Formosa marble from Germany. The columns are Bewnou marble from France, that of the pilasters of Breche Coraline from Italy.

The stones in the construction of the capitol are varicolored, employing shades of marble, granite, and limestone from eight states from different quarries and seven foreign countries.

Four imposing murals occupy the walls of the chamber with the visitor's first impression attracted to the one he first encounters on entering the chamber. Straight ahead above the judicial bench centered in the dais is "The Signing of the Constitution." All the paintings are the work of Albert Herter of New York. The remaining walls contain his "Roman Law," "The Signing of the Magna Carta," and "The Trial of Chief Oshkosh by Judge James Duwayne Doty"; the four paintings illustrate the laws of Rome, England, the United States, and Wisconsin.

The dignity of the judiciary is characterized in the mahogany and leather furnishings on the gold-colored rug of the chamber which is surrounded by the seven justices' suites finished in quarter-sawed oak.

The Senate chamber, south wing, is circular in shape with a corresponding skylight 31 feet above the red-colored carpeted floor. The walls are Tavernelle marble in a soft cream yellow. Matching columns and pilasters are Escalette marble from France. At the head of the room, between the columns, are three murals by Ohio artist Kenyon Cox titled "The Marriage of the Atlantic and Pacific." The murals symbolize the opening of the Panama Canal. The center mural shows the ceremony of their union and the side panels welcome the nations of the world to the ceremony.

The Assembly chamber is the largest room with the highest ceiling on the second floor occupying the west wing. With rectangular dimensions of 73 feet by 68 feet, its skylight, 41 feet above the floor, admits daylight through its leaded glass dome. An elliptical arch is on each side of the room and the one above the carved oak wainscoting behind the speaker's platform contains another of Blashfield's paintings, "Wisconsin."

Measuring 16½ feet by 37⅔ feet, the painting's setting is a pine forest with "Wisconsin" seated off-center, right surrounded by persons representing her past with fur traders and Indians; her present with lumbermen, miners and farmers with families; and her future, a single figure shielding the Lamp of Progress being cautioned by Conservation.

The north wing of the second floor is given over to the Hearing Room, whose design is much different from the others discussed above. It is in a brilliant, harmonious color scheme with walls of yellow Verona marble with the space between the pilasters carrying panels of black and gold Porte d'Or Italian marble. The coves of the ceiling contain paintings of the four methods of transportation in Wisconsin. By Charles Turner of New York, the four murals, in order, represent Indian travel by horse and travois, travel by canoe, by stage coach, and by auto and railway.

Besides the spectators' galleries for each of the legislative chambers on the second floor, the east wing of the third floor contains the State Law Library.

The fourth floor's north wing was designated as the G. A. R. Memorial Hall Museum by the Wisconsin legislature in 1901. Over the years the museum has become a landmark within the capitol. On permanent view is the Wisconsin Memorial Collection of artifacts, battle flags, uniforms, weapons, and historical displays of the Civil and Spanish-American wars. Renovated in 1965 by the State Historical Society, among the new exhibits displayed is a diorama of the Battle of Gettysburg.

The remaining space in the capitol's five stories and basement is given over to storage, offices, committee rooms, hearing rooms, and the government's supporting services.

Elevators run from the basement to the fourth floor. A snack bar on the basement floor is open during business hours as is the information and tours office on the ground floor.

WYOMING
The Equality State

HEIGHT: 146'   FACADE: 300'   DEPTH: 120'

When the United States acquired the Louisiana Purchase in 1803 the region encompassing Wyoming was included. After its acquisition a territory was created and General James Wilkinson was named its governor in 1805.

Prior to the nineteenth century several Europeans may have seen the mountains of Wyoming. French-Canadian fur trappers Francois and Louis La Vérendrye are believed to have been two of them.

In 1807 an American trapper, Edward Rose, left his party and settled in the Big Horn Basin in northwest Wyoming. He is credited with being the first settler in the state.

Another American trapper and former member of the Lewis and Clark expedition, John Coulter, discovered what became Yellowstone National Park in 1807.

With the Europeans crying for hats made from beaver skin, trapping for beaver fur became a lucrative business for those who managed well, hired industrious trappers, and organized them into groups that eventually remained in the Wyoming Rockies through the winters, holding their furs to sell or exchange for more supplies during a summer rendezvous. The first such rendezvous was organized by Thomas Fitzpatrick and held on the Green River in 1824.

In 1834 William Sublette and Robert Campbell built a trading post at the juncture of the Laramie and North Platte rivers. Named Fort William and renamed Fort Laramie, it became a stopover place for missionaries and pioneers on the Oregon Trail. The route was first used in 1812 by a group led by Robert Stuart of the American Fur Company.

In 1843, the year Jim Bridger built Fort Bridger in Wyoming's southwest corner, John C. Frémont was sent west to establish a line of military posts toward territorial expansion. There followed two important transactions toward Wyoming's statehood: in 1846 a treaty with Great Britain established the United States' claim to Oregon which included northwestern Wyoming; and in 1848 Mexico ceded southwestern Wyoming to the United States and the Oregon Territory was organized to include Wyoming.

Thereafter, in succession, Wyoming, or parts of it, were included in the Utah Territory, 1850; the Nebraska Territory, 1854; the Dakota Territory, 1861; and the Idaho Territory, 1863.

With an advance surveying party of the Union Pacific Railroad, its chief engineer, Grenville M. Dodge platted the town of Cheyenne in 1867. Towns were laid out across southern Wyoming along the railroad's proposed route. Following the discovery of gold in the Carissa lode, people swarmed into the area.

The following year on July 25, 1868, the Wyoming Territory was created. Cheyenne was designated its capital when the territory was organized a year later (May 19, 1869) and, after J. A. Campbell was appointed governor, peace treaties were signed with the Indians at forts Laramie and Bridger.

Soon after they organized, the territorial legislature gave women of Wyoming the right to vote December 10, 1869, and Esther Hobart Morris of South Pass, Wyoming, became the first woman justice of the peace. These events led to women serving as jurors for the first time in the United States.

Twenty years later, July 10, 1890, Wyoming was taken into the Union as the forty-fourth state. The capital remained in Cheyenne. Francis E. Warren was the first governor and it was he who had pressed legislation for a capitol.

During its 20 years as a territory, the government entities had met in rented quarters scattered over Cheyenne. Communication between departments was inconvenient, time consuming, and financially wasteful. Speaking to the Ninth Territorial Legislature, Governor Warren pointed out the inconvenience and proposed a building which would bring all departments together and be an investment for the people of the territory.

The legislature passed a bill, which Governor Warren signed March 4, 1886, authorizing such a building at a cost of no more than $150,000. A five-member Capitol Commission was immediately appointed with instructions to have the capitol ready for the 1888 legislature.

Deciding upon a French Renaissance design for the statehouse, that April the commission selected and paid $13,100 for a building site. After advertising for an architect, they agreed upon David W. Gibbs of Toledo, Ohio, and instructed him to draw plans for a capitol upon which additions could be built as needed.

Advertisement for bids resulted in the commission contracting with Adam Feick & Brother of Sandusky, Ohio, for the construction cost of $131,275.13. Ground was broken September 9, 1886, and the cornerstone was set the following May 18, 1887, in a celebration requiring several weeks of planning. All the citizens of the territory were invited to participate in the festivities, as were neighbors from Nebraska and Colorado.

Seating was provided for 400 people at a time. A cook house was built and an 80-foot shed covered a 50-foot barbecue pit five feet wide. Cheyenne's streets were draped with flags and festive bunting and, with all in readiness, the people waited for the great event.

That day finally came. It dawned bright and clear for throngs, arriving by train or whatever means available, to witness and take part in a parade through Cheyenne's gaily decorated streets. The bands, soldiers, societies, city and territory officials, members of the Grand Lodge, A. L. 5887, and other Masonic groups finally reached the site of the unfinished capitol. With a copper box containing the territory's most thought-of objects safely placed beneath, a sandstone block from the Rawlins area was set in place while the crowd cheered.

From the temporary platform the throng was addressed by several eminent persons, one of which was Wyoming's delegate to Congress, Judge Joseph M. Carey. Finished with the preliminaries, the throng turned to the main event and feasted upon barbecued beef, pork, and mutton served with bread and "cornerstone pickles" quaffed with lemonade. The day ended after the evening's grand ball sponsored by the Irish Benevolent Society.

With the central part and dome of the capitol finished, before the Capitol Commission's final report March 31, 1888, the legislature had already passed a bill for $215,000 for public buildings. Of that amount, $125,000 was set aside to construct the wings of the capitol. Vetoed by Governor Thomas Moonlight, who claimed the building was large enough for six more years, the legislature overrode his veto. The reluctant governor was authorized and instructed to appoint another Capitol Commission.

Selecting Gibbs as the architect, the commission contracted with Moses P. Keefe of Cheyenne to build the wings for $117,504 and accepted the completed wings April 4, 1890, a few months before Wyoming was admitted to the Union.

The building was modern with respect to those times, wired, plumbed, and ducted for heating and ventilation; but during the 1950s the exterior's Rawlins sandstone was deteriorating and required a stucco covering.

By 1913 the building was crowded. Governor Joseph M. Carey told the legislature the problem was becoming serious and requested their action, but he was ignored. Two years later (1915) when Governor John B. Kendrick repeated Carey's message and added his own concern, action was taken and another capitol Building Commission was appointed.

Awarding the architectural part to William Dubois of Cheyenne, the legislature gave the construction contract to John W. Howard of Cheyenne on a bid of $140,790. Completed, the two wings were accepted March 15, 1917. The final additions lengthened the facade 300 feet, the depth to 112 feet exclusive of approaches.

Outside, the gilded dome rises 146 feet into the sky. The most salient feature of the capitol today, it was first copper-covered which, with time, produced an unsightly oxidized green. In 1900 it was covered with 24-karat gold leaf. New gold leaf was applied over that in 1924 and 1953; but in 1979 the original was removed and regilded. It was regilded again with gold leaf in 1986 for the capitol's centennial. It was applied from rolls one-half inch wide by 67 feet long. It is said that less than one ounce of gold was used.

At the main entrance a heavy portico, its pediment peaking at the rooftop, is supported by stone pillars through the first floor with Corinthian columns taking over to the base of the arch above the second.

Fronting the main entrance facing the street, a monument contains the statue of women's rights champion Esther Hobart Morris.

A second monument, "The Spirit of Wyoming," represents Wyoming and praises its people: past, present, and future. Designed by Utahan Ed Fraughton, this remarkable creation of a "bronco buster" in action weighing 4,500 pounds, is over 13 feet high. The horse is balanced on one foot atop a five-foot pedestal and is found between the capitol and the Hershler Office Building.

The rotunda, inside the main entrance, is 30 feet in diameter. It ascends 54 feet to the stained glass dome above. Imported from England, the glass is two-sided with blue and green shades on the inside and red, orange, and yellow on the upper side.

On the right, entering the rotunda, is the Governor's Office which Wyoming governors have occupied since 1887. In the rotunda are a mounted elk and a bison, the former a big game attraction in Wyoming, the latter adopted as Wyoming's State Mammal in 1985. Corinthian columns support second and third floor balconies overlooking the rotunda's black and white checkered marble floor from which stairs rise to the second floor and the legislative chambers.

The work finished in 1917 created the legislative chambers, the House chamber in the east wing and the Senate chamber in the west. Each chamber contains four murals painted by artist Allen True; and each depicts an era of treasured Wyoming history.

The Senate chamber is adorned with paintings of "Indian Chief Cheyenne," "Frontier Cavalry Officers," "Pony Express Riders," and "Railroad Builders — Surveyors."

A fifth painting, "Along the Little Big Horn," is by Joseph Henry Sharp. Purchased in 1915 by Governor John B. Kendrick for his daughter, Rosa Maye, the painting was later donated by Miss Kendrick to the state's art collection.

The four by True in the House chamber are "Cattlemen," "Trappers," "Homesteaders," and "Stagecoach." Besides the murals there are two paintings by the Sheridan artist, E. W. "Bill" Gollings. Centered in the House chamber's elliptical-shaped, stained-glass skylight is the Great Seal of the State of Wyoming, adopted in 1893. Two dates on the seal, 1869 and 1890, indicate the years of territorial organization and statehood.

The Senate chamber's rectangular-shaped skylight displays two seals, longitudinally centered. Both skylights have Plexiglas roofs allowing daylight through the stained glass while protecting it from weather conditions.

The chambers' galleries are gained by stairs from the second to the third floor. In Room 302, unveiled in February 1982, is a mural, "Wyoming, the Land, the People." Painted by Mike Kopriva of Powell, Wyoming, it depicts Wyoming's culture and life styles through its history.

Also unveiled later that year on September 2 was the official portrait of Nellie Tayloe Ross by Randall Lake. Mrs. Ross was elected governor on November 9, 1924, following the death of her husband, Governor Ross, October 2, 1924. She became the first woman governor in the United States.

The corridors and rotunda walls of the capitol are trimmed throughout with delicate, hand-painted scroll work complemented by rich cherry wood, paneled wainscoting brought from Sandusky, Ohio.

Renovation of the capitol, beginning in 1974, was completed in 1980. Its refurbishing included refinishing the wood surfaces dulled over the years by subsequent coats of varnish and re-stenciling the original frieze. The checkerboard marble floors were raised and the wood floors and beams replaced with steel and concrete. The utility systems were modernized to include air conditioning and the House chamber had to be enlarged because of reapportionment.

The capitol welcomes visitors during business hours and especially during the legislative sessions.

Appendix

Territory and Statehood Dates.

State	Territorial Date	Statehood Date	Order
Alabama	03-03-1817	12-14-1819	22
Alaska	08-24-1912	01-03-1959	49
Arizona	02-24-1863	02-14-1912	48
Arkansas	03-12-1819	06-15-1836	25
California	See notes	09-09-1850	31
Colorado	02-28-1861	08-01-1876	38
Connecticut	Colony	01-09-1788	5
Delaware	Colony	12-07-1787	1
Florida	03-30-1822	03-03-1845	27
Georgia	Colony	01-02-1788	4
Hawaii	06-14-1900	08-21-1959	50
Idaho	03-04-1863	07-03-1890	43
Illinois	02-03-1809	12-03-1818	21
Indiana	05-07-1800	12-11-1816	19
Iowa	06-12-1838	12-28-1846	29
Kansas	05-30-1854	01-29-1861	34
Kentucky	See notes	06-01-1792	15
Louisiana	03-26-1804	04-30-1812	18
Maine	See notes	03-15-1820	23
Maryland	Colony	04-28-1788	7
Massachusetts	Colony	02-06-1788	6
Michigan	01-11-1805	01-26-1837	26
Minnesota	03-03-1849	05-11-1858	32
Mississippi	04-07-1798	12-10-1817	20
Missouri	06-04-1812	08-10-1821	24
Montana	05-26-1864	11-08-1889	41
Nebraska	05-30-1854	03-01-1867	37
Nevada	03-02-1861	10-31-1864	36
New Hampshire	Colony	06-21-1788	9
New Jersey	Colony	12-18-1787	3
New Mexico	09-09-1850	01-06-1912	47
New York	Colony	07-26-1788	11
North Carolina	Colony	11-21-1789	12
North Dakota	03-02-1861	11-02-1889	39

Appendix

State	Territorial Date	Statehood Date	Order
Ohio	05-07-1800	03-01-1803	17
Oklahoma	05-02-1890	11-16-1907	46
Oregon	08-14-1848	02-14-1859	33
Pennsylvania	Colony	12-12-1787	2
Rhode Island	Colony	05-29-1790	13
South Carolina	Colony	05-23-1788	8
South Dakota	03-02-1861	11-02-1889	40
Tennessee	06-08-1790	06-01-1796	16
Texas	See notes	12-29-1845	28
Utah	09-09-1850	01-04-1896	45
Vermont	See notes	03-04-1791	14
Virginia	Colony	06-25-1788	10
Washington	03-02-1853	11-11-1889	42
West Virginia	See notes	06-20-1863	35
Wisconsin	04-20-1836	05-29-1848	30
Wyoming	07-25-1868	07-10-1890	44

Notes: The Colony states were admitted in the chronological order they ratified the Constitution of the United States. California, won from Mexico in 1849, was declared a republic. Kentucky was a part of Virginia. Maine was a part of Massachusetts. Texas declared itself a republic, separated from Mexico. Vermont was a part of New Hampshire and New York. West Virginia was a part of Virginia.

Bibliography

Books

Ashbaugh, Don. *Nevada's Turbulent Yesterday.* N.p.: Westernlore Press, 1963.

Baxter, Elaine, ed. *Iowa Official Register Abridged Edition 1989–1990.* Des Moines: Secretary of State, 1989.

Bearse, Ray, ed. *Vermont: A Guide to the Green Mountain State.* 2d ed. Boston: Houghton Mifflin Co., 1966.

Bode, Carl. *Maryland: A History.* New York: W. W. Norton & Co., 1978.

Brown, Dee. *The Westerners.* New York: Holt, Rinehart and Winston, 1974.

Brown, Glen. *History of the United States Capitol.* 2 Vols. Washington, D.C.: U.S. Government Printing Office, 1900–1903.

Carruth, Gordon and Associates. *The Encyclopedia of American Facts and Dates.* 7th ed. New York: Thomas Y. Crowell, 1979.

Catton, Bruce. *Michigan: A Bicentennial History.* New York: W. W. Norton, 1976.

Chappelle, Suzanne Ellery Greene, et al. *Maryland: A History of Its People.* Baltimore: Johns Hopkins University Press, 1986.

Conley, Patrick T.; Jones, Robert Owen; and Woodward, William McKenzie. *The State Houses of Rhode Island.* Providence: Rhode Island Historical Society and Preservation Committee, 1988.

Current, Richard Nelson. *Wisconsin: A Bicentennial History.* New York: W. W. Norton, 1977.

Daniel, Jean Houston; and Daniel, Price. *Executive Mansions and Capitols of America.* Waukesha, WI: Country Beautiful, 1969.

The Delaware State House. Dover: Hall of Records, 1976.

Documentary History of the Construction and Development of the United States Capitol Building and Grounds. Washington, D.C.: U.S. Government Printing Office, 1904.

Dykeman, Wilma. *Tennessee: A Bicentennial History.* New York: W. W. Norton, 1975.

Edgar, Jim. *Handbook of Illinois Government, 1989–1990.* Springfield: State of Illinois, 1989.

Fairman, Charles E. *Art in the United States Capitol.* Washington, D.C.: U.S. Government Printing Office, 1978.

Fant, Christie Z. *The State House of South Carolina: An Illustrated Historical Guide.* Columbia: R. L. Bryan Company, 1970.

Fleming, Thomas. *New Jersey: A Bicentennial History.* New York: W. W. Norton, 1977.

Fletcher, John Gould. *Arkansas.* Chapel Hill: University of North Carolina Press, 1947.

Fowler, Charles F. *Building a Landmark: The Capitol of Nebraska.* Lincoln: Nebraska State Building Division, 1981.

Frary, I. T. *They Built the Capitol*. Richmond: Garrett & Company, 1940.

Galbraith, Christine; and Miller, Barbara. *Historical Documentary Research Project, 1902 Florida Capitol Restoration*. Tallahassee: Historic Tallahassee Preservation Board, 1979.

Giles, F. W. *Thirty Years in Topeka*. Topeka: Crane & Company, 1886.

Gruening, Ernest. *The State of Alaska*. New York: Random House, 1968.

Hadley, C. J.; and Sprout, Janine, eds. *History of the Nevada State Capitol and Governor's Mansion*. Carson City: Governor Richard H. Bryan, 1988.

Hamilton, James McClellan. *From Wilderness to Statehood*. Portland, OR: Binfords & Mort, 1957.

Hamlin, Talbot Faulkner. *The American Spirit in Architecture*. New Haven, CT: Yale University Press, 1926.

_____. *Greek Revival Architecture in America*. New York: Dover Publications, Inc., 1944.

Hatcher, Harlan, ed. *The Ohio Guide*. 2d ed. New York: Oxford University Press, 1962.

Havighurst, Walter. *Ohio: A Bicentennial History*. New York: W. W. Norton, 1976.

Hitchcock, Henry Russell; and Seale, William. *Temples of Democracy*. New York: Harcourt Brace Jovanovich, 1976.

Hitchins, Sinclair H.; and Farlow, Catherine H. *A New Guide to the Massachusetts State House*. Boston: John Hancock Mutual Life Insurance Company, 1964.

Hunt, William R. *Alaska: A Bicentennial History*. New York: W. W. Norton, 1976.

Jensen, Richard J. *Illinois: A Bicentennial History*. New York: W. W. Norton, 1978.

Kelly, J. Wells. *First Directory of the Nevada Territory*. Los Gatos, CA: Talisman Press, 1962.

Laxalt, Robert. *Nevada: A Bicentennial History*. New York: W. W. Norton, 1977.

Mack, Effie Mona; and Sawyer, Byrd Wall. *Here Is Nevada: A History of the State*. N.p., n.d.

Margolis, Susanne. *Adventuring in the Pacific*. San Francisco: Sierra Book Club, 1988.

Mathewson, James L., et al. *The Missouri State Capitol*. Jefferson City: Senate Administration Committee, 1989.

Merk, Frederick. *History of the Westward Movement*. New York: Alfred A. Knopf, 1978.

Mockel, Myrtle. *Montana: An Illustrated History*. Chicago: Sage Books, 1969.

Morison, Elizabeth Forbes; and Morison, Elting E. *New Hampshire: A Bicentennial History*. New York: W. W. Norton, 1976.

Morris, Allen. *The Florida Handbook*. Tallahassee: Florida Peninsular Press, 1980–1982.

Morrissey, Charles T. *Vermont: A Bicentennial History*. New York: W. W. Norton, 1981.

Moser, Don. *The Snake River Country*. New York: Time-Life Books, 1974.

Naske, Claus M.; and Slotnick, Herman E. *A History of the 49th State*. Grand Rapids, MI: Wm. B. Eerdmans, 1979.

New York Capitol Commission. *The Master Plan for the New York State Capitol*. Albany: Temporary State Commission, 1982.

O'Brien, Joy J.; and Pert, Edwin H., eds. *Senate and House Registers, State of Maine*. Augusta: State of Maine Legislature, 1989.

O'Brien, Robert ed. *The Encyclopedia of New England*. New York: Facts on File, 1985.

Paxton, John. *The Statesman's Yearbook, 1989–90*. 126th ed. New York: St. Martin's Press, 1989.

Perkins, Robert L. *The First Hundred Years*. New York: Doubleday, 1959.

Peterson, F. Ross. *Idaho: A Bicentennial History*. New York: W. W. Norton, 1976.

Placzek, Alfred K., ed. *Macmillan Encyclopedia of Architects.* 6 vols. New York: Free Press, n.d.

Pratt, Julius W. *Expansionists of 1898: The Acquisition of Hawaii and the Spanish Isles.* Baltimore: Johns Hopkins University Press, 1936; reprint, Gloucester, MA: Peter Smith, 1959.

Preuss, Charles. Erwin G. and Elizabeth K. Gudde, translators and eds. *Exploring with Frémont.* Norman: University of Oklahoma Press, 1958.

Reese, Lisle M. *South Dakota: A Guide to the State.* American Guide Series. New York: Hastings House, 1938 (revised ed. 1952).

Remele, Larry, ed. *The North Dakota State Capitol: Architecture and History.* Bismarck: State Historical Society, 1989.

Roberts, Kenneth. *The Battle of Cowpens.* New York: Doubleday, 1958.

Roth, David M. *Connecticut: A History.* New York: W. W. Norton, 1979.

Rubin, Louis D., Jr. *Virginia: A Bicentennial History.* New York: W. W. Norton, 1977.

Salley, Alexander S. *The State Houses of South Carolina, 1751-1936.* Columbia: South Carolina Historical Commission, 1957.

Shettleworth, Earle G., Jr.; and Beard, Frank A. *The Maine State House: A Brief History and Guide.* Augusta: Maine Historic Preservation Committee, August 1981.

Socolofsky, Homer E.; and Self, Huber. *Historical Atlas of Kansas.* 2d ed. Norman: University of Oklahoma Press, 1972, 1988.

Spence, Clark C. *Montana: A Bicentennial History.* New York: W. W. Norton, 1978.

Sprague, Marshall. *Colorado: A Bicentennial History.* New York: W. W. Norton, 1976. Copyright: Nashville: American Association for State and Local History.

Titus, Harold, ed. *Michigan: A Guide to the Wolverine State.* 2d ed. New York: Oxford University Press, 1956.

Trover, Ellen Lloyd. *Chronology and Documentary Handbook of the State of Alaska.* Dobbs Ferry, NY: Oceana Publications, 1972.

Van Dusen, Albert E. *Connecticut.* New York: Random House, 1961.

Vexler, Robert I., ed. *Chronology and Documentary Handbook of the State of New Hampshire.* Dobbs Ferry, NY: Oceana Publications, 1978.

_____. *Chronology and Documentary Handbook of the State of New Jersey.* Dobbs Ferry, NY: Oceana Publications, 1978.

_____. *Chronology and Documentary Handbook of the State of New Mexico.* Dobbs Ferry, NY: Oceana Publications, 1978.

_____. *Chronology and Documentary Handbook of the State of Tennessee.* Dobbs Ferry, NY: Oceana Publications, 1978.

Wall, Joseph Frazier. *Iowa: A Bicentennial History.* New York: W. W. Norton, 1978.

Wilkins, Robert P.; and Wilkins, Wynona H. *North Dakota: A Bicentennial History.* New York: W. W. Norton, 1977.

Williams, John Alexander. *West Virginia: A Bicentennial History.* New York: W. W. Norton, 1976.

Wilson, D. Ray. *Nebraska Historical Tour Guide.* 2d ed. Carpentersville, IL: Crossroads Communications, 1988.

Woodward, Lucinda. *A Documentary History of California's State Capitol.* Sacramento: California State Capitol Restoration Project, October 1981.

Wright, Louis B. *South Carolina: A Bicentennial History.* New York: W. W. Norton, 1976.

Zorn, Walter Lewis. *The Capitols of the United States of America.* Monroe, MI: Edwards Brothers, 1955.

Booklets, Brochures, Leaflets, Monographs, and Pamphlets

Adams, Tom. *Florida's Historic Capitol.* Tallahassee: Secretary of State, n.d.
The Alabama State Capitol. Montgomery: Governor's Office, 1988.
Allen, William C. *The United States Capitol: A Brief Architectural History.* Washington, D.C.: Office of the Architect of the Capitol, 1989.
Architects of the Capitol. Washington, D.C.: The Architect of the Capitol, 1974.
An Architectural Tour of the New Capitol. Jackson: Mississippi Department of Archives and History with the Secretary of State, n.d.
The Architecture of the United States Capitol. Washington, D.C.: The Architect of the Capitol, 1979.
Arizona State Capitol Museum. Phoenix: Archives and Public Records, 1989.
Begin with Maryland. Annapolis: Travel Division, Dept. of Economic Development, 1972.
Billings, Judith A. *Stalwart Stone.* Olympia: Superintendent of Public Instruction, 1989.
The Botany of the Washington State Capitol Campus. Olympia: Office of the Governor, 1986.
California: The Golden State. Sacramento: California State Senate, 1972.
The California Legislature. Sacramento: California State Assembly, June 1988.
California State Capitol Museum. Sacramento: Department of Parks & Recreation, 1989.
Capitol Building and Grounds / United States Capitol. Washington, D.C.: Architect of the Capitol, 1988.
The Capitol of North Carolina. Raleigh: Department of Cultural Resources, 1989.
Clark, Jan. *State Capitol South Dakota.* Pierre: Department of State Development, 1990.
Connolly, Michael Joseph. *The Massachusetts State House.* Boston: Secretary of State, 1982.
The Corydon State House: A Hoosier Shrine. Indianapolis: State Department of Conservation, 1930.
Edgar, Jim. *Unveiling of Artwork for the Illinois State Capitol.* Springfield: Secretary of State of Illinois, 1989.
Frazier, Calvin M. *Colorado State Capitol.* Denver: Colorado Department of Education, n.d.
Graves, Bill. *Kansas Capital Square.* Topeka: Secretary of State, 1987.
Hawaii: The Aloha State. Honolulu: Hawaii Visitors Bureau, 1987.
Hawaii's State Capitol and Government. Honolulu: Department of Accounting and General Services, State of Hawaii, n.d.
A History of the Arkansas State Capitol. Little Rock: Secretary of State, n.d.
Hixson, Vernon J. *Our Idaho State Capitol.* Boise: Hixson, 1986.
Illinois State Capitol. Springfield: Secretary of State of Illinois, 1989.
The Indiana State Capitol Building: A Centennial Restoration. Indianapolis: Indiana Historical Bureau, 1988.
Kentucky's Capitols. Frankfort: Office of Historic Properties, 1989.
Landmarks of Pennsylvania's Capitol Complex. Harrisburg: Department of General Services, 1988.
Legislative Building History. Olympia: Office of the Governor, 1989.

Legislative Office Building. Connecticut General Assembly. Hartford: Sweet Printing Company, 1988.

McKinney, Sandra Kay, ed. *South Carolina – State Symbols and Emblems*. Columbia: House of Representatives, n.d.

Maryland at a Glance. Annapolis: Tourist Division, Dept. of Economic Development, 1969.

Meyer, Clancy; and Murin, Susan M., eds. *Pennsylvania House of Representatives*. Harrisburg: B S C Litho, 1988.

Michigan . . . A Home to Be Proud Of. Lansing: V. J. Ehlers, 1988.

The Michigan State Capitol. Lansing: Department of State, 1972.

Michigan's State Capitol – History Art & Architecture. Lansing: State of Michigan, 1986.

Mickelson, George S. *South Dakota State Capitol*. Pierre: Executive Office, 1989.

Miller, Sam. *Capitol: A Guide for Visitors*. Tallahassee: Historic Tallahassee Preservation Board, Department of State, 1982.

Minnesota State Capitol. St. Paul: Minnesota Historical Society, n.d.

Mississippi. Jackson: Secretary of State, Documents/Publications Division, 1990.

Mississippi State Historical Museum. Jackson: Mississippi Department of Archives and History, n.d.

Missouri State Capitol and Missouri State Museum. Jefferson City: Dept. of Natural Resources, n.d.

Missouri State Capitol and Museum. Jefferson City: Department of Natural Resources, 1989.

Nebraska State Capitol. Lincoln: Department of Administrative Services, 1988.

New Mexico Capitol. Santa Fe: Tourist Division, Department of Development, 1970.

North Carolina "The Goodliest Land." Raleigh: Department of Conservation and Development, n.d.

"North Dakota State Capitol." *North Dakota Centennial Blue Book*. Bismarck: State Historical Society, 1988.

Notes on the Historical Background of Buildings in the Honolulu Civic Center. Revised. Honolulu: State Archives, 1966.

The Official Flag of the State of Washington. Olympia: Secretary of State, 1989.

Olympia – History of the Capitol City Area. Olympia: Office of the Governor, n.d.

Olympia: Washington State Capitol. Olympia: Office of the Governor, 1989.

Proceedings Connected with the Laying of the Cornerstone of Mississippi's New State House. Jackson: Tucker Printing Company, 1903.

Que Pasa. San Juan, Puerto Rico: Ramallo Brothers, May 1990.

Report of Nebraska State Capitol Commission to the Fiftieth Session of the Nebraska State Legislature. Lincoln: Capitol Commission, 1935.

The Rhode Island State House. Providence: Kathleen S. Connell, Secretary of State, 1989.

Rolde, Neil. "How Augusta Became and *Stayed* the State Capital." Address (given before the Kennebec Historical Society on 150th Anniversary of the Maine State House). Augusta: Maine State House, February 24, 1982.

The Senate of Pennsylvania. Harrisburg: B C S Litho, 1989–90.

Shettleworth, Earle G., Jr.; and Beard, Frank A. *The Maine State House: A Brief History and Guide*. Augusta: Maine Historic Preservation Committee, August 1981.

Some Interesting Facts about Alaska. Juneau: Office of the Governor, 1989.

"South Carolina's First Two State Houses." Columbia: Excerpted from book (Ch. 1) Department of Archives and History, n.d.

A Souvenir Guide to Missouri's Capitol. Jefferson City: Missouri Dept. of Natural Resources, n.d.

The State Capitol. Connecticut General Assembly. Hartford: Sweet Printing Company, 1988.

The State Reception Room. Olympia: Office of the Governor, 1989.

Territorial and International Affairs. U.S. Department of the Interior. Washington: U.S. Government Printing Office, 1989.

Texas Capitol Guide. Austin: Travel & Information Division, Dept. of Highways and Public Transportation, 1987.

Tower on the Plains: The Nebraska State Capitol. Lincoln: Nebraskaland Magazine, 1978.

Utah: A Guide to Capitol Hill. Salt Lake City: Office of the Governor, 1990.

The Virginia State Capitol. Richmond: Department of General Services, 1983.

A Visit to the Idaho State Capitol. Revised 1987. Boise: Legislative Information Center, 1987.

Visitor's Guide to the New York State Capitol. Albany: Office of General Services, 1987.

Warner, Lee. *Building Florida's Capitol.* Tallahassee: Historic Tallahassee Preservation Board, 1977.

Welcome to Oregon's State Capitol. Salem: Legislative Administration Committee, 1989.

Welcome to Pennsylvania's Capitol. Harrisburg: Department of General Services, 1988.

The West Virginia Capitol: A Commemorative History. Charleston: Senate of West Virginia. 1982.

Wyoming's Capitol. Cheyenne: The Wyoming State Press, 1987.

Your State Capitol — A Walking Tour. Lansing: House of Representatives, 1989.

Your Voice in Annapolis. Annapolis: The Maryland General Assembly, 1972.

Journals, Magazines and Newspapers

"California's Capitol Returns to Glory." *Sunset Magazine,* January 1982, p. 44.

"Capitol Being Restored for Future Generations." Michigan Capitol Committee. *Capitol Restoration Times,* Jan. 1990, p. 1.

"Capitol Visiting in the 13 Western States." *Sunset Magazine,* January 1982, p. 40.

Cooley, Everett L. "Utah's Capitols." *Utah State Quarterly,* n.d., pp. 258–273.

"Debugging the Capitol." *Time,* April 15, 1985, p. 73.

Dyrka, Paul. "A Stately House: Texas Capitol Photo Contest." *Texas Monthly,* May 1988, p. 88.

Fehrenbach, T. R. "The Living Stone of the Capitol." *Texas Monthly,* May 1989, p. 104.

Fergusen, Henry N. "Is Our Capitol Haunted?" *Boys' Life,* July 1982, p. 12.

Gabiou, Alfrieda. "The Burning of the First Capitol." *Gopher Historian,* Fall 1968, pp. 5–8.

Gadski, Mary Ellen. "The Tennessee State Capitol: An Architectural History." *Tennessee Historical Quarterly,* Summer 1988, pp. 67–120.

Glass, James A. "The Architects Town & Davis and the Second Indiana Statehouse." *Indiana Magazine of History,* Dec. 1984.

Goeldner, Paul. "The Designing Architect: Elijah E. Myers." *Southwestern Historical Quarterly,* Oct. 1988, pp. 271–287.

Goldberger, Paul. "Capitol Extension Is Somewhat True to Classical Design." *New York Times,* circa 1987, p. H1.

Green, William Elton. "'A Question of Great Delicacy': The Texas Capitol Competition, 1881." *Southwestern Historical Quarterly*, Oct. 1988, pp. 247–270.

Hoobler, James A. "Afterword: The 1984–88 Capitol Restoration." *Tennessee Historical Quarterly*, Summer 1988, pp. 121–123.

Johnson, Kathryn. "Statehouses: The Rescue of Architectural Treasures." *U.S. News & World Report*, July 29, 1985, p. 48.

Johnson, Kirk. "Museum Seeks Pay for View." *The New York Times*, May 2, 1989, pp. A14, B2.

McGinty, Brian. "Pierre Charles L'Enfant: Designer of the Nation's Capital." *American History Illustrated*, April 1988, p. 44.

Malan, Rian. "Past Perfect: It Took Six Years and $87 Million for California to Finally Treat Its Capitol Right." *California*, Dec. 1981, p. 114.

Mechem, Kirke. "Skeletons in the State House Closet." *The Kansas Teacher*, Nov. 1950, pp. 38–40.

"Meticulous Mr. Meigs." *American History Illustrated*, Nov. 1980, p. 34.

"Michigan State Capitol — Grand Old Dame Reaches One Hundred." *Michigan History*, Nov.-Dec. 1978, pp. 14–21.

"New York Capitol Stays Watertight." *American City & County*, March 1989, p. 56.

O'Dwyer, Jessica. "On the Western Front." *Americana*, May-June, 1987, p. 8.

Powers, Alice L. "In Capitol Heaven." *Americana*, Dec. 1988, pp. 46–47.

Reed, J. D. "Cheers for a Born Again Capitol." *Time*, Jan. 18, 1982, p. 64.

"Restoring the Capitol II." *Sacramento Bee*, Jan. 3, 1982, pp. CL 10ff.

Richmond, Robert W. "Kansas Builds a Capitol." *The Kansas Historical Quarterly*, Autumn 1972, pp. 249–267.

Robinson, Willard B. "Pride of Texas: The State Capitol." *Southwestern Historical Quarterly*, Oct. 1988, pp. 227–246.

Ross, Margaret. "Chronicles of Arkansas." *Arkansas Gazette*, July 3, 1960.

Rush, Richard. "The Order and the Awe." *Progressive Architecture*, June 1982, p. 80.

Sanders, John L. "The North Carolina State Capitol of 1840." *Antiques*, Sept. 1985, p. 474.

Schriever, George. "Decoration of the Missouri Capitol." *American West*, June 1987, p. 74.

Shapiro, Joseph P. "Free for All Over Shoring Up Shaky Capitol." *U.S. News & World Report*, May 23, 1983, p. 78.

Sorenson, Mark W. "The Illinois State Capitol." *Illinois History*, Dec. 1988.

"A State Capitol's Fiery Past." *Southern Living*, June 1988, p. 48.

Stutler, Boyd. "West Virginia's Magnificent State Capitol." *West Virginia Review*, Vol. IX, July 1932.

Tucker, John G. "Steady Job." *Interior Design*, July 1985, p. 208.

"Uncle Sam's Islands. *The Economist*, May 6, 1989.

"U.S. Capitol Freshens Up for Company." *U.S. News & World Report*, April 2, 1984, p. 84.

Viladas, Pilar. "Grand Dame." *Progressive Architecture*, Nov. 1983, p. 96.

Vyzralek, Frank. "North Dakota's First Capitol Building, 1883–1930." *Plains Talk*, Spring 1970, pp. 5–7.

White, John G. "How Denver's Dome Got Gilded." *Americana*, Sept.-Oct. 1981, p. 75.

Winship, Stephen. "At the Bend in the River." *Concord Monitor*, July 14, 1983, N.p.

Wood, Ernest. "Building for Empire." *Southern Living*, July 1986, p. 114.

"Wyoming's Elegant Capitol Gleams Again." *Sunset Magazine*, Sept. 1988, p. 46.

Encyclopedias, Directories, etc.

Carrens, William Carlton et al. *The Book of the States.* 1988–89 ed. Lexington, KY: Council of State Governments, 1988.

Carruth, Gordon. *The Encyclopedia of American Facts and Dates.* 8th ed. New York: Harper & Row, 1987.

Collier's. New York: Macmillan Education Company, 1986.

Encyclopedia Americana. Danbury, CT: Grolier, 1986.

Encyclopaedia Britannica. Chicago: Encyclopaedia Britannica, 1987.

The Europa World Yearbook. London: Europa Publishers, 1989.

The New Caxton Encyclopedia. London: Caxton Publishing Company, 1987.

World Book. Chicago: World Book, 1989.

Index

297

Index

308   Index